Off the Record

"*The music business is a cruel and shallow money trench, a long plastic hallway where thieves and pimps run free, and good men die like dogs. There's also a negative side.*"

—Hunter S. Thompson

Off the Record

David Menconi

Writers Club Press
San Jose New York Lincoln Shanghai

Off the Record

Writers Club Press
an imprint of iUniverse.com, Inc.

For information address:
iUniverse.com, Inc.
620 North 48th Street, Suite 201
Lincoln, NE 68504-3467
www.iuniverse.com

ISBN: 0-595-13330-4

Printed in the United States of America

ACKNOWLEDGEMENTS

Grateful thanks to the following for assistance, advice, encouragement and pick-me-ups as needed: Geoff Edgers, Suzanne Brown, Mary Cornatzer, Peggy Neal, Corey Lowenstein, Eric Frederick, Judy Ogle, Ken Cartner, Tim Gray, Dan Gearino, J. Peder Zane, Juliet Wittman, Richard Kilgo, Charles Dainoff, Matt Brown, Ben Goldberg, Jeff Calder, Peter Blackstock, Jeff Wooding, Ginger Watson, Sara Bell, Michael Skube, Parker Williams, Rick Cornell, Bridget Booher, Jackson Griffith, Jim Desmond, Dave Burris, Mimi Chapman, Jeff Long, Patti McDougal, Chuck Twardy, Ed Ward, Scott Timberg, Dana Kletter, Dave Dunton, Caroline Carney, Chris Babcock, Mike Milligan, Bart Bull, Godfrey Cheshire, Chris Clark, Jim "Wannabeast" Maynard, Ed Pierson, Alyson Poole, Chris Stamey, the Lakeside Lounge and of course, Scott Huler.

Above and beyond the call of duty: Steve Knopper, Leland Rucker and Gil Asakawa, (the other three-fourths of the Colorado Media Mafia); Van Alston, Renaissance Man of Raleigh, North Carolina; John Schultz, for taking this seriously when no one else would; Kenny Roby, father of Ray among many other things; Jon Wurster, for introducing Ronald Thomas Clontle into my life; Holden Richards, pagan god of the world wide web; Andy Menconi, who is an even better brother than he is a graphic artist; Larry and Rosemary Menconi, my first and still best cheerleaders; Laurie Mitchell, glad to have you back; Aaron, Edward, Claudia and especially Leigh Menconi, for putting up with me through

it all; and last but not least, Brian Zabcik, whose time and devotion to
this project was exceeded only by the author himself.

PROLOGUE

Dribbling to his right, Gus DeGrande head-faked an imaginary opponent, pulled up at the free-throw line and launched a jumpshot. He followed through, fingers splayed, wrist cocked just so, eyes staring intently at the flight of the basketball...

Clank...

The shot glanced off the rim at an ugly angle. Gus started to give chase, then slowed to a walk as the ball bounded toward the other end of the deserted gym. He broke into a trot as he reached the opposite free-throw line, picked up the ball and dribbled back, heaving a prayer from just inside half-court. The shot appeared to be on line, but...

Clank...

It smacked the back of the iron, rattling the glass backboard.

"Shit," Gus murmured. He stopped and bent over, gripping the front of his shorts. Perspiration soaked the frayed Rolling Stones T-shirt that rode up over his belly, a bead of sweat dropping onto his custom-made Nikes. But he was still less winded than jangled. Usually, these late-night basket-shooting sessions calmed him down. When the other nineteen rooms of his mansion got to be just too quiet—the kind of quiet that stereos and TV sets and telephones couldn't drown out—he retreated to his windowless private gym in the back for a little one-on-none.

Tonight, however, he could not unwind. His schedule had offered up the usual array of booking agents to cajole, band managers to schmooze, buildings to rent, tickets to sell, underlings to berate, competitors to browbeat. All in all, a typical day in the life of a concert promoter. Over the course of the afternoon and evening, Gus had consumed too much cocaine and not enough food. The two belts of Scotch he'd just thrown down hadn't dulled his restlessness...

Clank...

...But they'd sure as hell dulled his shooting touch. As another shot rattled out, Gus turned and kicked the ball away. It flew the length of the gym and hit the far wall with a satisfying *boom,* just missing a couple of framed platinum records. So many of these music-industry trophies already covered the walls of his office, living room, bedroom and even bathrooms that he had taken to hanging them out here. He owned a lot of these tokens because bands never forgot Gus, not if they knew what was good for them.

Both the bands and their platinum records arrived on a schedule, like clockwork. The bands, he booked into stadiums and arenas. The commemorative mementos with their personalized nameplates— "Presented to Gus DeGrande and Grandiose Concerts to mark the sale of three million units of the Poly Brothers Records album *Body Odor"*—he hung up wherever he could find empty wallspace. And for Gus, booking the bands was scarcely more complicated than hanging their tributes. The business had become easy for him. Too easy...

Clank...

Still another shot missed, to DeGrande's amazement. Forty-eight years old and roughly pear-shaped, he was no athlete. But he still prided himself on his shooting touch. There weren't many people who could beat him at horse. The promoter even installed basketball goals backstage at his venues so he could take on all comers—the bands, their managers, the roadcrews. Tonight, Gus couldn't throw it in the ocean. He tried bearing down harder...

Clank...

Clank...

Clank...

Roaring in frustration, Gus slammed the ball down so hard it hit the ceiling on the bounce. Then he started running, dribbling as he labored back and forth around the gym. He wondered how long he could keep this up. Then he wondered if he kept running laps for days—and he almost felt wired enough to do that—whether anyone would even miss him at the office, since by now Grandiose Concerts practically ran itself.

Gus had the business of promoting concerts down to a science. Who to book and where; how much to charge; when and how much to advertise; what to do to protect his territory from competitors. Grandiose Concerts wasn't a company, it was an empire. DeGrande was wealthy, powerful, feared—enough so that he rarely had to get his hands dirty anymore.

Earlier in the evening, however, he'd had to do that for the first time in quite a while.

Gus had been keeping an eye on Jay Simmons since the day the young man went to work for him in Grandiose Concerts' marketing department. Fresh out of college, Jay was an ambitious young man with big plans. When he applied for a job, Jay submitted his MBA thesis—a business plan to diversify a large concert promotion firm by starting an artist management division. But it soon became apparent that Jay did not intend to stay anyone else's employee for very long.

"I'd watch that kid if I were you," a band manager told Gus. "He's smart, but not as smart as he thinks. He told me he might be going out on his own soon, and that he hoped 'we can continue working together.'"

The manager and Gus had a good laugh at the young man's naivete. And sure enough, in no time at all Jay was running a hustle out of his office—booking club shows of his own on the sly, thinking DeGrande wouldn't notice. The promoter didn't bust him right away, instead waiting to see just how far his subordinate would push it. He finally went too far when he booked a rising rhythm & blues singer named Luther

Maxwell into a large downtown Raleigh nightclub, The Vibe. Jay even bought some ads on local radio stations, and bragged about the show to a co-worker.

Gus waited until the evening of the show to put the hammer down, showing up at The Vibe as a line queued up outside. Jay was standing on the sidewalk by the door, and his face fell when he saw a Mercedes pull up and the passenger side window hum down to reveal his boss glowering at him.

"Howdy, Jay," Gus called out, eyeing the line of people snaked around the block. "Nice crowd."

Knowing he'd been caught red-handed, Jay didn't answer.

"You want to talk about this?" Gus asked. "Get in the car, Jay."

Jay didn't move, even after DeGrande raised an eyebrow and leaned forward.

"Gee, Jay, it sure would be a shame if somebody called in a bomb threat on this place," Gus said, and still his prey stood frozen. Finally, when DeGrande picked up his cellular phone and reached for the speed-dial button, Jay stepped woodenly off the curb and into the car. The promoter pulled away from the club, headed north.

"Where are we going?" Jay asked, nervously licking his lips.

"To the office," Gus said evenly.

"Why?"

"Because I'm firing you and I want you to clean out your desk. Then we're coming back down here and you're gonna hand over every dime from the door. That ought to cover what you've been ripping me off doing these shows behind my back."

"Listen, Mr. DeGrande, this is all just a misunderstanding. I don't know what you're—"

"Don't even try it," Gus interrupted. "You're a shitty liar, Jay, and you're not much good at the truth, either."

Several minutes went by before either spoke again.

"Gus," Jay said in a weak rasp, "I can't give you the door."

"You don't seem to understand, Jay. *Not* giving it up is not an option."

"But the door isn't all mine. I owe some people."

"Who?" Gus asked.

"Some people."

"So you had to borrow the guarantee. How much was it?"

Jay mumbled something. "Speak up," Gus said, elbowing him in the shoulder.

"Ten thousand dollars," he said, and the promoter laughed harshly.

"Jay, you are one stupid son of a bitch. Ten-grand is at least double what that guy is worth. You'd never make it in this business."

"Oh, yeah?" the young man bristled. "Well, the show's a sellout. Once I pay everybody off, I'm gonna clear five-grand. I'll make more in one night than you pay me for a couple of months."

Gus pondered that for a moment. Then he pulled into the empty parking lot of a bank, stopped the car, opened his console and removed the 357 Magnum he kept for occasions like this, jamming the barrel up against Jay's throat.

"I've got some bad news, Jay," DeGrande said. "You're not gonna clear five-grand tonight. In fact, you're probably not even gonna live until tomorrow morning. Either I'm gonna kill you, or the drug dealer you borrowed ten thousand dollars from will. So shut the fuck up."

When they arrived at the office a few minutes later, DeGrande drove into the underground parking garage and stopped. "Okay," he said, "you have exactly two minutes to go get what you want out of your desk. I expect you to be back in this car by then. Trust me, you don't want me to come looking for you. Now go."

Once Jay was out of sight, Gus drove back out and headed downtown. After arriving at The Vibe, he asked the girl at the door for "Jay's partner," then approached the stylishly dressed young man she pointed out.

"You Jay's backer on this show?" Gus asked.

"Who wants to know?"

"Well, Jay works for me, and I thought you'd like to know I heard him bragging about the scam he's gonna pull here tonight. He's setting you up for a bust so he doesn't have to pay you."

The young man's eyes narrowed as he gave the promoter a nasty look. Then he took a quick look up and down the block—and saw that police cars were indeed at both ends, just barely visible around each corner. They were there because Gus had called the dispatch operator while driving downtown and asked if two squad cars could park there for ten minutes.

"Why should I believe you?" Jay's partner asked, returning his gaze to Gus.

"In the next five minutes, Jay's gonna come barreling down here in a cab. He'll want to go settle up right away, back in the office. But the cops are watching, and they'll move in once they see you go inside with him. Jay's deal with the cops is he gives you up, plants something if he has to—and keeps all the money. You don't want to believe me, fine. It's your ass, not mine."

Not waiting for an answer, Gus turned and walked away.

"Why you tellin' me this?" Jay's partner called after him. "What's it to you?"

DeGrande kept walking, got back in his car and drove off. He went around the block and into a parking garage across the street, parking in the shadows where he could watch the club without being seen. Two minutes later, a speeding cab skidded to a halt in front of The Vibe, ejecting a flustered-looking Jay Simmons onto the sidewalk. He went directly to his partner.

"Yo, Rufus," Gus heard him say. "Can we go talk for a minute?"

"Sure."

"Let's go in the office."

Rufus stopped, turned and gave Jay a look. "Nah, let's go for a ride instead," he said, taking his partner by the elbow and guiding him into a red Porsche that was parked in front of the club.

Gus figured that would be the last anyone ever saw of Jay. The promoter went back to his office and spent a couple of hours on the phone. Then he came home, puttered around his house for a while, went out to the gym—and discovered lids on the baskets, as he threw up one brick after another.

At first, Gus chalked up his agitated state of mind to that evening's events. The most annoying part was that, thanks to Jay, Luther Maxwell's booking agent would expect at least ten thousand dollars for his next show. Except for the financial inconvenience, however, DeGrande felt curiously indifferent. Once upon a time, solving a problem like Jay would've given him immense pleasure. Tonight, fending off the latest challenge to his territory left Gus feeling…bored.

That occurred to Gus as he jogged laps around his gym, that he really was bored out of his mind because promoting concerts was no longer a challenge. Despite his money and influence, despite the fact that he had worked with every significant rock act of the past quarter-century, DeGrande was still just a glorified member of the service sector economy. An employee. No, not even an employee, an independent contractor who could be replaced if he let his guard down for a second.

But what if?… Gus wondered, then lost his train of thought when he bounced the basketball off his foot. He retrieved it and resumed dribbling at a walk.

"What if…I became a boss?" he asked, thinking out loud. No, that wasn't it. He already was a boss.

"What if…I became an owner?" he asked again, which was closer to the mark. He already owned some things—buildings, companies, contacts, contracts. But what he didn't own was the one thing he actually sold: music. The promoter found his mind returning to Jay's proposed business plan.

What if, Gus thought as he hoisted another shot, *I owned a band?*

The ball settled into the net. Gus looked at it and blinked, realizing he liked the idea of band ownership. However, it begat a follow-up question.

But which one?

CHAPTER ONE

Right before shows was always the worst time. But it wasn't due to simple stage fright. The pre-show ritual Tommy Aguilar put himself through was more like preparation for offering himself up as a human sacrifice.

To get centered enough to crank up to full candlepower onstage with his group, Tommy Aguilar Band (TAB), he would first descend into something like catatonia. It required careful timing, so he could get all the way there and back on schedule. Anyone not familiar with the routine might easily mistake the bandleader's metamorphosis for a seizure. More than once, an unwary clubowner barged in on Tommy backstage shortly before showtime, and had to be talked out of calling an ambulance, or the cops, or both.

"Oh, there's nothin' to worry about," Ray the drummer would reassure unwanted intruders while shooing them out. "He'll be fine. He's just a little nervous, that's all."

Actually, nerves had little to do with it. Tommy had Lead Singer Syndrome, which was common enough—over the years, Ray had seen enough flaky pre-show routines that they barely registered anymore. Even so, Tommy was in a class by himself.

It always began on the way to the club, when Tommy would start out talking a mile a minute about some song he'd just heard, some girl he'd just seen, some asshole who'd just pissed him off, anything. Gradually, he wound down and stopped (he could never be trusted to drive), lapsing into a stupor by the time they arrived. Sometimes, Ray even had to carry him in along with everything else, since Tommy obviously wasn't much use for hoofing gear.

Once inside, Tommy would find the nearest TV set, tune it to an empty station ("The PFFFFFFFSH Channel," he called it) and sit staring at the static before eventually lurching off into a corner, curling into a fetal position and shaking. Violently. The first time she saw this, TAB's bass player Michelle thought he was dying. Rehearsals with the boss of her new band were weird enough, but this was downright creepy.

"God, what's wrong with him?" she asked Ray, who shrugged nonchalantly.

"Just wait," the drummer called back from the stage, hoisting Tommy's amplifier into place. "He'll be fine."

About twenty minutes before showtime, Ray instructed Michelle to prod Tommy awake. As she discovered, this was something you wanted to con someone else into doing, because the prodder was likely to be attacked—or, as happened to Michelle that night, vomited upon (a doubly nasty proposition due to Tommy's customary pre-show meal of sardines, to lubricate his throat). Over time, rousing the bandleader from his pre-show trances became a hazing ritual for new members of the TAB touring entourage, not to mention obnoxious club-owners or anyone else foolhardy enough to violate the backstage sanctum.

Once on his feet, Tommy would pace around chewing on a towel, loudly humming scales to himself. This delicate transitional state presented its own special problems, since it tended to be when clubowners came backstage with last-minute instructions or requests—and disturbing Tommy before he was ready to be disturbed could lead to disastrous consequences.

Ray and Michelle tried to run interference, but there were times when intruders insisted on speaking to Tommy directly. In Greenville one night, a clubowner demanded that the band play "Happy Birthday" for his girlfriend, who he said was turning twenty-one. Deep into his pre-show funk, Tommy greeted the man's request with a thousand-yard stare of incomprehension.

"You retarded, boy?" the clubowner asked, cocking his head to one side.

"He's, uh, not feeling too well tonight," Ray said hastily, putting an arm around the clubowner and guiding him out. "But don't worry, he'll be okay. I'll see what we can do."

That was the night Tommy unveiled a new song, one Ray and Michelle had never heard before.

"I just wrote this backstage," Tommy announced, "in honor of a certain under-aged homewrecker's birthday tonight. It's called 'Jailbait Blues,' and it goes somethin' like this. Ah, *one-two-three-four!...*"

If everything went well and he was left alone, Tommy usually finished his towel-chewing about five minutes before Zero Hour, then vanished. He would reappear just in time to walk onstage—wild-eyed, but in control—and by the time he was in front of people and actually playing, he was usually okay.

But not always. Some nights, his pre-show trauma spilled over from behind the backstage curtain, with bizarre results. One night in Wilmington, Tommy claimed his guitar was talking back in an evil and argumentative manner. So he decided to teach it a lesson, shoving the neck through an amplifier and starting an electrical fire. As flames shot out and wires crackled, Tommy gripped the instrument by the neck, raised it above his head and did a two-hand smash onto the stage. Breaking a guitar is harder than most people realize, but after a dozen swings Tommy managed to reduce it to an unrecognizable mass of wood, strings and wires. No encore for *that* show.

Then there was the night in Fayetteville when Tommy walked onstage, gazed out at the crowd, and decided he did not like its looks. So he went into Heavy Antagonism Mode, sending out ear-splitting shrieks of feedback from his guitar.

"Are we, um, trying to clear the room?!" Ray asked, shouting to be heard over the feedback, but Tommy didn't answer. Ray shot an inquisitive look over at Michelle, who was also baffled. Finally, they both shrugged and began flailing away themselves.

It took just under five minutes to chase everyone out. As soon as the last person left, Tommy began to play an actual song. Ray and Michelle picked up on it and fell in behind him. But as soon as people started trickling back into the room, Tommy went back to metal machine music. Again, the white noise drove the audience from the room. Ray was having a blast, battering his drumkit so hard he cracked the high-hat. Michelle settled for breaking a bass string; at least there was no rush to change it. This game of keep-away went back and forth a couple of times before the clubowner decided he'd had enough and pulled the plug. It was a tossup who was more enraged—the owner, or the head-liner whose show TAB had ruined.

"What the *fuck* was that?!" the clubowner screamed.

"It was their fault," Tommy said. "Too much ambient negative commentary. Besides, this will work out great. Next time we come back, I guarantee a full house."

"'Next time'? What 'next time,' are you out of your fucking mind?! After what you just did, you think I'd ever book you again?!"

"If we don't draw the crowd for you," Tommy shrugged, "we'll just draw it for somebody else."

Ray was alarmed to see that this guy carried a gun and seemed angry enough to use it. Fortunately, they were saved by an unsatisfied and extremely drunk customer, a Fort Bragg enlisted man who chose that very moment to express his dissatisfaction by driving a Chevrolet pickup through the club's front door. Miraculously, no one was hurt—except for the clubowner, who collapsed clutching at his left arm and had to be rushed to the hospital.

Well, Ray thought as he watched the paramedics take the man away, *better a coronary than a murder beef.*

But Tommy's prediction was correct. Six weeks later, TAB came back and confounded an overflow crowd at a larger club across town. Expecting another freak show, people came ready to attack. Instead, they saw TAB play a brilliant, flawless performance.

Whatever his personal faults, and they were many, Tommy was almost never random. But unless you operated on his same demented wavelength, it was almost impossible to decipher the method to his madness, at least not until much later.

Even when Tommy was behaving, being his bandmate wasn't easy. In rehearsals as well as onstage, he never used a set list; just started each song and expected Ray and Michelle to figure it out and keep up. That was no simple matter, since Tommy never played anything the same way twice and used a lot of chords and tunings that didn't really exist. Sometimes, his bandmates would think they were playing one song and not realize they'd guessed wrong until halfway through the first verse.

Whenever that happened, catching up involved punishment. Rather than act nice and let his bandmates recover, Tommy kept going, playing faster and harder. It was like being herded toward a cliff. But if they could hang on, interesting things usually happened. Tommy had written entire songs based on such mistakes.

The most potentially humiliating situation was when someone— usually Ray—managed to keep up with Tommy, and they then ganged up on whoever was unfortunate enough to be on the wrong track, usually Michelle. While she was the band's most technically proficient musician, her classical background was a handicap when it came to improvisation.

If Michelle recovered quickly, it was merely like getting run over by a truck. But there were times when the resulting horrors reminded her of something she once saw at summer camp years earlier, as a kid, watching a lake full of carp during mating season. Swarms of the male fish would corner the females against the shoreline and gangbang them, sending up geysers of water. That's what being attacked by Tommy and Ray could feel like: being violated, underwater, in excruciating slow motion.

It happened the first and last time Michelle's parents came to see her play with TAB. Their only comment afterward was, "I don't remember your cello recitals ever being so…loud."

Half the time, Michelle felt more like a hired hand than an actual band member. It all seemed a little unreal. She first met Tommy in the middle of one of TAB's shows, while buying a beer. She turned around and there he was, standing right in front of her, power-chording away. He was using a guitar with a wireless remote transmitter rather than a cord, which gave him free run of the place. So he wandered over during the instrumental bridge to have a look-see at the tall red-haired girl at the bar, the one he'd seen playing in another band a few months earlier.

"Hello," Michelle said, puzzled.

"Howdy!" Tommy yelled back, not missing a note. "Sorry, can't talk now. Busy."

"Um, so I see."

They were far enough from the stage that Michelle could hear the plink of his guitar pick hitting the strings separately from the amplified sound. It made for a peculiar sort of delay effect. Tommy smiled when he saw that she noticed it.

"Before I go," he said, "one question: You play bass, right?"

"Yeah," Michelle said.

Tommy nodded, turned and left. He strode back toward the stage, strumming as he went, then stopped playing when he reached the front. Ray and the bass player continued for a few bars without Tommy's guitar, before stopping in confusion. That was when Tommy yelled at them, "You guys fuckin' *suck!*"

A week later, TAB's old bassist, Gary, was out and Michelle was in. She still wasn't entirely sure how it happened, or why. She suspected Tommy thought he could push a girl around, although he rarely tried it. Her looks—bookish, but attractive in a behind-the-glasses kind of way—didn't hurt, nor did her occasional harmony vocals a perfect split-octave above Tommy's range.

Michelle's best attribute, though, was her classical training, which was the perfect foil for Tommy's psychotic flights of guitar fancy. She'd studied cello for a year at North Texas State's music school before dropping out and moving back home, disillusioned with her own mediocrity as a classical musician. But then she discovered her true calling as a bassist in rock bands. Suddenly, she went from being the worst musician in the room to the best.

Tommy's music demanded bass support that was structurally sound enough to withstand his gale-force tangents. In fact, bass was the hardest spot to fill in TAB. It only involved four strings, but only people who'd never played bass thought it was easy. You had to know how chords and notes fit together to drive the groove, and Michelle had put in the practice time with a metronome to become a real bass player. There was nobody better.

Between Michelle's classical training and Ray's checkered past in some of the most awful metal bands in town, TAB was a power trio that covered a lot of ground. Ray was one of the workhorses of the local scene, the guy everybody called to fill in when their regular drummer couldn't make the gig. That's how he wound up playing with Tommy at first, as a temporary replacement. After a while, Ray figured that Tommy didn't actually have another drummer, which meant he was in the band. Fine by him. Ray didn't demand much beyond loud and weird, and TAB pushed both those buttons.

TAB had gone through a half-dozen bassists and even done some time as a guitar-drums duo, but the lineup never quite clicked until Michelle joined. It was an ideal, once-in-a-lifetime musical fit, and Michelle knew it. When TAB really connected, it was a rush that playing in a string quartet could never match, not in a million years.

Still, it was a tossup whether the kicks compensated for the unavoidable drawback of spending a lot of time around a card-carrying sociopath. Although they'd only been together for six months, things were already getting unacceptably weird. Their last weekend roadtrip had been a disaster, in part due to Tommy's unfortunate habit of leaving behind suicide notes instead of thank-you notes for the people whose floors they slept on. Written in blood, "from the heart," as he put it. One of the recipients was Michelle's old college roommate, who was still pissed at her over it.

Tonight, however, probably wouldn't be one of TAB's weird shows. In fact, Tommy had even declared there was to be "no fuckery"—an odd command, given that the bandleader himself was invariably the one who started anything of the sort. But that night's show opening for Driveby Drowning was TAB's first gig at Each, the best club in Raleigh. Each's owner, Bob Porter, would be there, and so would that newspaper critic Ken Morrison.

Tommy had his sights on both of them.

CHAPTER TWO

Ken Morrison left his apartment just before ten that night and headed for Each. The walk wasn't far, maybe a mile. But that wasn't why he left his car at home. Since getting popped for driving under the influence a few months earlier, he tried to be more careful about drinking and driving. That lapse had cost him twelve-hundred bucks and a weekend in the clink.

But the worst part of the entire episode was seeing his name in print as something other than a byline. Anytime a *Daily News* employee got so much as a traffic ticket—even the lowly rock critic—a story about it appeared in the newspaper. It was company policy, as the employee handbook explained. Ken pleaded for mercy with the explanation that drinking in nightclubs was a necessary part of his job, to no avail.

"Can't have our readers thinking we're above the law, or the news," the publisher told him, then winked. "Don't get caught next time."

There was a special gleefulness to his readers' hate mail that week, and the venom still hadn't quite subsided two months later. Ken figured at least one person at Each was going to call him jailbird that night.

Ten minutes later, Ken arrived at Each and found a young man sitting on a stool in the doorway, eating a slice of pizza. He appeared to be about ten years Ken's junior, in his early twenties, and looked like a Goodwill classified ad come to life. He wore tattered jeans and a

"PARENTAL ADVISORY: EXPLICIT LYRICS" T-shirt, and his scruffy dark hair hung just below the collar of a black leather jacket that had surely seen at least one motorcycle wreck.

Ken stopped and waited for him to move out of the way. Instead, the kid sat there, chewing his pizza crust and impassively looking up from behind his mirrored Ray Bans. It was odd that he wore shades after dark. Odder still, the music on his headphones was loud enough to be heard halfway across the parking lot. Duke Ellington didn't seem like anything that triple-digit decibels of volume was going to improve.

Finally, the kid took one last bite of his pizza and stood up, dropping the rest of the slice on the concrete sidewalk. He then looked Ken up and down before announcing, "He lied and said he was alive."

Next, he solemnly took Ken's hand into his own and bent down as if to kiss it, but kissed his own instead—a very old gag made famous by Little Richard—and stood there refusing to let go.

"Um…thank you," Ken finally said, befuddled.

His mysterious new acquaintance smirked and turned Ken's hand loose, stuck a cigarette in his mouth and lit up, exhaling a large cloud of smoke at point-blank range. "You'll do fine," he said, patting Ken on the shoulder and walking away. "Just fine."

Inside, the air was already close to toxic from cigarette smoke, even though most of the evening's crowd had yet to arrive. Long, narrow and low-ceilinged, Each was practically ventilation-proof. But it was the best-sounding room in town, and a coveted gig for local bands.

"Hey," Ken said when he found Bob Porter behind the bar, "what's up with your new doorman?"

"He's not the doorman," Bob said, passing a bottle of beer over the bar. "That's tonight's opening act. Tommy Aguilar. His band is called TAB."

Ken was surprised; Bob's intolerance for flaky artistic temperaments was legendary.

"When'd you start doing outreach for the state hospital?" Ken asked, taking a sip.

"You watch," the clubowner said, "he'll be headlining by next month."

"Really?"

"Oh, yeah. I'm surprised you haven't already heard about this guy."

"Why?"

"He goes around handing out tapes of himself."

"Handing out tapes, as in giving them away?"

"Yep," Bob said. "Real primitive stuff, sounds like it was recorded on an answering machine or something. But still lots better than most of what I hear in here every night."

"Hmm. How come he hasn't played here before?"

"He has, sort of. I first noticed him hanging around a couple months back. Then three weeks ago, there's a knock on my door and it's him, holding out a tape. He doesn't say anything, so I take it and tell him thanks, the schedule's pretty tight right now but I'll be in touch if you sound like something I'd want to book. Then I close the door. Two minutes later, another knock on the door. I open it up and it's him again. And he says, 'I didn't give that to you to get a show. I just wanted to give you one, Bob.'

"A few nights later, Frag the Lieutenant is playing. It's a Tuesday night, maybe twenty people in here—and this guy Tommy shows up, jumps onstage between sets with an acoustic guitar and starts playing…I dunno what to call it, this weird space-age shit. No amps, no mike, but it didn't matter. The crowd went completely ape-shit. I tried to throw him out, the band tried to get him off the stage, but the crowd wouldn't let us. Damnedest thing I ever saw.

"So the Frag guys are pissed, their show is fucked, but what could they do? Tommy plays for ten minutes or so, then jumps off the stage in mid-song and goes running out the door. Just vanishes. An hour later, everybody's gone and I'm about to lock the door when he shows up again. 'Did you like my tape?' he asks. 'I hadn't gotten to it yet,' I said, 'but after what you did tonight, I was just about to play it.'

"And he goes, 'Forget it. I want my tape back.' The only way he let me keep it was to give him a gig. So I did, with the promise that he wouldn't pull his hit-and-run act again. He said okay, so here we are. I can't wait to hear him with a band."

"Wow," Ken said, intrigued. "What's he sound like?"

"I can't even begin to describe it," Bob said. "Besides, that's *your* department, sport."

Standing centerstage, Tommy strummed and crooned lightly, unaccompanied, just gliding along and not bearing down on either his voice or Gibson Firebird guitar. His bandmates waited silently, at ease in a perfect triangle. Directly behind the guitarist, Ray toweled off and lit a cigarette. Michelle stood to their right, perfectly still, listening for her cue.

Tommy rarely sang in this higher part of his range. His voice was clear and dry, with the faint burning scent of the barest hint of vibrato. Each word emerged the way you might blow a soap bubble, wobbly and floating, buoyed by his feathery strums. The music and words seemed almost weightless as they floated away.

Comin' down
   Comin' down
      Come on dooooooooooooown,
         Tooooooooooo the outside.

Nominally, this was rockabilly, a variation on that classic Bo Diddley backbeat. But this song wouldn't stay anything so easily identifiable for much longer. Tommy loved rockabilly, the music of the early mad geniuses of rock 'n' roll—a style that had seemingly been encased in amber since Elvis Presley and Carl Perkins and Jerry Lee Lewis. But then

Tommy got ahold of it and discovered that rockabilly was the ultimate base material. Played slow and dirty, it could become funk. Played soft and clean, like he was doing now, it could pass for country:

> Comin' round
>> Comin' round
>>> Come on rooooooooooound
>>>> Tooooooooooooo my bad side.

Play it hard, though, and rockabilly could be heavy metal or punk (and TAB's set list had the Sex Pistols covers to prove it). And if played even harder still, it would mutate into something else entirely. Tommy was about to do just that.

The notes and tones and syllables he'd been throwing into the air hadn't drifted away at all. Instead, they clustered behind the crowd for a surprise attack, waiting only to be summoned. Tommy began to strum a bit faster, taking his guitar from jingle-jangle to chucka-chucka as Ray took up a pair of brushes and stoked the tempo by drumming on his cymbals. Line by line, the tension built. Less atmospheric and more distinct, the words and music weren't so much floating as taking flight.

After arranging everything just so, Tommy snapped it all into place and sent his concoction into orbit. He reared back and escalated from a soft croon to a hell-hound shriek that made every hair on the back of every neck stand up:

> What's the use o' lovin' you, *baby,*
>> If yoooooooooou're gonna do me like
>>> *ttttttthhhhhhhhAAAAAAAAATTTTTT???!!!*

Michelle's bass rose up from beneath, dive-bombing into the song at precisely the right instant. It was like sleight of hand—no bass one moment and there it was the next, sliding in mid-scream so that no one noticed its entrance. Her timing was pinpoint.

Ray traded his brushes for sticks and, with a mischievous smirk, hit the bass drum with a thunderous *whomp* that reverberated in every cranium in the room. Drummers like nothing better than to hit things really, really hard.

Now for the tricky part. In the span of a millisecond, each player threw out separate squalls of barely controlled noise that tore a hole in the sonic fabric Tommy had so painstakingly woven. But just as the cacophony seemed about to implode, all three crash-landed on the same riff at the same time. Harnessing the force of the collapse they'd halted mid-note, they used it like an interstellar slingshot to launch the song into a pulverizing triple-time raveup. The room was so full of sound that it seemed to be pushing the walls outward.

Each note chased the previous one around until the music became a blur of crashing white noise, catapulting from person to person and feeding off the crowd's energy. A small cluster of people thrashed wildly in a mosh pit in front of the stage, but most of the audience was content to just stand there, entranced as TAB's spell washed over them.

Tommy's guitar was actually setting the tempo more than Ray's drums, pushing and pulling first ahead of and then behind the drumbeat (a trick he'd learned from careful study of Roy Orbison's "Pretty Woman," although this song's tempo was a rocketship compared to "Pretty Woman"'s Sopwith Camel). It was like the Doppler shift of an approaching siren. Even though Ray kept a consistent tempo, Tommy's guitar bouncing back and forth across the rhythm made it seem to oscillate between a controlled martial stomp one moment and a full-on frenzied rampage the next. It was dizzying.

Michelle was perilously close to dizziness herself, head down as she rode shotgun between Ray's jackhammer pounding and Tommy's howling guitar. She would've been angry, if she could have spared any concentration from hanging onto her bassline for dear life. This was a song they'd played just twice in rehearsal, and only at a fraction of this speed. Tommy was pushing his bandmates again, rewriting the song as he went, tinkering with the geometry of the notes to see what new shapes could be conjured. Michelle's bassline was the only thing standing between the song and total chaos, a bridge she frantically struggled to throw together over a deep, dark chasm even as Tommy rushed forward, heedless. She was barely keeping up and didn't know how long she could.

But this was why Michelle put up with Tommy. As maddening as he could be, he knew how good she really was. Where the other bands she'd been in barely trusted her enough to plunk away at a simple root, Tommy trusted her enough to risk disaster onstage. The crowd only noticed his spectacular guitar fireworks, but the song's true burden was falling on Michelle. If she faltered for even an instant, everything would fall apart.

Michelle risked a glance at Tommy, who was lost in following one note after another after another, further and further out, seeing how far this song could be pushed without collapsing. He seemed to sense her gaze and looked up to meet it.

His lips curling into a smirk, Tommy began to thrash his guitar even faster.

Standing in the crowd at Each, Ken was so awestruck he stopped drinking once TAB began to play. He'd never seen or heard anything like this band before, and was having difficulty believing that the guy onstage was the same self-conscious put-on artist he'd met earlier.

In a way, TAB was as derivative as any cover band. They played a lot of them, for one thing, but not covers you'd expect. Tommy seemed to have every song written over the last century stored on his mental rolodex, which he raided at will. While it was hell on Ray and Michelle, their on-the-fly improvisations were fascinating to watch.

The cover choices were amazing, too. "Holidays in the Sun," Ken hadn't heard that one in years. From there, they segued into a medley of "Minnie the Moocher," "Blank Generation" and "Close Up the Honky-Tonks"—all played at extreme volume and tempo in a weird style Ken could only describe as jacked-up interplanetary rockabilly. In Tommy's hands, unthinkable combinations fit together with a musical logic that seemed inevitable, flowing together as naturally as creek to stream to river to ocean. All you could do was stand and stare and wonder what on earth the kid would come up with next.

Tommy's originals were even stranger. Every band Ken ever interviewed talked the talk about having a wide range of tastes and influences. But TAB was the genuine article, seamlessly meshing everything from the softest Tin Pan Alley pop to the harshest rock, tempered with soul, country, funk, the Beatles-Stones-Who classic-rock axis, even shades of rap and jazz. There didn't appear to be anything Tommy couldn't do.

The kid was so good, he could even make playing out of tune seem like an act of genius. Small wonder, as Ken soon discovered, that every other musician in Raleigh loathed Tommy. In a town full of self-consciously incompetent college-kid musicians all pretending to be insane or artistic or both, Tommy was the real thing.

Ken decided to pay a rare backstage visit after TAB's performance; rare because, after getting beyond the basics—"Nice set," "When's your next show?" and "Got a tape?"—the small talk was usually pretty awkward. But Ken had a feeling TAB would be different.

Seemingly every woman in the joint was packed into Each's small, dank dressing room. They all crowded around Tommy, asking for autographs, but nobody had anything to sign. Finally, one girl stepped to the front of the mob and handed Tommy a dark blue Sharpie felt-tip pen.

"Here," she said, pulling down her T-shirt to expose an ample left breast. Tommy looked puzzled for a moment before realizing what she wanted him to do.

"Oh," he finally said, cupping the breast in his right palm and signing his name as he leered deep into the autographee's eyes. But before he could pursue any seduction options, everybody had to have a breast autographed. So they all queued up with their shirts askew—up, down, unbuttoned. It looked like a line of breast salutes.

Tommy spied Ken as he moved through the line, and waved. Leaning against a wall by the door, the critic waved back.

"Nice set," Ken called out.

"Really?" Tommy asked. He had a way of seeming genuinely interested in other people's opinions, especially when he himself was the topic.

"Oh yeah," Ken said. "That was great."

"Thanks a lot," Tommy said, continuing to sign. He was about to ask what Ken's favorite part of the show had been, when his bandmates walked into the room. Ray snickered at the breast-signing spectacle, while Michelle blanched.

"God, you're sick," she said, fuming, and stalked off.

Tommy shrugged, and Ray noticed the media's presence in the room.

"Well, well, well, if it isn't Mr. Poison Pen himself," he said with a bow. "What brings you out to our humble performance?"

The drummer hated all critics on general principle but especially Ken, going back to a particularly caustic review of one of Ray's former bands. Privately, he would've been the first to admit that particular band was worthy of disdain. But Ray was never going to give Ken the satisfaction of telling him he'd been right.

"Heard you traded up, and had to see for myself," Ken said.

"And?"

"My sources spoke the truth."

"You just be sure and speak the truth, too, then."

"Hey, it's what I do."

"Yeah, right," Ray smirked.

TAB's titular leader finally reached the end of the autograph line, dotting the 'i' in 'Aguilar' with a flourish. The girl looked at Tommy, glassy-eyed, and leaned forward to whisper something in his ear.

"Your voice," she murmured, just loud enough for Ken to hear, too, "makes me wet."

Before anyone could answer, there was a commotion outside. An extremely large, loud drunk came charging backstage, none too pleased about seeing another man's signature on his girlfriend's chest. He intended to lessen Tommy's attractiveness by rearranging his face.

Tommy saw the guy coming just in time and ducked under his roundhouse right. The drunk's fist crashed into the cement wall of the dressing room and shattered, swelling up to the size of a volleyball. His caterwauling rivaled the volume level of TAB's performance earlier.

"Be seein' you," Tommy told Ken, hastily packing up his guitar and escaping, once again, into the night.

CHAPTER THREE

That Friday, Ken Morrison published the first of what would be many TAB reviews in his *Daily News* column, a short item under the heading "New Faces." He wrote:

> One of the most intriguing new acts in town has to be TAB (an acronym for Tommy Aguilar Band), who opened for Driveby Drowning at Each on Tuesday.
>
> Pagan god guitarist Tommy Aguilar leads this power troika, playing thrashy, jacked-up bubblegum rockabilly embellished with side dishes from a veritable buffet line of musical styles. It's not often you run across a guitar player capable of quoting both Jimi Hendrix and Django Rinehardt, and who can get them both just right.
>
> TAB's influences are so diverse and at such apparent cross-purposes that, on paper, it sounds like a messy recipe. But with the able backing of classically trained bassist Michelle Rubin and sledgehammer drummer Ray Roby, Aguilar interweaves everything so seamlessly that his combinations come out sounding perfectly organic—as well as both timeless and thoroughly up-to-date.
>
> Volume, speed and amazing improvisational skills by all three players were on abundant display Tuesday night as

TAB ripped through a spellbinding 40-minute set. Framing their originals were fascinating interpretations of songs made famous by the Sex Pistols, Cab Calloway, Richard Hell, Buck Owens and Fats Waller. If that sounds like a confusing hodgepodge, all I call say is that it worked brilliantly.

Around these parts, at least, TAB won't stay an opening act for long. Remember, sports fans: You heard it here first.

Ken expected to hear some reaction from Tommy about this. One way or another, he usually heard from his subjects. In the past, he'd gotten everything from thank-you notes to death threats. Still, he never got a response quite like the message Tommy left on Each's answering machine for Bob Porter to pass along.

"You tell that Morrison guy," Tommy said in his best Marlon Brando rasp, "to deal with his own manifestations of insecurity before worrying about mine."

The clubowner was happy to convey that little tidbit to Ken (who couldn't decide if Tommy was kidding or not). Bob liked the recording so much, in fact, that he put it on Each's concert hotline for callers to hear before TAB's next show.

At the time he first met Tommy, Bob had been running Each for about six years—although, when he first took over, it was actually called The Beach, complete with a green-and-pink neon sign on the roof. No one could remember if the name was a reference to "Beach Music," the supper-club rhythm & blues of Southern coastal resort towns; or a previous owner's long-forgotten private joke, seeing as how there wasn't a beach within a hundred miles unless you counted the fake gravel one out at Lake Johnson reservoir (and nobody did).

But that became a moot point after a forcible name change, which followed a heated argument over a band's guarantee. Bob did what he always did when anyone asked him for something he considered unreasonable: folded his arms, glared and shook his head no. When it became clear no more money would be forthcoming, the band stormed out under a cloud of expletives. As their battered blue Dodge van churned through the potholes in the parking lot, the drummer leaned out a window and launched an empty brown Budweiser bottle toward the club's roof. His Hail Mary shot crashed into the "B" of the sign, exploding in a shower of sparks. Broken glass tubing tinkled onto the pavement as the van hit the street and sped off. The other letters in the sign sputtered and smoldered, but somehow didn't go out.

THE BEACH had become THE EACH.

"Fuckers," Bob grumbled, watching the smoke rise. Muttering something about having to change the club's name, he shambled back inside. The next day, he called the *Daily News'* advertising department and did just that. The club became "Each, formerly The Beach," and eventually just "Each."

The broken sign actually suited the club, which occupied a low-slung building on the edge of the downtown warehouse district. From the outside it looked like an oversized double-wide trailer made of soot-stained bricks. Inside, it felt more like a submarine—cramped and narrow, with pillars in strange places. On nights when Each drew its capacity of three hundred people (or four hundred, when the fire marshal wasn't around), it was not a place for those with a history of claustrophobia or respiratory problems.

But the club wasn't without its advantages. Bob had turned it into the best-sounding room in town by installing baffles and acoustic ceiling tiles to eliminate standing waves. If a band couldn't sound good at Each, they couldn't sound good anywhere.

Each had actually been in Bob's family for more than a decade. Under the previous owner, his cousin Mitch, the club was a house of ill repute, surrounded by persistent rumors that it was really just a front for a drug ring. The rumors were confirmed early one morning when a

DEA assault team paid a visit to Mitch's house and caught him loading a dozen bales of marijuana into a rented Ryder truck. Mitch turned state's evidence, testified at the trial of his mob-connected supplier from behind a curtain and entered the witness protection program. Bob never saw him again. The last rumor he heard was that his cousin was living two time zones away and working as a greenskeeper for a country club golf course. What no one knew was that he spent his evenings tending to a small patch of reefer deep in the out-of-bounds woods behind the 13th green (just enough for personal use, so Mitch's parole officer looked the other way).

Bob had an air-tight alibi that kept him clear of the bust. At the time, he was recuperating in a military hospital in Texas. After he got out, Bob moved back to Raleigh and surprised everyone by deciding to take over the nightclub. Nobody else wanted the building or the land, which was right next to some railroad tracks (fortunately, most of the bands that played there were loud enough to drown out the passing trains). So after negotiating a transfer of the club's liquor license, Bob moved a cot into the office, plugged in a coffee machine and plunged into the club business with feverish intensity. He was a novice, but he learned quickly.

At that point in his life, Bob needed something that would demand all of his concentration. He'd left the military following one of those abbreviated police actions that seem to flare up every few years. Before the conflict, Bob always thought the military would be his long-term career. But those forty-eight hours of combat were enough to turn him off soldiering forever.

All it took to escape with an honorable discharge was some shrapnel in his right shoulder and left leg, which Bob still carried around. It could have been much worse for him. The other six guys in his Bell-Huey helicopter all died when a friendly-fire mortar round exploded directly beneath the chopper as it hovered at treetop level, knocking it out of the sky in pieces. The last thing Bob remembered was hurtling sideways and down, before waking up covered in gore. By the time the corpsmen arrived to pry him out of the wreckage, he was screaming soundlessly and lacerating himself trying to scrape pieces of what used to be his co-pilot—and his best friend, dating all the way back to basic training—off his skin. The medics had seen this before. "Pulling a Lady MacBeth," as they called it, was a sign of severe shock. Despite his mangled shoulder and a broken leg, getting Bob still enough to load into a Medivac chopper required a stiff sedative and restraints across his stretcher. That was the last time he ever set foot in a helicopter.

Bob never told a soul about any of this. Quite by accident, Ken was one of the clubowner's few current acquaintances who knew anything about his military background. Ken came across an old newspaper article about the accident in an electronic database while doing a cross-referenced computer search for information about helicopter-related deaths in the music industry. Since the story was missing all the uglier details, Ken was oblivious to the whole truth; just enough to surmise where Bob's moodier tendencies came from.

To the rest of Each's patrons, Bob was just the crusty older guy behind the bar. People came back because he ran a good club and usually treated people fairly. In fact, Bob was the closest thing Ken had ever known to a popular clubowner—meaning he was the only one in town who wasn't universally reviled. While Bob could be surly and tightfisted, his club was still one of the few in Raleigh that gave unknown bands a shot and actually paid them for playing.

But six years of running Each had made Bob weary of the night-in, night-out grind. It would be a luxury to keep daytime hours and go to sleep before dawn, to work someplace other than a loud smoke-filled room, to not be surrounded by the constant temptations of running a bar. Many nights, he found himself drinking too much out of simple boredom.

While Bob looked down on most musicians as lazy and undisciplined, he respected the good ones. He'd even dabbled on the creative side himself. Occasionally serving as Each's live sound engineer led to the studio, where he produced rudimentary demo tapes for local bands. And dealing with incompetent band managers convinced him he could do that better than most so-called professionals.

So it happened that Bob Porter was looking to give artist management a try at the same time that Tommy Aguilar wandered into his field of view. Their meeting was well-timed. Tommy just happened to be in need of a manager.

"So I dunno, man. I still don't understand what it is a manager does."

Bob and Tommy were in Each's office with the door closed. Bob had just made his pitch to manage TAB's business affairs and provide some speculative financial backing, even offering to do it for ten percent of gross—less than the industry standard of fifteen. Tommy was going to say yes, but didn't want to appear too eager. So he played dumb.

"Detail work, mostly," Bob explained. "A manager handles things you don't want to deal with yourself. Business stuff, booking, logistics. I'd be your go-between on the business side, and try to do some long-term career planning. And I could…well…you know, help things go smoother. Maybe with a few less riots."

"Hey," Tommy said, "what's wrong with a little riot every now and then?"

Bob started to laugh, then stopped himself when he saw his would-be client appeared to be serious.

"Do you really like the shows that end in riots?" he asked. "Even that one in Greensboro a while back where you almost got the shit beat out of you?"

"Well…yeah," Tommy said, fingering the faint remnants of a black eye. "The way I see it, riots can be really cool. They keep things interesting. And if I get smacked around a little every now and then, that's just a price I'll have to pay."

"Look, Tommy, I like the occasional riot as much as the next guy. But you can have too much of a good thing, because you seem to cause 'em damn near every night—not just every now and then. I know cops who call you a riot enabler, and that's bad for business."

"Maybe that's bad for *your* business," Tommy shot back, "but not mine."

"And your business is what, then?"

"You wanna be my manager, you tell me."

"Your business is…well, leading a band," Bob said hesitantly, unsure how to respond. "Playing guitar, writing songs, doing shows, rehearsing…"

"No, no, no," Tommy said with an impatient wave of dismissal. "You don't get it at all. That shit's all just…what'd you call it? 'Detail work'?"

"Detail work. Okay, then, what's the big-picture answer?"

"If you have to ask, I could never explain it in a way you'd understand. Closest I can come is, being me. Sounds retarded, I know. But as long as I'm doin' my thing and not getting distracted by that other bullshit, all the details will sort themselves out. The songs will get written, the shows will get played, the band will…well, the band will be the band. My band."

Tommy paused to light a cigarette.

"But right now," he continued, "you have to ask yourself whether or not you really want to get into this with me, Bob, because there's one other thing. Give me half a chance and I'll always fuck up, just on general principle. Always."

"Why?"

"Just because. I sometimes have to burn everything down and start over."

"That can be messy," Bob said. Tommy shrugged.

"Yeah, it can, but that's me. Take it or leave it."

Bob thought for a moment before answering, and tried to choose his words carefully.

"Tommy," he said, "you are the strangest fucker I've ever met, here or anywhere else. I have no illusions we'll be best buddies because you're just too weird. But I don't care about that. What I do care about is that TAB is the best band I've ever booked in here and I think you can go a long way—far enough to get me out of this place, because I'm tired of running a bar. So yes, I'm sure this will be an exasperating experience. But I'm still interested."

"You sure?"

"Yes."

"This will probably be a very strange trip. Things are likely to get complicated, fucked-up. Maybe even scary."

"Believe me," Bob said, "it won't be any scarier or more fucked-up than anything I've seen before."

Tommy hesitated for a moment, then reached across the desk. The clubowner took his hand, and they shook.

Bob tried not to feel like he was shaking hands with the devil.

Three days after Gus DeGrande fired Jay Simmons, the Raleigh police department came calling. Homicide detective Jeeter paid a visit to Gus's office and conducted a brief interview.

"You and Simmons were seen leaving the club together at about nine o'clock. Where did you go?"

"Back here to my office," Gus said, "to discuss some last-minute radio spots."

"How long were you here?"

"Not very. Jay left before I did and took a cab back downtown. When I went down there later, I couldn't find him. But I did talk to his partner on the show, a guy named Rufus."

"Rufus Wilson?" Jeeter asked, showing DeGrande a photograph.

"Yeah, that's him," Gus answered.

"What'd you and Rufus talk about?"

"Where Jay was, and when he might show up. He never did, so I left."

"Where did you go after that?"

"Back here."

"And what did you do?"

"Made some phone calls."

"At ten o'clock at night? To whom?"

"People in the music business keep weird hours, detective. I called some booking agents on the West Coast, mostly—you can check the phone records—then went on home about midnight."

Jeeter closed his notebook. This interview was strictly a formality, open and shut, and so was the case. As the detective explained to Gus, Jay had been shot execution-style in the back of the head at about eleven that night, and his body was found in a dumpster. The murder weapon was a gun that police later found on Rufus Wilson's body, after *he* was shot to death the next day.

"Sounds like you guys had a busy weekend," DeGrande said. "Any suspects for who shot Rufus?"

"Nope. A drive-by, somebody shot up his car while he was in it. A real shame, too. A beautiful Porsche, just trashed."

"That is a shame," the promoter clucked. "Say, detective, can I set you up with tickets for anything?"

DeGrande had carefully avoided going anywhere near Jay's desk until talking to the police. After Detective Jeeter left, the promoter took a trash can into his late subordinate's office to clean it out. There wasn't much—a rolodex, some posters, a pile of compact discs, a potted plant, a calculator, a jar of candy. Gus pitched all of it.

Jay's file drawer was stuffed with folders for the different advertising accounts he'd handled, all routine. But the drawer yielded one interesting document, a file labeled MANAGEMENT. Inside the folder were notes and newspaper articles about various bands. Glancing through the papers, Gus realized that all the groups were local.

In the middle of the stack was Ken Morrison's first column on TAB.

CHAPTER FOUR

Thomas Wayne Aguilar made his first grandiose attention-getting gesture at the age of nine months, when his beleaguered mother Rita was trying to ignore his crying and take a nap. He shut up just long enough to get out of his crib and crawl out a window of their third-floor walkup apartment in San Antonio. Once on the ledge, he began crying again. His mother had to call the fire department to rescue him. The lights, noise, excitement and most of all the attentive hysteria of his mother—who refused to let Tommy out of her sight for the rest of his infancy, to the point of sleeping in the same bed for years—implanted the message early on that the ends justified the means. Throughout his life, Tommy's attention-getting strategies never got much more sophisticated than the ones he used as an infant.

Young Tommy came from a home that wasn't broken so much as smashed, turned to pulp by the shotgun his father used to commit suicide when Tommy was four years old. Very messy, especially since no one had any idea why he did it. The suicide note only revealed that he'd planned on killing his wife and son, too.

The cruel uncertainties of why Anthony Aguilar decided to spare his family but not himself—or why, as Tommy's mother viewed it, they'd been rejected as unworthy of accompanying him to the Great Beyond—drove the already-frail Rita Aguilar completely around the bend. She spent the rest of her days in the state hospital in Austin, rarely speaking.

When she did break her silence, it was usually to rail at her long-dead husband for "cheating" her.

Tommy used to visit his mother at the hospital, until he got old enough to resemble his father as she remembered him. On his final visit, Rita began shrieking at her son as if he was a ghost: "Why did you come back again?! Why?! You already killed yourself and left us, now you're back—*Why?!* Can't you leave me in peace? *What do you want from me?!...*"

When he was old enough to understand what happened, Tommy coped by telling himself that his father simply forgot to take his family with him. An oversight. Somehow, it made the whole thing easier.

Tommy passed his childhood bouncing from one foster family, orphanage and halfway house to the next. He was variously diagnosed as autistic, dyslexic, schizophrenic, psychotic and even retarded. But he always managed to function well enough to avoid being institutionalized. Though never a good student, he always picked up just enough in school to pass year-end equivalency tests and move along to the next grade.

At age twelve, Tommy was living with a foster family in Kansas City when he found a dusty, beat-up old guitar under a bed. He picked up the instrument, wondering how to play, and discovered he already knew (even though he was left-handed and the guitar was strung for a right-handed player). While he never learned how to read music, Tommy could play along with songs on the radio and quickly turned himself into a child prodigy musician.

Unfortunately, Tommy soon had to move again after he was caught setting fire to his junior high school to get out of detention. Fortuitously, he was sent to live with a college professor in Kentucky, a man who had an enormous record collection. Tommy spent the next two years in the professor's basement listening to every single record in alphabetical order, from Abba to ZZ Top—even the bad ones—playing along on guitar. By the time he dropped out of high school, Tommy had given himself a first-class musical education.

Had Tommy been honest and self-aware enough to communicate it, his personal history would have made for great biography. Ken found him eerily fascinating, but had a hard time pinning Tommy down about specific personal details. Just as he never played any song the same way twice, TAB's leader rarely gave the same answer to any given question—especially interview questions. Ask about his childhood and he was likely to launch into a monologue about his sheepherder parents in the Australian outback, or claim to have grown up as the secret love child of a disgraced Benedictine monk:

"Reverb is my life. Echo effects changed everything for me. *Everything.* You ever been in one of those Spanish monasteries where they chant, man? They're like echo chambers, creepiest places you've ever seen. But you can get some great vocal effects there. My dad taught me everything I know about singing. Wasn't much of a guitar player, though. That damn robe always got in the way, and he kept wearing it even after they kicked him out…"

It made for entertaining conversation, but bewildering interviews.

"Ah, you reporters just make it all up, anyway," Tommy chided when Ken complained about his tendency to fictionalize his past. "Anyway, if anyone's gonna make up things about me, it should be me because I make up better shit than you do."

True enough, Ken had to admit. It was why Tommy got away with so much—lying, cheating, stealing, wearing dresses (or nothing at all) onstage, acting crazy, frequently smelling bad. Maddening as he was, Tommy nevertheless possessed a near-lethal combination of charm, talent and entertainment value. It took the psychological equivalent of grueling physical labor to stay mad at the guy for any length of time.

Plenty of people were willing to put in the work, of course, starting with every other musician in town. Stories of Tommy ruining other bands' shows were legion, either by forcing his way onstage for uninvited cameos or playing three-hour sets as an opening act. He got away with it because he was better than anyone else; he knew it, and so did they.

At any given moment, several-score young women were actively pissed at Tommy, too. He had two words tattooed on his knuckles: TEMPT on the left hand, ME on the right. He liked how the tattoos looked when he cupped large breasts in his hands, especially ones he'd never held before. This happened often enough to get him into lots and lots of trouble with lots and lots of people.

But girls still flocked to see TAB play, and there was always at least one brave or foolish enough to venture up to the bandleader afterward. Tommy would be happy to buy her a drink, chat her up, get real friendly. Autograph her breast, even, or some other equally secret place.

"Songs are all over the place, and writing them is just like fishing," Tommy said. "There are a couple of 'em, big as trout, in this room right now. Lazy fuckers just floating there, I can almost hear them. If I got a guitar and noodled around, I bet I could catch us one."

Ken looked over at a guitar in a corner of the room, an old Martin twelve-string. It was broken, the neck snapped off.

"Guess you can't do any fishing with that one," he said.

"What, that one?" Tommy scoffed, and lit another cigarette. "It was catching too many I didn't like. So it had to be punished. It's in the penalty box for now. But if it convinces me it deserves another chance, maybe I'll get it fixed and try again. If not, winter's coming. Right now, though, it still needs to shape up 'cause I don't much like its attitude.

"And the real shame," he concluded, exhaling a cloud of acrid smoke, "is that it's not even my guitar."

"Oh…"

Next to the shattered guitar was a four-track tape deck, also in pieces.

"What happened to the tape deck?"

"Ken," Tommy said, "you don't even want to know what that damn thing said to me the last time I tried to use it."

You are so right, the critic thought to himself, listening to Tommy launch into an explanation of how he called other people's answering machines to record song fragments and ideas.

"Yep," he concluded with a smirk, "I got me demo studios all over town."

Ken tried to get the interview back to a level he could control, or at least comprehend. "Which do you write first," he asked, "the words or the music?"

This was the worst hack question in the world, and Ken was filled with embarrassed self-loathing for asking it. But he couldn't help himself. Tommy was such a bizarre interview experience that Ken wanted to see if he could turn even this turd of a question into something interesting.

"The music, of course. Words suck."

"Words suck?" Ken repeated. As someone who knew a lot more about words than music, he was almost offended.

"No one can hear 'em, which is probably a good thing," Tommy explained. "But words suck because they can tell you lies. Little lies, big lies, I-love-you lies, which are the worst kind of all. I don't like lies, even though I tell a lot of them. Just can't help myself because it's such a kick, you know? It's fun, especially when you get away with it and I usually do 'cause I'm good at it. Better than most people. So…that's why words suck.

"Music, though…" Tommy paused to smoke some more, exhaling for punctuation—"…does…not…lie."

"It doesn't?" Ken asked, thinking he had him here. "But I hear fake bands all the time. They sound completely phony and false as soon as they start playing, before they say a word. So are you saying they're telling the truth?"

"Well, no," Tommy backtracked. "You're right, some people are so evil or twisted or mediocre that they can tell lies with anything, even music. This town's full of jerkoffs like that—shit, we've opened for most of 'em, which has been a drag. But at least we showed them up for the truthless bastards they really are."

"But you, you're different?"

"Yep. I, myself, can't lie with music."

"Can't, or won't?"

"Can't. Understand, now, it's not because I'm any less of an asshole than anybody else. But I just don't know how to lie musically, and I'm scared to try and figure out how. Because if I *did* figure it out, I'd probably do it all the time. Just for the hell of it."

"So, Tommy, are you lying now?"

Tommy didn't answer; just lit another cigarette and gave a sly grin. Ken shifted uncomfortably on the battered Naugahyde couch, glancing at his watch as he tried to stifle a rising panic.

They'd been sitting in Tommy's living room and talking for over an hour, the critic's tape deck on the coffee table recording their conversation. Deadline loomed three hours away, and Ken didn't yet have a single useable quote. Or rather, he didn't have a single quote he believed to be completely truthful. That was probably the case with most interviews, he had to admit, but the bullshit was rarely this blatant. It broke down to about ninety percent lies and ten percent psychotic hallucinations, he figured.

Most maddening of all, Ken still couldn't decide how much of his interview subject's craziness was genuine, or a self-conscious put-on. Conversation with Tommy was like listening to a politician make a speech that sounded perfectly reasonable—until you suddenly realized halfway through that he was nude from the waist down behind the podium.

At one point, while speaking to the pros and cons of different guitars—"Rickenbackers are too jangly, got no guts. If they didn't look so great, nobody'd ever play one"—Tommy stopped smoking long enough to reach into a pocket of his jacket and remove a bundle wrapped in an old rag. The lump turned out to be a pistol, which he unwrapped and began casually wiping off with the rag.

"…Fenders, I don't like them much, either," he continued, as if cleaning a handgun was the most natural thing in the world to do while making guitar talk. "They clang too much and have this piercing tone that just sorta dissolves. They're not as bad as Rickenbackers, but they're still too trebly and high-end, and no crowd worth a damn ever showed up for treble. They come for treble, they're gonna just stand there and that's no good…"

Ken never took his eyes off the gun. Tommy went right on talking and wiping, oblivious.

"…You know, I can tell what kind of crowd it's gonna be just from watching heads in the audience, whether they're paying attention to the bass or the drums. Drum crowds are easy. They'll go for big, obvious, stupid shit every time."

He finished wiping the gun, pointed it out an open window and drew a bead on a large elm tree in the front yard.

"…Bass crowds, though, you've got to work a little harder on."

Tommy pulled the trigger, filling the house with the roar of the gun's report. Ken felt as if the bullet took all the air in the room out with it. Through the window, he could see bark turn to dust on the tree trunk, which appeared to be scarred from many such shots.

"Bass crowds are the shows where I usually wind up rolling around in broken glass or something," Tommy continued, pocketing his gun with a satisfied nod as a flock of birds fled the tree, screaming for vengeance. "That's why I like Gibson guitars. They sound like a chainsaw if ya hit 'em just right; got that thick, fat, dirty tone and they're more forgiving—and forgiveness is something I need a lot of, obviously.

"Say," he concluded, "can I get you a beer or anything?"

If nothing else, after this Ken could honestly say he'd conducted an interview at gunpoint. Equally unnerving were the surroundings, a small shack at the edge of a tobacco farm in rural Wake County. Tommy lived there rent-free, serving as on-site caretaker. Mostly, his duties consisted of keeping trespassers away and making sure nothing burned down.

Ray dubbed the rundown little cabin "The Crypt," and it looked like something out of *The Texas Chainsaw Massacre.* Animal bones covered the wall above the fireplace, dominated by a large cow skull with a bullet hole between the eyes. Antique farm implements hung here and there, including a scythe that looked like it would do for weaponry if Tommy ever ran out of bullets. The Weather Channel flickered soundlessly on the television set in one corner. On the walls above it were various pilfered highway markers, an upside-down American flag, a velvet Elvis painting, a poster-sized photo of a young Johnny Cash shooting someone the bird and a 1940s-vintage "Roy Acuff for Governor" sign.

The Crypt doubled as TAB's rehearsal space, and piles of records, tapes, books, beer cans, liquor bottles and electrical cords were strewn carelessly about. An ancient personal computer that looked as if it hadn't been functional in years sat on a desk, next to a plastic DNA helix model—the kind science students studied in biology class.

"I use that as a songwriting aid," Tommy explained. "Music is history—you've got to know the history or you're doomed to repeat it, and I'd rather make it rhyme, as Mark Twain used to put it. But music is also the most numerical of all the arts. So if you think about it in terms of geometric relationships, you can maybe figure out different ways to get from Point A to Point B. That's where the chromosomes come in."

Ken had no idea what the hell Tommy was talking about.

In the next room, Ray's drums were already set up for a TAB rehearsal scheduled to begin as soon as he and Michelle arrived. Ken had planned to hang around after the interview and listen to a few songs. But now, he was thinking it might be better to leave before Tommy decided *his* tape deck said something untoward and felt compelled to teach it a lesson, too.

"Listen, Tommy," he said, shutting off the recorder, "I've probably got enough here, so I think I'll take off."

He stood and began gathering his notes and papers together.

"You sure about that?"

"Oh, yeah," Ken said, looking up. "And if I think of anything I forgot, I can always—"

Tommy had pulled the gun out of his pocket and was idly passing it from hand to hand as he eyed the critic. For the first time, Ken noticed Tommy's TEMPT ME tattoos; he decided not to take their advice.

"Oh. Well…Um, maybe I don't have enough after all," he said, hastily sitting back down. "Just found another couple questions here I forgot to ask, in fact."

Ken replaced his tape recorder on the coffeetable and turned it back on. "Now then, where were we?"

Chapter Five

After much agonizing, Ken gave up and wrote the story with what he had. There was little else he could do. He tried to talk his editor into canceling the TAB feature, but she asked why and he made the mistake of telling her about Tommy's gunplay.

"Are you kidding?" she asked incredulously. "Somebody pulls a gun on you in the middle of an interview, that is *not* a story you kill. That's your lead! So write it up. Now."

Ken figured there was no way the accompanying pictures could be as weird as his story, but underestimated Tommy's determination. To his astonishment, Tommy posed with a gun. He even stuck the pistol in his mouth and pretended to pull the trigger for the camera—the orphan's tribute to his late father, even if no one else realized it. Horrifying as it was, the picture made for one attention-getting image. It also gave Tommy's peers something else to hate him for. Once again, he'd beaten them at their own game.

"No offense, but I'd rather have a great picture and a shitty review than a great review with a shitty picture," another local musician once told Ken. "Let's face it, nobody remembers the words—just the pictures. Except for 'All you need is love,' and him saying the Beatles were bigger than Jesus, does anybody remember anything John Lennon ever said? Uh uh. But they sure do remember him naked on the cover with Yoko."

Tommy was not yet naked on the cover with Yoko, but Ken still shuddered when he saw the picture and his TAB piece in the *Daily News*. Even soft-pedaling the weirder stuff and using as few quotes as possible, he couldn't keep TAB's bandleader from coming across as a monstrous, egomaniacal sociopath.

But as he told Bob, he just wrote what Tommy told him. Ken was thankful he had the whole thing on tape, so there'd be no disputing who said what.

"Save that tape," Bob advised. "Especially the part with the gunshot. One day, that might be worth something."

No doubt. Ken figured there would be room for it on a future TAB rarities collection: *The Answering Machine Tapes*.

As the rock critic for the only daily paper in town, Ken Morrison occupied a peculiar station in the local music community. He served as its official chronicler, interviewing national touring acts that passed through the area, and reviewing concerts and records. He also covered the local scene in a weekly column, in which he was part critic, part journalist and part self-conscious raconteur.

Translating *the* charms of a bunch of loud, scruffy bands for *the Daily News'* quarter-million readers involved some special challenges, because straight-up journalism just wasn't designed to accommodate rock 'n' roll. Yet except for his reviews (which were carefully labeled "opinion," with a timid disclaimer that the views expressed therein were "not necessarily those of management"), Ken had to operate within some very inflexible and old-fashioned rules regarding what he could and couldn't get into print. If someone agreed to be quoted by name about a controversial situation, that was "on the record." Everything else was "off the record" and therefore off-limits, including anonymous quotes and sources.

The paper's political reporters cited anonymous sources all the time, with the full blessings of their editors. As the state's governmental paper of record, the *Daily News* went out of its way to cover politics aggressively. Libel suits from politicians were practically a badge of honor. The music beat, on the other hand, ranked just south of high school soccer in terms of importance. The last thing management wanted was for its rock critic to get them sued, so Ken had to stay within much narrower boundaries. That was frustrating, because there were many occasions when "on the record" was just a polite term for "face-saving bullshit."

Like when Pasture Bedtime broke up. Ken heard what happened through the grapevine: The lead singer was screwing the wife of the bass player, who caught them in bed together and attacked his bandmate with a knife. The singer escaped by jumping out a second-story window, breaking an ankle while making his getaway, and that was the end of the band. Because the bassist's wife was also the group's manager, there were whisperings about financial hanky-panky, too.

But of course, everything was off the record, and Ken ran into a brick wall when he tried to confirm the story's juicier details. The official, unanimous party line on the breakup was "artistic differences." The critic approached all four band members, and got this same answer four times.

"You know and I know that is just not true," he pressed each one.

Everybody nevertheless gave the same reply: No comment.

Nobody else in the band's inner circle was talking, either, and there were no lawsuits or police reports, hence nothing in the public record to fall back on. When Ken explained the situation to his editor, she refused to back him up.

"Unless somebody is willing to talk about this on the record," she told him, "I'm afraid you're stuck. Sorry, but you know the rules."

So the column item about Pasture Bedtime's demise attributed their split to that ancient warhorse, "artistic differences." Ken tried to effect a dubious tone, but skepticism was no substitute for the truth. The worst part was that, for weeks afterward, people kept sidling up to him to smirk, "Jesus, Morrison, didn't you hear what *really* happened?"

Yeah, yeah, yeah…

As Bob was fond of saying, the real truth is always off the record.

Ken had fun with this boundary when he could, such as the time a hotshot local guitarist unexpectedly married a woman who was not his girlfriend—but who was, nevertheless, visibly pregnant at the wedding ceremony. The ensuing column item read:

> In this week's nuptial news, your faithful correspondent has three pieces of information to impart:
>
> (1) Wedding bells chimed last weekend for Joey Spangenberg, lead guitarist for Bug Parts.
>
> (2) The bride, however, was not Spangenberg's longtime sweetheart Brenda Myrick. Instead, the lucky gal was Suzanne Anders.
>
> (3) I can't. I just can't. Sorry…

Another way around the attribution dilemma was for Ken to make himself the news. He did this by turning himself into a minor celebrity, creating a flamboyant in-print personality with little relation to who he really was. He wore a fedora and a Blank Generation stare in his column's mugshot, and did his best to live up to his byline's glib persona.

On the rare occasions when he performed in public, Ken's dual identities intersected. His first time onstage was with a band called the Guidance Counselors, who invited Ken to do a "performance art" version of his column during a show. So he dragged an old Smith-Corona typewriter onto Each's stage for their encore one night and attacked it like Jerry Lee Lewis at a piano. As the band slaughtered the old Wilson Pickett standard "Land of 1000 Dances," he dashed off a post-verbal masterpiece that began:

opietr [pouiyuw/po90df qweer09ug9u8asd-06-03485;-
l'erkklnZXc kleryierulkgi v78eiot gpiou-itpiog. Fktkgj v
iodj5iut5, jktrklvuikrm589w70 23lf I rfirui dfjertmvj tru-
imgv egrjkpoeirtu vorpjhdiouir.

"Whattaya know, one of your columns that actually makes sense,"
Bob smirked. He claimed to prefer this raw first-draft version to the
Daily News column Ken later wrote about the experience.

Bob also served as co-conspirator on Ken's follow-up performance.
During Arrowhead's "Ravage America" tour, there were rumors the band
would play some unannounced club shows along the way. Since one of the
tour's open dates fell on the night after Arrowhead played Raleigh's Carter-
Finley Stadium, Ken decided to take advantage of the buzz.

"You didn't hear this from me," he told a few people, "but it'll be
worth your while to show up at Each Thursday night."

Word spread, especially after the big local rock station picked up
on the rumor, and an overflow crowd turned out at Each. But instead
of an intimate performance by the most popular rock 'n' roll band on
earth, the evening's entertainment was Ken Morrison in costume,
playing air guitar to a scratchy Arrowhead bootleg. Following a brief
medley of Arrowhead's biggest hits—"Stain," "Panty Church,"
"Vagaboned" and "Eleven O'Cock High"—the critic fled before the
angry mob turned into a riot.

This time, Ken's editor didn't let him write about the experience. She
did, however, suspend him for a week without pay.

In his own way, Ken was as much a huckster as the bands he
covered. Like them, he yearned for his big break. One moved up the
rock journalism totem pole by way of the big national magazines.
Despite scoring some freelance articles for trade papers and smaller
magazines, he had yet to crack the really big ones. He didn't have the
New York or Los Angeles connections to get the easy stories—the

record reviews and softball rock star profiles with which bigtime critics earned a living—nor did he have a regional story so undeniable the slick-page magazines just couldn't turn it down.

Tommy Aguilar, he hoped, would be that story. Here was someone perfectly willing to make his psychotic tendencies upfront and on-the-record, and who was going to be a huge star. Of that, Ken had no doubts whatsoever. And with his proximity, Ken had a headstart on every other critic in the country. If he played his cards right, he could crack the glossy magazines with this one; maybe even score a book deal.

"I saw rock 'n' roll's future—and its name is Tommy Aguilar."

Too bad that line had already been used on Bruce Springsteen decades ago. Ken was tempted to resurrect it anyway. Such a declaration was the secret vice of every rock critic—to be the first to declare an unknown artist's genius, in hopes it would confer genius upon the critic, too.

Ken had almost but not quite dropped all pretensions to genius by then. He grew up in the middle-class suburban environs of Charlotte, North Carolina, where some of the few thrills to be had involved scanning the AM radio dial when he was supposed to be sleeping. The strange, faraway noises from New York and Chicago made the rest of the world sound lots more interesting than where he was, especially late at night at a hundred thousand clear-channel watts.

At age twelve, he made an ill-fated attempt at learning to play violin. His instructor was a terrifying old man with a thick accent of indeterminate European origin, whose teaching method consisted of swatting his pupils' knuckles with a ruler when they botched their scale exercises. Following a couple of lessons that left his hands bruised and bleeding, Ken decided he'd rather play basketball.

That didn't take, either, thanks to Ken's clumsiness and tendency to back-talk coaches. His athletic career ended when the freshman basketball coach cut him, after which he joined the staff of the high school paper. He broke into the record review rotation at the University of

North Carolina's *Daily Tarheel,* and discovered he had a gift for enraging people.

After dropping out of UNC, the budding young critic found employment at the *Raleigh Daily News,* although he neglected to tell his employers he never actually completed his degree (like Tommy, Ken wasn't above fudging his own personal details when it suited him). One of his occupation's major perks was that drinking on the job was a requirement. It didn't always work, but Ken discovered that people were more willing to talk and less likely to notice his notebook when he was as drunk as they were. He just had to stay sober enough to hold onto his pen.

While Ken wasn't a musician, he could hold his liquor and liked music almost as much as gossip. He wrote passably well, with knowledge that was broad but not deep. Put him in any given situation and he could usually write his way out of it, and even convince most people he knew what he was talking about.

Rock criticism sure wasn't brain surgery. You went to a concert or listened to a record or took down some quotes, came up with a few wry adjectives or clever comparisons, and tried to avoid spelling anybody's name wrong. Since he worked at night, Ken didn't spend much time in the office. As long as his byline showed up in the paper a couple times a week, no one cared much where he spent his time. It was, he had to admit, a pretty cushy regimen.

"What you do is baseball cards," Bob once scoffed, when an argument with Ken reached the stage where they felt compelled to take cheap shots. "Does knowing somebody's batting average mean you can hit a curveball? Of course not. You just know a bunch of useless shit nobody else cares about, because you didn't get out of the house enough when you were a kid. Where the fuck would you be if you actually had to *do* something for a living?"

"This from a man who pours beer for a living," Ken shot back. But Bob's accusation stung because it was true.

Ten years of covering a thoroughly corrupt industry hardened Ken into something like a jaded war correspondent. Beneath his glib exterior, he felt himself going numb, depressed by the local music scene's endless cycle of futility. It was a vast wasteland populated by a few good bands and a lot more awful ones, all going nowhere fast and caught up in vicious backbiting over who was and wasn't "selling out." And they all seemed to think Ken was their publicist.

"Ninety percent of music is publicity and gimmicks," the leader of a particularly atrocious band once told Ken. "Gotta have a good gimmick or you're fucked, especially in this town."

Such people made Ken feel that if he had a shred of dignity, he would lay down his pen and do something honorable for a living. Dig ditches, steal purses, give blowjobs, stick up banks. Anything.

Instead, he tried to get along by going along, immersing himself in the scene, prowling the local club circuit almost every night, losing himself in tracking the endless stream of details. He perfunctorily reviewed the records local bands made and reported on their comings and goings, their many failures and few successes, their breakups, their reformations. Who got signed, who got dropped, who hit, missed, opened, closed, broke up. Who was doing what with whom, and how often—but almost never why, because *that* was off the record. Who was on the way up, down, out. Rumors, gossip, lies, dreams; pipe dreams, lots of those.

It was easy to do, the detail work. Ken could do it in his sleep—had been doing it in his sleep for quite some time. That was the path of least resistance and no one seemed to notice one way or the other, least of all Ken himself. There were no percentages in bucking the tide, as Ken discovered several years back when he got a little too carried away with keeping everything on the record.

Charlie Holmes played guitar in one of Raleigh's less illustrious bands, the Potshots. The group did have its fans, a few dozen loyalists who came to every show. But between their small following and general suckiness, Ken had long before filed the Potshots in the category of Safe To Ignore. Then Charlie turned up dead with a syringe in his hand, victim of a heroin overdose. The only surprise was that it didn't happen sooner. The last time Ken saw Charlie, on-stage at Each maybe three months before he died, he looked scarcely able to stand up.

Heroin terrified Ken, mostly because of the needles. Years earlier, in college, he watched someone he knew take a dose and it was the most horrible thing he'd ever seen. The burning odor of cooking the drug smelled like death—like cremation, almost—and the injection itself looked as if his friend literally had sucked a quantity of life out of his arm with a syringe. Declining an offer to shoot up a dose himself, Ken fled.

Charlie Holmes wasn't the only local musician with a drug problem. So Ken decided to use his death as a news peg for a column on the dangers of heroin. The only problem was that nobody wanted to talk about it. Bandmates, relatives, friends—not one person was willing to say a word, even off the record.

Somewhere in the back of the critic's mind, a voice told him to back off. Instead, he went down to the Wake County medical records department and looked up Charlie's death certificate: heart failure. Not many twenty-seven-year-olds die of heart failure, so Ken called the medical examiner who performed the autopsy.

"That kid," the man told him, "had enough smack in him to kill a horse."

Ken played that quote prominently, right below a lead he was rather proud of. It hit just the right tone of sorrow and outrage, he thought:

Nobody wants to talk about it, but this is the truth: Charlie Holmes died of a heroin overdose. And unless some folks wise up, he won't be the last one in this town who does, either.

For once, the ugly truth was actually on the record. Ken thought this was the right thing to do, holding up Charlie as a cautionary example. Maybe it would even save someone else's life. But the family and friends of Charlie Holmes didn't quite see it that way. To their way of thinking, it wasn't anybody else's business how he died. He was hardly a public figure—outside of his relatives and the Potholes' twenty-four-person fanbase, nobody even knew Charlie's name. He was just a guy who waited tables at the Vertigo Diner, played guitar in a band that was little more than a hobby, and had a dangerous private habit. Because that habit killed him, it became public news and therefore fair game, according to the rules of journalism.

But textbooks didn't cover how to deal with the flood of angry phone calls, letters, faxes and e-mails that poured in. "Ghoul" was one of the more polite things Ken was called, along with "sensationalist muckraker," "hypocrite" and "asshole."

"Why don't you just fucking piss on his grave while you're at it?" read a letter signed by Charlie's Potshots bandmates.

Several days later, the torrent was just beginning to subside when Ken answered his phone—and felt his stomach clench when an older female voice said, "This is Edna Holmes." Charlie's mother was still crazed with grief, and very angry.

"How is it," she sputtered, "that you can put these lies in the paper?"

"I'm…I'm sorry," Ken said, "but it wasn't a lie. It was the truth. The medical examiner said—"

"No it's *not!*" Edna howled. "It's not, it's *not,* it's *not!* It was a mistake, my son was *not* a *junkie!*"

Ken tried to reason with her, to tell her he only reported what he'd been told, but the woman refused to let him pass the buck. Sobbing hysterically, bordering on incoherent, she rallied enough to pronounce a curse that would haunt him the rest of his days.

"I just wanted you to know how much you've hurt me," Edna Holmes said in a terribly still voice that sounded like the eye of a hurricane. "Even though I don't expect you to understand. But I just hope…that someday, somebody else hurts you just as bad. And then…"

The pause was so long, Ken wondered if she was still on the line. He would've hung up, but found he could not move.

"…You'll know," Edna finally continued, almost whispering. Something in her voice seemed to crack, and she gave in to her urge to scream again.

"You *bastard!* God *damn* you! God damn you straight to *hell!!*"

And she slammed the phone down.

That happened just after 11 a.m. on a Tuesday. Ken took the rest of the day off and drank. Heavily.

About a month later, Ken was sitting at his desk reading a magazine when he heard a calm voice say, "My mother is dead."

He looked up to see Madeline Holmes, Charlie's sister, standing over him. Her eyes didn't just stare, they bored right through him. Every curve of her body asked: *Well?…*

Ken took a deep breath and tried to swallow. All the fluid in his body seemed to be rushing from his mouth to his palms. He didn't know what to say.

"I'm sorry," he finally managed, knowing that was pathetically inadequate. Madeline began to laugh, an awful sound, then shook her head.

"You're sorry, huh?" she hissed. "Yeah, you got that right. So are you gonna do a column about her, too?"

Ken had no answer for that, either, or for the next thing Madeline did. She reared back and slapped him across the face so hard it made his teeth hurt.

"That was for Charlie," she snarled, then spat in Ken's face, "and that's for my mother."

Then she turned and stormed off, slamming a door on the way out. Everyone else in the newsroom just gaped.

Ken left the office early that day, too.

CHAPTER SIX

Ostensibly, the news hook for Ken's first big TAB profile was the band's first real tour. They'd already done numerous short jaunts to towns a few hours away, but never an extended roadtrip of more than a day or two.

Making a record and hitting the road were steps one and two in their new manager's master plan. As soon as he took over, Bob postponed a few weeks' worth of shows and sent the band off to Tommy's shack for some intensive rehearsals. Bob instructed the trio to take their best original songs, tear them apart and put each one back together in battle-tested arrangements.

After the first week, Bob started coming to the practices, carefully listening to the eleven songs TAB played over and over. He couldn't define precisely what he was looking for, only that he'd know it when he heard it—the perfect song to record as a quickie seven-inch vinyl single.

TAB's first single was to be a calling card. So it had to be good, but not too good. Attention-getting, mostly. You didn't want to burn your best material on a self-produced cheapo single that you wouldn't get much out of besides club dates, publicity and (if you were lucky) some college radio airplay. Few stores even handled the antiquated seven-inch format anymore, but singles remained a cheap and effective way to get a few songs out there. Most college stations and rock critics still had turntables.

Bob finally settled on "Rock Hit Back to Black," one of the most energetic rave-ups in TAB's live set. Though it was a dependable crowd-pleaser, "Rock Hit" wasn't one of Tommy's better songs. It did, however, have a signature gimmick in the lyrics' nonsensical wordplay, which he turned into a Buddy Holly tribute by hiccuping the title chorus.

More importantly, "Rock Hit Back to Black" was relatively simple: three chords, four-four time, verse-chorus-verse. It would be easy to record, and difficult for Tommy to screw up too much if he went off on one of his tangents in the studio. Bob fervently hoped to avoid a knock-down-drag-out on their very first record—Tommy was spoiling for a fight, ever since Bob nixed his idea of just putting out one of TAB's home-recorded demotapes.

"It's too much, Tommy," the manager told him. "Better we should start with a small taste. Besides, those demos are some of your best songs. We might want to use them later, on a full-length album."

"But what if I don't wanna do anything else with those songs?" Tommy whined. "Half of 'em already bore the fuck out of me."

"Then write some more. Look, you just worry about that 'Big Picture' stuff and leave the detail work to me—because that's what this is, detail work. Trust me, this won't be a mistake."

After forcing TAB to practice "Rock Hit Back to Black" so many times everyone was sick of it, Bob hustled the band into a sixteen-track studio whose owner owed him a favor. They ran through the song repeatedly, eventually settling on take number six (out of eleven). To loosen everybody up, Bob opened the session with a surprise one-take recording of the Sex Pistols chestnut "Holidays in the Sun," a song TAB occasionally covered live but never practiced. That gave them a B-side as attention-getting as the A-side.

The session went off without incident, except for Tommy's insistence on "cleansing" the studio of any evil spirits before he would play a note. So he turned out the lights and performed a quasi-voodoo ritual with an incredibly noxious-smelling incense. One unexpected benefit was that everyone worked faster and more efficiently—they all wanted out of there and away from the stench as soon as possible. Ray could taste it for days afterward, while Michelle's clothes reeked so badly that her parents asked if she'd taken up peyote.

Tommy had numerous ideas about the cover, most of them involving expensive color reproductions of one of his paintings. His manager dutifully listened, then pleaded the indie-rock dough-ray-me amendment: We ain't got none. Instead, Bob used a stark black-and-white photo he had taken of TAB their first time onstage at Each. Total production costs came to fifteen cents, inserted into the copy machine at the Winn-Dixie grocery store.

Bob got a cut rate at a small pressing plant near Greensboro and ordered five hundred copies. They needed to put a record company name on the label, so Bob dubbed the venture TABeach Records. He didn't bother with a "Produced By" credit on the back cover, instead listing the single as, "Recorded by Bob Porter." He mailed the records to clubowners, college radio stations and rock critics. The whole thing cost about three thousand dollars, which Bob paid out of his own pocket.

Then he started running up his phone bill, booking dates. From their previous weekend roadtrips, TAB retained just enough non-antagonized club contacts to form the outlines of a regional tour. So while Bob went fishing for dates farther afield, he sent TAB out to play their familiar haunts in nearby towns. This was the band's first concentrated dose of playing every night—hard work compared to the leisurely schedule they used to keep, practicing a couple evenings a week with a show every other weekend.

TAB covered the Carolinas and Virginia in just under two weeks. By then, Bob had lined up another month's worth of dates through the rest of the South, some Northeastern cities and as far west as Kansas City. He was able to get the shows because he knew almost every other clubowner in America, and because he offered the band at the cut rate of fifty dollars plus a percentage of the door. That made TAB a no-risk proposition. A club they played only had to sell a couple dozen beers to break even on the night.

It didn't hurt that, wonder of wonders, both "Rock Hit Back to Black" and the "Holidays in the Sun" B-side were getting some airplay. TAB sounded like nothing else out there—weird, raw, bubblegum-punk rockabilly. Anybody who didn't know better would swear the record was at least forty years old, yet it didn't sound the least bit retro, either. It made a great change of pace for radio segues. The single began to register with stations reporting to the college radio trade papers, which listed it on their airplay charts. That got some nibbles from smaller independent record labels, who were calling Bob at Each (he thoughtfully included a phone number in the credits).

Music writers in other cities picked up on TAB, too. Between the single and Ken Morrison's TAB profile (which virtually every newspaper critic in the country saw, after the *Daily News* sent it out over the Associated Press wire), they were intrigued. Journalists like nothing better than an easy, juicy angle, and gun-wielding rockabilly psycho Tommy Aguilar was a story that could write itself.

So Tommy began doing interviews, usually from truckstop phone booths. Sometimes, Bob coordinated them via conference calls through his office phone and furtively listened in. He even devised a form to keep track of who interviewed Tommy for which publication, and how the conversation went: "Normal (So To Speak)," "Fair," "Not So Good" and "Venus." The manager quickly learned to judge how things were going by the tone of Tommy's spewing to the media. Relatively normal interviews meant all was well. But fair interviews were almost worse than bad ones, because they meant the bandleader was bored—probably watching The Weather Channel and looking for storms to chase for inspiration. And when Tommy checked in from Venus, Bob could usually count on making a late-night wire transfer so the band could pay off the cops, an angry clubowner or a bail bondsman.

Nobody would have called these shows "prestige gigs." Mostly, TAB opened for other bands in small rooms—lots of campus coffeehouses, basements, warehouses close to railroad tracks.

"Just like Each," Bob told Tommy during one of his check-in calls. "You should feel right at home."

"Sure."

The routine went: Pull into town, find the club, maybe get to do a soundcheck (if the headlining act was merciful), then nap on the floor until it was time for Tommy's pre-show voodoo. Frequently, that was the only sleep they got. After playing, TAB hoofed their gear back into the van, settled up for a pathetically small amount of money and took off for the next town.

Between all-night drives and tending to equipment failures, there was little time for sightseeing beyond watching what went by outside the window—although Tommy could always find time to visit famous morbid landmarks. TAB paid their respects at the corner of Hillcrest and Bartlett in Macon, Georgia, site of Duane Allman's 1971 motorcycle wreck; left some pocket change on Hank Williams' gravestone at Oakwood Cemetery in Montgomery, Alabama; and spent so much time one afternoon trying to find a certain highway crossroads near Clarksdale, Mississippi, that they were almost late for that night's show down in Jackson.

"You keeping some kinda list here?" Ray asked.

"Just hopin' something rubs off."

Michelle decided it was best not to ask just what that "something" was.

Occasionally, some kind soul offered to put TAB up for the night. Sometimes, that even happened on a night when they could accept the offer. Once a week, they splurged on a motel room to take showers, wash clothes and sleep in a bed. But that was a luxury, because gas to get down the road was always priority number one. Even eating took a backseat, so they depended on the kindness of strangers for food. It was amazing, Michelle reflected, just how good pizza tasted when you couldn't afford it, and some wonderful mensch took pity and gave you a slice.

Things started out slowly, moving Ray to dub their roadtrip the "Dead As This Room's Ever Been Tour." After one especially disheartening night, Michelle scribbled on the dressing room wall, "Never have so few worked so hard to entertain even fewer." A grand total of two paying customers had shown up.

"Nothin' like being on a first-name basis with your audience," sighed Ray.

Halfway through the tour, though, the crowds grew noticeably bigger, thanks to steadily increasing airplay on the single. The band wasn't seeing any more money, of course—"Wow, I never knew forty people could take up so much room," Ray sarcastically told one clubowner who was obviously shorting them—but it beat playing to empty rooms.

After the shows, people came around to ask where they could buy the single. They'd heard it, but "Rock Hit Back to Black" wasn't in stores. On the band's next long-distance report to Bob, Tommy asked, "Shouldn't we be selling the single at shows or something?"

"No, this is perfect."

"It is? Why?"

"'Cause we're building demand," Bob explained. "Kinda like planting seeds. I know this is hard right now, but look what's happening: People are hearing about something they can only get by coming to see you, and right now TAB is much better live than on record. So don't worry about it. By the time you get back to these places again, you'll have something to sell."

While things were going according to plan, Michelle was nevertheless miserable. She'd never endured this kind of intensive low-budget touring with her other bands. And unlike her vagabond bandmates, she was accustomed to relative middle-class comfort. The exhausting stretches of travel, lack of basic necessities and, most of all, uncertainty—not knowing where their next meal was coming from, or where they would sleep or bathe or even go to the bathroom—were exacting an awful toll.

By contrast, touring agreed with Ray, a seasoned veteran of the punk-rock chitlin' circuit. This was both good and bad—good because Ray was useful to have around, bad because he was wholly unsympathetic to anyone else's discomfort.

"You think this is bad, you ain't seen nothin'," he taunted his bandmates. "Jesus, I'm in a band with total *pussies*."

When Michelle asked how things could get much worse, the drummer just smirked and told her she didn't want to know. If touring was like boot camp, Ray served as a particularly sadistic drill sergeant.

Offstage and on, Ray was the engine that powered TAB—timekeeping drummer, de facto road manager, kicker of asses, and a crackerjack mechanic to boot. Put enough coffee in his mug and bad heavy metal on the stereo, and he was a drive-all-night machine. More than once, his stash of tools, spare parts and other paraphernalia saved the day. After their Dodge Roadstar van conked out climbing a steep Appalachian highway pass, the drummer astounded his bandmates by not only diagnosing the problem as a bum alternator, but producing a spare from under the seat.

"Always carry an extra alternator with Dodges," he said, swiftly ratcheting the new part into place and heaving the old one over a cliff. "Good vans, but their electrical systems ain't for shit. Look at 'em wrong and poof, off they go…Okay, gang, let's hit it and quit it, we're burnin' daylight."

Nothing phased Ray, not even the time a would-be robber approached them at a West Virginia rest stop with a bulge under his jacket. Correctly guessing that the man was unarmed, Ray called his bluff and chased him off with a sixteen-inch flashlight that still had "Dallas Police Department" etched into its base.

"Speak softly and carry a large flashlight," Ray said afterward. "Besides, that guy was a stupid fuck—it's not like bands ever have any money. What'd he think he was gonna steal from us, blood?"

As for Tommy, the road just seemed to make him squirrelier. One night when they were in a motel room, Michelle awoke to find him sprawled across the bathroom floor, frantically filling in the cracks between tiles with toothpaste.

"What the hell are you doing?" she mumbled groggily.

"Trying to keep the worms out," Tommy whispered, wide-eyed. "Christ, they're everywhere, can't you see them? Look out, *don't step on them!!*"

Bob also worried about Tommy, because his client began giving him trouble before the tour even started—when he insisted on putting together a "contract rider" of technical and equipment specifications. Bob knew it would simply be ignored and tried to keep it simple, although he did add one stipulation of his own: No green stage lights ("Makes you look diseased and ugly"). Ray the equipment snob insisted on no Peavey amplifiers ("Chump, amateur gear"), while Michelle asked for single-edged razor blades and number-two pencils. That was a trick of the trade; when applied to tuning pegs, pencil graphite shavings kept bass and guitar strings in tune longer.

Tommy's contribution was to demand a dozen oysters for his voice, one tube of hot pink lipstick (cruelty-free); a box of birthday cake candles; and a six-pack of beer with two bottles of Budweiser and one each of Shiner, Corona, Rolling Rock and the nearest regional microbrew.

"What, no ban on brown M&M's?" the manager sighed, referring to Van Halen's legendary backstage requirement. Bob quietly left

Tommy's demands out of the rider, and he forgot all about it by the time the band left town.

Sending TAB out without a handler was risky but unavoidable, because they couldn't afford another person on the road. The one advantage to the grueling schedule was that Tommy didn't have much time to get into trouble with women. Even so, he required near-constant supervision. New York City was the most unnerving date, as it coincided with TAB's only day off on the tour. Originally, Bob was going to fly up to see how things were going and lend moral support. But he had to bail at the last minute when one of his Each bartenders quit unexpectedly. That left Tommy at loose ends in the big city.

He called Bob from a seedy Times Square motel, saying he was going out alone for a bite to eat. An hour later, Tommy called back to ask his manager which motel he was staying in: "It's moved, it's not where it was before." An hour after that, he called yet again to ask what restaurant he'd called from earlier. After making his way back to the motel, Tommy realized he left his wallet at the restaurant—but couldn't recall either its name or location.

"Goddamn," Bob sighed after finally getting Tommy and his wallet safely back to the motel. "It's like baby-sitting the devil."

Michelle would have appreciated that analogy, especially after an incident a week later in Bowling Green, Ohio. She'd gone out to the van after soundcheck, looking for a pen to write some postcards ("Having a horrid time, wish I was anywhere but here"). She opened the glovebox, rummaged through it in the dark and hit something sharp.

"Owww!" Michelle yelped, and jerked her hand out—then shrieked bloody murder when she saw a syringe sticking out of the meat of her palm. Ray heard the scream and came running outside.

"What the fuck?!" he panted.

Michelle didn't say a word, just looked at him with her eyes spread all over her face and held up her hand. Ray lunged forward, yanking the needle out while looking over his shoulder.

"Jesus, don't let anybody see that," he growled, pitching the syringe into a nearby dumpster. "You trying to get us busted? These small-town cops would love that."

Michelle stared at the small drop of blood on her hand. She looked up.

"Ray…Why is a syringe in here?"

"Why do you think?" he asked, then anticipated her next question. "Not me, hell no. It ain't my drug and besides, needles creep me out. Him."

The drummer nodded toward the dressing room, where Tommy was well into his pre-show ritual.

"How long?…"

"Not very. Claims he doesn't have a habit, just a hobby. Near as I can tell, he's still a weekend user. He hasn't done it much this tour. But that scene in the bathroom a while back, with the toothpaste and the 'worms'—I'm pretty sure he took a shot that night."

"And it never occurred to you that this was something I, you know, might want to know about?" Michelle asked, her initial fear giving way to anger.

"I figured you already knew," Ray shrugged. "Hell, just watch him for a while. How could you *not* notice?"

Michelle felt numb.

Heroin, she thought. *Great. Just…great. I haven't eaten or slept in a day and a half, I have no money and probably no job—all so I can be in a band with a raving lunatic who likes guns and has a drug problem…*

"Ugh," Michelle said, feeling lightheaded. "I must be out of my fucking *mind*…"

"C'mon," Ray said, taking her by the unstuck hand. "Let's get that bandaged up."

Stoned or straight, there was no denying that Tommy and TAB sounded better than ever. Playing every night for a month tightened them up, and also attuned them to each other's quirks—the unconscious double-time snare flourish Ray liked to play coming out of the break; Tommy's penchant for banjo riffs; Michelle's preferred cruising space in the pocket a quarter-beat behind the rhythm, just like the old soul bassists James Jamerson and Duck Dunn. Michelle had become especially adept at keeping up with Tommy's off-the-wall changes. He rarely fooled her anymore, but she had yet to beat him to the punch herself. Until that night in Bowling Green, when the bassist was playing angry.

Tommy tried to pull a fast one toward the end of the set, segueing a half-bar early into the next song without stopping—only to find Michelle already there, waiting on him. Watching his fret hand, she figured out what he was about to do a full bar before he actually did it. The guitarist made the change a little too casually and gave a start when he realized Michelle beat him to it and was pushing him. He was so surprised, he briefly faltered.

Tommy's bandmates had been waiting for this moment since the day they joined TAB. Leering like jackals, they pounced all over Tommy, pushing him around the way he'd done to them. Michelle leaned forward, leveled the neck of her bass at the guitarist like a shotgun and blasted away. Tommy tried to regain control of the tempo by throwing out a withering volley of chords, but he was off-balance and Michelle beat him to that one, too.

The bassist laughed wildly and hammered away, pressing even harder as Tommy struggled to keep up. He seemed like a boxer on the ropes, reeling as he thrashed out one bum note after another. But Michelle would not relent and Ray stayed right with her; he wanted to see how this turned out.

They had taken the song so far from its original arrangement that there was no possible way they could find their way back without stopping and starting over. Michelle kept up her assault, cutting off every avenue of escape whenever Tommy tried to move the music back toward order. This was a reversal of their usual roles, and she was determined to force him to admit defeat…

…Just when she thought Tommy was about to surrender, his eyes narrowed and he gave her a sly little grin. And he stepped over to the microphone and began to sing the song's first verse.

What?!…

Now it was Michelle's turn to falter as she realized they had suddenly, inexplicably arrived back at the song's original melody line. They were even in the correct key and tempo. Stunned, she looked over at Ray, who appeared equally bewildered. They'd been so busy beating up on Tommy, trying to smother him with noise, that neither one noticed the trap he led them into. His seemingly random thrashing hadn't been accidental at all, instead traveling a circuitous route back to the precise place they started from.

Planned out ahead of time, this would have been impressive. Made up on the fly, it was genius-level musicianship—plus one hell of an acting job. Feeling as if she'd been suckered in a very expensive hand of strip poker, Michelle barely made it through the rest of the song, mechanically thumping away at the root.

"Thank ya very much," Tommy crooned as the crowd cheered wildly. Then he turned toward Michelle and said, off-mike, "Hey, we should do that one like that every night."

Two hours later, they were fifty-seven miles down the road. Ray drove, Michelle rode shotgun, Tommy was sprawled unconscious in the back. Nobody said a word after the show.

"You okay?" Ray finally asked.

She nodded. They drove in silence a few more miles.

"Your hand hurt?"

"A little," Michelle said, shrugging.

"Well," Ray said, "now you know."

"Know what?"

"Why he does smack."

"So he can play like that? Bullshit. You were up there, that should have been impossible. I still don't know how he did it. And you're telling me it's the drugs? No way. Heroin would only get in the way."

"That's right," Ray said. "The heroin isn't so he can play like that. It's so he doesn't hear it in his head all the time."

CHAPTER SEVEN

Six weeks, forty shows, forty cities, nineteen states and 11,389 miles later, TAB's first "real" tour came to a merciful end. They played the last show in Columbia, Missouri, and turned for home, only stopping for gas and to nap a few hours at a highway rest stop after even Ray couldn't keep his eyes open anymore.

Their battered van limped into Each's parking lot late the next night. The tires were bald, and several fresh cracks spidered across the windows. Road grime was caked on so thick, the vehicle looked brown instead of metallic blue. The van was burning more than a quart of oil per tank of gas, and dangerously overheating. They'd had to run the heater so it wouldn't boil over, even though the outside temperature was almost ninety degrees.

Onstage inside, Bug Parts was about to start its encore. Bug Parts' lead singer was a former bandmate of Ray's, and gave the drummer a shout-out when he saw TAB walk through the door: "Ladies and gentlemen, let's have a warm welcome for road warriors TAB, back in the house from the Western front!"

He pointed, and the small crowd murmured and turned as one to look—then recoiled in horror. All three TAB members had lost weight on the road and looked alarmingly gaunt, even the muscular Ray. The crowd grew hushed and stared, parting before them. It was like watching the scene in *Lawrence of Arabia* where Peter O'Toole comes out of the desert.

Always a show-stopper, Ken thought. Tommy looked right through him as he passed by, and appeared not to recognize anybody in the room.

Tommy, Ray and Michelle went behind the bar and into Each's office. Bob followed.

"Hey, Bob," Ken called out, "better go a little easier on 'em next time or Amnesty International will be all over you. Jesus, they look like they just came through a war."

"They did," Bob said, closing the door.

The first order of business was settling up profits from the tour. TAB came back with a grand total of $77.90 after expenses. Bob's ten percent came to $7.79, leaving $70.11 to be split three ways. Each member's share came to $23.37.

Twenty-three dollars and thirty-seven cents.

Averaged over the six weeks they'd been gone, that came to not quite $3.90 a week...

...Or fifty-seven cents for each show they played.

A month and a half of miserable insanity, and they each came away with enough cash for cheap dinner and a movie.

Reminding himself that far bigger careers had started with less, Bob sighed and briskly counted out everyone's shares: twenty-three bucks and change for each of them; and $7.79 for him, to go toward the three thousand dollars he'd spent on singles and postage (not to mention an astronomical phone bill).

"Don't spend it all in one place," the manager quipped, trying to lighten the mood. No one even cracked a smile.

Bob told them to stay completely out of touch for at least a week. He needn't have bothered. After six weeks in the cramped confines of their van, they couldn't wait to get out of each other's sight.

Michelle went to her parents' house, ate every scrap of food in the refrigerator, took a two-hour bubblebath and went to sleep for a day and a half. When she woke up, she got a trash can and burned all the clothes she took on tour, using her twenty-three dollars to start the fire. She was tempted to throw in her bass, but resisted the impulse.

Ray went home and slept for about five hours. He arose early the next morning and set to work on the van, replacing the water pump and flushing the radiator. He hit a junkyard to scavenge some new tires, which took twenty bucks of his $23.37. Then he called a pal who owned a machine shop, making arrangements to take the van there later that night to start on a ring job. That would solve the vehicle's oil-burning problem. He arrived at the machine shop around midnight, after spending the day hanging around Dick's Drum Head instrument store. Ray also spent part of his evening at HammerJack's nightclub, sitting in with some friends from another of his former bands, Dopplegangbanger.

Ray never did have much use for time off.

As for TAB's spiritual leader, Tommy lost his $23.37 somewhere between Each and his shack. Once home, he collapsed and slept the sleep of the drugged. When he finally awoke the next day, Tommy brooded. He didn't go out or answer his phone, which wasn't unusual. But he didn't pick up a guitar, either, which was. Bob figured he and his client needed to have a heart-to-heart debriefing soon, but gave Tommy his week off first. In the meantime, the manager encased his own $7.79 tour share in an amber block and put it on his desk as a paperweight. Someday, he hoped everyone would find it an amusing artifact of TAB's humble origins.

On the seventh day, Bob drove his battered Chevy pickup out to The Crypt for an attitude check. He arrived late in the afternoon to find Tommy sprawled on his couch, engrossed in a thick book. *Moby Dick,* of all things.

"Oh, the 'Asshole Chases Whale' book," Bob said, walking through the open front door without knocking. "What page you on?"

"One-twenty-four."

"Here, I'll save you some time," Bob said as he lowered himself into a chair. "No one gets out of it alive."

"The Doors," Tommy sneered, identifying the source of his manager's paraphrased quote. "I didn't know you listened to that old shit."

"I don't, and besides, what've you got against 'old shit?' You're the one who still plays Cab Calloway and Hank Williams covers."

"Got more life left in 'em than the friggin' Doors."

"No doubt."

Tommy set the book down and went to his tiny kitchen, returning with two cans of Budweiser. While Tommy was out of the room, Bob studied the elm tree in the front yard. It looked pretty ragged from all the target practice.

"So," Bob said, opening his can, "how you feeling?"

"Like, with my hands?" Tommy grinned briefly, then resumed frowning. "Okay, I guess. Although my hands…haven't, um, had that much in them worth holding lately, if you know what I mean. But I'm all right. Mostly just tired. Don't know how long it'll be before I want to do *that* again, you know?"

Bob nodded sympathetically.

"Unfortunately, that's part of the gig," the manager said. "It's a tough business. A lot of work."

"But that's just it," Tommy said. "You know, that word."

"What, 'work?' "

"No, 'business,' " Tommy sneered. "The whole 'music business' thing of 'building an audience.' After going out and doing that, I just think the whole thing is kind of…demeaning."

"Especially when you bust your ass for a month and a half, and come home with twenty-three bucks. Right?"

"Well, sure, that sucked. But that wasn't the worst part."

"What was?"

Tommy paused and bit his lip, gazing at the skull above his fireplace.

"Bob," he finally said, "people were yelling for the single."

" 'Rock Hit Back'?"

"Yeah," he muttered gloomily. "Every night, crowds yelled for it. Over and over and over."

"Cool," Bob said, misreading his mood. "A dinky little single we just sent to some radio stations, nobody can even buy the thing, and people somehow still knew about it. Next time, we'll do even better."

"That's what I'm afraid of," Tommy said, exasperated. "You don't understand, Bob: People were yelling for that song every night, and it bugged me. I mean, it *really* bugged me."

Bob ran a hand over his face and counted to ten. Breathe in, breathe out.

"Let me get this straight," the manager said. "You just came back from a tour where you were working for a nickel an hour, maybe—and you're telling me you're upset because too many people heard one of your songs on the radio?"

"Well…"

"So do you want smaller crowds showing up?"

"Maybe."

Bob closed his eyes, this time counting to twenty. Then he opened them back up and opted for a less-direct tack.

"Tommy, what do you do for money?"

"Lately, not much. I was washing dishes at the Rathskeller for a while, but I got fired. So I do odd jobs here and there. Yardwork, mostly. Some errands. I painted somebody's house a while back. I don't need much to live on."

"Okay, then, let's go back to this single. You recorded a song, and people heard it and liked it enough to pay money to hear it again. As complicated and mysterious as the music business seems to be, that's the whole thing right there. If you write enough songs people want to hear, you get to have a career. You can play, make records, tour—or not. If you're successful enough, you can do as much or as little as you want."

"See, I don't know if I believe that," Tommy said. "If I ever had a big hit record, wouldn't that just be a trap?"

"How so?"

"Look, it's not like 'Rock Hit' was a gigantic top-forty hit or anything, right? But people were still yelling for it everywhere! So does that mean I have to play it every goddamn night now? Fuck that. There are some nights I want to just make some weird, fucked-up noises and see what happens, but I can't do that if the crowd is a bunch of asshole fratboy pinheads who'll go away pissed off if they don't hear the one song they came for. And it's not even that great a song! It's just a stupid brain fart I wish I'd thrown away because it's following me around like a, like a…like a goddamned white whale!"

Tommy nodded toward *Moby Dick*.

"Okay, Ahab, so how come you were all upset you didn't have any copies of it to sell?" Bob asked, playing his first trump card.

Tommy thought for a minute. "Probably because I was hungry," he said. "If I'd had a couple of singles, I could've traded them for something to eat. Hunger makes people do some strange shit, Bob, you know that."

"Really? Is that all?"

"Yes…"

Bob dealt trump card number two.

"Because if these crowds were pissing you off so much, it's not like you don't know how to clear a room. You've done that before, part of this 'I reserve the right to fuck up' clause of yours. But I also remember you telling me you wanted a bigger audience, and were tired of being broke all the time. Any of this ringing a bell?"

"Okay, sure," Tommy backtracked. "I haven't exactly sorted this out yet. All this really means is that I had to play 'Rock Hit Back' every fucking night, and it pissed me off because I didn't want to. You've got to understand, Bob, I didn't start playing music because of 'business' or to turn it into a 'career.' I play because…well, it's what I do. And I don't know anything else *to* do. Do you know what I mean?"

"Yes."

"So you tell me taking care of business can be painless, and here our very first record almost wrecks my life. Makes me wonder if I want to do this."

"But don't you remember all that stuff you were telling me about riots and how people shouldn't hold anything back? That goes both ways. If you don't want anyone else to hold back—your audience, Ray, Michelle, me—you better not be doing it, either."

"What the fuck are you getting at?" Tommy asked angrily. "Am I just supposed to go ahead and sell out, is that it?"

"Selling out has nothing to do with it. This town is full of shitty bands who can't wait to sell out, if only somebody was buying. No, I want you to cut the crap and decide what you want. Do you want a big audience? Okay, let's go out and get you one. Or do you want to be this cooler-than-thou indie-rock fuckup? Yeah, you can do that. But you can't have both."

"What if I don't know?"

" 'Don't know' don't cut it."

"But I don't!"

"Then decide."

"But—"

"But nothing. Tommy, your musical instincts are better than anyone I've ever seen. The only way you can fuck it up is if you keep trying to have it both ways. If you want your manager's advice, it's time for you to quit half-assing around and take your shot. I think this is about reaching as many people as possible. Isn't that why you play? To be heard?"

"I don't know. I'd never really thought about it like that before. I think I could be just as happy playing for myself. If nobody else ever heard me, I'm not so sure I'd mind."

"Bullshit," Bob said, dealing trump card number three. "Look at yourself, you've got TEMPT ME tattooed across your knuckles. That ain't the sort of thing one does if one plans to avoid temptation—like, say, becoming a 'rock star.'"

He drained the rest of his beer and crumpled the can.

"Now, then," Bob continued, "I believe we can be successful without turning you into a whore. In fact, I'm counting on it. Unless we can all feel good about this, we're not doing it. I didn't become your manager to turn you into some pathetic top-forty jingle asshole. Sure, I'd like to get rich. But if I do right by you, I figure I'll do right by me, too. So it's up to you. We can get back to work. Or, if you really want, you can just play Each once a month for the rest of your life. Lots of bands do that, but only because it's as far as they can go. You, on the other hand, would be a chickenshit because you'd be settling for a lot less than your potential.

"Anyway," he concluded, "how can you stop now? Don't you want to see what happens next?"

"Well…" Tommy said. "Yeah, I guess I do."

He paused. "Just one thing, Bob. Let's make sure we stay on top of things. If anything happens, I want it to be something we can control."

"Fine by me," the manager said. "And while we're on the subject of speed, I want you to hold up your end of the bargain. Don't go slowing yourself down."

Tommy's eyes narrowed. "What do you mean?" he asked, a little too innocently.

"Don't give me that shit," Bob said. "You know exactly what I'm talking about."

"No, I don't."

The manager gave his client's eyes a good, long stare, until Tommy finally looked away. Then Bob dropped his empty beer can on the floor with a clatter, stood up and walked into the bathroom. Humming loudly, he rooted around the medicine chest and closet until he finally located the stash of syringes he figured would be there—after hearing the rumors and taking a good look at Tommy the night TAB arrived back at Each. Bob had been around enough junkies to recognize the symptoms.

He carried a syringe back into the living room and threw it needle-down, like a dart. It stuck in the wood floor, quivering.

"That," Bob said, "is what I'm talking about. I don't want you doing *that* anymore. It's a stupid habit."

"But I don't have a habit," Tommy protested. "I just…you know…do it every now and then to relax."

"And you can quit anytime, right?" Bob sighed. "You know, it's funny how nobody ever has a 'problem' with smack. It's always just a little something they do 'every now and then.' Ain't no big thing, they can stop whenever they want—and then one day they turn up dead. You may think you've got it under control, but there's no such thing as careful enough with that shit. Leave it alone. I mean it."

Bob knew he wouldn't catch his client red-handed again so easily. Thinking he had everyone fooled, Tommy had been cocky and therefore careless. He would, the manager knew, be craftier about hiding places from now on.

"I'm warning you, stop it," Bob said, extracting the syringe from the floor and snapping it in half for emphasis. "Capece?"

"Capece."

By the time Bob arrived back at Each to prepare for that night's show, Ken was already inside nursing a beer. The club wasn't yet open, but the critic was one of several regulars who knew how to jimmy open the bathroom window to break in. Finding the front door locked and no one around, Ken came in the back way and helped himself to the bar.

"You're here early," Bob said.

"Couldn't sleep."

It was 4:15 in the afternoon.

"Maybe you could if you were sober. Jesus, Morrison, I know you keep vampire's hours, but doesn't your editor ever get suspicious?"

"Long as I chew some gum before going to the office, nobody notices a thing."

"Don't count on it. How many you had, anyway? Just because you know how to break in here doesn't mean you get to drink for free."

"Put it on my TAB," Ken smirked, and Bob winced.

"Sounds like a few. Drunk before dark, that's one of the classic alcoholic symptoms. You ought to slow down."

"Oh, c'mon. It's not a problem."

"Second time today I've heard that," the clubowner sighed.

Ken was so eager to ask his next question, he didn't even notice this very large softball of a hint Bob dropped in his lap.

"So how is he?"

"How is who?" the clubowner deadpanned, watching the hint bounce up and roll away. Now Ken would have to earn his dish.

"Aw, come oooooooooon, Bob," he whined. "Don't play hard-to-get."

"I got no idea what you're talking about," Bob said, turning away. Ken trailed behind him into the office.

"Tommy, TAB, the tour—what happened?"

"Oh, that," Bob said innocently, settling in behind his desk. "Why didn't you just say so? Went great. Decent crowds, good shows. Even made a little money."

That was all literally true; he just didn't specify exactly how "little" money was involved.

"And?"

"And what?"

"Bob, what are you hiding here? They came in here last week looking like they'd just taken the redeye from Stalingrad. And you're telling me this was a tour that 'went great?'"

"Depends. Are we on or off the record?"

That was startling. The clubowner had always been one of Ken's best sources. It wasn't like him to clam up when there was good dish to share.

"Damn, Bob, you've changed since you graduated from bars to bands. Tommy make you take a blood oath or something?"

"Or something, yeah."

The critic sighed, hating to give up some potentially juicy column material. But he also wanted the information badly enough to agree not to print it, at least not yet.

"Okay," he said reluctantly, "we're off the record."

"Well, they had a pretty rough time," Bob said. "Six weeks is a long time to be out there playing shit gigs for fifty bucks a night, but I wanted to see how they'd hold up. I knew Ray would do fine, I was worried about Michelle and had no idea about Tommy—and if this didn't break 'em, nothing will. Compared to what they just lived through, every other tour from here on out will be a breeze.

"I've heard nothing but good things about how they played. One night, two people showed up—that's two, as in one-two—after the band had driven four hundred miles for the gig. And they still did an amazing show. Guy who owns that place told me he'd never seen anything like it in twenty years: 'TAB has three big fans in Harrisburg now, two paying customers and me!' Tommy might be a strange bunch of guys—"

"I'll say," Ken interjected with a smirk; Bob ignored him.

"—But when it comes time to get out there, he does his job. Ray and Michelle, too, they're all pros. I'm really proud of them."

"I heard the single's been getting some decent airplay, too."

"Number twelve in CMJ," Bob said, referring to College Media Journal's chart measuring college radio airplay.

"And you didn't even put it in stores, right?"

"Right."

"That's amazing. So how's Tommy liking his first taste of stardom?"

"Well...okay, I guess."

"Just 'okay?' I figured he'd be turning handstands."

"Not exactly," Bob said. "He likes the abstract idea of being famous, especially the girls-on-demand part, but the reality of it freaks him out. He's never thought through what happens when you actually become famous; just figured that if you go from one to ten, you get ten times the money and pussy, and everybody loves you ten times as much. It hadn't occurred to him before now that there's a downside."

"And this surprises you?"

"I'd be more surprised if Tommy didn't feel weird about this. He's used to people treating him like a freak, and doesn't trust anybody who shows signs of liking him—which is why he's always yankin' my chain, and why he pulled out the gun when you did that interview. He thinks everyone is trying to push him around. You wouldn't believe how pissed he got that people were yelling for the single."

Ken laughed. "We should all have such problems."

"Yep," Bob said. "If all goes according to plan, we'll have more such problems soon."

"What is the plan, anyway?"

"Same thing it always is: We go out and do it all over again. And again. And again. And if it still hasn't happened by then, we just do it again again."

CHAPTER EIGHT

TAB's three principals recovered quickly. Regular sleep and food did wonders for Michelle, who returned to her job at the bookstore. Even if the bassist's real last name had officially disappeared into her new identity as "Michelle From TAB," it was nice to be back home and having conversations about normal things like the weather, Sylvia Plath or where to go for coffee. On the road, typical tour chatter tended to center on which convenience store looked easiest to shoplift dinner out of.

If Michelle was glad to be home, Ray couldn't wait to get back on the road. The drummer resumed his weight-lifting regimen and quickly bulked back up. In short order, he also had TAB's van running like a top again. He even gave it a polish-and-wax job, and added some new camouflage—American flag decals and NRA bumper stickers to deflect the attention of authorities. For a scruffy rock band, counter-cultural bumper stickers were an open invitation to be pulled over.

After his talk with Bob, Tommy made the latest in a series of resolutions to quit heroin. He preferred booze anyway, he told himself; it wouldn't be hard. So he flushed his stash down the toilet. Or rather, he almost did.

A part of his mind believed he really poured it into the water and flushed it away. But when the time came to let go, something made

Tommy's hand pull away and put the plastic bag back under the loose floorboard tile in the bathroom closet.

I won't do any of it, he thought to himself. *I'll just…hang onto it. Keep it right here, maybe even give it away. I know a lot of people who need it worse than me. But I won't do it.*

Tommy kept that promise for as long as he could.

Ten days after coming off the road, TAB resumed rehearsals. The first practice started tentatively, slowed down by cobwebs and rust. Michelle was amazed and depressed at how quickly a band's precision could decay. But it only took a few hours for the trio to slip back into the unconscious groove they'd developed on the road.

Band practices went well after that, as Tommy went on another song-writing binge. During the tour, a certain part of his musical brain had been switched off, as he channeled his energy into live improvisation. With his compositional lobe reactivated, Tommy cranked out song after song at a dizzying pace, each one more twisted and inspired than the one before.

One day, Michelle arrived at practice to find the guitarist picking out an oddly familiar-sounding figure. It was something she vaguely remembered from her days as a classical music student—a Bach concerto. Tommy had figured out how to transpose it to guitar, by ear, and somehow turned it into a pop song.

"Where," she asked in wonder, "did you hear *that?*"

"WUNC," Tommy said—the local public radio station.

"Oh," she said. "Well, I like it. It's…different."

"Yeah. Wicked hook, innit?"

After two weeks of practices, TAB came out of hiding to play a Friday night show at Each—the trio's first performance since the tour. Bob booked it mostly to dispel the breakup rumors that swirled around town following the band's bedraggled reappearance. Ken gave TAB a day-of-show preview in his column, recounting some of the band's on-the-record touring experiences (Tommy: "Playing at the same club where Jaco Pastorius was beaten to death, wow, what a thrill *that* was"). But the show didn't need any plugging to draw a capacity crowd. The locals were curious.

TAB played wonderfully that night, unveiling a half-dozen mesmerizing new originals and closing with an amped-up rockabilly-punk/free-jazz cover of the Doors' "Light My Fire"—a private joke Tommy intended for Bob, who got it.

The rest of the crowd didn't, but went crazy anyway.

There was, however, a dark lining to the evening's silver cloud, which revealed itself shortly before TAB went onstage. Bob and Ken were standing just outside the door, trying to escape the heat and cigarette smoke inside, when a black stretch limo wheeled into the parking lot. They looked at the massive car (the first limo Bob could remember darkening Each's parking lot), then at each other and shrugged.

The back door opened and Gus DeGrande emerged. Ken would've been less surprised to see the Pope himself. The critic rarely saw the promoter from any closer than all the way across an arena or football stadium, when Gus would come onstage between acts to plug upcoming events. The distance between them was no accident. Gus came from the old school, which held that you treated the media with contempt. The review tickets he gave to critics were always in the back row, even if the venue was deserted. Petty though it was, Ken appreciated the gesture. Every time he reviewed a Grandiose Concerts show, his seats in the rafters served to remind the critic who his friends weren't.

Though wide of girth, the promoter was not as large as he seemed. Even his ample belly spilling over his designer jeans didn't account for the volume of his presence. Any room Gus occupied always felt overcrowded, no matter how empty, because he always took more than his fair share—even when it came to oxygen. The promoter's bald head was vaguely fist-shaped, barren as the moon, with deep-set craters for sockets. His eyes didn't just glower, they scalded.

"To what do we peons owe this honor?" Ken asked, bowing theatrically as the promoter approached Each's entrance. Gus didn't bother answering, just frowned as he slapped a five-dollar bill on the counter by the door.

"That's okay, Mr. DeGrande," Bob said, handing the bill back. "On me. Come on in."

"Thanks," Gus growled, nodding as he took his money back and moved inside.

"Do you know what you just did, Bob?" Ken asked, watching DeGrande make his way toward the bar. "You just comped a fucking war criminal."

In years to come, Bob would remember not keeping that five-spot as the first of many mistakes he made with Gus DeGrande. He was still luckier than most—few people lasted beyond their first error with the promoter.

He had been born Giusseppe DiGiacomo forty-eight years earlier in Chicago. When he was still in diapers, his father Vincent drowned in Lake Michigan. That was what the coroner's report said, anyway. There was no mention of the twenty-three bullet holes in him, or the territorial dispute that led to Vincent DiGiacomo's untimely demise. Likewise, control over territory was to be a recurring theme in his son's life.

Young Giusseppe was adopted by an aunt and uncle who anglicized his surname to DeGrande, and moved him to Atlanta with their family. Growing up in the South, Gus learned the valuable protective coloration of passing for a yokel. He noticed at a young age that people tended to equate a thick drawl with stupidity. That could be convenient, so he developed one. About the only time Gus's drawl disappeared into his native Midwestern cadence was if he drank excessively (all the more reason to stick to his preferred poison, cocaine).

Like Ken Morrison, Gus discovered his calling after an unsuccessful stab at sports. He went out for football his sophomore year of high school and failed miserably. After getting cut, he became the team's equipment manager and unofficial social director. Mostly, that consisted of putting on post-game parties. Gus knew a few people in garage bands, which he hired to play for the free booze. Then he charged people who wanted to come hang around the players a couple bucks each, to "cover overhead." Since these parties took place in basements or backyards and most of the alcohol was stolen out of parents' liquor cabinets, "overhead" was virtually non-existent. Somewhere in Gus's head, a lightbulb went off.

This party scam led to an even more lucrative brainstorm—selling autographed pictures of the team's dreamboat quarterback to swooning girls. Gus split the money with the quarterback fifty-fifty, surely the last time he ever gave anybody else that good a split; a rookie mistake, he decided in retrospect. But the budding young promoter learned some important lessons from the arrangement: that it was easy to manipulate people through flattery; that the real money in any enterprise was in secondary merchandise; and most of all, that he could increase his own share by lying about how much money was coming in.

Hello, music business. DeGrande gravitated toward it like a vulture to a squashed rabbit.

Gus studied carefully and selected a college based primarily on location and social life. He wound up in Chapel Hill, and went to work for the student-run University of North Carolina's program council. At the time DeGrande began college, most of the area's concert business was in the hands of a pair of aging hipsters who ran a small promotion firm called Jekyll & Hype Productions. He worked closely with them throughout his college years, booking and co-producing rock concerts from tiny nightclubs up through huge stadiums. It was the best on-the-job training he could've asked for.

Upon his graduation, J&H Productions offered Gus a job. He turned them down and went into business for himself, hanging out a shingle with an audacious name: Grandiose Concerts. His former mentors had a good laugh over the young man's brashness, and told each other that Gus DeGrande hadn't been that good a concert guy, anyway. He would never last.

That was exactly what Gus wanted them to think.

Within three years, Gus put Jekyll & Hype out of business. They ran a sloppy ship and were constantly on the verge of bankruptcy, so it hadn't been hard. After that, it didn't take long for DeGrande to bankrupt the university program council, too—the same one from which he learned the business. But now that he was no longer enrolled, Gus looked at it as just another competitor. Co-producing shows with the program council meant cutting them in on profits, and the promoter refused to do it.

By the time he was thirty, Gus owned the rest of the Carolinas, too. He repeated the same pattern city by city, town by town and venue by venue, moving in and waging holy war until the opposition caved in.

By the time he was forty, Gus owned most of the Eastern and Central time zones. His genius was to expand along the path of least resistance, taking the territory nobody else wanted. DeGrande confined his efforts to what the record company hacks called "Flyoverland," medium-sized cities and towns off the beaten path, where competition was minimal. But these places all had cable TV, and bored kids with money to spend on concert tickets and overpriced black T-shirts. Gus had thrived over the past twenty-seven years by choosing his fights carefully and avoiding warfare with any opponent he couldn't beat. So he stayed away from the big cities, which was all part of the code. The concert business operated on a sort of "Monroe Doctrine" in which all the big promoters defended their fiefdoms with Mafia-esque zeal.

When it came to competitors, real or imagined, Gus was utterly ruthless. Bands certainly knew the score. They were free to play wherever and for whomever they wanted during the small-club phase of their careers. But once an act got far enough along to show up on the Grandiose radar screen, major unpleasantness would ensue if they played for anyone else in what the promoter defined as his territory.

Gus's tentacles seemed to reach everywhere. Rival promoters frequently turned up as targets of out-of-nowhere IRS audits, invariably at a time when cash flow was tight; or the subject of a fire department inspection (or an anonymous bomb threat) on the one night of the month they exceeded their building's legal capacity. A band's instruments and gear might turn up inexplicably missing, or a group might arrive at a venue to find it burned to the ground.

When all else failed, DeGrande could fight with figurative as well as literal fire. If anyone else had the cojones to book an act he wanted, he'd simply bury them—schedule acts that would attract the same audience immediately before and after his competitor's show, and undercut their prices. That hurt Gus, too, and bands were never happy about being used as pawns in his turf wars. But he was a troll that everybody, one way or another, had to pay.

By Gus's mid-forties, the frontier was closed. Grandiose Concerts had expanded as far as it could. Trying to go further meant jeopardizing everything, and this Gus could not afford. So he tended to business, and fidgeted. During the day, he puttered around his lavish office, playing with his toys and barking at his secretaries while wheeling and dealing over the phone. If something displeased him, he unwound by feeding live goldfish to the piranha he kept in an aquarium by his desk.

By night, Gus prowled around his mansion. Dubbed the Creepshow Palace by his numerous enemies, the estate occupied three wooded acres in a gated country club subdivision outside Cary.

Scattered among its nineteen rooms were a half-dozen big-screen televisions, which he liked to leave on with the sound turned off. His children were grown and scattered, his long-suffering wife banished years before (though still exacting revenge via alimony payments). So Gus had the place to himself.

The promoter was bored stiff, wondering what to do next. Then he had his midnight brainstorm in the gym: He needed a new world to conquer.

Gus's empire consisted almost entirely of hardware. His primary company, Grandiose Concerts, had divisions handling concert-booking, production, sound, lights, vending, security, catering, even limo rental. He had hundreds of employees, and owned everything he needed to put on a concert—except for the software. The promoter had always depended on his contacts with artist managers and booking agents for access to talent. But owning an artist himself would add the final piece of the puzzle, giving him a way into new and untapped realms for his empire: records, publishing, merchandise.

Thanks to a tip from the late, lamented Jay Simmons, Gus already had his eye on the piece of software he wanted, an up-and-coming local band. A trio by the name of TAB.

Gus tended to think in tactical military terms, which was why he seldom lost. Where others were content with mere survival, DeGrande never settled for anything less than unconditional victory. And if he had to scorch a little earth to get it, well, that's what it was there for.

Tommy Aguilar presented an entirely different sort of challenge. Gus would have to cut through some artsy-fartsy "no-sell-out" bullshit (a mindset he found unfathomable), and do so with subtlety. Paradoxically, DeGrande's usual full-frontal assault wouldn't work on TAB because the power imbalance was too great. The promoter knew he'd have all the leverage in any working relationship with the band. If he approached them, they'd know it, too. But not if they came to him.

Making that happen would take trickery, and all Gus's powers of deception and flattery.

It was a tall order, but a challenge Gus relished as he settled in to watch TAB play at Each that night. He'd already done some background work. Discreet inquiries yielded the information that Bob was managing TAB without a written contract, most likely based on promises and a handshake. Legally, at least, stealing the band away would be simple. DeGrande might have to grease some palms to salve guilty consciences and wounded pride, but these were amateurs. They would settle for a laughably small sum.

Part one, check.

Neither would it be difficult to convince Tommy that Gus was a more efficient starmaker than Bob. Sure, TAB's first single and tour demonstrated that the clubowner was well-connected at the independent underground level (or the pissant wannabe beginner level, as DeGrande regarded it). But Gus had the juice and the chits to put together a major-label record deal with a few phone calls, and make sure all the right buttons got pushed.

Part two, check.

Part three, though, was more complicated. He had to convince Tommy that he wouldn't just be a better starmaker than Bob, but also a better nurturer. DeGrande just wasn't the nurturing type. So he came to Each that night in search of an angle.

But first, he had to get past his initial reaction to hearing TAB play. Gus was a tightly wrapped control freak, and the abandon at the heart of Tommy's music made him viscerally uncomfortable. He coped by drinking, and dispassionately concentrating on the mechanics of the performance.

Profiting from music he couldn't stand was nothing new for the promoter. So he downed one scotch after another, and listened. And the more he watched and drank and heard, the more he found himself drawn in. Not by TAB's music, which he didn't like or understand, but by Tommy's presence. Gus had never seen anyone whose aspirations of stardom were more transparent. This kid didn't just crave success, he wanted enormity—significance, importance, respect. He wanted the hall of fame. Tommy had the charisma to pull it off, too, which was as easy to read as a neon billboard. Even that damn-fool newspaper critic had figured that much out.

But there was also a conflicted aspect to his star-tripping, which took Gus most of the show to pick up on. Tommy constantly pushed, seeing how much his bandmates could do and the audience would take. It was part of what made his performances so unpredictable, and powerful. If you knew what to look for, it was also manipulative and self-conscious. Tommy wasn't just pushing, he was testing.

More than once, when the guitarist seemed to be completely caught up in a musical moment, Gus caught him taking little sidelong glances to see how a certain move or riff was going over. Everybody else seemed too busy trying to keep up to notice. But at those moments, the nervous twitch in Tommy's eyes betrayed a glimmer of doubt that everyone else would continue pushing back.

Far beneath the swaggering exterior, Tommy didn't just expect they wouldn't follow his lead—he hoped they wouldn't. Which would, in the peculiar way his subconscious had worked everything out, set him free from the burden of other people's expectations.

So Tommy Aguilar could want to be a star, without seeming like he wanted to be one; an important line to walk in the world of underground rock bands. He was hardly the only performer who wanted it both ways, the perks of stardom without the stigma of "selling out." But his orphan's craving for guidance and approval added still another layer of complications. DeGrande knew about that, too, having already looked into the bandleader's personal background. To Gus, Tommy's ambitiousness had the feel of a dutiful son fulfilling an unwanted obligation. It seemed to be what everyone else expected of him. So he compensated by unconsciously hedging his bets, insuring he'd have someone else to blame no matter what happened.

If the audience let him down and didn't come around, well, that couldn't be helped. But what he really wanted was for someone else to step in and orchestrate the whole thing—million-selling albums, magazine covers, the works—and then take the blame for the inevitable, ensuing corruption. Either way, Tommy himself would be off the hook.

Bob had figured out the first part of this equation, that Tommy wanted a father figure. It would be Bob's misfortune that he hadn't yet deduced that his client also wanted a fall guy. In a strange way, Tommy wanted to go home again. Betrayal was the only home he'd ever known, going all the way back to his father pulling the trigger.

Gus knew a thing or two about betrayal beginning at home. And if that's what Tommy wanted, that's what he was going to get. The promoter smiled and emptied another shot glass as the guitarist blazed away.

Springing his trap would take time and planning, so Gus didn't bother paying a backstage call. Instead, he contented himself with contemplating TAB from afar while downing a half-dozen shots of scotch (which Bob gave him on the house, despite Ken's disgust at this "professional courtesy"). The promoter retreated right before the first encore, stopping to speak to Bob at the bar on his way out.

"You should go far with each other," he said, nodding toward the stage as he extended his hand.

"Hope we do," Bob said, shaking hands. "Thanks for coming."

"My pleasure," Gus said, presenting a business card. "If I can ever be of any help…"

"Yeah…Thanks…" Bob said to the back of DeGrande's head as the promoter slid out the door. Then he looked down at the card, which had Gus's unlisted home number (something many people would have killed to get). By the time he looked up again, the black limo was pulling away.

"Jesus," Bob murmured. "I wonder what the fuck he wants?"

"Your ass," cracked Ken. "I suggest you cover it while you still can."

Gus was deep in conversation on the carphone before his limo even reached the end of the parking lot.

CHAPTER NINE

Most nights, Tommy was ricocheting off the walls after a show. But he was unusually subdued at Each that night. Part of it was thinking about the contents of the bag under the loose tile in his bathroom closet. So far, he'd kept his promise to Bob. So far.

But it was getting harder, gnawing at the back of his mind. Making him cranky, paranoid.

Sure could use a blast right now, Tommy thought. He'd been compensating by drinking a lot, but that only made him surlier. So while Ray hoofed all the gear offstage, Tommy sat in Each's backstage room and brooded, idly re-stringing his guitar. It kept his hands busy, if not his mind.

"Hey, Tommy," Ray called as he wheeled his bass drum into the room, "you see that old bald guy over by the wall?"

The bandleader shook his head no.

"The scary-looking fucker throwing down all the shots?"

"Uh uh."

"Well," the drummer said, "we must be getting famous. That was Gus DeGrande. You know who he is?"

"Satan," Ken Morrison interjected, sticking his head through the door. The rest of his body followed into the room, uninvited.

"Mr. Reporter Boy!" Ray crowed with a smirk, leaning against his drumkit. "You bring your tape-recorder tonight?"

"Forgot it, sorry."

"Aw, too bad. And here I even felt like talking on the record for a change. That was one *cute* little story you did on us. Really captured the flavor of our traveling lunatic asylum."

The critic felt himself blush as Ray laughed. He looked over toward Tommy, who seemed not to have heard and continued re-stringing his guitar.

"So," the drummer asked, "what've you got against DeGrande, Morrison? He gives you tickets, and aren't the freebies all you media weasels care about?"

"Ray, Gus DeGrande has never given anything away his whole fucking life. Remember that the next time he shows up."

"You think I don't know that?" Ray scoffed. "Hell, *you* never worked for the man. When I was with Dopplegangbanger, we got to open a show at the Enormodome once, and we went over the time he gave us by two-and-a-half minutes. So Gus comes back afterward, all steamed—steam is literally coming out his fuckin' ears—and whips out a calculator. Says he's gonna have to fine us because we made the show run late and into overtime, and he was having to pay all the stagehands union scale. Not his decision, venue policy, it was all on page 119 of the contract, blah blah blah. Anyway, he punches on the calculator for a while, mumbling to himself the whole time, and tells us it comes to $110—and he was only paying us a hundred bucks to play the gig. Then the fucker puts his hand out and asks for ten bucks!"

"No shit?" Ken asked, wishing he had his tape recorder.

"No shit. At first, we laughed and thought he was kidding, but he did not put his hand away. I was gonna go get some change, give it to him in rolls of pennies. Finally, he says, 'I'll let you off this time, but it better not happen again. Now pack your shit up and get outta here.'

"God," Ray concluded, "it was soooooooo showbiz. Being stiffed on the gig and then read the riot act by El Sleazeball, that's gotta be the closest thing there is to being a rock star."

"So who is this guy, anyway?" Tommy finally piped up.

"You really don't know?" Ken asked, and the guitarist shook his head no.

"He's only the biggest concert promoter in the state," Ray said, and Ken laughed.

"More like the whole East Coast," the critic said. "Hell, he's as big as anybody in the country. You ever start playing in places any bigger than this, you'll have to deal with him."

"Is he good?" Tommy asked, surprising Ken.

"You'd have to define 'good': Competent, or non-evil?"

"Competent."

"Sure, he's good. He knows a lot of people and sells a lot of tickets. And if anybody crosses him, he's an absolute ball-buster. The way Gus looks at things is that somebody's gotta win, and somebody's gotta lose—and he don't ever lose."

"You don't like him, do you?"

"I've got my reasons. He doesn't like me much, either."

"Does he scare you?"

Another surprising question. Ken had to think before answering. "Maybe a little, yeah," he said.

"Why?"

"I dunno, he just does. He seems kind of…predatory. Like a shark looking for his next snack. You should've seen him watching you tonight."

"Why? You think he's interested in us?"

"Oh, he probably heard something. Maybe he needs an opening act for another of his shows out at the Enormodome."

"Maybe I can get fined again," Ray said.

"Yeah," Ken quipped, "and maybe you'll be able to afford it this time."

There was another reason for Tommy's subdued mood, a face he'd seen in the crowd. Susan. She was back.

Tommy hadn't seen Susan in close to a year. Not since she shot him, in fact. She hadn't meant to do it, and the bullet just grazed him in the side. But still, it was her gun and she was holding it when it went off. They'd been at a party, both quite drunk, and Susan tended to get even crazier than usual when she drank.

That night, she pulled a pistol out of her purse and started waving it around as she danced; one of the table-dance gyration routines she did for money at strip joints. Tommy was as drunk as she was, rubbing up against her as she swayed.

"I didn't know you carried a gun," he whispered into her ear. She didn't answer and he was about to tell her about the gun he kept at home, only he never got the chance. The last thing he heard was, "I love you"— and then the gun went off.

Tommy had never seen a room clear out so fast in his life. He figured somebody must have bumped into him because he wound up sitting on the floor, unable to remember how he got down there, looking up at Susan. A look of horror was spreading across her face, and he didn't realize why until he looked down and saw the blood soaking through his shirt.

"I think the love," he said right before passing out, "has gone out of our relationship."

Tommy did not wake up until the following afternoon, in a bed at the intensive care unit. It was just a flesh wound and the bullet left behind little damage beyond blood loss, but the hospital insisted on keeping him overnight.

Susan had disappeared, which was actually a relief. She was the closest Tommy had ever come to having a real girlfriend; not that he was trying. Getting shot was the farthest he'd ever had to go to rid himself of anybody.

Tommy never initiated breakups himself. Instead, whenever a woman lingered longer than he wanted, he had ways to drive her away. Step one was to dye his hair some garish color, usually orange or purple, and demand his partner do the same—"It's the only way I can be sure I'll always find you in a crowd."

If that wasn't enough, he would invite himself over for dinner, drink himself blind and trash the house. Insisting on three-way sex with a friend or roommate had worked before, too. So had asking if he could carve his initials into a girl's arm, or stomach.

The final mutual-assured-destruction option was to ask that they do heroin with him. Nobody had ever called that bluff before, until Susan.

Susan not only went along with everything Tommy demanded, but gave as good as she got. When he dyed his hair green, she dyed hers the very next day. When he came over for dinner, she got even drunker than he did and they wound up competing to see who could be more pointlessly destructive (a contest Tommy won by throwing her TV set out a window). When Tommy suggested broadening their small circle of friends, Susan brought along a friend as well as her roommate; damn near killed him. She not only let Tommy carve "TA" into her stomach, but embellished his handiwork by adding a small heart. And when he proposed they shoot up together, Susan was so enthusiastic that it scared him a little. Especially since Tommy had never actually done heroin before.

But once he made the offer, there was no turning back. So Tommy journeyed over to the housing project in Durham where all the first-timers went to cop, came back to The Crypt with a syringe and enough smack for two—and discovered that he really liked it. A lot.

So did Susan, which soon became a problem. She'd been working at The Doll Palace, the "upscale" strip joint in town. But then she began hanging around Tommy and turned up with green hair, scar tissue and needlemarks, which was just a little too hardcore. So she got busted down to Crazy Ladies, which was more of a white-trash joint. And Tommy didn't know what to do to make her go away, until an errant pistol shot intervened. Nobody was ever more relieved to get shot.

Tommy hadn't given her a thought in months, until tonight—when he looked over toward Michelle and caught a glimpse of Susan lurking near the stage, staring up at him. The prospect of seeing her again filled him with dread, so he stayed in the back room as long as he could.

But when he finally walked outside at about 3 a.m., there Susan was in her midnight-blue Camaro, parked across the lot with her window down. Tommy could see as he approached the car that her hair was back to its natural jet black. She still looked good.

She still looked like trouble.

"Hey, sailor," Susan called out as soon as she saw him.

It was toward dawn before Tommy and Susan finally untangled. They started by drinking the better part of a fifth of bourbon on the drive out to The Crypt, then they screwed for what seemed like hours. Then they dipped into Tommy's heroin stash—Susan's idea—and rolled around some more, feeling stuporous.

Tommy wanted to just pass out for a couple of days. But if he did that, he knew Susan was never going to leave. So he made his move. He got up from the mattress and left his bedroom for a minute, then came back in with his gun and a red bandanna.

Half-asleep, Susan snapped awake when she saw Tommy's gun. At first, though, she was not alarmed.

"That a pistol in your hand or are you just glad to see me?" she cracked, then giggled. "Wait, let me get mine, too; we'll draw at twenty—"

Susan stopped talking when she saw Tommy tie the bandanna around his scalp. He opened the gun to show that it was empty, then put in a single bullet, snapped it shut and spun the chamber. Then he put the gun to his head and pulled the trigger.

Click.

The only way he could do it was fast, impulsively, without thinking. He looked into Susan's eyes as he pulled the trigger, and her face seemed to collapse. It was, he realized, the first time he'd ever seen her scared. Her fear had a scent he could smell, and it turned him on. He suddenly wanted to screw her again, almost as much as he wanted her to leave.

Instead, Tommy knelt down on the mattress, placed the gun in front of her, held out the bandanna and said, "Your turn."

Susan stared at him for a full minute. Tommy had no idea what she was going to do. Even so, she surprised him. She picked up the gun, placed it against his forehead and pulled the trigger before he could do anything.

Click.

It was a tossup which Tommy came closer to doing, dying of heart failure or ejaculating.

"You like that, huh?" Susan said, keeping the gun trained on him. Then she pushed Tommy down, put her head in his crotch and began to suck. Hard. Eventually, she climbed on top of him and raped him.

That's what it felt like, anyway, because she never lowered the gun. As they started in, she began to mumble. Her voice rose as they got going, until she was finally hollering as loud as she could:

"FUCK ME FUCK ME FUCK ME FUCK ME!!!..."

They heaved toward climax together. As she started to come, Susan pulled the trigger again.

Click.

Tommy didn't know what to do. There was nothing he could do, actually. Susan had him pinned down, trapped beneath her hips—and still had the gun on him.

"FUCK ME FUCK ME FUCK ME FUCK ME!!!..."

Click.

Now Tommy was starting to panic. The trigger had been pulled four times, and one of the two remaining chambers had a bullet. Susan showed no signs of stopping.

"FUCK ME FUCK ME FUCK ME FUCK ME!!!..."

Trying to time it just right, between thrusts, Tommy made a desperate lunge for the gun. But he couldn't wrestle it away from her. Four
hands gripped the pistol, the trigger got pulled again.

Click.

Tommy let go then because he wasn't going to get the gun away from
her. If Susan wanted to shoot him, there was nothing stopping her.

Once she knew there was a bullet in the chamber, Susan seemed to lose
interest in the sex and finally stopped moving. She sat there on top of
Tommy for a minute, breathing hard. Her eyes seemed to be twitching.

Susan then leaned back, raised the gun to her own head and looked
down at Tommy. Her pupils looked as dark and fathomless as the eyes of
a hammerhead shark.

It took every ounce of strength Tommy could summon to lunge
upward and knock the gunbarrel away from her head just in time.

Blam!

The shot echoed in the room. Shattered plaster rained down from
the ceiling as the noise subsided. Tommy couldn't have moved right
then even if the house was on fire.

Slowly, Susan got to her feet and threw Tommy's gun across the
room. Then she stood there, ran her hands through her hair and
moaned, an awful sound.

"You know what you are, Tommy?" she asked, bending down to hiss
in his face. "You're death on a stick."

He didn't know what to say to that.

"Well, if it's death you want to fuck," she said, "be my guest."

After Susan left, Tommy took another shot. Just to recover, he told
himself. Just like old times.

CHAPTER TEN

Bob wasted no time getting TAB back into the studio, this time for something a little more ambitious—a five-song mini-album CD they would actually try to sell. As usual, Tommy just wanted to tweak some of his demos and release those.

"They're what we really sound like, Bob," he argued. "They're honest, they're pure—and I don't want to put out some slick shit that don't sound anything like us."

Bob decided he had to distract Tommy by throwing him a bone: T-shirts. It was time for TAB to start putting its name out there, so he told Tommy to go design a shirt.

Few civilians had any idea of the lofty financial place T-shirts occupied in the music industry, especially for underground bands. T-shirt money was just another bucket of gravy for the big boys, the huge arena acts playing to twenty-thousand people and selling a hundred grand worth of shirts every night. But for bands at TAB's level of vagabonding around the country playing in bars, money from T-shirt sales was frequently the only touring cash they ever saw.

The reason was simple: overhead. It cost almost nothing to design and make T-shirts, but it cost lots of money to make records. So while they sold for about the same price, T-shirts yielded many multiples more profit per unit sold. By contrast, the profit margin on records was so low that you had to sell a ton of them just to break even.

As TAB's first tour demonstrated, there was virtually no money in an unknown band going on tour. But the reason bands recorded and toured was to sell T-shirts. You made the record, even though you probably wouldn't break even on it, so you could get press and airplay and go on the road, even though you'd barely break even on that—all so you could sell shirts. This tertiary level of merchandise was where you could make money (and lots of it), selling T-shirts and hats and keychains and other gewgaws plastered with a band's logo. There was gold in them there useless accessories.

Bob's plan for round two was to put out an EP and tour behind it, hitting most of the same cities as before and going a bit farther west. If he couldn't arrange retail distribution of the disc, then TAB would hawk copies from the stage at shows. T-shirts fit into the picture, too, and for more than just financial reasons. Stories in the business were legendary about bands coming to the attention of record label recruiters because they kept seeing an act's logo on shirts.

Short-term, Bob hoped that letting Tommy design a T-shirt would buy his cooperation on the record. Whatever Tommy came up with, Bob figured he could use the results to his advantage. If it sold enough to bankroll this tour, great. And if it flopped, he'd have some leverage to rein Tommy in on the next project.

Of course, the manager had to live by the same rules. It was important that the band like this EP, even after going out and playing its songs every night for months. Bob had to be careful to keep it gimmick-free; a repeat of "Rock Hit Back to Black" would be disastrous. If the single had been TAB's personal ad, Bob wanted the EP to be a modest, no-pressure first date. Lunch or mid-afternoon coffee, perhaps, to do some sizing up; something to get people both inside and outside the industry interested, but not frenzied.

It was too soon to start a bidding war just yet.

As **Bob** expected, Tommy's first proposed T-shirt was a little...strange. He took the photo that ran with Ken Morrison's TAB profile in the newspaper—of himself holding a gun in his mouth—and rendered it in a garish red-toned watercolor. In the painting, he power-chorded a guitar with his free hand. There was also a caption: WE'LL DIE TRYING.

"Um, Tommy," Bob said, rubbing his eyes, "just what is it you're trying to say with this?"

Tommy made no mention of Susan, the painting's spiritual inspiration, who was gone again but not forgotten.

"That we're serious," Tommy said. "You know, we're not fuckin' around. We'll do anything, whatever it takes to get the job done. Don't you think it's cool?"

"Well, sure. In fact, I'd like to hang it on my wall right here...well...maybe not. But that isn't the point. The point is, we're gonna, you know...have a really hard time selling this in Peoria, that's all."

"I don't fucking care what anybody in Peoria thinks, Bob."

"Yeah, I know you don't. But right now, unfortunately, you have to. This is the shirt you do when you don't have to care anymore, so save it for then. Try again."

With much grumbling, Tommy went back to the drawing board. A day later, he called the manager to say he'd come up with the perfect T-shirt design and would bring it right over. He arrived a half-hour later, literally bubbling with excitement. Bob braced himself for another gruesome concoction, but was surprised when Tommy uncovered his canvas to reveal a simple isosceles triangle, blood-red on a black background, with one tip pointed downward.

Bob stared for a few minutes, trying to figure it out. He couldn't, which was one reason why he found the image appealing.

"I like it," he said. "I think. Does it actually mean anything?"

"Yeah, it's the band," Tommy said, then pointed to each side as he explained. "One side is me, one is Ray and one is Michelle. See, the three-piece is the perfect band setup because it's perfectly balanced, especially when the two people out front are left-handed and right-handed—"

"—Like you and Michelle," Bob finished. Tommy was left-handed, Michelle right-handed. They always played with the necks of their instruments pointing toward each other.

"Right," Tommy said, nodding. "In a triangle, everything balances out."

"But what makes a trio any better than, say, a four-piece? Isn't a square balanced, too?"

"It can be, yeah, but only if all four people are equal and it's almost impossible to find four different people who are that well-matched. Besides which, a square is dull."

To demonstrate, Tommy picked up a red pen and drew a perfectly symmetrical square on Bob's desk blotter calendar.

"See, a perfect square is too clean. Boring. That's no good, and besides, it almost never works that way."

He sketched out another four-sided shape with one side much longer than the other three, yielding what looked like a flat-topped pyramid.

"Usually, what happens with a four-piece is that one side is longer than the others and it turns into something like this. It's unstable, and not much more interesting than a perfect square because you just wind up paying attention to that one long line—like Creedence Clearwater Revival, John Fogerty was the only guy in that band worth a shit. Usually, the best you can do with four is a rectangle, if you've got two studs and two good role players, like the Beatles."

"Well, what about a five-piece?" Bob asked, picking up a green pen and drawing a rough pentagon.

"You just answered your own question," Tommy said, gesturing toward Bob's rather lopsided pentagon. "That's hard to draw, right? Because it's too complicated. Too many angles intersecting, too many places for things to go wrong. With a five-piece, you'd almost be better off drawing it as a star, which is *really* unstable—lines going off in different directions all over the place, really sharp angles—but it's fun while it lasts. Anything five and up, drawing it the way you did there, it starts to get almost like a circle."

"What's wrong with circles?"

"A properly drawn circle is infinite and perfect, but there's no such thing as infinity or perfection in music. It's all about where you start, where you stop and getting something interesting out of your mistakes. Sure, you can strive for a circle; but you'll have to accept that it's a goal you'll never reach. Maybe you could do it if you cloned yourself. That's what all these one-man studio bands try to do, with their synthesizers and shit. But different people can't interact without angles."

Tommy drew an oval racetrack shape.

"This is probably as close as you can get to a circle, if you had two really well-matched people—Burt Bacharach and Hal David, Sam and Dave, Mick Jagger and Keith Richards, Gram Parsons and Emmylou Harris."

Then he drew a lopsided egg shape.

"But most duos turn out more like this, because one person is usually stronger than the other. It's sort of like an oval trying to turn into a triangle—the perfect band shape. Trios are best because a triangle absorbs stresses and flaws without collapsing better than any other shape. It directs energy inward, and it's the best setup to have if one side is longer than the others."

Tommy sketched a series of warped triangles with the baselines progressively longer.

"The only thing that can fuck up a triangle is if one side gets so much longer that the other two have to stretch too far to connect. If one of the lines becomes infinitely long, a triangle will collapse into a straight line. Sort of like a black hole—infinity. But like I said, there's no such thing as infinity in music."

"I see you've got all three sides of equal length here," Bob said. "Very democratic of you."

"Gotta keep the troops happy, boss," Tommy said, shrugging.

"Why's it tilted?"

"So it's not perfect. That's kinda like the grain of sand that gets turned into a pearl. Also, I didn't want anybody thinking it's a pyramid. I'm not into any of that mystical Egyptian bullshit."

"Oh, no," Bob laughed, "this isn't mystical in the slightest. But it is…interesting. Dunno if I buy the theory, but it looks good and might work as a record cover, too. Red on black, it might even sell."

"Not important," Tommy said.

"Maybe not to you, but it is to us detail guys."

Three days later, Bob was having a hard time swallowing his client's stability-of-trios theory. TAB was back in the studio and they couldn't get out of their own way, or even agree on anything. Everything the band tried was too weird for Michelle, not weird enough for Tommy and didn't rock hard enough for Ray.

As for Bob, playing referee was about as much fun as a trip to the dentist. Sitting in the control room and watching yet another take disintegrate, he took stock. His original plan was to record live with minimal overdubs. But TAB couldn't even get through the first verse of the first song without erupting into endless bickering over mechanics—tempo, chord changes, even lyrics. If this kept up, Bob faced the unpleasant prospect of piecing each song together in the editing room, splicing segments of different takes. At least he had a lot to work with. They were already up to take number seventeen with no end in sight, and had yet to reach the end of the song.

Bob diagnosed the problem as hyper awareness of the recording process. It had been one thing to rush in and knock out the single's two songs in one overnight marathon. But this was the first of a planned week's worth of sessions: a song a day for five days, and two for mixing and tweaking. Although this was very small scale compared to the months or even years that major-label acts spent in the studio, it was still enough to paralyze Tommy, Ray and Michelle with self-conscious-ness. There was, the manager decided, only one solution—make them stop thinking about it. Make them stop thinking, period.

Bob opened the control room door and ventured into the studio as Ray tried to convince his bandmates that the rimshot he kept playing over and over was just the right cue for a verse-chorus transition. The song was "Come Go Away," and the lyrics were about drawing someone in only to push them away. The drummer insisted that a jarring down-beat on the "go" would accentuate the title chorus.

"See?" he said, booming out another bone-rattling *thwack*. "It's per-fect! Gives it just the right push there going into the chorus."

"But that 'push' is totally wrecking the tempo, Ray," argued Michelle. "If I have to keep up with Tommy and wait for you to do that, I'll have to completely rewrite the bassline—and it's going to make the song at least a minute longer."

"Well, let's just play it faster, then," Tommy said, absent-mindedly strumming his guitar.

My my, thought Bob. *What a mess.*

Ray's suggestion actually wasn't a bad one. But it was still a distrac-tion, a detail they were wasting too much time over. They'd have to get the ship upright and floating before trying to scrape the rust off.

"Okay, gang," Bob announced. "Let's drop this one for now. It ain't working."

Michelle sighed and started to take off her bass.

"But don't go anywhere. We're not stopping."

The bassist looked at Bob, puzzled.

"Go ahead, put it back on," he said. "All right, then, here's the problem: You're thinking too much about this. All of us are, way too much. And let's face it, nobody in this room is exactly a genius."

"Speak for yourself," Ray cracked from behind his drums.

"Okay, Mensa Boy," Bob said. "See if you can handle this one: Quit thinking and just play."

"Play what?" Tommy asked.

"I don't care, anything. Surprise me. It doesn't even have to be a song you know—or a song at all. Try to clear the room. That's something I *know* you can do."

"But the only one in the room is you," Michelle said.

"So?"

Ray grinned. "You'll be sooooooooooooory," he crooned.

The bassist began to say something else, but her words were drowned out when Tommy turned his amplifier all the way up, windmilled down on his guitar and let out a lightning bolt of white noise. Michelle howled in pain as she stuffed her earplugs back in, then retaliated by turning her own amp all the way up and hitting an E-chord with a rumble that shook the floor. It felt like an earthquake. Like most drummers, Ray never wore earplugs as a point of pride (and had the tinnitus to prove it). He beamed and began to flail away—overplaying the sort of florid arena-rock fills he never got to do anymore, now that he was no longer in a metal band.

Bob fled back to the control room and closed the door, watching TAB's war of sonic attrition play out through the vibrating window pane. All three of them were irritated and played like it—even Ray, who was getting his way. Things could never be noisy enough for him. The manager crossed his fingers and waited. Five minutes later, he got his wish. As often happens with bands that have been together long enough, TAB eventually fell into a groove almost in spite of themselves. And since "Come Go Away" was the song they'd most recently tried to play, that was it (albeit in almost unrecognizable form).

After working it over for another ten minutes, the three of them finally lurched to a halt. Bob seized the moment, switching on the microphone and rolling tape.

"All right," he said, "I think we're ready. Tommy and Michelle, turn your amps down just a little, okay? What you just did, do that again—only this time, Tommy, sing the words. Do it now, do it fast and most of all, don't think about it."

Rimshot and all, take number eighteen was a keeper.

After that, the rest of the EP came pretty easily, although it took more time than Bob planned on. In fact, he had to book an extra day to finish up, which secretly pleased him because it gave him an excuse to do the final mixing alone and unassisted. Mixing involved adjusting the volume and placement of each song's different tracks and sounds on the final master tape. The process seemed simple enough, but was also the easiest stage at which to ruin a record. Bob had seen it happen many times, almost always because everyone was hanging around looking over the engineer's shoulder and demanding their parts be turned up louder.

Bob didn't plan on anything too fancy, but it would've been impossible with the band in the room. His basic rule of thumb was to turn the vocals and bass up, and the drums and guitar down. Tommy's guitar was the tricky part, because it tended to drive the songs. Unlike most bands, in TAB, the rhythm section took its cues from the guitar.

Such a mix represented a calculated risk, but one the manager thought would pay off. Tommy was an inspired guitarist, but a preternatural singer. His voice was the most accessible part of TAB, even if few people realized what a great singer he was because of the shitty acoustics of most clubs the band played. A guitar-focused record would be what the previously converted expected. Unfortunately, TAB didn't have enough of those just yet.

No, it made more sense to key the record around Tommy's voice and leave live shows as the primary venue for his guitar-wanking. Most bands only went as far as their vocalists could take them, so this was a logical decision. Of course, Bob knew what the band's initial reaction would be. They'd hate it—which was most musicians' stock response to anything, especially somebody else's mix of their record. Getting it by them would take a selling job.

Or some subterfuge.

Ken Morrison was dying to go meddle during the recording sessions. Between the new songs he heard TAB do at their last Each show, the burgeoning size of the band's audience and Gus DeGrande's apparent interest, he was anxious to solidify his claim as official critic of record. Just about the time he was trying to think of excuses to show up at the studio unannounced (maybe he could offer to play a typewriter cameo?), a compact disc arrived in his mail at home. There was no return address and the CD was unlabeled, but Ken recognized Bob's handwriting on the envelope. Besides, there was no doubt who it was as soon as he cued up the first track in his stereo.

From the first listen, the critic was floored. This was about the last thing he expected out of TAB: a pop record. Not that it was slick, exactly, just cleaner than he ever imagined they could sound. Mostly, that came from the mix, which placed Tommy's voice top dead center with the other instruments fanned out in more subordinate roles than usual.

Ken had never heard TAB this catchy before. Tommy played a skronky guitar, but he had a bell-clear choirboy voice. With his singing taking up so much of the mix, this glowed with actual melodic hooks. Grooves, too. Like most non-musicians, Ken didn't fully appreciate just how good Michelle was. But there was no missing it in this mix, which gave her bass as much volume as Tommy's guitar. Since she was the most technically skilled player in TAB, the songs sounded that much more grounded. This was some brilliant studio tweaking—almost as good as the songs, the singing and the playing. Ken was on the phone dialing Bob's number halfway through his second listen.

"Each."

"Did you do this?"

"Did I do what?"

"Hell, Bob, don't start with the name-rank-and-serial-number routine again. *This!*" he hollered, holding the phone up in front of a speaker to blast a verse.

"So what do you think?" Bob asked after Ken turned down the music.

"It's great."

"Really?"

"Yeah, really. I just want to know how you talked them into it."

"With a two-by-four to the back of the head."

Ken laughed. "I can't wait to hear Tommy's version of that."

"Funny you should mention that," Bob said. "You can't say anything to Tommy about this yet."

"Why not?"

"Well…" There was a pause.

"Well, what?"

"Well…See, Tommy hasn't heard it yet, exactly."

"He hasn't?"

"No. That's a preliminary mix. It hasn't been approved by the band and if they don't like it, I'll have to start all over. The record we put out may not sound anything like that. So you can't write about it yet."

Ken was flabbergasted. "Are you serious?! Bob, this is literally the best thing I've heard all year. No matter what they tell you, if you don't put this out as-is, you're out of your fucking mind!"

"Maybe so," the manager said, "but I just sent that as a favor, and it's still embargoed until I say so. Off the record, sport."

"Aw, come oooooooon, Bob," the critic whined. "You have to let me write about this! Trust me, I'll make you a star."

Oh, I'm counting on it, Bob thought.

"No can do," Bob said. "Besides, star-making is *my* department. So—nope, sorry. Not yet. You're just gonna have to wait."

He hung up before Ken could say anything else. Listening to the dial-tone, the critic was annoyed.

"Well, fuck 'em, then," he muttered. "If he didn't want it reviewed, he shouldn't have sent it."

Ken turned the volume on his stereo back up to annoy-the-neighbors range, sat down at his desk and began to type.

Just as Bob knew he would, Ken devoted his next column to a preview of TAB's upcoming mini-album—a four-star rave predicting that, if released as-is, the EP would be the biggest thing to come out of North Carolina since a nationwide salmonella outbreak was traced to a chicken-processing plant near Kinston eight years earlier.

The review appeared in print the day after Bob played his final mix of the EP for the band. As he expected, they utterly loathed it. Two of them did, anyway. Ray was apoplectic, declaring he would've joined a "foo foo haircut cover band" if he wanted to sound this limp-wristed. Tommy was right behind him.

"Jesus, Bob," he protested, "you made us sound...pretty. How could you do that? What's next, fuckin' violins?"

Michelle alone liked it, but her bandmates were so angry that her vindication was short-lived. All three of them departed Bob's office in a huff.

The next day, Ken's review showed up in the newspaper. The morning deejay on the big local rock radio station read it on the air, claiming he only did so "because Morrison hates everything, and I just can't believe he likes anything this much." Then he played *Come Go Away* (a disc of which had, coincidentally, just arrived at the station), and the phone lines lit up with calls from listeners wanting to know when and where they could buy the record.

"It pains me to admit it," the deejay said, "but Morrison might actually be right about this one."

Bob was up early and captured the whole thing on tape, including the deejay's instructions for listeners to turn to the station's full-page advertisement in the *Daily News*. The ad was on the page facing Ken's column, and if you folded it just right it read, "FUCK KEN MORRISON."

CHAPTER ELEVEN

Thud...

A heavy hardback book hit the counter right beside Michelle. Startled and a bit annoyed, she looked up from her paperback, and was surprised to see Bob.

"I'll take that one," Bob announced. Michelle glanced down at the book he dropped, and laughed. It was a Bible.

"Oh, my. The Old Testament."

"Yep," said the manager. "I don't go for any of that feel-good, New Testament bullshit. I always went more for the vengeful wrath-of-God shit, the famines and plagues and disasters."

"No wonder you manage a rock band," Michelle sighed, her smile fading a bit. "Although you never struck me as the least bit religious, Bob."

"I'm not," he said. "This is research. Gotta keep up with my client's ever-changing mindsets."

Michelle laughed again, this time mirthlessly. "If you're talking about Tommy," she said, "that will take some doing."

There was a pause while another customer approached the counter to make a purchase. A self-help title, *How to be Rich and Guilt-Free Forever.* Michelle made a face at the buyer as he walked away. To her disgust, such books seemed to be all that college kids bought anymore. They bugged her almost as much as the pretentious art-major types who came in wanting to "borrow" volumes of Joyce or Kerouac to read at the coffeehouse next door.

"So, boss," she said, turning back to Bob, "what can I do for you? Any other liturgical needs I can help you with, or did you really just need an extra copy of the Old Testament?"

"Yeah," the manager said, "you can reassure me about this tour."

"So I figured."

"I…ah…know it's nothing you're looking forward to."

Michelle didn't say anything, just made a face and shrugged.

"Look," he said, "I know that last tour was harder on you than anyone else. That's what happens when you're the only sane person in the van."

"Well, Bob, the gap must be closing because a truly sane person would've quit by now. And I'm still here, right?"

"But you do know that TAB wouldn't work without you," he pressed. "I mean, you've heard the record, and—"

"And I don't know that you did me any favors there," Michelle interrupted. "I mean, yeah, I was glad you did it. Sort of. It's nice somebody finally figured out how hard Tommy is to keep in line, and who has to do it. But he and Ray still aren't speaking to me. They act like this record was something I put you up to."

"I know, I know," the manager conceded. "I've told them both I did it completely on my own, and I'm still not sure they believe me. But you watch, they'll come around. Everybody who's heard this record loves it, and once you get out there in front of some bigger crowds, they'll come around. By the time you get back, they'll be arguing over whose idea it was to turn you up."

"I'll believe it when I see it."

"Trust me, it'll happen. But they're not the ones I'm worried about. You are."

"Me?" Michelle asked.

"Yep, you."

"Okay, let me guess: Now that you've taken this chance on me, you'd like a little reassurance about my commitment to the cause. Right?"

"Something like that."

"God, Bob," she laughed. "What am I gonna say? 'I'm louder than anybody else on the record, nyah nyah nyah—and just to rub it in, I quit. You boys go on out there alone, have fun.' "

Now Bob laughed, too.

"Besides," Michelle continued, "girls aren't the ones who have problems with commitment. Assertiveness, maybe, but never commitment. That's always the boy's problem. Don't you know anything?"

"Guess not."

"Wow," she whistled with mock awe. "First time I ever heard a male authority figure own up to *that*."

"Well, I know when I've been shown up."

"Sure you do. But anyway, to answer your question: Yeah, I'm in. For the time being, anyway."

"Willingly? No bullshit?"

"Willingly, no bullshit," she said. "Honestly, though, I don't know how much more touring I can take, if it's anything like that last one."

"It won't be."

"Promise?"

"Promise," Bob said, solemnly laying his left hand on the Bible and raising his right hand as if testifying. "From here on out, no more death marches. The tours will be better, and easier."

"I'll hold you to that," Michelle warned. "I expect clean motel rooms and regular meals."

"Done."

"So while we're negotiating, Mr. Manager, I have another request."

"Name it."

"I want to play El Paso sometime soon."

"El Paso? Why?"

"Because," she said, "I hear lithium is in the water down there, and I want to see if it calms Tommy down any."

Bob laughed. "El Paso's kinda out of the way, but I'll see what I can do," he said. "Anything else?"

"Yeah. Did you mix the record this way to guilt me into staying in the band?"

"Yes and no. Yes, I do think it's important to keep you in TAB because you're the only bass player who's ever been able to keep up with Tommy. But honestly, I was just trying to make the best record I could with what we had—and your bass and his voice are the two best things we got going. So it really was a big-picture decision. And I figure if I keep making the right big-picture decisions, you'll want to stay."

"We'll see," Michelle said. "I have to admit, I'm curious to see how this goes. But a lot depends on Tommy and how he manages…um, you know, certain habits."

Bob was leaning on the counter and drew closer, lowering his voice.

"I think that's under control," he said. "At least I hope so. We've had a couple of long and unpleasant talks about it, and I think I was able to scare him enough to make him stop."

"I wouldn't be so sure of that," Michelle said. "And now that you've sworn on that Bible, I'm afraid you've gonna have to buy it."

Two days later, Michelle sat reading Ken Morrison's column over her Friday morning breakfast. The critic was basically harmless, she thought, although she didn't entirely trust him. It took the better part of a year for her anger over the Charlie Holmes fiasco to subside. She and Charlie had briefly played together in the Potshots, with Michelle filling in on a few shows when they were between bass players.

Ken was definitely easier to take if he liked the band you were in. This week's column led with another fawning TAB item, about the tour that was to start the following week. Below that was a couple of paragraphs about another of the bassist's former bands, Dangermouse. Michelle almost choked on her Cheerios when she saw that Dangermouse was finally breaking up. Then she cackled evilly.

Ah, sweet revenge.

Dangermouse was among the first bands Michelle joined after returning home from dropping out of North Texas State. She considered the group a blot on her resume, mostly because the blowhard ringleader Todd was such a pretentious twit. Todd was always trying to write, sing and play songs he had no chance whatsoever of bringing off. It just wasn't in him. And there was nothing sadder, Michelle thought, than someone as mediocre as him trying so hard. All his songs were seven minutes long and full of phrases like "magenta fecundity," at weird tempos and in nonexistent tunings. Whenever she raised objections, the bandleader turned into a pompous college professor right before her eyes.

"Michelle," he said at rehearsal one night, "this isn't music school with all your safe little 'rules.'"

"I know, Todd, but out of tune is out of tune."

"You're missing the point," he sniffed condescendingly. "Maybe out of tune is what this song needs. I want it to paint a Picasso, not a Norman Rockwell."

"No, *you're* missing the point," Michelle argued. "If you're going to break the rules, you've got to know what they are first. You have to learn how to play tight and in tune before you can get away with out of tune."

The bassist watched Todd's back stiffen. Having just challenged his ability to play, she expected his response to be hostile, patronizing or both. He did not disappoint her.

"Michelle," he began, with elaborate feigned patience, "do you have some insecurity issues we need to talk about? Because nobody else here seems to have a problem with this. Are you just more comfortable following rules? Is that it? Are you not...*adventurous* enough to play in Dangermouse?"

At that, Michelle burst out laughing. It was really too much—this twenty-one-year-old English lit major who thought he was so cutting edge because he'd read *On the Road* and wasn't registered to vote.

"Todd," she said, struggling to maintain a civil tone, "I can't do this anymore. I guess you're right, I'm not 'adventurous' enough for Dangermouse. So, um…I'll be seeing you."

She packed up her bass and left.

Three weeks later, Michelle was at the Vertigo Lounge with her friend Sarah, who chanced to have overheard Todd talking about his band's former bassist earlier that day at the Record Hole.

"He was talking about me?" Michelle asked, taken aback. Since walking out of rehearsal that night, she hadn't given Todd or his band a second thought. She was relieved no one from Dangermouse had asked her to reconsider. "What'd he say?"

"You're, um, not gonna like it," Sarah said.

"Wow, what a shock," Michelle sighed. "Well?"

"Well…He was in there to take down the flyer they'd put up, looking for a bass player."

"Who'd they get?"

"I didn't catch his name," Sarah said. "But that wasn't the bad part. I heard Todd tell some guy that they kicked you out of the band."

Michelle laughed a bit at that. "Well, if Todd wants to think they kicked me out," she said, "I guess that's fine."

"But that's not all," Sarah said, looking embarrassed.

"It's not?…"

"No. Todd said they kicked you out because…well, because you kept coming on to everyone else in the band."

"*What?!*"

"Uh huh."

"Why, that little—"

"Wait," Sarah said, raising a hand, "it gets worse."

"It does?!"

"Uh huh. According to Todd, you have 'a real thing about being tied down.' And he said…um…he said…"

"What?"

Sarah had turned bright red. The only way she could continue was to lean across the table and lower her voice to a murmur. "Todd described you as, quote, 'the most aggressive fuck I've ever had,' unquote."

Michelle couldn't breathe. She sat with her hands on the table, color draining from her face, white with rage. Then she began to laugh, hysterical waves of guffaws so loud that everybody else in the bar turned to look. Sarah caught her laughter, and they cackled together for a while.

"Sarah," Michelle began when she could speak again, "you don't…"

"Oh, no!" Sarah said, then lowered her voice and deadpanned: "But I did like the part about the handcuffs."

The two women had finally reached the point where they could look at each other without dissolving into giggles, when who should walk into the Vertigo but Todd. He saw Michelle and ambled right up to their table.

"Hey, Michelle," he said, smiling broadly.

Michelle was so surprised to see him that, for a long moment, she just stared. Then she forced a smile of her own onto her face.

"Hey, Todd," she said. "So what's new…*prick?*"

"Excuse me?" Todd said, cocking his head as Michelle snickered from behind her hands.

"You heard me," she said, lowering her hands. "I called you a prick. There's a few other things I wish I could call you right now, too, like 'dead' or at least 'maimed.' But I'll settle for 'gutless, stupid little shithead.'"

"Michelle," he said, a note of condescension entering his voice, "are you still pissed about us kicking you out of the band?"

"Uh, I hate to intrude on your hallucination, Todd, but you didn't kick me out. I quit, remember?"

"Yeah, I remember," Todd said. "But it actually worked out okay 'cause we'd decided to kick you out when you quit. So it was less messy.

And no hard feelings, because we already found another bass player. Somebody better."

"Somebody better," she repeated. "And who would that be?"

"Jerry Huff."

Michelle gave a dismissive nod. Jerry Huff was another pathetic little wannabe with a goatee. He'd fit right into Dangermouse.

"Jerry Huff, eh?" she asked.

"Yeah," Todd said. "We're playing Duke Coffeehouse on Saturday. You should come. I'll put you on the guest list."

Michelle took a gulp of her scotch and water, then a deep breath. "Well, Todd," she said, "speaking as 'the most aggressive fuck you've ever had,' I think I'll say no thanks because I've already heard more than enough of your bullshit."

Todd got a funny look on his face. He'd come looking for Michelle so he could gloat about Dangermouse's new, improved bassist. He hadn't counted on his sexual wishful thinking getting back to her.

"So you've been telling people you threw me out of your shitty little band, and that you fucked me," Michelle continued. "I can't decide what's more ridiculous—that you actually seem to believe I'm not good enough to play in Dangermouse, or the idea of you even touching me, much less fucking me. Sarah, what do you think?"

"Sounds like a toss up to me," Sarah replied, lighting a cigarette with a conspiratorial wink.

Todd didn't say anything. He just stood there, frozen, like a rat caught in a flashlight beam.

"Anyway, Todd, I'm glad to hear I was such an important part of your band's lore," Michelle continued. "The communal hose beast. Yeah, that's rich. But there's one thing I'd like you to think about: You've been lying about me all over town. Well, two can play that game, motherfucker. I'll see you around."

Michelle stood up, threw the rest of her drink in Todd's face and stormed out of the Vertigo. Then she went right home and called

Jennifer Marino. She didn't know Jenny well, but then again, nobody did. There was only so much of her to go around, and everybody knew Jenny at least a little. She was practically a one-person wire service. If you wanted a piece of information to get around fast, you told Jenny. It was cheaper than buying a billboard.

Jenny answered her telephone and did what she always did, started talking so fast that the caller could barely get a word in edgewise. It was one reason Michelle rarely called her—she seldom had an hour she could waste on the phone, saying little beyond "uh huh" and "yeah."

Michelle let her go on for a while, waiting her out. Finally, almost twenty minutes into the conversation, Jenny gave her the opening she was looking for: "Say, Michelle, what's this I hear about Dangermouse giving you the boot?" The rest of Todd's lie, which Jenny had already heard via a clerk at the record store, lurked unspoken behind her words—a tacit offer to disseminate Michelle's side of the story. Michelle took her up on it.

She told Jenny that Todd had tried to rape her. For the first time Michelle could remember, Jenny was actually speechless.

"Please, Jenny," she pleaded, "don't tell *anybody*. Especially because…"

Michelle stopped talking and made some weird gurgling noises in her throat, as if choking back sobs.

"What? Michelle, what is it?!"

The suspense, Michelle could tell, was just killing her.

"Well…" Michelle said. "This is just between us, right? Can I trust you not to tell anyone about this? Not a soul?"

"Michelle, I swear, it goes no further."

"Okay, then…Jenny, you just wouldn't believe what a small dick he has."

Before dawn, the news was all over town: Todd Blackwell was an attempted rapist, and had a three-inch penis.

The next morning, Michelle took a drive over to Durham and headed for Duke. Todd had put up some flyers for Dangermouse's Duke Coffeehouse show around campus. On every flyer she saw, Michelle wrote in large red letters: RAPIST.

Michelle took one flyer off a telephone poll and put it in an envelope with another piece of paper, on which she'd typed, "This band's singer attempted to rape one of his former bandmates." She took the envelope to the student union building and put it in the mail slot for the Duke University Feminist Alliance.

Dangermouse's show that Saturday night was a disaster. With everybody whispering about Todd, nobody much wanted to go see his band—especially since a dozen women were picketing the club with signs that read, TAKE BACK THE NIGHT and RAPISTS OUT OF DUKE. When Dangermouse began their set, the picketers went inside to boo and hiss and heckle. The band tried to play, but finally gave up three songs in, after a chant went up from the protesters:

"NEEDLE-DICK RAPIST! NEEDLE-DICK RAPIST! NEEDLE-DICK RAPIST!..."

Dangermouse more or less ceased to exist after that. They continued to do the occasional show, just enough to keep up the pretense of still being a band. But most people shunned them, and felt none the poorer for it—it's not like they'd been any good. And now, a year and a half later, here was their on-the-record obituary notice in Ken Morrison's column:

> Well, it seems the breakup bug has claimed yet another band, one of the longer-lasting in town—Dangermouse, best-known by now for TAB bassist Michelle Rubin's brief tenure...

Ha, Michelle thought, *Todd's gonna love that.*

> Frontman Todd Blackwell attributes the split to the usual reasons. 'It's just time,' he says. 'We had a good run, but all of us are into different things nowadays.'
> As for future plans, bassist Jerry Huff has already began playing with the Leechmen and drummer Marty Caruthers is moving to San Francisco with his girlfriend. Guitarist Ryan Adams says he's putting together a new, as-yet-unnamed band. And Blackwell says he's through with music—he'll return to NC State next semester to finish his English degree.
> 'The music business is just very tough,' says Blackwell. 'Especially if you're trying to do something creative and non-mainstream, like we were. But at least we're going out with our dignity intact.'

"That's my boy Todd," Michelle sighed, tossing the newspaper aside. "Full of shit to the bitter end."

CHAPTER TWELVE

From the day TAB left town on their second tour, strange and awful things happened. Instruments and equipment malfunctioned or disappeared, boxes of T-shirts and CDs turned up missing or ruined, the van had one expensive breakdown after another. Invariably, each disaster struck at the worst possible moment, wiping out whatever cash they'd managed to accumulate.

There were bizarre miscommunications, too. More than once, TAB showed up at a radio station for a scheduled interview, only to be told it was canceled. The same thing happened with some shows, usually after they'd just spent their last few dollars and were counting on the canceled show's guarantee for gas to the next destination.

It was never entirely clear why all these miscues kept happening, because the band never heard the same excuse twice. Either they were expected on another day, or the person in charge had never heard of them, or whoever scheduled them had quit or been fired or disappeared. All they knew was that in one city after another, they burned time, energy and money to get to events that didn't happen.

Ray had suffered through some hideous tours in the past, but nothing like this comedy of errors. Literally everything that could go wrong, did—spectacularly. Because he was a drummer and therefore paranoid (an occupational hazard), Ray found himself wondering if TAB had fallen under the spell of some particularly sinister curse.

Their very first night out set the tone. It was in Athens, Georgia, not quite a day's drive away, in a club where they did well their last time through. So they expected to draw at least respectably, even on a Monday night. Things got off to a promising start when they heard the University of Georgia radio station play "Come Go Away" as they drove in for soundcheck. But when the deejay announced the cut afterward, he made no mention of TAB's show in town that night.

That was curious. But the curiosities were only beginning.

The advertising the club promised to do never materialized, the venue having blown its advertising budget on another show two nights earlier. That was for Plurabellum, a buzz band of the moment, whose flyers were omnipresent and impossible to miss. So were the preview stories and pictures of Plurabellum in all the local papers. To top it all off, Plurabellum tickets were expensive, which left the local club-going population broke until next payday.

Ray smelled disaster. TAB's mood was grim during load-in, and even grimmer after playing a half-hearted set in an echo-filled room. The biggest cheer of the night wasn't for anything they did onstage, but for the football game on the TV set behind the bar. The clubowner refused to turn it off, sneering that he had more money riding on the game than on TAB's show.

The evening's events left Tommy depressed and Michelle sullen. Having borne most of the asshole clubowner's petty humiliations, Ray was livid. He took it out on Bob during the nightly postmortem phone call.

"Bob," he barked into a payphone, "what the fuck happened?! Nobody showed up!"

"What?" Bob was shocked. "What was the count?"

"More than six, less than eight."

"Seven? Are you serious?"

"Yep. Seven people, none of whom bought a shirt or a record. And they were a lot more interested in the goddamn football game than in us. Hey, that's something we need to add to the rider—no fucking TV sports on while we're playing."

"Yeah, good idea," the manager said mechanically, his head swimming. He couldn't figure out what went wrong; after all the advance work he'd put in for this date, he expected to hear good news when the phone rang. "Was there anything about the show in the papers down there?"

"Fuck no," Ray snarled. "Everybody had their dick in their hand for Plurabellum. They were in every paper, and their flyers are on every goddamn telephone pole and wall in Athens. Kinko's must be out of paper."

"We were supposed to have flyers up, too," Bob said. "I know I sent them. When was Plurabellum down there, anyway?"

"Two nights ago."

Now Bob was getting worried. Plurabellum hadn't been booked anywhere near Athens when he scheduled this show.

"What about radio?"

"Yeah, they're playing the record. We heard it."

"Well, at least that came through."

"Not really. They didn't say anything on the air about us being here tonight. Didn't you let them know about the show?"

"Yeah," Bob said, "I did."

"Not a word. I sense a pattern here. What the hell happened?"

"You got me. Everything was all taken care of. You were supposed to get radio, flyers, advertising, pictures in the papers—and no competition. When I booked this show, Plurabellum wasn't coming anywhere near there. Jesus. What a clusterfuck."

"Clusterfuck is right," Ray said. "We made twenty-eight bucks."

Bob stared at the phone. Twenty-eight dollars. After gassing up the van, they would barely have enough left over for cheese and crackers. Cash being tight, the manager sent TAB off with just enough money to get through the first show. He booked this date without a guarantee in order to get more of the door. That was a mistake, one he would have to pay for very soon.

"How are Tommy and Michelle taking it?" he asked nervously.

"Badly," Ray said. "Tommy's still in his catatonic mode. He never really came out of that pre-show trance he does. And Michelle just seems pissed off."

Bob winced. Here it was their very first night on the road, and he was already breaking his promise. TAB would have to sleep in the van.

"Ray," he said, "I'll make this up to you. It's only one night. We're off to a slow start, but it's gonna get better. Promise."

The next day, when he called to check with the Athens radio station playing TAB's record, Bob was told they'd been informed a week earlier that the band's show was canceled—although nobody could say by whom. The program director was surprised to hear TAB had already come and gone. At least he promised to keep playing the record.

The manager scraped together enough cash for the band to get a decent meal and a motel room, and wired it down to the Western Union office in Atlanta. Unfortunately, TAB didn't get to use the money for creature comforts. Instead, they had to spend it on a new alternator and battery for the van, which died on a remote stretch of highway.

Usually, such a breakdown wouldn't have been a problem because Ray always packed spare parts. But when he went to look for the backup alternator, it had mysteriously vanished along with his tool kit. So they had to get the van towed. Thirty-seven miles. The tow truck charged by the mile.

"Looks like bread and water again," Michelle sighed over the phone later. She called in after the Atlanta show, which went better than Athens. At least there'd been no televised sports to compete with. The crowd cracked three figures and was enthusiastic. But the van breakdown and ensuing cash crunch put a damper on any good feelings.

"Could be worse," Bob said.

"How?"

"The bread could be stale, maybe?"

"That's not helping, Bob."

"Sorry," he said. "Shit, this tour has already made a liar out of me."

"Expectations suck, Bob. As bad as that first tour was, this one is already worse because we thought it would be better."

"It will be."

"Promise?" she asked. They both laughed—Michelle bitterly, Bob nervously.

"Maybe I shouldn't do that just yet, but this is nothing more than rotten luck," he said, trying to sound upbeat. "We're getting all the bad breaks out of the way early, so think of this as inoculation. I don't see what else can go wrong."

Three days later, TAB finally got to spend the night in a motel. But the pleasure of sleeping in a bed didn't last, because Michelle's bass amplifier turned up missing. When they went to unload their gear at the next show, it wasn't in the van.

"Did you forget it last night?" Ray asked, accusingly.

"No," Michelle said, flustered. "Tommy helped me carry it out and we put it in the back here, same place it always goes."

"So where is it?"

"I...don't know."

"Are you telling me," Ray said slowly as he leveled a killing glare at her, "that somebody picked this lock, broke into the van and didn't take anything except the heaviest, hardest-to-pawn thing in it?"

Michelle bit her lip and turned away without answering. She and Ray had no way of knowing it, of course, but that was exactly what happened.

It would be many more nights before they slept in another motel room.

Strangely enough, as mishap followed mishap, Tommy was the one cheerful camper in the van. In fact, the more the situation decayed, the better his mood seemed to get. Tommy appeared perfectly happy to accept whatever came his way—like the night a clubowner refused to pay TAB in money. Instead, he offered a small quantity of hallucinogenic mushrooms, which the bandleader enthusiastically accepted. Michelle was furious.

"You *asshole!*" she screamed. "Now what are we supposed to *eat?!*"

Tommy didn't say anything, just giggled and stared. As his snickering grew more unhinged, it finally dawned on Michelle that her bandmate had already eaten some of the mushrooms and wanted her to do the same. That made her even angrier, and she stormed off to call Bob. As Michelle stood at a payphone and dialed, Tommy stumbled up behind her, in the early stages of a giddy mushroom high.

"Be sure to ask Bob…" he stammered between paralyzing waves of laughter, "…if he wants…his ten percent…"

Michelle slammed the phone down so hard she cracked the receiver, then whirled around and shoved Tommy into a wall. He flattened against it, slid down in a heap and lay on the sidewalk, giggling.

"Oy fuckin' vey," she snarled, rolling her eyes skyward, and went to find Ray.

"I don't get it," Ray told Bob several nights later. "In all the time I've played with Tommy, I've never seen him like this. He's damn near bubbly. I didn't think he'd even live through that last tour, and this one is worse—a lot worse. But he seems to think everything's just peachy."

"How's he playing?"

"Great. Nobody except me and Michelle there to hear it most nights, but he's never sounded better."

The manager was worried. "This may sound weird, but you need to keep a close eye on him," he said. "Closer than usual."

"How come?"

"You know how some people get real cheerful after they've decided to commit suicide?"

"Aw, c'mon," Ray scoffed. "Even for Tommy, that's out there. He might pretend he's gonna pull a Cobain to impress some girl, but off himself for real? Nah, I don't think so. You don't spend your own money to have your teeth capped if you've got a real death wish. You really think he'd try it?"

"Well, that does run in his family, you know."

"Yeah, I know—his dad."

"But I'm actually thinking more like career suicide," Bob continued. "Tommy's always saying he'd be perfectly happy playing for nobody, which you know and I know is bullshit. But it sounds like he's got himself temporarily convinced that he's enjoying this starving-artist routine. Once the crowds start getting bigger again, look for some major flakeouts."

"Think so?" Ray asked.

"Bet on it. Now, an awkward question: Is he clean?"

"As far as I can tell, yeah. He's hardly been out of our sight the whole time, so he hasn't had many chances. He still does his weird pre-show thing, and he's been drinking more than usual. He can be a mean drunk, but lately that just makes him happier, too."

"Fuck."

"Although he does seem grumpy about one thing," the drummer said.

"What's that?"

"Smaller crowds mean fewer girls to get into trouble with."

"Well," Bob said, "thank God for small favors."

"But you don't understand," Ray said. "That's making *me* grumpy, too."

Gus DeGrande hung up the phone, leaned back in his desk chair and allowed himself a brief interlude of satisfaction. He was, for the moment, as content as his pet piranha after a goldfish snack. Of course, just as the fish would be hungry again soon, the promoter's sanguine mood wouldn't last.

But things were going fabulously in the sabotage department, which was enough for now. Gus's network of spies had been on the case early: A truck driver for the local beer wholesaler who owed DeGrande a favor, and was a real crackerjack when it came to picking locks, heisted a copy of TAB's tour schedule from Bob's office. So Gus knew their routing well in advance. He had also heard their EP almost as soon as a copy came off the assembly line (thanks to a mole at the pressing plant), and knew from his record company contacts that TAB's name was making the rounds within a few A&R departments.

That forced the promoter to accelerate his timetable a bit, since it looked as though TAB might stumble into a record deal sooner than expected. Once the group had any sort of binding contract with someone else, seizing control would become complicated and expensive. So Gus buried TAB's tour the way he buried competing promoters. Touring wasn't hard to figure out. You made money playing where you already had a draw on weekends, then used less-lucrative weeknights to establish beachheads in new markets. Since Bob was running low on cash, he had gambled on the big nights of this tour bringing in enough money to tide them over for a while. He'd again offered the band for small guarantees, but against a larger percentage of the door. If big crowds showed up, the strategy would pay off.

Instead, the tour had been a financial catastrophe, thanks to DeGrande's string-pulling. Picking his spots with care, the promoter shadowed TAB the whole way with a half-dozen better-known acts— one of which always seemed to show up in the same city as TAB almost every night. Attendance at TAB's shows was sparse, which also meant nobody was buying their T-shirts or CDs. For good measure, Gus had his minions steal several boxes of the *Come Go Away* discs, which he stashed behind a locked door in his office closet.

Booking the right competing shows was relatively simple, orchestrating the automotive breakdowns even more so. But the real masterstroke had been stealing Michelle's bass amp and Ray's toolkit out of the van. That brought on still more financial ruin, and made everyone in the band edgy and paranoid.

Everyone except Tommy. Gus had just gotten off the phone with a clubowner in Little Rock, where TAB played the night before. Thanks to yet another high-dollar show there with Plurabellum the night before, TAB's total attendance was twenty-one people, resulting in another pitiful fifty-dollar payday.

"The kid acted like I just paid him a thousand bucks," the clubowner marveled. "Just grinned like an idiot the whole time. If I'd given him a quarter, he probably wouldn't have noticed the difference. That guy must be nuts."

"He is," DeGrande said, mentally noting how well his fall-guy theory explained Tommy's seemingly incomprehensible mood swings. The tour wasn't going well—but that was somebody else's fault, even if he didn't know whose. So the pressure was off, and Tommy was enjoying himself.

At a certain point, however, he'd start to get antsy again. His malcontent side would elbow its way to the foreground, making Tommy potentially receptive to an overture. Not the final hardball pitch, but a preliminary courtesy toss.

Gus expected that to happen sooner rather than later, thanks to a little bonus vandalism courtesy of the Little Rock clubowner. In exchange for a couple of larger theater shows DeGrande cut him in on as co-producer, the man destroyed a box of brand new TAB T-shirts with a small bottle of hydrochloric acid. It ate a tennis ball-sized hole through all fifty shirts, which Ray wouldn't discover until they were down the road the next day.

It was time for Gus to figure out where and when to make his move. He opened a desk drawer and pulled out a U.S. road map in which TAB's tour itinerary was outlined in red ink.

CHAPTER THIRTEEN

"Folks," Ray announced even though nobody was paying attention, "we are fucked."

The only answer came from a nearby crow, which continued cawing at regular intervals, steady as a metronome. The sound had all the soothing charm of an alarm clock.

"F. U. C—"

"We get the picture, Ray," an irritated Michelle interrupted.

"Well, we've got no tools or parts, we're down to pocket change and we're stuck in the middle of nowhere. What're we gonna do?"

"Hey, it was *your* idea to get off the interstate and take this 'shortcut,'" she said.

"Which, if you'll remember, seemed like a good idea when we were stuck in traffic. I didn't hear any objections out of you back there."

"Oh, piss off."

"Hey, good idea!"

Ray walked to the front of the van, unzipped his fly and began to urinate all over the drivers side tire. Steam rose as it dripped onto the pavement.

"God, you are just gross," Michelle said with disgust.

"Thank you," the drummer smirked, zipping his pants back up.

"I, um, don't think that's gonna get the van running again."

Tommy's interjection surprised both his bandmates. He usually showed little interest in transportation issues, especially when it came to mechanical breakdowns.

At the moment, dusk was falling on this isolated stretch of Illinois blacktop. The van had just up and stopped. Fuel pump, Ray guessed, diagnosing the cause as the cheap gas they'd been buying. Actually, the egg that had been stuffed down the gas tank the night before had a lot more to do with it. Pickup trucks were passing by at the rate of one every five minutes. Since the van died, three had roared by without even slowing down.

"The master speaks!" Ray declared, bowing sarcastically in Tommy's direction. "You got any suggestions, sir?"

"Nope. You're the mechanic."

"Yeah, and you're the idiot genius boy."

"And we've got soundcheck in an hour and a half."

"Why, excuse me! I didn't realize we weren't keeping up with your timetable. Tell ya what, I'll get right on it, Mr. Rock Star."

"Fuck off," Tommy mumbled, "I ain't no 'rock star.'"

The drummer laughed derisively. "Yeah, sure you're not," he said. "Gimmie a fuckin' break, all you ever do is sit on your ass. You're too busy being an 'artist' to do any of the work."

"Ray, what does any of this have to do with getting the van running again?"

"And now all of a sudden, we're Mr. Pragmatic! Here you've never once lifted a finger during load-in, 'cause you have to do your nervous-breakdown routine before every show—and now that we're stuck out here in Bumfuck, you turn into General Patton."

"I've had about enough of your shit, asshole."

"Oh, you haven't even had the *beginning* of it," Ray growled, taking a step toward him.

"Come on, fucker," Tommy said.

Michelle was incredulous. Apparently, her bandmates were going to have an actual, honest-to-God fistfight right here on the side of the highway.

"Um, guys?" she said, raising a hand. Tommy and Ray both stopped. "What the hell is the matter with you? Are you gonna, like, *hit* each other now?"

"Not exactly," Ray said. "I'm gonna hit Tommy, but he ain't hittin' nothin' except the pavement."

"Think so, huh?" Tommy said, taking another step and clenching his fists.

"Bring it on, motherfucker," the drummer said, striking a pose he'd once seen in a karate movie.

"Oh, puh-*leeze*," Michelle groaned. "Both of you, spare me."

Just then, a car appeared on the horizon, speeding toward them. A large black car. A stretch limousine.

The three of them watched it go barreling by and were about to turn back toward Tommy and Ray's confrontation when the car suddenly slowed, pulled onto the shoulder of the highway and came to a stop down the road. Then it backed up until it was next to them. A darkened window in the back hummed open.

Sitting inside, trying his damnedest to look surprised, was Gus DeGrande.

"Getting off the interstate was smart," DeGrande said. "We gave up on it, too. All that construction, and there's too damn much traffic. If you know where you're going, the backroads are faster."

"They're faster if you've got a car that actually moves," Michelle sighed, looking out the window at the darkening twilight. Amber waves of grain all around. "We wouldn't know."

"Bad luck," the promoter shrugged. "It happens."

"Don't we know it," she replied

Tommy and Michelle rode in the back of the limo with Gus, and all their instruments and gear packed around them. The trunk was full, too, and there was just barely enough room. Most of the drums were stuffed into the front seat with Ray, who drove. DeGrande ordered his driver to stay with TAB's van, and called for a tow truck on his cellphone. They would all rendezvous at the club in Chicago later.

"Anyway, we do appreciate you doing this," Michelle said, giving Gus as warm a smile as she could muster. The hint of wariness in her voice did not go unnoticed.

"My pleasure," he said. "Glad to do it."

"So…this is a long way from Raleigh. What brings you all the way out here to the great heartland?" she asked.

DeGrande laughed, wondering if TAB had any suspicions about who was causing all their recent troubles. "I'm co-promoting some shows in St. Louis and Chicago," he said. "I flew into St. Louis, had some business in Springfield on the way and some reading to catch up on"—he held up a stack of trade magazines—"so I decided to hire a limo to make the trip. Same as you, we were looking for a shortcut."

"Well, we're glad you showed up when you did," Tommy said. "Good timing."

"Good timing," the promoter repeated, nodding.

"I'll say," Michelle smirked, remembering the narrowly averted roadside fisticuffs. Now that the heat of the moment had passed, both would-be combatants felt sheepish about it. Tommy was glad Ray was in the front seat, on the other side of a pane of glass.

"So how long've you been out?" Gus asked.

"Three weeks."

"Things going okay?"

There was a pause, after which Tommy and Michelle spoke in unison.

"Great," he said.

"Awful," she said.

Struggling mightily to keep his poker face in place, DeGrande gave them a quizzical look. "Can't be both," he said, "so which one is it? Great or awful?"

"Actually, it is sort of both," Tommy said. "The music's been great. I mean, we've never played better. But we...ah...haven't been drawing for shit."

"Oh, no?" Gus asked, feigning surprise. "That's odd. Why not?"

"You name it," Michelle said dolefully. "Everywhere we go, something seems to happen. Either the clubowner forgot to advertise or the radio station forgot to play the record or something disappears or somebody huge just played there—or the van breaks down. It's been one disaster after another."

"Well, I'm...surprised to hear that," the promoter said carefully. "I really expected you'd be a bit further along. Maybe even moving up to bigger places, given how much I've been hearing about you."

That got Tommy's attention. "What do you mean?" he asked, a little too eagerly for Michelle's taste.

"People in the business, I hear them talking about your record."

"Really?"

"All the time," DeGrande nodded.

"Well, they must be the only ones who've heard the goddamn thing," Tommy grumbled, "because it hasn't been selling, either."

"Hmm," Gus said. "It's a good record, too."

"You've heard it?" Tommy asked, surprised.

"Mmm hmm. Pretty impressive, considering you made it on the cheap, right?"

"Right."

"Be nice to hear what you could do on a real budget," DeGrande said.

"Hell, yeah! But you really liked it?"

Seeing that his bullshit was working, Gus poured it on even thicker. "Oh, yeah," he said. "A lot of promise there. You deserve every bit of the buzz you've got going now."

"'Buzz?'" Tommy asked in wonderment. "We've got 'buzz?'"

"Sure do. Coin of the realm in the music business, the elusive buzz. Cherish it while it lasts."

"Well, if we've got all this 'buzz,' how come nobody's showing up?"

"Hard to say. Sometimes the buzz doesn't necessarily lead to anything—at least not right away. It's a tough business and things never happen as fast as you want. But I'd say you're on the right track, if you keep at it."

"Yeah, that's what Bob says."

"He's a good man," Gus said. "Seems to know what he's doing."

The promoter let that one sink in for a few moments, knowing that the band couldn't help but hold Bob at least partly responsible for their touring misadventures. He allowed Tommy and Michelle's unhappiness to fester a bit more before delivering his next jab.

"Did Bob book this tour?"

"Yeah," Michelle side.

Inside, Gus was mentally spiking a football, since the grimace on her face told him everything he needed to know. Outwardly, he just gave them a pained smile and nodded sympathetically. They rode on in silence for a few more minutes before Tommy spoke up again, returning to one of the bugs Gus had put in his ear.

"So you really liked our record, huh?"

"Yeah," DeGrande lied again.

"Anything about it you'd change?"

Gus laughed. "C'mon, Tommy," he said, "you're gonna get me in trouble with your manager. I wouldn't want him to think I was meddling."

"No," Tommy said, "just between us."

"Well…"

"What?"

"…I really shouldn't say anything."

"Please."

"Well…okay," the promoter said, then leaned ever-so-slightly forward and uncrossed his arms. "If it was up to me, I think I might've had more guitar on it."

"You see?!" Tommy crowed triumphantly, elbowing his bandmate on the arm. "I knew it!"

Michelle looked darkly at Gus. If a sharp object had been within reach, she would've ripped his throat out right then and there.

A heavy and awkward silence had descended over the back of the car by the time Ray steered it into the club's parking lot. They were late and the clubowner was standing outside the front door, waiting impatiently. Tommy had moodswung back into gloom, while Michelle was surly—she couldn't decide who she was angrier at, the promoter or her bandmate. As for Gus, he was having difficulty concealing his euphoria. He couldn't have asked for more out of this mission.

There was one more piece of business to take care of. DeGrande pulled Ray aside during load-in.

"Here," he said, pressing three hundred-dollar bills into his hand. "That ought to cover the van and leave enough to get something to eat—looks like you could all use it. There's a pasta joint right down the street that I'd recommend, Milano's. Tell 'em you know me and they'll take care of you. If you ask for the veal tenderloin and specify 'the way Gus likes it,' you can't go wrong."

Wide-eyed, the drummer looked at the money in his hand. It was more than they'd grossed on any show on the tour. He couldn't believe that the same man who tried to fine his previous band a ten-spot for playing two minutes too long was doing this.

"Wow…thanks. I, uh, don't know how we can repay you."

"Don't worry about it," the promoter said with a dismissive wave. "I look at that as a down payment. Before too long, I expect I'll be booking you into bigger rooms. I'll make it back then."

"I hope that'll be soon," Ray said. "Can you stay for the show?"

"Afraid I can't. Gotta go keep an eye on my associates and make sure they're not rippin' me off," he said with a conspiratorial wink. "Be seeing you. Take care of those two."

"Wilco," Ray said, watching him go. He looked again at the $300, not realizing just how much of a down payment it really was.

That night, for the first time on the tour, Tommy played angry. Not simply cranky, but genuinely enraged in a way his bandmates hadn't witnessed in a long time. Maybe ever. It was as if the guitarist was channeling every hostile vibe from the greater Chicago metro area, and spraying it like blood through his instrument. The clamor was deafening. It didn't help matters that his bandmates both had a bad night, Michelle especially. She dragged behind the beat and was off on her changes, to the point that Tommy grew impatient and started pushing her around again.

TAB's set ended earlier than planned, when Tommy snapped two strings in frustration. He didn't feel like changing them, so he decided to do away with any notions of encores. He unslung his guitar and destroyed it, swinging it down over his head like an ax. Feedback echoed through the room as Tommy stalked off the stage in barely controlled fury. Ray and Michelle looked at the splintered wood and wires, wondering how they were going to do the following night's show.

On the upside, the crowd was happy. They rewarded the spectacle with their most enthusiastic applause of the evening, parting to let the guitar destroyer pass by.

"Sounds like somebody needs to get laid," Ray muttered, watching the back of Tommy's head disappear out the door.

CHAPTER FOURTEEN

With the courtship phase going according to plan, Gus DeGrande turned his attention to the next step—TAB's record deal. He already had a rough framework in place.

Several years back, the promoter signed a production agreement with a major label, Poly Brothers Records, as a minor amendment to an entirely separate business deal. The record company wanted to put four of its new acts on the road together as a package tour; to insure DeGrande wouldn't sabotage the venture, Poly Brothers hired him to book and produce it.

Almost as an afterthought, Gus asked for a production deal as part of the bargain. So Poly Brothers set up an imprint, Grandiose Records, for which the promoter would recruit and sign talent. Poly Brothers retained right of first refusal on any act DeGrande signed, and would distribute, market and promote whatever Grandiose releases it deemed worthy. Such deals almost always favored the larger distributing label. But the opposite was true in this case because Gus was the only one paying attention during negotiations. Poly Brothers' lawyers were only humoring him over something they figured wouldn't cost them anything. So far, it hadn't. Grandiose Records still did not exist as anything beyond a name on some legal documents, and the label had yet to submit any artists or records for the Poly Brothers pipeline.

TAB would be the first.

DeGrande dialed the A&R department of Poly Brothers Records' offices in New York. "A&R" stood for "artists & repertoire," which was an anachronism—a throwback to the early days of the music industry, when singers sang and writers wrote and neither tried to do the other's job. Back then, a key A&R task was finding songs for artists to record; hence the "repertoire" part of the title. With the rise of self-contained acts that wrote most of their own material, A&R became simply talent scouting. But the profession's old name had stuck, with all the attendant jokes: "Angst & Rejection," "Assault & Robbery," "Attitude & Revulsion" and so on.

"A&R," answered the receptionist at Poly Brothers.

"Yes," the promoter said, "is Craig Padgett in?"

"He no longer works here." Her voice almost sang the answer as a single word, *Henolongerworkshere,* which came out sounding like a question.

"Oh," Gus said. "How about Lydia Hagerty?"

"Shenolongerworkshere."

"Okay; Tom Cordero?"

"Henolongerworkshere."

"David Fuller?"

"Henolongerworkshere."

"My my," he clucked. "Sounds like you've had some turnover."

"You could say that," the receptionist said in a flat voice. She'd been having this same conversation a lot lately.

Actually, Gus wasn't surprised. A&R careers were notoriously short-lived. A typical A&R person got one or two shots and unless one of them hit, they were usually gone. Poly Brothers hadn't had many hits lately, so every A&R person the promoter knew there had been disappeared.

"Sir," the receptionist asked with a hint of impatience, "is there something I can help you with?"

"Afraid not," Gus replied, and hung up.

Although well past its heyday, Poly Brothers Records was nevertheless one of the big boys—the handful of major labels that collectively controlled most of the market for popular music in America and the rest of the world. Including its publishing arm, it was still the third-largest label in the country.

It wasn't much of an exaggeration to claim that the history of Poly Brothers was the history of American popular music. The company had been founded over a century earlier by two young brothers from Eastern Europe, Nikolai and Yuri Polydoroff, old-country carpenters who emigrated to America not long after the Civil War. Soon after landing in Brooklyn, the brothers hung out a shingle with a shortened surname, rolled up their sleeves and set to work making furniture.

Since the war had just smashed up virtually every stick of furniture in vast areas of the country, their venture was well-timed. Within a decade of their arrival, Poly Brothers furniture factories dotted the East Coast, turning out cheap-but-durable tables and chairs and beds and dressers. By the turn of the century, business was good enough that they were looking for sidelines to expand into.

Since Yuri liked music, one spinoff they tried was mass-producing pianos. But they quickly abandoned that because the instruments were too costly and difficult to make. Their brief foray into piano-making did, however, introduce the brothers to the sheet music business. The Poly Brothers Music Publishing Company became a highly profitable subsidiary, and an early player in America's then-embryonic music industry. A shrewd man, Yuri intuitively understood that the real power and money lay in ownership of the music itself rather than the paper it was printed on. If you controlled the right to sell the music, each copy sold would generate pennies of royalties that eventually added up to many, many dollars.

Yuri Polydoroff went on to become one of the music industry's original robber barons. He was a major force behind the Copyright Statute of 1909, lobbying Congress on numerous points of the law; he was even said to have actually written much of it. Legend held that Yuri intentionally made U.S. copyright law so Byzantine that he alone truly understood all its mysteries.

By the time Poly Brothers started producing record players, it was only natural that the company would make phonograph records to play on them. Thus was born Poly Brothers Records. It started as a small record shop next door to Poly Brothers' flagship furniture store in Brooklyn, with a cramped recording studio in the back. They would hire pickup bands to record the popular songs of the day—preferably songs they owned through their publishing company—then press up records at a small pressing plant they owned nearby, and sell them at their furniture stores.

This vertical integration enabled the Polydoroffs to undercut their competition's prices, and entice people in the door to buy record-players. Many decades before mass-merchandise retailers got the bright idea to sell compact discs at loss-leader prices to get people to buy expensive stereos, Poly Brothers was doing the same thing with 78 RPM shellac records and windup Victrolas.

Nikolai and Yuri were careful to keep ownership of their growing empire within the family, passing it intact to the next generation. But Poly Brothers would not fully blossom until another generation passed and Yuri's grandsons, Adolph and Nehi, entered the picture. They grew up haunting the Poly Brothers record store and recording studio, and were far more interested in producing music than furniture.

Like their grandfather, the young Polydoroffs were fortunate to be in the right place at the right time—and shrewd enough to make the most of the opportunity. It was shortly after World War II and the major labels of the day weren't interested in black rhythm & blues, condescendingly labeling it "race music." Adolph and Nehi had no such prejudices, and Poly Brothers was one of the first white-owned labels to release music by black artists. The label had even fewer qualms about rock 'n' roll, signing up numerous early rock acts while bigger record companies were still writing the style off as a passing fad.

The Polydoroffs knew better because they had the most precious commodity in the music industry: "ears," the knack for finding hits. Each brother was also smart enough to stick with what he did best. Studio hound Nehi served as staff producer for most of the label's records, while Adolph handled the business end. What they didn't know how to do themselves, they hired capable people to handle.

Most unusual of all, Poly Brothers had a reputation for taking care of its artists. Although this was truly novel among music labels of the day, it still had less to do with altruism than self-interest—the fact remained that the Polydoroffs always took care of themselves best of all. Early on, they figured out that it didn't take much to make musicians happy. As long as they paid more than the competition, they could get away without paying their acts what they were really worth, and no one was the wiser.

Only their bottom line knew for sure, and it wasn't talking.

The hits rolled in, elevating Poly Brothers Records to the status of a bonafide major label by the end of the 1950s. From the '60s through the '80s, the label rode the same tidal waves of shifting popular tastes and technological advances that lifted every record company in America to astounding heights of profitability. By then, everybody wanted in. The music business was attractive because startup costs were relatively low, compared to the movie industry, with potentially unlimited returns. If a record hit, it quickly covered its costs and generated revenue with virtually no expenses for years—decades, even. Spend a hundred grand, make millions. Pure profit.

All that, and you got to hang around rock stars, too. Record labels made so much money so fast that Wall Street began looking their way during the 1990s. In an incredible buying binge, foreign-based multinational conglomerates spent billions snapping up every formerly independent American record label. Poly Brothers was the last to go. After years of rebuffing every potential buyer who came courting, Adolph and Nehi finally accepted an offer from the Japanese electronics giant Sapporo for the perverse sum of $666 million. They insisted there was no significance to the figure other than it being what the company was actually worth.

The agreement specified that the Polydoroff family would continue to run the label with full autonomy. But Poly Brothers went from being a gigantic fish in a small pond to a place to round off on Sapporo's balance sheet. Unaccustomed to answering to superiors after a half-century of independence, Adolph and Nehi chafed under the new regime. It didn't take long for the aging brothers to cash in their chips, take eight-figure buyouts and promote themselves to largely ceremonial positions on the company's board of directors.

Before taking their leave, however, the brothers exacted an act of revenge against Sapporo by installing one of their own as new label president—Mo Polydoroff, their thirty-one-year-old nephew. Mo was not well-regarded in the business. In fact, the joke went that "Mo" was short for "Moron."

Behind closed doors, debate raged within the industry over the meaning of Mo's ascension. One popular theory was that it was proof of the elder Polydoroff's encroaching senility. Another school of thought held that Mo was meant to serve as a kind of neutron bomb, taking Poly Brothers down without harming its franchise artists. That would enable Adolph and Nehi to take as many of their old company's acts as they could and start another label under a new name.

Mo was an amiable sort whose biggest flaw was not realizing how far in over his head he was. That he had shown no particular skill for music or business was secondary to the fact that he had never shown any aptitude for anything, ever, except perhaps drinking—and, more recently, losing enormous sums of money. After scraping through Rutgers, Mo pulled gentleman C's at NYU law school. He was toiling in well-deserved obscurity as a Poly Brothers vice president for legal affairs when his destiny was thrust upon him. Anyone possessing a lick of self-preservation instinct (or sense) would have recognized a setup and turned the job down cold. The nephew, on the other hand, considered it his due.

Things had not gone well for Poly Brothers on Mo's watch. In fact, if not for the guaranteed annual revenue from its far-flung publishing holdings and huge catalog of classic older r&b, jazz and rock recordings (which continued to sell, year after year), the label would have foundered long before.

There had been some spectacular failures, virtually all of them Mo's fault. One of his worst missteps was to shift the label's focus away from building up new bands. Instead, he went after expensive, already-established free agents—most of whom were well past their prime. Mo rescued one act after another from the where-are-they-now file, and had nothing but an embarrassing string of high-priced flops to show for it. Wags joked that Poly Brothers was becoming a retirement home for unwanted rockers; its scripted "PB" logo, they said, actually stood for "Pre-Burned."

Just one of the president's high-profile signings had panned out, and only because of morbid curiosity. He signed a well-known band for a five million dollar advance, unaware that the group's lead singer was dying of AIDS (an open secret in the business, and the reason they were available in the first place). The band quietly took the money and ran to the nearest studio, knocking together an album against the clock.

Mo launched the album with a lavish release-party gala on a cruise ship in New York harbor. The boat's ballroom was divided into cubicles, each with a different kinky motif featuring scantily clad women: an aquarium with a "mermaid," a petting zoo with women dressed as "pussycats," a physician's office for "playing doctor" and so on. The T&A simply demonstrated Mo's cluelessness, as he was also unaware that his band's lead singer was gay (and too ill to attend, anyway). For the grand finale, a fireworks display depicted the band's logo above the Statue of Liberty as the boat floated by.

Total cost of the party came to five hundred thousand dollars—more than the band spent on recording costs—and it didn't do a thing to prevent the album from stiffing. After the singer died of AIDS-related pneumonia three months later, however, radio stations began playing the album's elegiac closing track as a tribute. That turned the record into a belated hit and also boosted sales of the group's back catalog, which Poly Brothers had acquired in the deal (an afterthought that turned out well). Death—the ultimate career move.

Still, a fluke hit like that would do little for Poly Brothers' long-term prospects. Neither would it earn Mo the respect he craved, or help him escape the long shadow of his famous uncles. With his label in trouble, Mo was growing desperate.

Gus DeGrande was a man who knew how to make the most of other people's desperation. He knew exactly what buttons he would push to sell Mo on TAB as Poly Brothers' salvation.

An hour after his initial call to Poly Brothers A&R, Gus dialed Mo Polydoroff's "Batphone" direct line. Sitting at his desk, Mo answered on the first ring. He was expecting a call from overseas.

"Mo Polydoroff."

"Mo, this is Gus DeGrande."

It took Mo several moments to place him, during which he wondered how this DeGrande person had come to have his private number. Gus never would've gotten past the president's secretary.

"Oh, yeah, right," Polydoroff finally said, regaining his footing. "Gus DeGrande, the concert promoter?"

"And small-time label president," Gus said, trying for disarming self-deprecation.

"That's right; we have a contract with you, do we not?"

"Yes, you do," DeGrande said.

"And your company is called?…"

"Grandiose Records."

Mo gave the sort of chuckle one hears on televised laugh tracks.

"That's good," he said. "I like that. We can always use more grandiose things here at Poly Brothers. So then, Mr. DeGrande—"

"—Please, call me Gus—"

"—Gus, then. What can I do for you?"

"I have a proposition."

"I'm listening."

"I realize I signed this deal with your uncles, before you took over the company, and a lot has changed since then. So I don't expect that anything like my little imprint would be much of a priority for you at the moment."

"Honestly, no," Mo said.

"I appreciate your frankness, and won't take up much more of your time. But please, hear me out: I'm about to sign an act I think will be worth making a priority. In fact, I'm guessing they can single-handedly save Poly Brothers Records."

As soon as the promoter launched into his pitch, Mo began readying his standard rejection speech—*we appreciate your thinking of us and thanks very much, but no; our release schedule is very crowded the rest of the year, we couldn't possibly work anything else in; I would encourage you to investigate other opportunities elsewhere…*—with which he hoped to get Gus out of his hair with a minimum of fuss. But those last four words tripped him up: "save Poly Brothers Records."

"Mr. DeGrande—"

"—Please, Gus—"

"—Gus, then. Poly Brothers has been around a long time. A lot longer than I've been running it, or you've been promoting concerts. So what makes you think this company needs 'saving?'"

Just as Gus hoped, Mo had taken the bait. He chose his reply carefully, dropping it casually for maximum impact.

"Oh, maybe the fact that I hear you're trying to sell off your publishing company."

Mo's knuckles turned stark white as he gripped the phone. It took an effort not to gasp. This was the Poly Brothers empire's deepest, darkest secret—that things were going so badly that they might have to sell off the publishing division to keep the record label going. Not even Sapporo knew about it yet. Up to now, all discussions had taken place in what the president thought was total secrecy. Apparently not.

"Mr. DeGrande—"

"—Gus—"

"—Don't 'Gus' me," Mo barked, trying to stifle his panic. "*Where* did you hear *that?!*"

No, DeGrande thought, *the guy is no poker player.*

"I have my sources," Gus murmured softly, after another perfectly timed pause.

"That is categorically untrue," Polydoroff said in as steady a voice as he could manage, shuddering at the consequences of his Sapporo superiors hearing this from someone else. "Furthermore, if you get any ideas about spreading any more fairy tales about Poly Brothers, be assured that the wrath of God and our lawyers will rain down upon you."

"My lips are sealed," the promoter said smoothly, unperturbed. "But there's one other piece of information you should know. I understand you have a potential buyer?"

Mo greeted this with stony silence, removing his glasses to rub his eyes.

"A German company, perhaps?" Gus continued.

"Mr. DeGrande—"

"—Gus—"

"—I really don't see the point of continuing this conversation, so I'm going to hang up now."

"Fine," DeGrande said. "But before you do, you might want to know who BMC really is."

The president gave a start upon hearing the name of Poly Brothers Publishing's supposedly confidential German suitor. *Sonofabitch...*

"I have no idea what you're talking about," Mo said through clenched teeth, stubbornly conceding nothing. But he did not hang up.

The promoter delivered his coup de grace.

"BMC doesn't exist, except on paper," he said. "It's a dummy shell corporation. Even though it's registered in Germany, it has no holdings there. It's a complicated chain of entities, but BMC is actually nothing more than an unnumbered Swiss bank account controlled by two people: Adolph and Nehi Polydoroff. Your uncles."

For a good ten seconds, Mo was speechless. He knew the music business was cutthroat and corrupt; that was part of the attraction. Nevertheless, he could not believe he was being double-crossed by his own uncles—who were still on the Poly Brothers board and would therefore be voting to approve the sale of Poly Brothers Publishing, secretly, to themselves for a literal and figurative song.

"How could they do this to me?" Mo asked incredulously when he could speak again. "How?...Why?..."

"Can't trust anyone in this business," Gus said sympathetically. "Not even your own family. Especially *your* family."

"Yeah..." Polydoroff said numbly.

"Look, Mo, you've got a problem: no new business. You're basically getting by with selling catalog, because nothing new has been hitting. Right?"

"Right," he answered, too dazed to argue.

"So your uncles see that and figure you're easy meat, even if you're a relative. They already cashed out once, and figure they can make another bundle picking up the pieces if you fall—especially if they're the ones giving you a shove. You've been set up."

"I've been set up," Mo repeated in a bewildered voice. Then he finally uttered the magic words the promoter had been waiting to hear: "So what do I do?"

Triumphant, Gus smiled and leaned back in his chair, planting his Gucci loafers on his desk.

"Screw 'em right back," he said. "And I just happen to have the perfect screwdriver."

After hanging up, Gus opened a desk drawer, which held a cassette recorder wired into his phone. He rewound the tape and jotted down a few notes on the label. Then he pocketed it for safekeeping, until he could get over to his safe deposit box at the bank. DeGrande taped everything, just in case. He also listened to his more important conversations afterward to see if he had read a situation correctly.

This one, however, was simple. Gus had serious misgivings about Poly Brothers. The fact that Mo would even consider selling the publishing company to salvage the record label was proof of his short-sightedness.

Record companies were more glamorous than publishing companies, but there was still more long-term value in publishing. You could always hire someone else to stamp the music onto tape or plastic or microchips, get the product to market and hawk it. Owning the information itself was the key. Mo was more interested in the pieces of plastic because they brought in big wads of cash right away. But the pennies generated by publishing were worth far more over the long haul.

DeGrande would find a way to use the label president's myopia to his advantage. With Poly Brothers in such dire straits, all he had to do was get a hit record into its pipeline. Then all of the label's still-formidable marketing machinery would be focused on his project.

Now he just had to get the right record, and the right band.

CHAPTER FIFTEEN

As Gus finished reeling in Mo Polydoroff, Ken Morrison sat at his desk dialing a number in Chicago. He spent the better part of each day with a phone receiver glued to his ear, checking in with sources and bands, and gossiping with his colleagues at other papers. Little actual work came of the endless hours the critic spent on the phone, but it at least enabled him to look busy at his desk.

"Martin P. McPhail," a businesslike voice answered on the third ring. One of *Chicago Times-Tribune* critic Marty McPhail's odder conceits was to use his formal name as a phone greeting, thinking it sounded more intellectual. It fooled about as many people as his hairweave did.

"Marty, Ken Morrison here." Ken refused to address McPhail with any sort of formality. He figured he was entitled, after the eventful evening they spent together while covering an industry convention in Texas the previous year. The night included several gallons of margaritas, after which Marty wound up down on all fours in an alley regurgitating everything that had gone down his throat the previous twenty-four hours.

But that was just a warm-up for the main event, in which McPhail fell down and fractured his hip without realizing what he'd done—until he stood up, passed out from the pain, fell again and managed to break his collarbone. Ken was also thoroughly intoxicated by then, and considered it a miracle that he got his colleague to the emergency room without inflicting further damage. While filling out the paperwork at the hospital, Ken put "bizarre gardening accident" as the cause of injury.

McPhail claimed he didn't remember a thing until he woke up in a hospital bed with two casts on. Memory loss, and rock critic workman's comp. It had been a bonding experience for the two of them.

"Hey, Ken. Funny you should call, I've been meaning to give you a holler. This band TAB, they're from down your way, right?"

"Raleigh's finest," Ken said. "That's why I'm calling. You go see 'em the other night?"

"Uh huh. They were great, in a…well, really bizarre sorta way. They do 'Little Deuce Coupe' every night?"

"The Beach Boys song?" Ken asked. "Not that I've ever seen. That must be a new one."

"It was really cool, even though I couldn't tell if they really even knew how to play it. They did a bunch of weird covers—or songs that sounded like they might've been covers, anyway. Then the guitar player broke two strings, got pissed and smashed his guitar, and that was it."

"That's my boy," Ken said, chuckling.

"He does seem like a strange one. Didn't you do a story on that guy where he pulled a gun on you?"

"Yep, that was him. Tommy Aguilar, fuck-up extraordinaire."

"Yeah, well, the guy must have his reasons for packing heat," McPhail said. "Especially if this was a typical night. He was hitting on somebody else's girlfriend."

"Ouch," Ken winced. "Wouldn't be the first time. Anybody I'd know?"

"No, but somebody who should've known better. This girl named Beth. Her boyfriend Carl plays in Basenji, and they opened the show."

Ken moaned. As deadly sins went, hitting on another musician's girlfriend—especially your opening act's girlfriend—was considered asshole star-tripping of the lowest sort. People had been killed for less.

"Carl was really pissed," McPhail continued, "and he can be kind of a hothead. If Aguilar ever comes back up here again, he'd better be careful."

"Oh, he won't," Ken sighed.

"Come back to Chicago?"

"No, be careful. The word is not in his vocabulary."

"Well, he definitely made a hell of an impression up here. You know they showed up in a limo?"

"Say what?" Ken said, laughing. "And I'd been hearing this tour wasn't going so well."

"Maybe it's not, because it wasn't actually their limo. I just happened to be at the club before soundcheck, and here comes this big ol' stretch limo with TAB and all their gear inside—and their drummer driving it. Apparently, their van broke down out in the sticks, and some high-roller guy showed up out of nowhere and gave them a ride. I heard he even sprang for getting the van towed and fixed."

Alarm bells started going off in Ken's head. "The guy who gave them the ride," he said, "was it anybody you recognized?"

"Nope."

"What'd he look like?"

"Oh, I dunno. Old and unpleasant, I guess."

"Scary, glowery-looking bald guy? Prison guard type who maybe enjoys the work a little too much?"

"Right. Angry-looking dude, too, even when he smiled. Why, is that someone you know?"

"DeGrande," Ken said. "Gus DeGrande."

"*That* was Gus DeGrande? The big-cheese fascist promoter you're always bitching about down there?"

"Uh huh, and a creepier fucker never lived. I wonder why he was up there? This is the second time I know about that DeGrande has been at a TAB show. A couple months ago, he actually came to see them play at a bar here—the first time I've ever seen him at a local band's show—and now he drops in on them a thousand miles away. What would he be doing in Chicago?"

"I dunno," McPhail said. "Wait a minute, yes I do—I think he's co-promoting some concerts here with Don Krishnard; maybe one in St. Louis, too."

Don Krishnard was Chicago's local equivalent to Gus DeGrande. There was no telling what behind-the-scenes blood-letting had gone on to compel him to cut Gus in on a show in his territory.

"Hmm," Ken said. "Maybe DeGrande is scouting for opening acts?"

"If he was, then they must've played a private audition. He didn't actually stay for the show."

"You know TAB's drummer, the guy you said was driving the limo? He told me once that DeGrande tried to fine his old band for playing two minutes too long."

"At least he didn't just break their wrists," McPhail said. "That's what Krishnard usually does when someone displeases him."

"Must be DeGrande's Southern gentility and refinement," Ken said.

"Must be. So does DeGrande actually have anything to do with this TAB band?"

"Not unless there's been a change I haven't heard about. As far as I know, a guy down here named Bob Porter is still their manager."

"Never heard of him," McPhail said. "He any good?"

"Seems to be. He just runs a bar where all these shitty local bands play. TAB is the best band down here, but managing them involves a lot of psychology. As you saw last night, they can be a pretty unstable bunch. I think Bob's doing a pretty decent job with them."

"Well," McPhail said, "I doubt Gus DeGrande was chauffeuring that band around in a limo to enhance his indie cred. Their manager better watch his back."

"I'll be sure and tell him."

Bob was worried, although not as much as he should've been. After hearing about Gus's limousine rescue, he called the promoter's office to leave a message of thanks and promised to repay the three hundred dollars as soon as he could. But first, he had to wire the band enough money for Tommy to replace the guitar he'd destroyed. The worrisome part was that Tommy's on-the-road antics took a turn for the worse after Chicago. At first, they didn't seem to be drug-related—just obnoxious, and sexual. After starting the tour on his best behavior, TAB's bandleader was once again a man on the make. The situation finally came to a head a week later in Cincinnati, in profoundly horrific circumstances.

For the first time Ray could remember, Tommy had foregone his usual pre-show trance ritual and disappeared. The drummer suspected the cause was a waitress with whom Tommy kept making eyes during soundcheck. Unfortunately, it was Michelle who discovered him locked in a carnal embrace with the woman—in TAB's van, which was parked behind the club.

That made Michelle angry enough. But what totally enraged her was the item Tommy was using for a makeshift blanket: the very garment she had walked out to the van to get, her last clean sweater. Between TAB's ongoing bad-tour karma and lingering bad vibes from Gus's hit-and-run visit, the bassist was already on edge. When she caught Tommy, she snapped, surprising everyone (including herself) by going blind crazy. First, Michelle dragged Tommy's nude sex partner out of the van by her hair, kicking and screaming, and chased her around the parking lot. After the woman fled, Michelle turned her wrath on her bandmate.

"You miserable fucker!" she screamed, lunging for Tommy's throat. "Ray was just gonna beat you up, but I'm gonna *kill* you!!!"

Struggling to get his pants on, Tommy made the mistake of laughing, which only increased Michelle's fury. His second error was to raise his arms to fend off her attack from his face. Stumbling backwards and flailing, he left just enough of an opening for Michelle to unexpectedly turn her attack southward. She latched onto his testicles and squeezed. Hard.

Like most musicians, Michelle had a surprisingly strong grip. Tommy emitted an animal howl that sounded as if it originated from within the deepest forest primeval. The harder he thrashed and struggled to escape, the harder she squeezed. The bassist held on with her right hand while warding off Tommy's blows with her left arm, standing him up against the side of the van as she dug in her nails. Alarmed by the agonized screams, people came running out to see what was the matter.

"Let's see you get a hard-on *now*, wonderboy," Michelle hissed as Tommy started to gag, his eyes rolling back in his head. She probably would've held on until he turned purple and passed out had Ray not intervened, prying her off.

"Jesus, Michelle," Ray yelped, walking gingerly in sympathy for his bandmate's private parts. "What the fuck are you doing?!"

"Something I should've done a long time ago," she answered in a weirdly calm voice, as Tommy fell in a heap. Michelle reached into the van to retrieve her soiled sweater and dropped it over his prostrate, semi-nude form.

"When he can stand up," she told Ray, "tell him he'll need to get that dry-cleaned."

Then Michelle went into the bathroom, locked the door, filled the sink with warm water and soaked her hands. She felt like Lady MacBeth, but somehow didn't mind at all.

In a first for TAB, the band played an almost entirely instrumental set in Cincinnati that night. Michelle's assault left Tommy incapable of speaking, let alone singing. Under the hostile glare of the waitress she'd chased around the parking lot, the bassist twice stepped up to the microphone to sing, and even swapped instruments with Ray to peck away at drums for a song. Mostly, though, they just played everything without vocals, adding a dash of twangy reverb so it would pass for surf music.

"Tonight," Michelle announced, "is our Ventures tribute set. I'm Jan, that's Dean on drums, and over there on guitar is Mr. Wang Dang Doodle himself, Tommy Boy."

She waved toward Tommy, propped up in a chair. He waved back weakly. He'd barely been able to make the walk from backstage, and played the set sitting down (another first). The guitarist could only watch helplessly as Michelle walked over to his amplifier and turned down his volume. All things considered, she thought, the show went remarkably well.

The next day, on their way out of town, TAB went to the cleaners to get Michelle's sweater dry-cleaned. One-hour service. Tommy even sprang for martinizing.

With Tommy's nether regions on injured reserve, Bob was concerned he might resort to another of his habits to fill the void. Sure enough, he was showing all the signs. People on the take emit a certain smoke signal visible only to people who can fill that need, and plenty of smoke and fire shrouded the final dates of TAB's second tour. His bandmates couldn't help but notice the symptoms, starting with the return of Tommy's sullen mode. Even after he physically recovered from Michelle's attack, after she admitted she overreacted and apologized, after they kissed and made up, he brooded. Entire days went by where he said almost nothing except for onstage patter.

The crowds were getting creepier, too; a lot of thousand-yard-stare types, burn-outs, vultures. They were even worse than record company A&R people about not respecting the backstage sanctum. Every night, after TAB finished playing, it was the same. Tommy would go off with some scary-looking vampire, leaving Ray and Michelle to deal with the record label types who were starting to show up.

The drummer did what he could to chase off the nastier-looking parasites, and he and Michelle both tried to discourage Tommy from indulging. The guitarist was indignant at their accusations, and insisted he wasn't partaking of anything stronger than beer. He was clever about covering his tracks, but the narcoleptic hazes gave him away.

All tour long, Tommy had said he couldn't wait to get to Kansas City for the barbecue. When they went to Arthur Bryant's Famous Rib Joint, he could barely stay awake. He actually nodded off in mid-sentence—"So what should we..."—his face coming to rest in a plate of ribs. His bandmates stared first at him, then at each other and then at the other customers in the restaurant, wondering what to do.

A minute and a half went by. Finally, right about the time they figured they ought to check for vital signs, Tommy raised up his head and resumed speaking, apparently unaware he had barbecue sauce running down his cheek and a pinto bean stuck to his forehead.

"...start with tonight?" Tommy concluded.

"How about a bath?" Ray asked, pouring a glass of iced tea over his head.

Gus was still on top of the situation, from a thousand miles away. His spies began reporting back on Tommy's growing sexual debaucheries after Chicago, up to and including his near-maiming in Cincinnati. When reports of heavier drug use started filtering back, the promoter decided to nudge the situation along. Among his far-flung connections were drug dealers in virtually every city and town in America—useful folks to know, if one conducted dealings with a certain class of rock star. DeGrande began sending them around to TAB's shows.

"Don't waste any time with the drummer or the bass player," he instructed. "Just the guitar player. Be generous. But don't make it free, just cheap. He doesn't have much money."

Not that Gus was doing anything to alleviate Tommy's destitution. By the time tour number two wound down and TAB staggered homeward, the promoter's manipulations had been almost too effective. Broke, exhausted and discouraged from a tour that seemed to lose ground from the start, the band was perilously close to imploding. True, a few things had gone right. They picked up good press and college radio airplay (though not significantly more of either than on the first tour), and word in the industry was definitely out. Record companies were sending scouts out to see the band, and calling Bob to ask about *Come Go Away.*

Curiously, despite all the attention, *Come Go Away* hadn't sold at all, although lots and lots of copies had seemingly vanished into thin air. The manager couldn't figure it out. They weren't sold, just gone, and nobody could explain where or why. Another financial black hole. Between postage and manufacturing, Bob was out five-thousand dollars on this record.

Throw in all the cash infusions to deal with one crisis or another, and he was just about broke—and all for a tour in which TAB brought home even less money than they'd made their first time out. Bob would've taken out a second mortgage on Each, if he could find a bank willing to give him one. Every banker he approached acted as if he was putting up a burning building as collateral.

Yet Bob's cash-flow difficulties were minor compared to another, far thornier problem. Tommy Aguilar's on-again/off-again drug habit was on again, this time for good.

CHAPTER SIXTEEN

For as long as he'd been at the *Daily News,* Ken Morrison had been doggedly trying to interview Gus DeGrande. Not through any burning personal desire to do one, but because his editor was positively obsessed with "getting" the legendary concert promoter.

"There's got to be some dirt on this guy," she insisted.

"Of course there is," Ken said. "He's in the music industry. And I'm sure he'll be delighted to tell me and my tape recorder all about it."

"There must be somebody who'll talk about him, so go find them," his editor commanded.

So the critic made inquiries, and saw every source disappear into the same black hole of attribution. Virtually everyone who ever had dealings with Gus clearly despised him, but feared him even more. Present and former employees, would-be competitors, bands who'd worked for him—every single person Ken approached flatly refused to say anything, for fear of reprisals. He even tried to guarantee anonymity (even though he'd never get that past his editor), just to see if it would loosen any lips. Nada.

Ken had never seen anything like it. Off the record and third-hand, he heard incredible gossip and tantalizing rumors about the promoter's thuggery, gambling habits, cocaine indulgences. But he never had any luck confirming any of it. All the critic had to do was

163

pull out a notebook, and everybody's mouth snapped shut tighter than a kickdrum.

With no one willing to talk on the record (including the man himself), Ken had no story. He'd never even been allowed past the front door of Grandiose Concerts' offices. Nevertheless, the critic felt compelled to give his editor the impression he was still chasing the story. So he went through the motions, dutifully putting in interview requests on a regular basis.

Mostly to keep track, Ken did it quarterly. Four times a year—the 15th of January, April, July and October—he called Grandiose Concerts, asked for Gus and wound up talking to his snotty secretary Natalie. He would ask for an audience with DeGrande, usually under the pretense of previewing or recapping some impending or recently concluded event. She would put him on hold, then come back on the line to tell him no dice, after which they always traded insults before hanging up. The critic maintained similarly abusive phone relationships with publicists all over the industry, most of whom he'd never actually met in-person.

Ken particularly enjoyed making the call on April 15, income tax day. He found the thought of Gus having to pay someone else lots of money immensely pleasing. But today, it was time for the fall solicitation.

He waited until ten minutes to five o'clock before dialing 555-7625 (ROCK), and asked the switchboard operator for Gus DeGrande.

"Mr. DeGrande's office."

"Hello there, Natalie," Ken said, sing-song. "Guess who?"

"Well, if it isn't everybody's favorite hack," she sneered. "Gosh, I was starting to think you'd forgotten us."

"Are you kidding?"

"Yeah, I suppose it was too much to hope for."

"C'mon, Natalie, you know I live for these little chats of ours. Rejection as consistent and loyal as yours is so rare nowadays."

"In your case," she purred, "I doubt that very much."

"Oooooooh," Ken moaned, mock-wounded. "Now coming from you, *that* hurts."

"Yeah, you're breakin' my heart here."

"This is the thanks I get for brightening your Ides of October? For being your very own personal autumnal equinox event?"

"Believe it or not, Morrison, it's nothing I set my calendar by."

"Oh, but I do. Although our rhythm does seem to be a little bit off today."

"Our 'rhythm?' "

"Yeah," Ken said. "We usually start out civilized, and don't get to the name-calling part until after you turn me down. I feel like we're, you know, smoking' the cigarette first, if ya follow me."

Natalie cackled a harsh laugh. "If that was a proposition," she said, "it's the most pathetic one I've ever heard."

Now it was Ken's turn to laugh. "You should be so lucky," he said. "Thanks, I can think of more cost-effective ways to bore myself to death—like covering your concerts. So go ask that bloodsucker you work for when he's gonna book something from this calendar century. And while you're at it, tell him the interview request still stands."

"One moment," she said through a sneer, putting the critic on hold.

It always amazed Ken that anyone who called Grandiose Concerts had to listen to canned elevator music when they were put on hold. Between that and the satisfaction Natalie was going to get from telling him no, he almost hung up.

After nearly three minutes of an interminable orchestral version of "Whipping Post," a voice finally came back on the line. But it wasn't Natalie's.

"Gus DeGrande," the voice growled.

Distracted from trying to think up a snappy retort to the secretary's anticipated smug refusal, Ken almost fell over. He gave a start and sat bolt upright, pulling his feet off his desk.

"Beg pardon?" Ken asked.

"Yes?"

"This is really Gus DeGrande?"

"Live and in-person," the promoter said impatiently. "What can I do for you?"

"Well…um…" This was, to say the least, unexpected. "Well, Mr. DeGrande, I'd like to interview you."

"Fine," Gus said. "When?"

" 'When?' Excuse me, did you just say 'when?' "

"Yes. When?"

Ken's head was spinning. "Oh, whatever's convenient for you," he said weakly, hoping for a date far off in the future.

"Be at my office in an hour."

Click.

Fifty-seven minutes later, Ken approached Grandiose Concerts' bunker-like office building as evening shadows fell, wondering what on earth to do. He'd been caught completely off-guard, with no questions or background research prepared. There had never been a reason to do any, the chances of Gus agreeing to an interview seemed so remote. Yet here Ken was, having initiated his own ambush. After turning down scores of prior requests, the promoter obviously had his reasons for agreeing to talk now—and not just now, but right now.

Inside the building, he asked the steely-eyed man behind the security desk for DeGrande.

"Second floor," he said, pointing toward an elevator. "You'll need to sign in first."

The critic autographed a piece of paper on a clipboard and pinned a yellow "VISITOR" badge onto his T-shirt at an appropriately crooked angle. He made his way past rows of offices full of well-dressed employees and gloomily rode the elevator up, listening to the same canned music that Grandiose played over the phone lines. Apparently, the selections began and ended with "Whipping Post."

On the second floor, Ken found himself in a carpeted hallway wall-papered with large photos of Gus in the company of famous, near-famous and infamous rock stars, actors, celebrities and politicians. A couple of presidents, even.

Ken paused before one oversize picture, a panoramic black-and-white shot of a crowded football stadium. He remembered this concert from four summers earlier—the Arrowhead show, the night before the critic earned his weeklong suspension by impersonating them onstage at Each—and the moment this photo captured. Gus had come onstage to speak before the band came out, and acted as if the show was a Christmas present he was about to give the crowd. It was a strange bit of vanity for someone who usually went out of his way to stay invisible.

From a vantage point behind and above the stage, the photo showed DeGrande's back. He wore shorts and a too-small T-shirt, and seemed to list to one side with his shoulders slumped as he gripped the micro-phone. The promoter looked obese and yet terribly small in front of all that humanity. It was the closest to vulnerable he'd ever looked, Ken thought. The critic was reminded of an off-the-record quote he once heard attributed to a rival promoter, that Gus was the craziest man in the music industry because he came by his dementia honestly.

"All that bastard does at night is putter around the house and cook shrimp," the quote went, "and he's *still* outta his fuckin' mind. Insanity like DeGrande's, you just can't explain with booze or cocaine. Food must have the same effect on that guy as acid."

Ken continued down the deserted hallway and finally arrived at a small lobby. Behind a desk sat Natalie—maybe thirty years old, dark-haired and smaller than she sounded on the phone, though not quite frail. The critic sized her up and decided she might qualify as attractive if she would only turn down the volume on her frown. She wore the demeanor of a disapproving librarian.

"We meet at last," he said.

"So we do," Natalie answered, meeting his eyes without enthusiasm.

"So you're the gatekeeper, huh? That must involve a lot of raw meat. What's it like working for The Great Satan?"

"Probably not too different from working for a newspaper, except it pays better and we piss fewer people off."

"Don't bet on it," Ken said.

"Oh, sorry, I forgot. You're a highly paid professional, right?" Natalie asked, looking scornfully at Ken's wardrobe—black T-shirt, frayed denim, black leather jacket, scuffed Converse All-Stars.

"That wasn't what I meant," the critic said, suddenly self-conscious about his scruffy appearance.

"Duh," Natalie smirked.

Ken couldn't help laughing. "You this friendly to everybody who comes to visit?" he asked.

"Nobody comes here to visit," she said, sounding as if that didn't displease her.

"Well, with your bedside manner, it's no wonder," Ken said, then turned for the door to DeGrande's office. "Wish me luck. You want me to ask him to give you a raise while I'm at it?"

"Hey, wait a minute," Natalie protested, vainly trying to stop Ken as he barged in without knocking. "You can't just…"

What the hell, the critic thought. *Might as well see if I can get myself thrown out of here. Save us all a lot of trouble.*

Inside his office, DeGrande was hunched over his desk with the phone to his ear, listening to an extremely irate band manager curse and holler. The blustering was so loud that Ken could hear it from across the room. Gus's eyes never moved and his face never changed expression as he watched Ken enter, close the door behind him and plop into a chair in front of his desk.

"Irving," the promoter finally said into the phone, "I'm gonna have to call you back—after you've calmed down."

He hung up without waiting for a response, interrupting a scream.

"Prick," Gus muttered. "And after everything I've done for him…" He pressed his intercom button. "Hold my calls until I tell you otherwise."

Then he turned his attention to Ken, who felt as if he was seated before a throne. Gus was ensconced behind a desk so large it only needed tailfins to be a Cadillac. The evening skyline was framed in the window behind him, either side of which was lined with more photos and the inevitable gold and platinum records. In one corner across the room sat a complete home entertainment center; in another, an aquarium with the promoter's pet piranha.

"Nice fish," Ken said, feeling as if the fish was watching him with predatory intentions.

"Thanks."

"Does it have a name?"

"Nope."

"Why not?"

"All it does is eat. It's not gonna come when you call it."

"Sounds like a metaphor," the critic said. "Gus DeGrande as carnivorous fish. That'd make a nice headline, don't you think?"

"Cute," Gus said, "very cute."

"I try."

"So why do you want to do an interview?"

"Funny," Ken said, "I was about to ask you the same thing."

"Why? You're the one who asked."

"Yeah, and I've been asking for years, and the answer has always been no. So why now?"

"Because I was busy every other time you called. But I'm not too busy now, so why not?"

"Why not?" the critic repeated. "Okay, why not?"

He opened his backpack and removed a tape recorder, set it on the desk and turned it on. Gus had already surreptitiously activated his own tape recorder with a foot pedal under the desk.

"First question: In ten years, I've been unable to find a single person willing to talk about you on the record. Any idea why that would be?"

By opening with a confrontational question, Ken was violating a cardinal tenet of interviewing—build trust and rapport with easy questions first, and save the potential interview-ending hardballs for last. He actually hoped DeGrande would cut the interview off and throw him out. No such luck.

"Nope," Gus said, shrugging. "You'd have to ask them."

Ken pressed on. "Well, most people seem to be afraid of you," he said.

" 'Afraid?' What do you mean?"

"Afraid they'll wind up blackballed, fired, their thumbs broken, things like that. It does seem that anybody who goes up against you always has bad shit happen to them."

"I've no idea why anyone would think that," the promoter said. "My reputation for nastiness is greatly exaggerated. All I can say is, if you're around long enough and you're successful enough, there will always be people who resent that. Anybody who thinks the music business is a popularity contest, I've got news for them—it ain't. I have no control over what people think of me, nor do I care."

"Obviously not, because a lot of people think you're the most ruthless bastard in the industry."

Gus laughed. "Not even close," he said. "Why would anyone think that? All I do is put on shows and sell tickets."

"Lots of people put on shows and sell tickets. Why is it that anyone who tries to compete with you never lasts very long?"

"Number one, because I put out a better product. I might not be so good at schmoozing the 'important' people like yourself, but I do take care of the kid who buys a ticket. And number two, because this business is very political. The relationships and connections—and money—that you have determine which acts you can hire. I've been doing this a long time, and I know every booking agent and band manager and building owner in the country. A lot of the bands, too.

That didn't happen overnight, and it doesn't happen overnight for anyone else, either."

"You've been promoting concerts for how long now?"

"Twenty-seven years."

"How has the business changed since you got started?"

"Well, like everything else, it isn't as personal as it used to be. I was just talking about relationships. As time goes by, those seem to matter less and less, and how much money you can pile on the table matters more and more. I do miss the old days, when things were simpler— there was more trust, you could do deals on a handshake. But just like record labels or car companies or whatever else, the concert business has gotten bigger and more corporate. Used to be that every city in America had a guy like me, its own Gus DeGrande. There aren't many independent promoters left anymore."

"Some people might say you yourself had a lot to do with that. Haven't you put a lot of other promoters out of business?"

"No, I wouldn't say that," Gus said. "Sure, Grandiose has expanded, and I've had to fight some fights to do that. Nothing underhanded about it, just competition. And where there's competition, one side wins and the other side loses. This is an expensive business and if you lose a few times in a row, you can go broke in a hurry. Anybody who went up against me and lost, they beat themselves. They made stupid bookings or paid bands too much or made tickets too expensive. I had nothing to do with it."

"So these take-no-prisoners stories about burning down buildings and sabotaging shows and strong-arming people…"

"Lies," the promoter said, with a Corleone-esque wave of dismissal. "All lies. You may not want to believe this because it isn't a popular viewpoint, but I'm not a bad guy. You keep telling me, 'People say this, people say that.' Who is saying what, exactly? Tell me something specific and I can respond. Otherwise, it's all just hearsay and scurrilous innuendo."

DeGrande smiled as Ken sighed. Was that what Gus had summoned him for? More names for his enemies list? Great. Just great…

The critic glanced at his watch. He had missed dinner and his stomach was growling. This was shaping up to be a long night.

"Don't you ever eat?" he asked

"All the time," Gus said. "But dinner's for losers who don't have enough to do."

Their interview lasted a long time, nearly three hours. For someone who never talked to the press, Gus gave good quote. Ken came away with lots of pithy soundbites, including the promoter's three ironclad rules for survival in the concert business:

"First, stay the fuck off of helicopters. Second: No glove, no love. And third, always remember, loyalty is a stupid emotion. Use it when you find it, but try to avoid it yourself and don't ever expect it from anyone else."

The critic asked the usual boilerplate questions about personal background, which DeGrande answered without volunteering much: place of birth (Chicago), place he was raised (Atlanta), education (business degree from University of North Carolina), family status (divorced), offspring (two grown sons), hobbies (cards), actual musical experience (none).

They also discussed the state of contemporary music. Ken didn't find Gus's disdain for it the least bit surprising.

"I think music's kind of stagnant right now," DeGrande said. "Seems like everything's a rehash of things that were done better by bands I was working with twenty years ago, or weird computer-type shit I just don't get and can't imagine will last. I don't see much out there that excites me. One of the few really good young new acts I've seen is this band from here, TAB. I think they're terrific."

The critic sat up and took notice of that. "You seem…interested in them," he said. "Haven't you gone to a lot of their shows?"

"Not exactly. I did go to one here in town a while back. And two weeks ago, I gave them a ride to Chicago because I happened to pass their van after it had broken down on the highway—I presume that's what you're talking about?"

"Yeah. So what's your interest in them?"

"Nothing, beyond thinking that they're a very fine band that should do well. I expect I'll be booking them into arenas in another couple of years."

"You don't want to get more directly involved than that?"

"Why would I? All I do is book concerts. And besides, TAB already has a manager."

Despite Ken's obvious skepticism, Gus knew his quotes about TAB would be played prominently in the story. The promoter had read Ken's rave reviews of TAB, and correctly gauged their undercurrents: The critic wanted this band to succeed, and wanted some of the credit for it, too. He would not pass up a chance to give them a plug this good.

As it turned out, Ken did more than just use DeGrande's quote in the *Daily News.* He wrote two different stories based on the interview—one for the newspaper and another for *Cashboard,* the music business trade paper. Virtually everyone in the industry read *Cashboard,* for its weekly sales and airplay charts if nothing else.

Ken had been a freelance stringer for *Cashboard* for several years, usually doing stories about the occasional Raleigh band that managed to get a record deal. The pay was abysmal, but the cachet of having bylines in "the music industry's Bible" had done wonders for his connections. The magazine was only too happy to have an interview with Gus DeGrande, one of a dying breed of maverick entrepreneurs in the concert business. The promoter never did interviews, and was as mysterious as he was legendary.

Cashboard's readers didn't have to get too far into the story to find DeGrande's opinion of TAB. Ken chose to lead with it:

While promoting concerts has made Gus DeGrande a behind-the-scenes power in the music business, he still doesn't think much of today's pop music scene.

"I think music's kind of stagnant right now," says DeGrande, a 27-year veteran of the industry. "Seems like it's all a rehash of things that were done better by bands I was working with 20 years ago, or weird computer-type [stuff] I just don't get and can't imagine will last. I don't hear much out there that excites me. One of the few really good young new acts I've seen is this band from here, TAB. I think they're terrific."

TAB, a space-age rockabilly power trio based in DeGrande's hometown of Raleigh, N.C., is as yet unsigned, although the band's self-released Come Go Away mini-album is garnering enthusiastic industry response. DeGrande predicts he'll be booking TAB into arenas before too long...

CHAPTER SEVENTEEN

Tommy Aguilar wasn't answering his phone again. Oh, he was around, all right—holed up and licking his wounds from TAB's latest touring misadventures. But he was staying out of sight and out of touch, which made Bob antsy. This time, he gave his client a couple of weeks to cool out before approaching. And for three straight days, he left the same message on the answering machine:

"Tommy, Bob here. Gimmie a holler. Time to figure out our next move."

The manager knew only one way to solve problems, by outworking them. Until the military, he'd never quit anything in his life. There were relatives he no longer spoke to after they allowed family members to give up when stricken with fatal diseases. His maternal grandparents still hadn't forgiven him for the chemotherapy regimen Bob insisted on for his own mother's cancer. It did her no good, but the son refused to budge.

Whether it was battling cancer or breaking a band, Bob was not going to fail through lack of effort. So they had to get busy and make another record, get back on the road, cross their fingers and hope the next tour went better. It couldn't possibly go any worse, although that was something Bob would hesitate to promise again. TAB was zero for two on tours so far.

That was discouraging, but the manager still believed things were moving in the right direction. Both inside and outside the industry, people were talking about TAB. That all-important "buzz" was growing. If the band could just avoid falling apart, and Bob could avoid bankruptcy, everything would come together. Not overnight, but sooner rather than later.

While Bob couldn't guarantee success, he did have a surprise lined up to lift the band's spirits. An honest-to-god, capital-P Producer was going to produce TAB's next record. Not just any producer, either: Clay Dickerson, grand old man of the local music scene.

Most locals still regarded Dickerson with something approaching awe, thanks to his tenure a decade earlier as bassist and lead singer of the Rampagans—one of the saddest should've-been stories in all of the music business. The Rampagans were one of the best live bands Bob had ever seen, as well as one of the loudest (even their between-song pauses seemed louder than anyone else's). The clubowner thought TAB was better, but just barely; something he made a point of never telling either Clay or Tommy.

Unfortunately, all the Rampagans' recorded efforts were the proverbial lightning bugs to their live shows' lightning bolts. As good as they were onstage, they never made an undeniably great album. They also had the regrettable habit of hiring friends, relatives and even significant others as managers. Dickerson used to joke that the Rampagans had more ex-managers than records sold to their credit.

End result, the Rampagans owned their hometown but no place else. Local heroes. The same sad fate as a thousand other bands in a thousand other towns. They came to an ugly and brutal end, crashing and burning beneath the weight of years of frustration. Dickerson once told Bob that the Rampagans' breakup was the most traumatic split he'd ever lived through, worse than either of his divorces.

Post-breakup, Dickerson embarked on a low-key solo career, releasing the occasional album whenever he could con a record company into paying for one. He also became a producer.

"Beats working," went his standard explanation. "Besides, I fucked up every record my own band ever made, so I figured I might as well see how many other records I could fuck up, too. You know, spread the love around."

Despite his self-deprecation, Clay Dickerson turned out to be an exceptional producer. He'd only produced a handful of big hits, but even fewer outright duds. Virtually every album on his resume was critically acclaimed. Though largely unknown to the public, he was highly regarded within the industry. His name on a record by a new, unsigned band would guarantee attention from all the right people. Which was a curious aspect of the record business, since nobody actually understood just what producers did.

Twiddling knobs and setting up microphones was only a small part of the Black Art of producing. The process was a lot like directing movies. Some producers were the equivalent of low-rent porno directors; they did little more than turn on the tape machine and keep out of the way. Others recorded take after take and then painstakingly pieced songs together a note at a time, which Dickerson scornfully compared to filming car wrecks by leaving cameras running on street corners. Still others went for big-budget special effects, layering in extraneous noises that few untrained ears would ever notice.

On the other hand, Dickerson made records that were more like Westerns—solid, competent and logical, with a beginning, middle and end. Although he was essentially a producer with an expensive hobby, Dickerson still considered himself a recording artist first and a producer second. Or as he put it, "I don't shave a producer every morning." He knew how to make bands feel like peers rather than underlings, even while whipping them into shape in ways that went beyond notes, chords and arrangements. Any band that made a record with Dickerson was going to come out of the experience better than before.

"Producing is basically medicine and physics," he was fond of saying. "There are just two things to remember. First, do no harm—don't fuck shit up worse than it already is. And the second is a corollary to the first: Every action has an equal and opposite reaction. So figure out where you want to go before you start pushing—and whether it's gonna take a shovel, a backhoe or a cattle prod."

Dickerson's production method was equal parts cheerleading, tough love and subterfuge. He could be a band's best buddy, just one of the boys trading war stories about getting busted for a marijuana seed at the Canadian border. Or he could be as brutal as a Marine drill instructor, putting musicians through the equivalent of forced death marches. Often, he had to use both guises during the same session. The trick was knowing when to bear down, and when to back off.

Mostly because he refused to work with the other crappy bands in town, Dickerson was one of the few established local figures that Tommy didn't hold in utter contempt. Ray practically worshipped the man, going back to when he snuck into Rampagans shows as a teenager. And Michelle would have guaranteed rapport with the producer, since bass players always stuck together.

Figuring that TAB could use some of the master's Zen discipline, Bob sent Dickerson a copy of the *Come Go Away* EP. Just as he hoped, Dickerson called back and offered his services.

"Hell, they've already made a better record than the Rampagans ever did. So let's see if we can top it." Dickerson agreed to produce TAB on a speculative basis, for no upfront money. He could afford to, since he had a twenty-four-track home studio in his own basement. Bob's plan was to release this record independently, too; maybe try to find a distributor to handle it, or put copies into stores on consignment. If they sold enough copies on their own, perhaps a record company would be willing to pick it up. Maybe even a big label.

If they could make the right record, the manager thought, they might—might—be able to accelerate the timetable. Bob's dream scenario was a record that sold enough to pay for itself, and maybe recouped some of the money he'd sunk into TAB.

But first things first. While he'd been tempted to give the band the good news about Dickerson early, Bob held off telling them until they returned from the tour. He wanted to hit them with it at the right moment, so they could get to work while everyone was still enthusiastic. The first thing the producer wanted to do was put TAB through two grueling weeks of pre-production rehearsals.

Now all Bob had to do was get Tommy on the phone.

When he didn't have a guitar in his hands, Tommy liked to take long, aimless walks. Destination unknown, no particular place to go, just random wanderings. He drifted around the woods surrounding the tobacco fields by his shack, which he could do so long as it wasn't hunting season—in which case he had to wear a ridiculous orange hat so he wouldn't get shot. That wasn't an option, because there was nothing Tommy hated more than looking stupid.

Going into town for a beer and an excursion to the record store wasn't much fun anymore. Things there had gotten...strange.

After TAB rose to the top of the local hierarchy, nobody wanted to talk about guitars or records or girls or anything else normal anymore. Instead, people asked Tommy weird and silly questions, like if it was true that some record company guy would be flying down from New York to see his next show—and whether or not he had an opening act for the gig yet. There was a grasping, jealous quality to these questions, which left Tommy certain that people were whispering nasty things as soon as he was out of earshot. It was as if he'd been convicted of some awful crime.

In a way, he had. The party line on TAB was that they were no longer cool, apparently because too many of the "wrong" people liked them.

Moreover, TAB had come too far too fast, and lost their once-proud sense of apathy. Tommy was too caught up in material concerns, they said; too concerned with becoming a "rawk star."

On its face, this was absurd. Tommy still played the same music he'd always played, way-left-of-center rockabilly space pop. True, it got prettied up a little on that record. But it was still weirder, more idiosyncratic—and, not coincidentally, better—than anything anyone else in town was doing. It wasn't exactly making anybody involved rich, either. Yet as soon as TAB started getting more attention than other bands, all sorts of motives were ascribed to Tommy that he didn't necessarily have.

Or did he?

This was not a simple either-or question. Deep down, TAB's leader was guilty as charged because he *did* want the carrot—just like everybody else, whether they were willing to admit it or not. But article one of the unwritten code of band ethics held that You Must Always Disavow and Shun Material Success. Why, Tommy wondered, was success inevitably tainted? What if you just did what you wanted, without compromising, and an audience came to you? What was wrong with that?

He couldn't figure it out. All Tommy knew was that he no longer had the energy to go to many of his old haunts anymore, especially Each. Last time he'd gone to the club, everybody stared at him as if he was a three-headed space alien who'd just beamed down from Saturn. Only one person other than Bob would even speak to him, a passing acquaintance he barely knew who cornered him for a lecture.

"Man," he slurred drunkenly, "you guys were a lot better before you got *good,* you know what I mean?"

"No idea," Tommy said, recoiling from his beer stench.

"There was more of a, a, a...purity to it before. Like, 'Here's what we do, take it or leave it and we don't give a fuck what you think.'"

"And you think I give a fuck now?"

The drunk only smirked, and Tommy turned to leave. But he couldn't escape the guy's parting shot.

"You need to go back to doing what you were doing before anybody else was telling you what to do, man!"

"Will do, asshole," Tommy muttered under his breath. "Will do."

Such encounters grated on Tommy far more than he let on. It galled him that people thought he was whoring himself, especially since nobody seemed to be buying his alleged "sellout." Okay, sure, TAB had a manager; they'd made a couple of records, been on the radio, gotten some nice reviews, toured, sold a few T-shirts.

So what? They were more broke than ever, and seemingly no closer to whatever it was they were trying to accomplish. The only thing going on the road had accomplished was to push TAB to the point of breaking up.

Well…Touring had done one other thing. The road's lethal combination of stress and boredom had made Tommy's cravings for heroin worse. A lot worse. The dabbling he began with crazy Susan was turning into an unmanageable beast. Although he spent most of his waking hours denying it to himself, Tommy knew he was becoming an addict. He hated himself for it, considered it a sign of weakness. Mistakenly, he thought he was strong enough to use smack without becoming addicted. Giving in to it reminded him of something his long-dead father would've done—only the son was killing himself slowly.

But a fix was the only thing he could make himself go into town for anymore, to a small dark house over on the poor east side where the only question anybody ever asked was, *how much?* Funny, he thought, how it was almost always the east side or the south side of every town. Must have something to do with the way rivers flowed. Tommy lived southeast of town and felt an upriver pull that grew stronger by the day.

Some days, he could resist. If he made three straight days, he considered that an accomplishment. And what better way to celebrate an accomplishment than with...?

Stop...

Right...

There...

It wasn't so long ago that Tommy had been able to go at least a week without using, no problem. But his weekend hobby had quietly accelerated into a twice-a-week habit, and daily was coming up soon. The path of least resistance went downhill, a downward spiral. He could not see the end of it, or a way out.

In his more lucid moments, Tommy wondered what to do. Methadone, perhaps; leech therapy; maybe chain himself to his bed long enough to go cold turkey.

In his less lucid moments, a single word burned itself into his brain, impossible to ignore:

Faster.

CHAPTER EIGHTEEN

TAB's three members convened at Tommy's house on a Tuesday afternoon for their first band meeting since limping home from tour number two. That had been almost a month earlier, and it was time to decide what to do next. Bob Porter's proposal was up for discussion. Frustrated because he couldn't find Tommy or get him to return phone calls, the manager finally left a rough outline of his plan on the bandleader's answering machine: Make the next record with Clay Dickerson, put it out themselves, get back on the road.

"I don't like it," Ray said. He paced back and forth in front of the couch where Tommy sprawled and Michelle sat, side by side.

"Why not?" Michelle asked.

"Do you want to go through that again?" the drummer asked. "We've done two of Bob's little club tours and they both sucked. We've made two records on our own, but didn't get jack out of either one. And now he wants to do the same thing all over again? Make another record nobody's gonna hear and then play for chump change in all the same places one more time? Uh uh, I don't think so."

"Well, it's not like any record companies are knocking our door down," Tommy said.

"That's what you think. You never stuck around during load-out, so the record label weasels always wound up talking to me. They were at some shows, and a few liked us enough to follow up. You know Casey, that weird old guy who comes into Each during the day to clean up? He told me he hears Bob on the phone all the time, talking to A&R guys calling about us, and Bob keeps telling them no. 'Thanks, but we're not ready yet'—that's what he's been telling everybody."

"Well," Michelle ventured, "maybe we're not."

"But what do we gain from waiting?" Ray asked. "What's the point? I don't know about you, but I'm sick of busting my ass for nothing, and I don't understand why Bob expects us to wait for him to wave his magic wand and pronounce us 'ready.' Fuck, man, Clay Dickerson wants to produce us, and we're somehow 'not ready' for a record deal?"

"Okay, genius," Tommy said. "What do we do, then?"

"I think we should call Gus DeGrande," Ray said.

"Gus DeGrande? But I thought all he did was concerts."

"Think about it. DeGrande has been around forever and knows everybody in the business. I bet he's got connections at record companies. If nothing else, he could book us a better tour than what Bob's been putting us through. And did you hear about that story in *Cashboard*? He thinks we're great!"

Neither of his bandmates said anything. The drummer looked first at one, then the other.

"I don't know," Tommy finally said. "Bob would freak…"

"Look, I love Bob to death, too," Ray said. "He's a great guy, works hard, seems to know his shit. But we're going nowhere with him. Face it: If we don't make a move now, we'll be stuck playing dumps like Each forever."

"I don't know," Tommy said again.

"Well, I *do* know," Michelle said. "Absolutely not. You may not think Bob is the best manager in the world, but he's always believed in us. He's also practically gone broke managing this band, and do you hear him complaining about it?"

"No," Ray said. "But if you go by that logic, you'll have to admit that DeGrande has got a lot more money to spend on us than Bob does."

"I don't care," Michelle said. "The man is a snake and I don't trust him."

"Why not? Because he thought your bass was too loud on the record?"

"No, asshole," Michelle shot back, "I don't trust DeGrande because he's a cheap thug. I can't believe you want to do this. Remember when he tried to shake down your other band for playing too long?"

"That was when I was in a band that sucked," the drummer said, shrugging. "This band doesn't suck. We deserve better and I think DeGrande can help us, that's all."

"Yeah, never mind that you used to call him 'El Sleazeball.' If he treats you better now, it's only because he thinks he can get more use out of you."

Ray shrugged again.

"Well, I still vote no," Michelle said, crossing her arms.

"And I still vote yes," Ray said, then turned to the bandleader. "Which leaves it up to you, boss."

There was more than a touch of mockery to his tone. "Your call, Tommy," he said. "You break the tie."

To Michelle's dismayed amazement, Tommy hemmed and hawed and finally sided with Ray—conditionally. First, he would talk to Bob. If the manager agreed to try to get TAB signed now rather than waiting, they'd stay with him. If not, they were going to approach DeGrande.

Tommy called Each and left Bob a message that he'd be in to see him early the next afternoon. As soon as Tommy walked into his office, the manager knew he was in trouble. His client plopped down in a chair across the desk and lit a cigarette. He left his mirrored sunglasses on.

"Howdy, stranger," Bob said.

Tommy just nodded and smoked. Three long, slow puffs later, he took the cigarette out of his mouth and finally spoke.

"Bob, the band isn't happy."

" 'The band' isn't happy, or *you* aren't happy?"

"The band. All three of us."

"Okay. 'The band' isn't happy. Why not?"

"Well…" Tommy paused to smoke some more. "We think things could be happening…you know, faster."

"How so?"

"Well, we really don't understanding what we're waiting for. I mean, you've got Clay Dickerson producing us, and that's great. But how come we're doing another record on our own when record companies are interested?"

"'Cause we've got no leverage yet," Bob said. "You want a record deal now? Sure, I could probably get you one—a bad one where you'd be totally at some label's mercy. Believe me, a bad record deal is worse than no deal at all. You'd get one shot, probably not even a fair one, and if it didn't hit you'd be out the door. That what you want?"

"Of course not," Tommy said. "But is that really the best we could do? It just seems like throwing another record out there on our own and then playing all the same places again won't really get us anywhere. Why don't we try making a video?"

"Do you have any idea how much that costs? Not some film-student jerkjob, but a real video good enough to get played on a real channel?"

"So let's sign with a label and get them to pay for it."

"But it's not time yet."

"So when will it be? Why not now?"

The manager wanted to scream. This was like explaining to a four-year-old why dessert came after, not before, dinner.

"Tommy," he said, "nobody just signs on the dotted line and then wakes up the next day with a number-one record and their face on magazine covers. If that's what you want, it takes work—and better you should do it than somebody else. Besides, I thought you didn't give a fuck about any of that. What happened to you being perfectly happy playing guitar on your porch, huh? You're playing what you want to play, isn't that enough? Why is it suddenly important that it be on some big record label? And what's wrong with playing clubs? Muddy Waters played shitty juke joints until the day he died."

As he spoke, Bob could tell this was going in one ear and out the other. Tommy did not appear to be paying attention.

"Bob," he insisted, "we've got to do something different."

"You're...not...*listening!*" Bob replied, fighting to keep his voice under control. "We *are* doing something different—making a better record, which we're gonna put out. Then we're gonna tour some more and build an audience, without any gimmicks. Staying in control, Tommy, remember that? Last time we talked about this, you said you wanted things to happen slowly enough to stay on top of."

"And I—we—still want that. We're not asking to start running. But we'd still rather walk than crawl. Is that too much to ask?"

"It is if you're not ready."

"We are."

"No you're not, and the fact that we're even having this conversation proves it. Trust me, how long you last on the back end is a direct result of how much work goes into the front end. The bands that come out of nowhere with videos and stupid gimmicks are the one-hit wonders. The ones that last build themselves up gradually. You build an audience one person at a time. So be patient, we've been working on this for less than a year."

"How much longer will it take?"

"If I told you I knew, I'd be lying. Maybe another two years. Maybe less, maybe more. I don't know."

"I need to know," Tommy said.

"Why this sudden urgency? Jesus, Tommy, you're only twenty-five years old."

"Twenty-six," Tommy said, looking down to avert his manager's eyes even though he still had his shades on. Bob sat for a moment with his chin in his right palm, his eyes burning into the top of Tommy's head, before speaking again.

"Well, happy birthday, then. When was it?"

"Last week."

"You celebrate?"

Tommy looked up. "What, with a cake?" he asked quizzically.

"No," Bob said, "with something a little…you know, harder."

"I don't follow."

"Uh huh. All of a sudden, this whole thing makes sense: You're still screwing around with smack, and it's getting a little hard to control. So now you're worried about how long world domination is taking. Right?"

"C'mon, Bob," Tommy said, fidgeting.

"Bingo," the manager sighed.

"Bob what does this have to do with anything?"

"You don't see it, do you? We've been arguing about short-term versus long-term. Short term, sure, it makes all the sense in the world to take the first crappy record deal that comes along. Just like it makes sense to keep sticking needles in your arm."

"I'm not sticking needles in my arm," Tommy insisted (which was true as far as it went; he had resorted to the backs of his knees, between his toes and even under his tongue to avoid leaving visible needle marks).

"Sure, you're not," Bob said sarcastically. "Is that why you're wearing long sleeves and sunglasses, or is it just more fashionable?"

"*Fuck you!!!*" Tommy suddenly shouted, slamming his open palm down on the desk with a reverberating boom. "Stop this shit *right now!* I did not come down here to argue about whether or not I'm doing drugs. I'm not. So drop it. Okay?"

Unconvinced, Bob nodded and let it drop. He was going to lose this battle. The only choice he had was what to lose it over.

"Okay, then," Tommy resumed, a little shakily. "We're not asking for much. Don't approach anybody, just talk to the labels that are already calling. Other than that, I don't think we need to do anything different. We make the same record we planned on, with Dickerson— that's a precondition of any deal. Why would that be a mistake?"

"Because," the manager said wearily, "you'd be giving up control too soon. Give it up now and you'll give up all of it, and never get it back. Besides which, you still can't seem to make up your fuckin' mind what you want. The deal you want today, you'll want me to get you out of tomorrow. You can do this on your own terms, or somebody else's. Get in a hurry, and I can guarantee it won't be yours."

"Well, right now, it seems to be on *your* terms, not mine. What's the difference? You go behind my back mixing that record, I hate it but get talked into putting it out—and it still gets us nowhere. I haven't even signed anything and people are already calling me a sellout. So fuck it, let's just go ahead and sell out. Maybe somebody will buy it. Aren't you tired of this shit?"

"Ah, Tommy, you're giving up way too easily," Bob said, sadly shaking his head. "Jesus, man, people are gonna talk. So let 'em. Don't let yourself be bullied into something as stupid as a bad record deal."

"Bob, we've made up our minds," the bandleader declared. "We've got to get a record deal. It's all we can do to keep from breaking up. You've been great for us. But right now, we need more than what you can do alone."

The manager sat quietly and weighed his options. For a fleeting instant, going along did flash through his mind. But the thought was gone just as quickly. One way or another, Bob was going to keep his word.

After a long moment, Bob hauled himself to his feet, walked to the door and opened it. He stood there holding it open.

"I quit," Bob said. "Now get out."

He wanted the declaration to sound strong, angry, defiant. It didn't, just mournful.

"This is it?" Tommy asked, taken aback.

"Afraid so."

"But why? After everything you've done for us, why do you want out now?"

"It's your life, Tommy," the clubowner said quietly. "You want to go over a cliff, be my guest. But I ain't driving the bus."

After Tommy left, Bob sat and stared at the amber paperweight on his desk; the one with his $7.79 share from the first TAB tour. After a while, he picked the block up and tossed it across the room, where it landed with a hollow clatter on a shelf where TAB mementos were accumulating.

Then he put his head down on his desk and, for the first time in years, allowed himself to cry.

Gus was just about to leave the office for the night when his phone rang. Natalie answered the call and buzzed him on the intercom.

"Mr. DeGrande," she said, "a Tommy Aguilar is calling."

"Put him through."

Thursday morning, Ken Morrison arrived at the office to find three messages on his answering machine. One was from a local band, telling him about an upcoming show and asking for a story or a blurb or a picture in the paper. Another was from an irate reader, still agitated over a concert review that had run earlier in the week.

But one was genuinely momentous and it came from Gus's secretary, of all people: "This is Natalie Petry at Grandiose Concerts. I just faxed over something that Mr. DeGrande thinks you may find of interest. If there's still time, perhaps you can fit it into this week's column."

The fax was in Ken's mail slot. It was a one-paragraph press release with the headline in all capital letters:

NEW COMPANY, GRANDIOSE MANAGEMENT, SIGNS FIRST CLIENT.

CHAPTER NINETEEN

Desperate to find out more, Ken Morrison called Grandiose Concerts under the pretense of asking for a quote. Natalie told him the promoter had nothing to say beyond the faxed statement. The critic tried Tommy, and got his answering machine. He tried Bob; no answer at Each. Attempts to track down Ray and Michelle were also fruitless.

Facing deadline, Ken banged out a neutrally worded one-paragraph item about TAB changing managers and tacked it onto the end of his column. He did it mechanically, his initial shock giving way to a dull ache in the pit of his stomach. This had to be some sort of horrible mistake.

DeGrande. Mother-fucking, goddamned…Gus…DeGrande. The ends justified the means, even if it meant signing on with the antichrist? Was that it? Ken could only assume that, with Joseph Stalin and Colonel Tom Parker both unavailable, Tommy had settled for the next worst thing in his suddenly naked quest for instant stardom.

The critic felt even worse when he pondered his own small role in this transition. DeGrande obviously had designs on TAB—it was why the promoter agreed to be interviewed, to lobby in-print for his first managerial client—but Ken was so positive that the desire would stay unrequited that he'd gone right ahead and played Gus's tune.

No way would Tommy leave Bob for DeGrande; that's what Ken thought. He couldn't decide if that was denial or stupidity on his part.

As soon as he could escape from the office, Ken headed for Each. He figured Bob was there, even if he wasn't answering the phone. Once there, the critic found both the front and back doors locked. So he climbed in through the bathroom window, took two bottles of beer from the cooler behind the bar and crept into the clubowner's office.

He found Bob sitting at his desk, staring at a wall. Ken walked in and sat in the same chair Tommy occupied a day earlier, opened both bottles and placed one in front of Bob, who appeared not to notice. There were already many empty bottles on the desk. The critic sat and drank for a while, waiting him out. The only sound was the hum of the cooler outside the office; the only movement the blinking red light of an answering machine on a corner of the desk. It blinked in a cycle, one flash for each call recorded but not yet played. Ken counted twenty-two of them.

"Bob," he said softly, "I think you've got some calls to return."

Blearily, the clubowner looked up without saying anything.

"Your answering machine," Ken continued. "It seems to be full. I tried to call, but didn't get an answer."

Bob nodded blankly. He looked as though he was straining to hear something at a great distance. When he finally spoke, his voice sounded as dry as a sand dune. "He kept calling," he said.

"What?" Ken asked, unsure what Bob meant.

"He kept calling."

"Who?"

"Tommy."

"Why?"

"I don't know. He just kept calling, and I finally had to tell him to stop. Some record company guys called, too, and a radio station. After a while, I got tired of arguing with Tommy between calls where I was trying to explain that I wasn't his manager anymore. So I just...quit answering. Figured everybody'd find out soon enough. Maybe I'll change the message on the machine: 'Sorry, but Tommy doesn't live here anymore. You'll find him over at Bloodsucker Enterprises, where Attila the Concert Promoter will be happy to take your money.'"

"Bob," Ken said, "are you okay?"

He appeared not to hear the question.

"Funny," the clubowner continued. "Just the other day, before any of this happened, I was thinking about the first time I ever heard Tommy play. When he crashed Frag the Lieutenant's show here, you remember that?"

"Only what you told me. I wasn't here that night."

"Tommy was lucky the Frag guys didn't beat the shit out of him," Bob said. "If I hadn't stopped them, they probably would've run him down and killed him. And the thing is, he deserved to get his ass kicked."

Bob finally laughed and so did Ken, relieved to see the clubowner wake from his stupor.

"That was the first time I ever bailed Tommy out of trouble," Bob said.

"And now, you kinda wish you hadn't?"

"Yeah, I guess so. It would've saved me a lot of grief—and money. Instead, I wound up becoming a fuckin' enabler. That was Tommy's first test, and I passed it."

Bob picked up the bottle Ken had brought in and took a sip. As much as he'd already poured down his neck, he couldn't believe he wasn't drunker. He did, however, have a wicked headache.

"But I didn't pass this last one," the clubowner concluded. "Anyway, I'm now officially the former artist manager known as Bob."

"Did they fire you?"

"Not exactly."

"You quit, then?"

"Well…both, sort of. They wanted to go one way and insisted on doing some things. I wanted to go another, so I refused. Before they could invoke the 'or else' part, I walked."

"What'd they want you to do?"

Bob hesitated, and Ken drew his notebook out of his jacket pocket and tossed it onto the desk. They were officially off the record.

"Mostly," Bob said, "they seemed to be mad because things weren't happening fast enough."

" 'Fast enough?' Christ, what the fuck did they expect?"

"Beats me," the former manager sighed. "I still can't figure out what the hell they want. They don't even know, Tommy especially. One minute, he claims he wants to starve for his art. The next, he wants to know where his million-dollar deal is."

"Sounds like he chose the million-dollar deal."

"Afraid so."

"So…what happens next?"

Bob shrugged again. "Not my problem anymore, so I don't care. Come to think of it, a lot of things aren't my problem anymore, like certain…Look, are we really off-the-record here? I mean, no bullshit? Not to be repeated or used as 'deep background' or anything like that?"

"Sure."

"Okay, then: Like certain chemical habits Tommy has picked up."

The critic blinked. "Does that mean what I think?" he asked.

Bob nodded, raising a hand to tap his thumb against the first two fingers—the movement one would use to manipulate a syringe.

"We went 'round and 'round about that. I could never even get Tommy to admit he's got a problem, so I never got anywhere convincing him to quit. I don't know that he ever will. I wish Gus DeGrande luck with that one."

The clubowner paused to take another sip.

"So yeah, Tommy has a habit that's turning into a problem, and it's not near as bad as it's gonna get. But that's down the road. Short-term, I had arranged for Clay Dickerson to produce their next record and maybe he still will. I don't know, that's up to them. I expect DeGrande will get them a record deal pretty quick. But I'll bet he gets 'em fucked before it's over with, too."

"What about the money? Don't you have a lot tied up in TAB?"

"More than I can afford to lose."

"So hire a lawyer and sue."

"We didn't have a written contract."

"You at least had an oral one, right?"

"Sure. But DeGrande can hire better weasels than I can. Dragging this into court would cost me more than I'd win."

"Dammit," Ken said, "this is not fair!"

"Nope," the clubowner said, "but it's over and done."

"Jesus, Bob. I can't tell you how sorry I am. I thought you were doing a really good job."

"So did I," Bob said, draining the last of his beer. "But not good enough, apparently."

"You want me to ban TAB from print? Never type their name again?"

"Nah, don't do that. From here on out, they're gonna need all the friends they can get. They've got no idea what they're in for."

With that, Bob stood up and walked unsteadily out to the cooler to get another beer.

Two days later, Bob was just about over his hangover when a check arrived in the mail. Before he'd sign anything with DeGrande, Tommy insisted that Gus pay off TAB's former manager. The check was for thirty thousand dollars—more than enough to cover Bob's investment in the band.

Bob stared at the check for a long time. It wasn't certified, and the letter hadn't been registered. In fact, it looked as if Gus had hastily scribbled it out, slapped a stamp on an envelope and dropped it in the mail, the way you'd pay your phone bill. It almost hurt to think about.

Thirty grand, Bob thought, exhaling. *More than I'll clear after taxes this year, and it's just petty cash to him.*

Bob made an enlarged photocopy of the check, which he put on his TAB memento shelf. Next, he took the check itself, shredded it into very small pieces and stuffed them back in the envelope, on which he wrote RETURN TO SENDER. He then taped the envelope shut and mailed it back to DeGrande.

Several days after that, someone left a mysterious message on Each's answering machine. Just two words: "Address unknown."

Bob thought the voice sounded a lot like Tommy's.

And so it came to pass that Bob's gradual growth curve for TAB mutated into Gus's blitzkrieg drive for world domination. Ray was ecstatic, Michelle moody and Tommy overcome with second thoughts. But once they took the jump, there was no turning back. DeGrande saw to that.

The promoter's price for buying out Bob was an ironclad contract binding TAB to him for seven years, plus options (all of them at Gus's discretion). Since the ex-manager didn't even cash his $30,000 check, this turned out to be the cheapest investment Gus ever made: Tommy signed himself over, body and soul, for the price of a postage stamp. He was still so guilt-stricken that it never even occurred to him to ask for some of his life back after Bob turned down the payoff.

By serving as both manager and record label, DeGrande set up a relationship with Tommy that was riddled with conflicts of interest. It was a great arrangement for Gus, putting his hand deep into literally every one of the band's pockets. Conversely, it was a rotten one for TAB.

"Don't think of our relationship as manager-client," Gus told the bandleader, "but as a partnership." That made it sound as if DeGrande was being generous. What the promoter didn't mention was that his definition of "partnership" meant he was entitled to at least half of the pie—and once the real money started coming in, he had no intention of stopping at fifty percent.

Tommy didn't realize that and probably wouldn't have cared if he did, because Gus made sure the magic phrase was scattered liberally throughout the contract's forty-seven pages: "artistic control." Once he saw that he "retained full artistic control," Tommy blanked out on all the rest. Thus, he didn't notice the arcane legal jargon elsewhere, which superseded all promises of "artistic control" and rendered them null and void at the manager's pleasure. Had TAB hired a lawyer, the group might have avoided the indentured servitude and unconscionable financial terms they were subjected to under this contract.

Actually, Gus would let TAB have artistic control—to a point. He'd let them handle what he thought they understood, which covered writing songs and recording basic tracks. Choice of producers, engineers, studio ringers and overdubs would be DeGrande's department. Same for all promotional and marketing decisions.

"Don't you sweat the details," he told Tommy. "Just remember, stars shine brighter when they're kept in the dark."

"**Mo Polydoroff.**"

"Mo, Gus DeGrande calling."

"Ah, yes. Mr. DeGrande."

"Please, call me Gus."

"Right. Gus. What can we do for you today?"

On one level, Gus admired the label president's penchant for getting right to the point with no small talk; it mirrored his own no-nonsense phone manner. On another, he found it irritating because he suspected Polydoroff refused to schmooze him out of snobbery. No matter, payback would be soon in coming.

"Well, I have my first act on Grandiose Records. That band from down here that I told you about, TAB…"

"Great," Mo said, without enthusiasm. He'd been grateful for DeGrande's warning about his uncle's scheming, but still didn't trust him.

"…And I wanted to let you know we're about to begin recording," the promoter continued.

"Great," Mo repeated.

"…So I'll be needing the first advance."

"Oh."

Gus heard some papers shuffling. Polydoroff had only been half-listening, but the word "advance" got his attention.

"Gus...I...um...What advance would that be?"

"The advance specified in our contract," DeGrande said, mentally adding, *which you still haven't bothered to go back and read, you stupid fuck.*

"Oh," Polydoroff said, shuffling some more papers. "Well...I don't seem to have a copy of that handy. How much are we talking about?"

"A hundred thousand dollars."

Mo nearly dropped the phone. In the overall scheme of things, a hundred thousand dollars wasn't much money—he probably spilled more than that much brandy any given year; it wasn't even an average major-label recording budget. But it still seemed like a lot to pay for a brand-new, unproven act on a brand-new, unproven imprint. Especially a band Mo had never heard of, and (more to the point) hadn't signed himself. So Mo chose to stall, and played right into DeGrande's hand.

"Gus, I don't exactly have that much cash on hand. I'll have to run this by some people on my end and get back to you."

"Fine," the promoter said and hung up, confident that Polydoroff would instantly forget all about this conversation. In fact, he was counting on it.

As detailed in the contract, Poly Brothers did have the option of not paying advances. But the fine print further specified that the clock began ticking as soon as Gus asked for the money (and a notarized letter to that effect was already in the mail). If the label failed to pay up within thirty business days, a number of clauses automatically kicked in.

For one thing, Grandiose would get a higher per-unit royalty rate on every TAB record sold through Poly Brothers distribution. An unusually high rate, in fact—the sort of rate labels generally only agreed to give established million-selling superstars. Furthermore, by refusing to pay anything upfront, Poly Brothers was also turning down its option on any of TAB's future publishing rights. A hundred grand was chump change compared to how many millions were potentially at stake. Gus was glad to forego the advance money, even if it meant he had to pay recording costs himself for TAB's album.

Now, all they had to do was come up with a record Poly Brothers deemed worthy of releasing.

After debriefing Bob, Ken felt worse than ever. Not angry, so much—that was already starting to ebb. His guilt, however, had legs, as did a persistent feeling of dread at what was about to happen. It galled the critic that DeGrande was going to profit from Bob's work with TAB. Moreover, he didn't see how Gus wouldn't be a corrupting influence. Getting into bed with an evil old-school huckster like him wasn't just compromise, it was capitulation. Ken was dying to interrogate Tommy, but TAB's bandleader had vanished from the radar screen.

Yet there was also a part of Ken that found it disturbingly easy to rationalize TAB's decision. Maybe they'd already paid enough dues. Maybe Bob was being overly cautious, even paranoid. Maybe Tommy really had the talent to succeed on his own terms, and the will to resist DeGrande's inevitable tampering. And maybe Gus was right: The bottom line was all that counted, and anyone else's notion of "artistic credibility" was just so much bullshit.

Maybe.

What was indisputable was that things with TAB were suddenly happening faster than ever—a record deal was in place, recording sessions were scheduled to start in New York soon—and Ken was still at ground zero, in a perfect position to capitalize on the buzz. He'd already done some TAB articles and reviews for smaller magazines, enough to earn the band's good graces. The critic had so many pieces in their presskit, in fact, that they whited out some of his bylines so he wouldn't look like their propagandist.

Once Gus took over TAB, he cut way down on media access to the band. Ken was the only critic who remained in the inner circle (mostly because of proximity), and that translated into opportunities at the bigger and more important glossies he'd never been able to crack.

There were two in particular, *Rock Slide* and *Bounce,* widely regarded as the top rock magazines. Ken professed disdain toward both, which was partly sour grapes. But he'd also heard just enough horror stories to know how thoroughly corrupt they were. Both magazines were run by egomaniacal, self-styled "star" publishers who weren't above using their own editorial pages to suck up to their friends and bash their enemies.

With its younger readership, *Bounce* fancied itself more cutting-edge and progressive. But the magazine's office was one of the most notorious boys' clubs in the music industry. The publisher was infamous for avidly courting young women to come work for *Bounce,* then ruining their careers if they rebuffed his sexual advances. A number of his former employees had filed sexual harassment lawsuits, but none had stuck. Thanks to a nine-figure trust fund (inherited from his arms merchant father, a certifiable war criminal), he had deep enough pockets to outlast his accusers in court.

As for the more staid *Rock Slide,* woe be to any rock star deemed to have snubbed the self-declared "Voice of Rock 'n' Roll Nation." When one well-known musician neglected to invite *Rock Slide's* publisher to his wedding, the magazine attempted an expose on the finances of his nonprofit charitable foundation (which had won awards for its work on environmental issues). After turning up nothing untoward, *Rock Slide* contented itself with a story poking merciless fun at the rock star's sullen public image—after discovering he'd actually been the happy, popular and well-adjusted president of his high school glee club.

Both magazines did have to tread a fine line, however. Much of their advertising revenue came from record companies, who were frequently unhappy with the coverage their acts got. The labels had to let most of it go, just for appearances sake. But they'd been known to put the hammer down.

One legendary off-the-record story involved an enormously popular but critically reviled act on Poly Brothers Records, during Adolph Polydoroff's regime as president. *Rock Slide* was all set to run a devastating review of the band's second album, which the label was releasing with much fanfare and touting as an artistic improvement over the group's huge-selling debut. *Rock Slide's* editorial offices happened to be in the same Manhattan skyscraper as Poly Brothers, and word leaked upstairs about the impending negative review. Adolph rode the elevator down from his top-floor suite, and paid a personal visit to *Rock Slide's* publisher.

They were old friends; belonged to the same country club, in fact. But just for good measure, Polydoroff laid a stack of advertising invoices on the publisher's desk—the ones Poly Brothers had paid to *Rock Slide* the previous year. The total came to more than two hundred thousand dollars. He didn't even have to mention the other high-profile releases the label had coming up, for which the magazine would want access for exclusive, timely interviews. Polydoroff was in a position to make that happen, or not.

The president let it be known there would be repercussions if *Rock Slide* went through with its unflattering review. He also told the publisher he'd appreciate it if his magazine's review included the phrase "a great leap forward," since Poly Brothers' marketing department already had trade paper ads with that phrase ready to go.

"It would look so much better coming from you than from us, don't you think?" Adolph cooed.

The publisher killed the bad review. Having heard the record, everybody else on the *Rock Slide* staff refused to touch it. So a hasty nationwide phone search was launched for a critic somewhere who would be willing to write a good review of the album—one that fit the headline "a great leap forward."

Ken was one of many critics to be unofficially interviewed for the job, though he didn't realize it at the time. A writer acquaintance he barely knew called him out of the blue from New York, and after some awkward small talk asked his opinion of the band in question. Ken said he thought they sucked, and the conversation ended soon afterward. It was only later, when comparing notes with other critic friends who had the same experience, that Ken figured out he was being sized up for the review, and flunked the audition.

Of course the poor guy who did end up with the job became a laughingstock, because everybody in the industry knew why he got the assignment. Ken's pal from Chicago, Marty McPhail, was apparently the only rock critic in America who hadn't heard about the original review getting killed.

Or maybe Marty just had less shame than anyone else.

Ken had a descent into shamelessness of his own to contemplate—an assignment from *Rock Slide* to do a short feature on TAB. For all his professed disinterest, the critic nevertheless lusted after a byline there. For one thing, it paid more than any other rock magazine. A buck a word, one thousand dollars for a story that would take one day to knock out. A thousand bucks, bigger than any check he'd ever seen in his life. And a byline in *Rock Slide,* still widely regarded as the rock world's "paper of record" and a magazine his parents had actually heard of. Given his conflicted loyalties about the situation, the temptation was killing him.

Which amused Gus DeGrande to no end, that a self-righteous dweeb like Ken Morrison could be tempted to sell out his alleged "principles" for such a pathetic amount of money. The critic assumed *Rock Slide* called him to write about TAB because he knew the band better than anyone else. Unbeknownst to him, DeGrande pulled some strings to get the magazine to commit to covering TAB, then pulled a few more to steer the assignment to Ken.

Gus figured he would be less skeptical and more supportive than any of the magazine's staff writers in New York, not to mention more discreet about Tommy's drug habit. Probably an unnecessary precaution, but the manager was taking no chances. In the post-Adolph era, Poly Brothers couldn't do as much to keep the likes of *Rock Slide* in line.

In the end, Gus was proven right all the way around. Just like Tommy, Ken's ambition finally won out and he took the assignment, though not without much sheepish rationalizing. First, he told himself that if he didn't do the story, somebody else would, only not as well. And when that didn't work, he told himself he was only doing what Bob told him he should.

Then he covered his bathroom mirror with a towel for a couple of days.

CHAPTER TWENTY

The first thing to change after Gus DeGrande signed on as TAB's Svengali was the size of the places they played. The promoter stuck them onto the bill as opening act for every big roadshow that came through town, with predictably erratic results. If Gus had his way, TAB would be playing for big crowds very soon; getting thrown to the wolves in low-pressure opening-act situations was good practice.

TAB's first arena gig left them bewildered. It was, by several multiples, the largest stage they'd ever played on. Michelle felt as if they were in three separate rooms, trying to play along to muffled echoes through walls. No soundcheck, twenty-minute set—they were done almost before they got started. It was the typical opening act's lot, only magnified by the larger surroundings.

This particular show found TAB opening for Arrowhead, a grizzled spandex-and-hairspray metal band from New York. Arrowhead had been around long enough to go in and out of style several times, from stadiums to state fairs and back again. Along the way, they'd destroyed almost as many hotel rooms as brain cells. Arrowhead came from the Old School.

All the years of self-abuse had finally caught up with them a decade earlier, when Arrowhead broke up long enough for all five members to embark on ill-fated solo careers. After everyone's album bombed, they regrouped for a much-ballyhooed comeback, and hit rock bottom.

Frontman Perry Rose marked the occasion of their first reunion show by getting so drunk he fell off the stage. This enraged the bassist and lead guitarist so much that they flung down their instruments, pulled the singer back onstage and pummeled him bad enough to put him in the hospital. Right there in front of fifteen thousand shrieking fans, while the drummer and rhythm guitarist played on.

This onstage brawl was the subject of much amusement in the business, the joke going that you never knew when a hockey game might break out at an Arrowhead concert. But it was symptomatic of some very unfunny problems—two members had nasty heroin habits, and all five were certifiable alcoholics. It soon became clear that the band was doomed unless everyone sobered up.

They each went through detoxification programs, some more smoothly than others. Rose had the roughest ride, needing four stays at the Betty Ford Center before he finally kicked smack. By the time TAB crossed their path, Arrowhead had pulled together and ironically was bigger than ever. The group's roadshow was also stridently chemical-free. Not even beer was allowed backstage.

But women sure were, which left Tommy feeling anxious and out of sorts before performing that night. He paced around the bowels of the Enormodome's backstage area, wondering what to do. It was still a little too early to start his usual pre-show ritual, but too late to go anywhere else. He could have used a drink to relax, especially given the backstage scenery. Arrowhead's style of cheeseball metal was a magnet for women who made a living by letting men ogle their bodies. It had a lot to do with the aging band's enduring appeal to teenage boys.

"Strippers," Ray declared as soon as he and Tommy walked backstage. "You can always tell the professionals from the amateurs."

"Cool," Tommy said, admiring several-score buxom young women with incredibly huge hair, chests that looked like the front end of a

'58 Buick, five-inch spiked heels and miniskirts small enough to fit inside a CD case.

"Gross," Michelle countered, turning on her heel to retreat into TAB's dressing room and slamming the door shut. Her bandmates looked at each other, shrugged and turned back to assess the situation.

Every female pleasure professional from the surrounding area seemed to be backstage, making the rounds among Arrowhead's various members. Perry Rose hid behind the darkened windows of a white stretch limo in the backstage area's VIP parking lot under the arena, entertaining women a pair at a time. Tommy lurked nearby and tried to look nonchalant as he put a watch to it. Every ten minutes, the door opened, two women got out, two more got in, and the door closed.

Now that, Tommy thought, was mighty keen. So keen, in fact, that he suddenly felt the urge to get up close and personal with some of the cleavage on display around him. So he casually wandered toward a knot of strippers gathered near the door of the Arrowhead drummer's dressing room.

"Evenin', ladies," Tommy said with a broad smile, tipping an imaginary fedora. Immediately, a hand clapped firmly onto his shoulder from behind. Tommy was about to say something belligerent until he whirled around and got a good look at the hand's owner, an extremely large individual known simply as Big Ed.

Big Ed weighed in at six-foot-six and two-hundred-ninety pounds, which had also been his dimensions during the eight seasons he anchored the offensive line for the Chicago Bears. Like a lot of pro athletes, he wound up in the celebrity security business after his playing days ended. He'd been Arrowhead's chief of security for fifteen years. One of his main responsibilities was to see to it that any and all women backstage remained unmolested by unauthorized personnel (which was anybody who was not a member of Arrowhead).

Big Ed's enormous head seemed to sprout directly out of his broad shoulders, sans neck. He looked so ominous that he rarely had to speak.

He didn't break his silence for Tommy, just shook his head and pointed a finger the size of an artillery shell in the direction of TAB's dressing room down the hall.

"Foiled again, eh?" Ray called out to his bandmate, who flipped him off and turned to go.

Muttering darkly, Tommy shuffled off while the women whispered and giggled, wondering who that scruffy little boy was. As Tommy passed by Rose's limo, the door opened again. This time, Rose himself stepped out.

He and Tommy eyed each other for a long moment, during which time Rose remembered his first trip through detox. He'd been a lot younger then; not much older than this kid appeared to be now, in fact. But the rock star's blood was so sludgy and full of toxins that the doctors actually had to replace it the way you'd change the oil in a car.

Even then, Rose didn't believe he had a problem. When the doctors found it necessary to change his blood again just six months later, it started to sink in. It still took a near-death experience in which he was rushed unconscious to the hospital before Rose finally got scared enough to kick for real. The forced withdrawal had been agonizing— the weak, disoriented, shivery feeling of going from frigid air conditioning to blinding heat multiplied by a thousand—and the singer still craved the drug. He was a vampire, and could detect the needle lust in others. Which was why he gave Tommy a longer look than most of the opening-act victims who came around to gawk enviously.

TAB's leader looked right back and was surprised at how…well…*old* Rose looked. From a distance, the man looked as though the previous two decades had never happened. Part of that was sleight-of-hand distraction. Wraithlike as ever, the singer kept his hair long and dyed jet-black. He wore spandex leggings, boots and a leopard-spotted vest over a ruffled white shirt, with brightly colored scarves and feathers. It was only up close that you didn't notice Rose's faux-gypsy wardrobe and saw the mileage he'd put on himself, mainly in the lines around his deep-set eyes. Makeup could only hide so much.

Rose and Tommy's respective radar waves pinged off each other, and they both knew why. Rose almost said something, and Tommy slowed his pace a half-step. But the moment passed in silence.

Rose held his tongue, and Tommy walked on by.

As usual, Ken brought along his binoculars to the Arrowhead show, expecting his customary back-row reviewer seat. To his surprise, he found himself on the floor of the arena, about halfway back. The critic wondered how long this particular perk would last.

The close-in vantage point gave Ken a better look at TAB, the first time he'd seen them play since DeGrande took over. Tommy seemed preoccupied, as if he were somewhere else, while Michelle looked as though she desperately wished to be anyplace else. But Ray appeared to be enraptured, hamming it up with the sort of cornball arena-rock flourishes he could never get away with in bars. Since he didn't get to do a drum solo, Ray contented himself with overplaying every song.

Tommy didn't put out enough to connect with a crowd that had come to see someone else. Most people in the arena regarded TAB with puzzlement as they hunted for their seats in the dark, or stood in line to buy Arrowhead's overpriced T-shirts. The applause was polite at best, but at least there was no heckling.

While TAB played, Ken used his binoculars to scan the peanut gallery in the side-stage wings, where the bigwigs generally hung out. DeGrande lurked just beyond the stagelights, looking malevolent as ever. It was obvious from his hunched, vulture-like posture that he did not find what he heard enjoyable.

Thieving bastard, the critic thought. *You could at least try to like your own fuckin' band, since you liked 'em enough to steal.*

Surrounding the promoter was what looked like a Secret Service entourage. You could spot the record company suits a mile away. Ken figured they were from Poly Brothers. He counted a half-dozen, all doing the Record Company Hokey-Pokey, in which industry hacks tried to demonstrate they "got" something: arms crossed or hands thrust deep into pockets, spine-crushing slump, heads nodding grimly to the beat with no sense of rhythm whatsoever.

The pump was already being primed.

One bonus of an assignment from a big magazine was traveling, which Ken got to do for his TAB story. He'd planned on just spending another afternoon over at The Crypt, watching Tommy shoot up some more trees. Instead, *Rock Slide* sent a plane ticket to New York so Ken could sit in on a day of TAB's recording sessions at Eccentric Landlady studios. First class, even. It was an absurd extravagance, but the critic wasn't complaining (although he would've felt a pang if he knew that DeGrande was actually picking up his expenses).

Clay Dickerson was still producing TAB's album, but almost everything else had changed from Bob's original plan. Instead of Dickerson's spartan home studio, they were recording in Eccentric Landlady's forty-eight-track splendor, at a cost of about a thousand dollars a day. Dickerson was being paid thirty-five thousand dollars upfront, but with no royalty points on the back end. Gus wasn't giving away any pieces of his act that he could keep for himself.

TAB had been recording for about a week when Ken showed up, arriving at the studio just as two-thirds of the band walked out.

"Where you going?" Ken asked. "Is something wrong?"

Michelle didn't speak and Ray just rolled his eyes, pointing a thumb back over his shoulder as he continued out. Inside the control room of Studio A, a heated argument between bandleader and producer was in progress. They were seated at the mixing board listening to the playback of a song called "Take It and Run," which was built around a fuzztone guitar riff layered with white-noise static. The static was the topic of their dispute.

To Dickerson, static was static. He thought it pointless, but was willing to give it a try. Tommy, however, was insistent that this song's static had to be tuned to a specific white-noise frequency, and turned up very loud. The volume was playing havoc with the rest of the track. Tommy wanted it to dirty up the song's guitar part, to contrast with his near-angelic vocal. But he also wanted the static so loud that it was all you noticed. Everyone who heard it came away with their teeth on edge.

"Tommy," Dickerson said, throwing a pair of headphones across the room in frustration, "this is giving me a fuckin' headache. How come you're jerkin' me like this? You did a beautiful vocal here, but nobody is gonna notice it because of this...this...*thing*."

"But that's the point. Anybody who wants to hear the singing will have to really pay attention, listen to it more than once. They'll have to earn it."

"'Earn it?'" Dickerson repeated, incredulous. "'Listen to it more than once?' What the fuck are you talking about? With that static, nobody is gonna listen to more than five seconds of it!"

"Take away the white noise," Tommy said, "and it's just too obvious."

"Take away the white noise," Dickerson said, "and it's a fucking hit record."

Neither of them noticed Ken quietly standing in the doorway to the control room, his tape recorder capturing the debate for posterity. Never having witnessed an actual in-the-studio argument over "the creative process" before, the critic was fascinated.

"So what?" Tommy retorted. "Who cares about hits?"

The producer shook his head, put his face in his hands and vowed to hold his tongue until after counting to twenty. He had just reached eleven when Ken finally cleared his throat and spoke for the first time.

"Howdy, guys."

Both combatants looked up, startled. They mumbled return greetings.

"Ken Morrison, right?" Dickerson asked. "The *Daily News* guy?"

"That's me."

"So, ah…what brings you all the way up here?"

"The record you're making," Ken said. "I'm doing a story on TAB for *Rock Slide*. Didn't anybody tell you I'd be coming?"

"Nope," Dickerson said.

Oops, the critic thought. But right then, Tommy had an idea.

"Hey, let's get some outside input," Tommy said. "Ken here has been reviewing us longer than anyone. So let's see what he thinks about this."

Dickerson tried to protest, but the bandleader was already cueing up the tape. He hit the play button, sat back on his hands and watched Ken listen. The lyrics were Tommy's typical stream of gibberish—"Take it and run/No, I ain't got a gun/Thought it sure might be fun/If you were the one/Who would shoot me"—sung in a high, keening voice.

There was little question about the subject matter: heroin. What no one else knew was that it was also about Tommy's recent game of sexual Russian roulette with Susan. He was having a high old time in New York, spending evenings scoring smack over in a decrepit Brooklyn neighborhood (under the watchful eye of Gus's lackeys, who discreetly shadowed Tommy to keep him out of trouble).

Despite the weird lyrics, Tommy's vocal performance was nevertheless terrific. You barely noticed the perfectly unobtrusive bass and drums, which propped up the guitar hook just so. Every piece was in place—except for that migraine-toned static, placed right in the listener's face. Dickerson was right; you had to strain to hear anything beyond it.

Ken felt both parties watching him and figured this was a test. Well, that was no contest. His very presence here was a compromise, and the critic was not one to compromise his compromises. He had more to gain from being on Tommy's good side than Dickerson's.

"I dunno," Ken said, almost wincing as he said it, "I kinda like the static."

Tommy smiled broadly and turned the track up even louder. Dickerson stood up, muttered something under his breath about ass-kissing jerk-offs and stalked outside for a smoke break before he smashed something.

It took three cigarettes before he felt up to going back in.

CHAPTER TWENTY-ONE

Unbeknownst to the band or the producer, the record they were working on would soon undergo a radical change in direction. Gus DeGrande had a secret weapon lined up: Geoff Baker, remix engineer to the superstars.

Pudgy and balding, Baker was the sort of middle-aged Englishman you'd expect to find puttering around a croquet lawn. Instead, he puttered around recording studios. His specialty was mixing records for radio, and he didn't work cheap. The engineer's going rate was seven thousand dollars per track, a figure that didn't include at least one major expense associated with every project he took on. Baker's contract specified that "a snowstorm" had to accompany his arrival in the studio, one that had nothing to do with cold fronts. He went through massive amounts of cocaine while he worked, which bumped his actual per-song cost up to around eight thousand dollars.

Yet Baker did not lack for work because his records were hits. Big hits. Most recently, he'd turned one of the worst songs anybody ever heard into a top-twenty single with some ingenious tweaking. The band was called Invasive Surgical Procedure, and their music was just as unpleasant as their name—especially "Lobotomy Shorts," the single Baker was hired to remix. The track was utter dreck, with a nonsensical chorus that went, "Lobotomy shorts squirts unto you."

It seemed hopeless, until Baker took a snort and set to work. First, he covered the weak vocal by copying it onto variable-speed digital tape (to alleviate the singer's wobbly pitch) and triple-tracking it, burying it with reverb and echo. The rhythm section was a mess, too, so he replaced the drum track with an electronic drum machine click track. Next, he fixed the bassline by taking the only verse in the song with a steady tempo, dubbing the bass part and looping it into the rest of the song.

Finally, it was time for one of Baker's signature masterstrokes. The engineer took a long hard listen to his work and decided it still lacked something. What it needed was…a glockenspiel. So he sent a gofer out to find one. It took some looking, but he finally came back with a beat-up glockenspiel with several cracked bars, purchased at an instrument store that catered to high school marching bands. Baker played around with this new toy for a while, figuring out different rhythms and how hard to hit the instrument to get certain tones. Then he sampled himself banging away on it in different patterns, and layered the off-kilter pings into "Lobotomy Shorts"—top dead center.

To the band's way of thinking, their song was wrecked. Invasive Surgical Procedure intended "Lobotomy Shorts" to sound menacing, but Baker's glockenspiel turned it into a goof. His tweaking also perfectly counter-balanced the ghastly noises elsewhere, and made "Lobotomy Shorts" a hit. If the group was nonplused, their record label was delighted.

That was Baker's gift. He could isolate odious sounds and find the complementary noises that would render them palatable. Baker had been known to use dialtones, running water, screeching tires, electric can openers and even human indigestion for such sound effects. The man's aural genius was, quite literally, his sole redeeming quality. The rest of his body, cocaine-ravaged nose and all, existed as a life support system for a pair of ears.

Given his track record, Gus figured Baker would have no problem squeezing hits out of TAB. It might not even take that much of his magical conjuring. But whether a mixing job was large or small, the engineer's price tag (and collateral chemical requirements) remained the same. DeGrande was glad to pay it. Having Geoff Baker's name in the credits of TAB's album would guarantee attention from radio programmers, just as Dickerson's name would lure the critics.

All part of the package.

When he heard the initial batch of rough tracks that DeGrande sent him, Mo Polydoroff found them quite strange. That was no accident. The main reason Gus sent him anything at all was to demonstrate that TAB was almost finished with the album. But the manager didn't want Mo to get too excited just yet—or to get any ideas about demanding a larger cut for Poly Brothers Records. So he sent Polydoroff the album's half-dozen weirdest songs (including "Take It and Run," white-noise static and all), but not the final radio-ready Geoff Baker mixes.

Even to Mo's untrained ears, there was clearly something to TAB. Mostly, it was the singer's voice. But Tommy's vocals were buried in weird, unearthly music that constantly seemed about to fly out of control. The combination of heavenly voice and hellish noise was unsettling. How, Mo wondered, was Poly Brothers going to sell this?

At the moment, however, the president had more pressing matters to deal with. A minor crisis had erupted after some Human Resources idiot sent out an "internal only" e-mail asking employees to stop using their magnetized company ID cards to cut lines of cocaine. Traces of the drug were making the office security system go haywire. While that was obviously not good, Mo sure didn't want it announced on-line (especially since, on occasion, he had used his own Poly Brothers ID for that very purpose).

A more serious problem was that Mo just had to fire one of his Poly Brothers vice presidents for repeated sexual harassment of underlings. The final straw came when the man's female secretary filed a $28 million lawsuit against the label, accusing it of condoning her boss's conduct by letting it go unpunished. The secretary's most lurid accusation was that he walked into her office one day with no pants on and masturbated on her desk, ejaculating onto a magazine she'd been reading.

The magazine in question was *Cashboard*—which, just to compound Mo's problems, had two absolutely ball-busting articles about his label on its front page this week. The first story detailed the secretary's sexual harassment lawsuit; the second recounted Poly Brothers' recent lack of success, and stopped just short of saying that Mo was running the company into the ground. Citing an "unnamed source," the article further hinted that a number of flagship Poly Brothers acts were displeased enough to break their contracts and go elsewhere.

"Anyone who wanted to leave would have grounds for claiming Poly Brothers is not the same label they signed to," said the source (Adolph Polydoroff, as it turned out). "Right now, things there really are that bad."

Mo's bosses at Sapporo were not happy, and made sure he wasn't, either. Now the label boss was not only unhappy, but scared. The combination fermented into rage, to the terror of the two-dozen Poly Brothers executives gathered in the main conference room for the weekly planning and marketing meeting. They all knew they were under suspicion as anonymous sources for the *Cashboard* stories, and each prayed he wouldn't be called out and accused.

Mo had already done damage control on the lawsuit, firing the executive and instructing his legal department to negotiate a confidential settlement. Topic A at the meeting was breaking a new act immediately—or else. It now went beyond financial necessity and into the realm of personal pride. Mo was going to show his uncles, by God.

"So what've we got coming up for spring quarter?" Mo asked, looking around the table. "New acts only, remember."

"Right now, we've got two," answered the head of product management.

"Who?"

"Well, one is this group TAB."

That, Mo thought, was less than ideal. "I don't know, I think that band is awfully…well, weird. I'm not sure they're the one to take a shot on. Besides, TAB is technically another label's act—we just distribute the imprint. I'd rather this be a hundred-percent Poly Brothers act. So who's the other band?"

A heavy silence fell across the room. Everyone avoided Mo's eyes as he looked from face to face, puzzled. Nobody wanted to answer his question.

"Well?!" the president finally asked with some exasperation. "Do we actually have anyone else, or not?"

"Plurabellum," a quiet voice at the other end of the table finally said. Mo turned crimson and fixed the man who had spoken (whose misfortune it was to have signed Plurabellum to Poly Brothers) with a glare that could have fried bacon.

Until recently, Poly Brothers counted Plurabellum as one of its bright hopes for the future. But two weeks earlier, the band's female lead singer had gone ballistic over one too many yank-jobs. Despite her reservations, she'd gone along with the label's choice of producer and material—which cast her as a slick diva rather than a singer in a band, against her wishes. She finally snapped after seeing a proposed video treatment for the album's first single. It had her singing while bound in chains with her hair teased out, Medusa-like, with snakes at the end of her locks. Underwater. Surrounded by sharks.

Mo made the mistake of writing a question in the margin: "How much nudity can we get away with on this one?"

Infuriated, the singer took her complaint straight to the top, catching a plane to New York and a cab to Poly Brothers' offices. She rode the elevator up, bluffed her way past Mo's secretary and stormed into his suite while he was meeting with an attorney from Sapporo. Then she leapt onto the president's antique oak and marble desk, dropped her cutoffs and pissed all over it. She'd been drinking heavily on the plane, so his desk got a thorough soaking.

"Here's 'how much nudity you can get away with on this one,' you fucking *bastard!*" she shrieked at Mo, then pulled her shorts up, stormed downstairs, caught another cab back to the airport and flew home. That would be the last time the two of them ever conversed directly. Mo counted it a small blessing that the incident hadn't shown up in either of Cashboard's front-page Poly Brothers stories.

Even so, he had every intention of exacting revenge. Plurabellum's album was in the can, and Poly Brothers would indeed release it—if throwing three copies out the window could be called a "release," which was more or less what Mo planned to do.

The label would provide no tour, marketing or video support, insuring the album's failure. Considering that the band had spent a half-million dollars of Poly Brothers' money and over a year making this album, it would be a horrible waste. Plurabellum would want to leave Poly Brothers and go elsewhere, but Mo planned to tie them up. He would reject all future recordings as unsatisfactory while refusing to release the band from its contract, keeping them in label purgatory. Eventually, Plurabellum would sue Poly Brothers to escape, citing the thirteenth amendment to the U.S. Constitution—the one prohibiting slavery. But it was no use. The label just stonewalled them in court until they went bankrupt and broke up, shattered from the experience.

That, however, was a long-term situation. Short-term, Polydoroff had a slot to fill and TAB was the only act available because their album was almost finished. So even though Mo didn't believe in their music, he nevertheless declared that the button was to be pushed. Poly Brothers was going to throw every ounce of its considerable marketing weight behind TAB: lavish videos, independent radio promotion, expensive advertising, prime retail placement. The major push Plurabellum was supposed to get, TAB would get instead.

"Whatever it takes," Mo told his assembled underlings, "we are going to break this band, or else every head in this room will roll. So go make it happen."

Later that afternoon, after hearing the report from one of his Poly Brothers spies, Gus DeGrande smiled an evil smile.

CHAPTER TWENTY-TWO

Somehow, TAB finished basic tracks by the appointed completion date. For reasons that weren't entirely clear to Clay Dickerson, they recorded far more material than they could use—about forty songs. Soon into the project, he called Gus to ask for some direction.

"I don't know what to do to rein Tommy in," Dickerson told the manager. "He's just all over the place. We're making three different records here, and I can't get him to make a decision on which one to do."

"Just let him go," DeGrande said. "Whatever he wants to do is fine. Record it all and we'll pare down later. If he's on a songwriting binge, let's not get in his way. Just make sure you get good vocal and guitar takes on everything. The rest, we can tweak later if we have to."

By the time they were done, the producer felt as if he'd lived through a month-long hurricane. He managed to keep everything moving along with an outward veneer of apparent sanity during the one day Ken Morrison spent in the studio to report his *Rock Slide* story—meaning that he refrained from throttling Tommy. The rest of the project was like being under siege, coping with a steady barrage of increasingly unhinged demands.

Tommy already sensed the rumblings of the machine gearing up to turn him into a pop star, so he tried to reassert control as best he could. Mostly, that took the form of what Dickerson called "method-acting bullshit." There was, for example, the song on which Tommy insisted that Michelle record her bass part while standing on her head. He was so adamant about it that Michelle actually tried to humor him—and nearly passed out after spending a half-hour upside-down against a wall. It took a couple of chocolate milkshakes for her to recover, then another three maddening, excruciating hours to get the part down satisfactorily. The residual headache lingered for over a day.

Another of the bandleader's bright ideas was to record "Go As You Are" in the nude, for reasons he refused to explain beyond saying the song "needed some skin." Everyone else was puzzled because the song's drop-dead lyrical sentiments and pulverizing arrangement were less sexual than actively hostile. Ray and Michelle demurred to disrobe, but Tommy stripped right down and cut the song's vocal in his birthday suit.

He was right in the middle of the outro chorus—in the vocal booth, howling "Go awaaaaaaaaaay" over and over and over—when someone knocked on the control room door. The gospel group recording over in Studio B picked that precise instant to inquire about borrowing some guitar strings, and were horrified to discover the pagan happenings right next door. Fear of reprisals from DeGrande was all that kept the studio manager from throwing TAB out.

Despite all the flakeouts, Dickerson coaxed inspired performances out of all three band members. He got Michelle to loosen up and Ray to tighten up, to the point that they'd never sounded better. And Tommy was, well, Tommy. In an odd way, Dickerson was glad the guy had been such a pain in the ass because it made him seem human. Otherwise, the producer might have been too awestruck at the sounds pouring out of the bandleader's voice and guitar to do his job. By the end of the project, he hated Tommy's guts.

However unpleasant the process, the results were spectacular. Even before final mixdown, this was the wildest-sounding record Dickerson had ever made. He got jittery just listening to the playbacks. Song after song, Tommy played chicken with his muse, pushing everything to the brink of flying apart and always pulling back at precisely the right instant.

The producer had adopted a working title for the album, *There's a Riot Goin' On*. It aptly described the chaotic goings-on in the studio, and also paid private homage to the classic Sly and the Family Stone album of the same name. *Riot* was a favorite of Tommy's, too. Then again, it would be—he was almost as fucked up as Sly had been in 1971, while making that album.

The bandleader's condition had grown progressively more alarming during the recording sessions. That was the problem with New York City: too much trouble to get into, and Tommy managed to find plenty. He'd become quite clever about slipping off unnoticed, disappearing for hours at a time.

His bandmates were all staying with friends in the city, but nobody had any idea where Tommy spent his time out of the studio. When asked, he just grinned and shrugged and told them not to worry about it. Some nights, he slept in TAB's van in the studio parking lot. Other nights, he was out and about until past dawn.

Tommy looked more and more bedraggled every day—functional, but just barely. As far as anyone could tell, he hadn't brought a suitcase or even a change of clothes to New York. No luggage at all, in fact, except for a couple of guitars; and the guitars weren't even his. Someday, he said, he planned to write a book: "How to be a Professional Musician Without Actually Owning a Single Piece of Equipment."

It was impossible to glean any of these juicier details from the "Newcomers" TAB piece that appeared in *Rock Slide* under Ken Morrison's byline. Typical for such stories, it focused instead on the "excitement" of an up-and-coming band making its first album, even though the critic thought the recording process was the most boring damn thing he'd ever seen. After several hours watching the band play the same thirty-second interlude over and over, he buttonholed the bandleader for an interview at a nearby diner.

But first came a strange detour. Tommy gave Ken directions and sent him ahead to the restaurant to get a table, excusing himself to hit the bathroom—then didn't show up for half an hour. Figuring he must've gone to the wrong place, Ken was just about to give up and return to the studio when his interview subject finally appeared, glassy-eyed.

"That must've been some trip to the bathroom," Ken said as Tommy slid into a chair with a look on his face suggesting an attempt to suppress something—panic, laughter, vomit, a gaseous emission. "Everything, um, come out okay?"

He hadn't really meant it as a joke, but Tommy nevertheless giggled maniacally.

"Ken," he said, looking right through the critic, "you kill me, man..."

Then Tommy looked at a bowl of potato cheese soup on the table; the diner's soup du jour.

"Those," he began, "are the most *pretentious* croutons I've ever—"

In mid-sentence, Tommy's eyes rolled shut and he made a sound like the air rushing out of a balloon as he slowly collapsed face-first onto the table. Fortunately, his head landed in a basket of dinner rolls, which cushioned the blow. But he was out cold.

Pretentious croutons, eh, Tommy? Ken thought, studying the scruffy top of the bandleader's head. *Well, you are definitely one for firsts. A new adventure with every interview.*

The waitress was growing concerned about having someone comatose and face-down on one of her tables, as dead people are notoriously bad tippers. Ken waved her away and wondered how he should handle this. Lead the story with it, probably. Gus would love that:

> Whether it's his music or his drug habit, Tommy Aguilar shows a complete lack of self-consciousness—so much so that he has no qualms about passing out in public.
> After a long day in the studio, he likes to kick back with a shot of China White, and doesn't care who knows it.

"Hey, man, whatever it takes; I've blacked out in some of the best restaurants in this town," he said, right after adding another notch to his syringe and doing a face-plant in a bread basket...

Jesus Christ. If he retained the slightest shred of dignity, Ken decided, he would just get up and leave before Tommy came to—before Tommy turned into Charlie Holmes. Tell Gus and Rock Slide and Poly Brothers and every other vulture with a stake in TAB to take their bylines and their money and their junkie junkets and get fucked, because he was through being their shill.

Instead, the critic kept the waitress at bay and sat quietly sipping his iced tea. While he was at it, he finished off his soup, pretentious croutons and all. After about ten minutes, Tommy finally stirred, raising his head and looking around blankly. At that moment, he looked like a fearful little child.

A boy with faraway eyes, Ken thought. That would make a helluva headline. One he knew he didn't have the cojones to use.

"So Tommy," he said, turning on his trusty tape recorder. "Are Michelle and Ray getting any more input on the songwriting these days?"

After the tracking, all that was left to do was pick out the final line-up of songs, then sequence and mix them. Dickerson assumed he'd handle mixing, which he never entrusted to anyone else on his projects. Gus had other ideas.

He told Dickerson to take a break and gave him a two thousand dollar tip and the use of his vacation house on Martha's Vineyard for a week. After a grueling month of hand-to-hand combat in the studio, the producer was happy to take him up on the offer. DeGrande kept TAB occupied, too, sending them out for some club dates down in Baltimore and D.C.

With the cats away, Gus whisked in his mouse Geoff Baker to wrap up the project. The engineer remixed the eleven songs the manager picked out, ranging from minor adjustments to major overhauls. He left the drum and bass tracks completely intact on six songs, and bolstered them with synthesizer overdubs on another two. Baker concentrated most of his efforts on three songs, radically recasting "Take It and Run," "Go As You Are" and "Love Buzz Off." If DeGrande had his way, TAB's album would have as many as a half-dozen singles. But these three were the money shots—the big hits, calculated to induce massive album sales through saturation airplay.

To get these tracks radio-ready, Baker went so far as to erase Ray's drums completely from two of them. The engineer substituted a mechanical drum machine on one; and on the other, a drum part played by a session drummer he often employed (a jazz hack slumming his way through another alimony payment). Baker also processed and compressed Tommy's guitar, trimming layers the way you'd slice fat off a cut of prime rib. He removed the static completely from "Take It and Run," turned Tommy's vocal tracks way up, and added keyboards throughout.

Keyboards. An instrument TAB had always proudly avoided, just on general principle. Keyboards so offended Ray's puritanical rock sensibilities that, when the band first arrived at Eccentric Landlady's Studio A, he refused to do anything until the piano was removed from the room.

Ray and Tommy may have been peeved over Bob's clean mix of their previous mini-album, but they were going to be genuinely enraged at this. So was Clay Dickerson, who showed up back in New York after his beach week tanned, rested and ready to begin mixing— only to be told that the project was done, the tapes already shipped off to be mastered.

Once he discovered that Geoff Baker had been at the studio, Dickerson figured out what happened. He called DeGrande from

New York, demanding that his name be pulled off the album. The manager told Dickerson to read the fine print of his contract, which he hadn't even looked at. Sure enough, the contract specified that he would not be allowed to disavow TAB's album by removing his name from the credits.

"Gus, you can't do this!" the producer protested.

"I already did. So go home, cash your check and keep your mouth shut. Trust me, you will not be sorry this record has your name on it. And don't make a stink, or you'll never produce another major-label record. I guarantee it."

"Is that a threat?" Dickerson asked heatedly.

"Yes," Gus said, hanging up.

The Geoff Baker mix of TAB's album was insurance of a sort. Gus decided he needed some actual life insurance on his client, with himself as beneficiary. After all, the manager had an investment to protect, and not a small one.

So he took out a policy on Tommy without telling him, purchased through the sort of agency not found in the phone book—a company in Las Vegas, specializing in high-risk policies. It was a three million dollar term-life deal, payable if the bandleader turned up dead or otherwise incapacitated.

The premiums were only eight hundred dollars a month with the non-smoker's discount, even though Tommy had a two-pack-a-day habit. Nor was that his only unhealthy habit. But DeGrande's personal physician took care of the physical. Or rather, signed the form; the doctor never actually saw the insuree. For bookkeeping purposes, the insurance premiums counted as another business expense, recoupable against anticipated income from TAB's record royalties. The manager did that with every penny he spent on the band.

Tommy didn't know it, but his band was already close to half a million dollars in the hole to Gus.

Ken was perturbed. TAB's record was finished and he knew it, but he couldn't get a copy—not from Gus, not from Poly Brothers, not from anybody in the band. This was a problem because he'd been commissioned to write the band's "official" record company biography, to accompany promotional copies of the album that went out to radio and press.

Ethically, this was crossing the line from journalist to flack. If Ken's employers at the *Daily News* were to find out, he would've been suspended at the very least. Instead, the critic quietly took the money and rationalized it by telling himself he was just maintaining his "access." This sort of thing happened all the time. The entire business of rock journalism was predicated on conflict of interest in the name of access.

Not that the access rationalization was working out. Here Ken had sold another chunk of his soul for a lousy hundred bucks to enlarge his cog in DeGrande's operation, and he couldn't even get a tape out of it. Instead, Ken was having to piece together the bio from his old clips and some canned quotes he'd been given. It was nothing personal, however—Gus was shutting out every critic in America. This was highly unusual. Labels and band managers were usually eager to get as much exposure as possible for a new act, and tried to drum up advance interest by sending pre-release copies months ahead of the street date.

But TAB's album was going to be released with virtually no advance fanfare, and the plants were manufacturing it under the sort of tight security usually afforded superstar releases. Mostly, that was because DeGrande didn't want any copies finding their way back to the band. To get Tommy off his back, the manager gave him a tape of eleven tracks of Dickerson's rough scratch mixes. It wasn't the album that was being released. It wasn't even the same eleven songs.

While the ruse bought him some time, Gus knew he didn't have long— a window of several weeks, during which Poly Brothers' massive marketing and promotional machinery was to kick in and blow TAB up overnight. DeGrande wanted it to happen so fast that Tommy wouldn't be able to do anything but go ahead and be a rock star. Then they'd let the press follow along and play catch-up.

That would be useful for distracting Tommy.

Gus had a scheme to prime the pump. It just so happened there was also an established act with a record in the Poly Brothers pipeline— Arrowhead, whose long-awaited new album was scheduled for release the same week as TAB. Arrowhead was one of Poly Brothers' few remaining cash cows, ringing up six million copies with their previous effort. But the label was about to lose the band. Their contract was up with this album, and the group's manager made it clear they intended to go elsewhere.

While Mo Polydoroff was glad to have one last big hit to milk, he was none too happy about Arrowhead leaving. So Gus concocted a little going-away present, based on the assumption that Arrowhead was going to sell millions of records. So many millions that nobody would miss, say, seventy-five thousand or so.

Poly Brothers was shipping three million copies of Arrowhead's album to stores. Of that initial shipment, seventy-five thousand were secretly printed up with the bar code of TAB's album and scattered in smaller cities and towns in the Midwest. So when store clerks in Cedar Rapids, Moline and Terre Haute rang up Arrowhead CDs, the computers that *Cashboard* used to compile its charts would register sales for TAB instead.

"That should get us off to a good start," DeGrande told Mo. "An out-of-nowhere high debut and a buzz at retail, and then the radio and video play will kick in. If it works, nobody will notice a thing." The manager didn't mention that these phantom sales also translated into an extra three hundred thousand dollars in royalties for Grandiose

Records. Since it came out of Arrowhead's pocket, Mo wouldn't have cared, anyway.

"Nice idea," the label president said approvingly. "Then we can put out the old 'Pressing Plants Working Round-the-Clock To Keep Up With Demand' story; that's always good for some press in the trades. It's brilliant. Don't know why I never thought to try this before."

Because you're a fuckin' moron, DeGrande thought, but held his tongue. The bar code bait-and-switch was one of the oldest tricks in the record business.

Officially, the initial pressing on TAB's *Chorus Verses Chorus* was two hundred thousand units, an almost unprecedented figure for an unknown new act. Then again, that wasn't how many were actually manufactured and shipped. Poly Brothers sent out twenty-five thousand legitimate copies plus the seventy-five thousand Arrowhead phantom copies, holding back a hundred thousand real ones to fill reorders once the marketing campaign kicked in.

Chorus Verses Chorus came out on Tuesday, February third. As DeGrande predicted, phase one worked perfectly. Enough of the phantom copies were sold that TAB entered the *Cashboard* album sales chart at number eighty-nine—a phenomenal debut for a band that few people outside of the industry had even heard of. Of the seventeen thousand copies of *Chorus Verses Chorus* sold that first week, only about fourteen hundred actual TAB albums sold. Business was strong in the band's home region of the Southeast, but slow elsewhere.

At the top of the chart, meanwhile, Arrowhead's *Rocks Off* easily debuted at number one, moving four hundred thousand copies in its first week. It would be several months before anybody noticed that the early reorder patterns on *Rocks Off* were strangely off-kilter in the Midwest. Stores in some secondary and tertiary markets ran out of copies, even though the computers insisted they should still have stock.

But by then, *Rocks Off* had sold over four million copies, and so many other things had happened that nobody paid it any mind.

CHAPTER TWENTY-THREE

Gus kept TAB out on the road continuously after they finished in the studio, alternating between headlining clubs and opening arena shows for their old pals Arrowhead—who Tommy despised more every time he saw them. Every Arrowhead show was identical, right down to Perry Rose's canned between-song chatter: "Good evening, [name of city]," "Oooooh, I *like* it when you do that," "Here's one we don't play much anymore," and so on. Being around their traveling medicine show was getting on Tommy's nerves.

So was Gus's doubletalk; Tommy couldn't get a straight answer out of the manager about anything, especially TAB's upcoming record. Everytime he broached the subject, DeGrande told him it was "in the pipeline" and met all questions about packaging, titles and song sequences with evasive answers.

"We'll sit down and figure everything out when you get back," he promised.

"Okay, then, when will we get back?" Tommy asked.

"Soon."

Aside from Tommy's restlessness, all was relatively calm. Even the ever-mistrustful Michelle had to admit that TAB's touring conditions improved once DeGrande took over. The crowds were decent and they were getting paid—or so they thought. With Gus filling multiple roles as promoter, artist manager and booking agent, far more of the money they generated was going into his pocket than theirs (plus he was count- ing the money he *did* pay TAB as a salary expense, recoupable against future royalties).

All they knew was that they got to sleep in motels rather than the van, and enough people showed up most nights to make the shows worth playing. This included an otherwise uneventful Tuesday night club show in South Bend, Indiana, on the same day that *Chorus Verses Chorus* slipped into stores without the band even being aware of it.

The next morning, TAB checked out of the local Days Inn and was about to hit Interstate Eighty for the next city on the itinerary: Des Moines, about nine hours away. Ray pulled into a gas station on the edge of town to fuel up. Tommy disappeared inside the bathroom, then spent a few minutes staring at a sunglasses display. He eventually settled on a garish pair of shades with pink frames in the shape of woman's breasts. Michelle wandered over to a record store in the shopping center across the street to buy something for the day's drive. Choice of music in the van was a constant issue, so they alternated control of the stereo. Today was her turn to play deejay, and she was bored with every disc she'd brought along.

Inside the store, Michelle was engrossed in reading the fine-print credits on a collection of string quartet pieces, wondering if something classical would be worth the wrath of her bandmates. Suddenly, she snapped to attention at the sound of a familiar bassline playing over the store's speakers. It was familiar because…she herself had played it. Sort of.

She listened intently. Yep, definitely one of hers. Seemed to be "Punk Song in A," which TAB recorded in New York for their record. But it sounded weird and different.

Fighting down a rising sense of panic, the bassist hurried up to the counter. There was a display with a "Now Playing" sign, which held the case for TAB's album. She had no idea where the title came from. But it was them, all right, even if you could barely tell because the cover shot was so blurry.

"When'd you get this?" Michelle asked the clerk.

"Just came out yesterday," he answered.

Michelle and her bandmates had been listening to a tape of what they thought was their album for weeks. This had different songs, and a radically different sound. Her bass and Ray's drums sounded quieter, oddly processed. Tommy's guitar was cleaner than she'd ever heard it. Plus this song had...what was that?

...*Keyboards!* OhmygodNO!!

Her eyes widening in horror, Michelle jerked the booklet out of the CD case and searched for the page of credits.

"Mother-*fucker!*" she hissed, throwing the booklet down. Then she reached into her purse, threw some bills onto the counter, grabbed an unopened copy of *Chorus Verses Chorus* off the rack and ran outside.

"Miss," the clerk called behind her, "your change?..."

Driving westward, TAB's three members listened in stunned silence to *Chorus Verses Chorus.* Twice. No one said a word. Halfway through the third play, Tommy took the disc and hurled it out the window like a Frisbee. It struck the "Iowa State Line" sign by the highway and shattered. Michelle threw the jewelbox after it, then ripped the CD booklet into tiny pieces and threw those out, too.

Another ten minutes went by before anyone said anything.

"You think this happens all the time?" Tommy finally asked. "You don't even recognize your own record?"

Nobody answered.

If Tommy disliked the album, he absolutely loathed the video for the first single, "Go As You Are." The videoclip was another of DeGrande's fast ones. When the manager sent TAB off to play during the week Geoff

Baker spent mixing the record, he arranged for their pre-show sound-checks to be filmed.

"Nothing elaborate," he told the band. "I just want to give the promo department at Poly Brothers a general idea of what you look and sound like. No one else will ever see this, so don't bother dressing up or anything."

That was a lie. These films actually formed the basis for TAB's first video (plus cover art for *Chorus Verses Chorus*). As put together by a hotshot editor, the finished clip was a back-and-forth montage. It alternated blurry black-and-white footage of the band playing in a series of dark empty rooms with garishly lit scenes of a crowd of freakish reprobates in a jam-packed auditorium—cheering wildly for three mannequins modeled on TAB's members, standing motionless with instruments on a stage. The video concluded with the audience spilling onto the stage, overwhelming the dummies in a surging wave of humanity and tearing them to pieces.

While the concept was pretty thin, the execution was brilliant. The dizzying jumpcuts back and forth grew faster and more jarring as the video progressed, building toward a release that never came. The overall mood was numbing. Detached, disembodied, bloodless. Ironic.

From the moment he laid eyes on it, Tommy was furious. "Go As You Are" had been warped into something he never meant, turned into a "statement" that seemed to have something to do with "alienation." Sitting in a motel room in Des Moines, Tommy put his head in his hands and moaned after watching it for the first time on The Video Channel. As the veejay noted afterward, TAB's album had just come out and "Go As You Are" was already in heavy rotation. A "buzzclip," no less.

"Goddamnit!" fumed the author. "I wrote that song about a crazy girl I wanted to leave me alone. It's got nothing to do with department store dummies or riots or…what'd that guy say just now? 'Irony.' Jesus, who came up with this shit?"

"The same guy you decided to hire as our bigtime new manager, smart guy," Michelle sighed, just as the door opened and Ray walked in. He had a big smile on his face, until he saw the rage on Tommy's.

"Whatsa matter?" the drummer asked.

"We just saw our video."

"You mean we *have* one?" Ray asked. "Are we even in it?"

"Sort of," Michelle said. "Remember those people who came around filming our soundchecks right after we did the record?"

"Yeah. So?"

"Well, they took some shots of us playing and some shots of a crowd cheering for some mannequins on a stage, and made a video."

"Who's 'they?'"

"DeGrande, I guess."

"Wow," Ray said. "I've never been in a band that had a video before."

His bandmates exchanged a look of disgust that went right by the drummer.

"So how is it?"

"How is it?" Michelle repeated, amazed at the question. "How do you think? Christ, it's awful!"

"Maybe so," Ray said, "but it does seem to be working. I was just at a record store at the mall over by campus, and they said they've already sold seven copies of our record since yesterday. We're that store's number-two seller!"

That got Tommy's attention.

"No shit?" he asked, and Ray nodded. "Who's number one?"

"Arrowhead."

Tommy put his head in his hands and moaned again. Then he went to the pay phone outside to make another call that Gus would neglect to return.

Later that same night, Bob Porter and Ken Morrison both had trouble sleeping. So they both happened to be channel-surfing in their respective dwellings at the same moment when they first saw TAB's video. They had the same reaction, albeit for different reasons.

Ken had talked to Tommy about "Go As You Are" before and knew what the song was about. In fact, he even knew *who* it was about—the infamous Susan—who Ken himself wouldn't have minded…well, you know. Then again, he didn't know her many facets nearly as well as Tommy did.

Knowing the background, Ken couldn't believe how badly the video misinterpreted this song. But Bob knew instantly that DeGrande hadn't misunderstood anything. Instead, Gus simply disregarded its meaning after concluding that a song about trying to chase someone off with a syringe was not the stuff of hit singles.

The hook, however, had "Big Hit" written all over it. So Gus simply reinvented the song as an underachiever's manifesto—"an ironic lost-generation peep show," the veejay called it—and obliterated its original meaning with overpowering visuals.

"Bastard," Ken and Bob both muttered, separately but simultaneously.

At that same moment, Tommy was half a continent away and also having a bad night. But his was far worse because it ended with a pair of handcuffs.

The bandleader hadn't wanted to play at all that night. He didn't want to hang around the Des Moines Civic Center and deal with Arrowhead, or their roadies or their groupies or their asshole road manager. Most of all, Tommy wanted no part of anybody who might show up wanting to hear "Go As You Are."

Anger like this called for booze. So Tommy locked himself into the motel bathroom and poured the better part of a bottle of tequila down his neck. Ray begged him to come out and finally broke the door down, forcibly carrying his bandleader to the van. On the way to the show, Tommy vomited out the window.

Once they were at the arena, the cajoling started all over again. Come showtime, Ray again resorted to physical force, dragging Tommy onto the darkened stage at the appointed hour and depositing him at the microphone. Michelle followed behind, more out of habit than conviction. She didn't much feel like playing, either, and couldn't understand why the drummer was suddenly so gung-ho.

"Ray," Tommy said menacingly, off-microphone, as the lighting tech flashed their cue from the mixing board, "don't make me do this."

The stagelights were coming on in ten seconds, at which point they were supposed to start playing so that the lighting would be in sync. The crowd buzzed with anticipation.

"C'mon, Tommy, it won't be so bad," Ray called back from behind his drumkit, then counted out the first song. "One-two-three-four…"

Michelle stood by, bass at the ready.

Thwap!

Ray hit his bass drum as the lights came up. The drum reverberated just like it was supposed to at the start of "Go As You Are," and then there was…nothing. No answering guitar riff, because Tommy still stood there empty-handed, glaring at his bandmate. As the lone drumbeat faded, the only sounds were the humming of inadequately grounded monitors, and the murmuring of a confused audience.

The drummer glared back at Tommy. "Well?" he asked with a shrug.

The corners of Tommy's mouth slowly curled into a smile so full of wicked intentions that Michelle shuddered just watching it form.

"Okay," Tommy said. "If that's what you want."

He walked back to his guitar, strapped it on and turned both the instrument and his amplifier up as loud as they would go. Then he strode back to the centerstage microphone and addressed the crowd for the first time.

"People," TAB's leader said solemnly, "it is time."

Then Tommy wound up and windmilled down on his guitar strings Pete Townshend-style with all the force he could muster, leaning into the onstage monitor to unleash a howling maelstrom of feedback. The screech was deafening, the sound of metal rending from a hundred-mile-an-hour head-on collision of locomotives. Michelle cowered back, covering her ears with her hands.

"It is time, brothers and sisters," Tommy went on after the noise died down, paraphrasing the gospel according to the original punk band, the MC5. "You must choose *right now* whether you are part of the *problem,* or part of the *solution.* And from the looks of you, right now I'm thinkin' you mother*fuck*ers are part of the *problem,* and you must therefore be *punished…* "

He hit the guitar another lacerating blow, so hard he snapped a string and cut the top knuckle of his left middle finger almost to the bone. The digit spurted blood as he held it high to signal FUCK YOU to the stunned crowd, who booed and would've given the bird right back—except no one wanted to risk uncovering their ears. People fled toward the concourse, seeking to escape the howling noise.

Tommy was just getting warmed up.

"Do you know," he began, "what Perry *fucking* Rose is doing backstage *right now?!* He's—"

Arrowhead's tour manager finally succeeded in pulling the plug on TAB at that moment, shutting off the soundboard and sparing the crowd the rest of the sentence: "—not sharing his groupies with me!" It took Tommy a few seconds to realize what happened. Once he did, the bandleader decided to moon the crowd.

"Hey," he called out, "wanna see my cock?"

Tommy was just about to drop his pants when the houselights came up, and he saw a gaggle of Arrowhead roadies sprinting toward the stage. So he leapt onto the drum riser and vaulted back toward the headliner's bank of keyboard synthesizers, which he took out by swinging his guitar like a sledgehammer. Then he knocked over every piece of equipment within reach and took off running, the roadies and a couple of cops in hot pursuit.

Ray had not moved since hitting that first drumbeat. He sat silently, open-mouthed. He didn't budge from behind his drums, not even when Arrowhead's tour manager ran up and began shrieking that they weren't just fired but busted and would never work again.

For her part, Michelle almost wished that was true.

Somehow, Tommy made it out to TAB's van and escaped his mob of pursuers, who dove out of the way as he burned rubber out of the arena's backstage area. He stopped at the first liquor store he came to and bought two fifths of cheap bourbon. He would've preferred the expensive kind, but didn't have enough cash on him and quantity was more important than quality. This was shaping up as a two-bottle night, at least.

Chain-smoking and swilling bad rotgut from the bottle, Tommy pointed the van north on I-35 in the twilight. Between cigarettes, he sucked on his finger, which throbbed from its cut. It took half a bottle of bourbon before the pain subsided. The only reminder was the sticky blood all over the steering wheel.

There was little traffic and Tommy made the hundred or so miles to Clear Lake in only seventy-five minutes, by which time he was into his second bottle. He got off the interstate and headed east toward Mason City, in search of a certain airfield. Somewhere in his mind was the thought that Buddy Holly's ghost might have something to say about this predicament.

Tommy figured he'd know what he was looking for when he saw it: the cornfield Holly's plane crashed into on a snowy February night in 1959.

"Gus, we got problems," Ray whined.

"So I heard. Where's Tommy?"

"We were hoping you knew. He took the van and hightailed it outta here a couple hours ago, and we haven't seen him since. We're back at the motel now and it doesn't look like he's been here."

"Damn." The manager thought for a moment.

"Okay, here's what you do: Pack up and get out of there. Go find another hotel and register under a different name, then stay there. Don't unpack because you'll have to be ready to roll with no warning. Call me when you get there."

Several hours later, Tommy was arrested after a brief, bizarre stand-off. He was drunk, naked, incoherent—and building a bonfire in a snow-covered field using a box of TAB T-shirts as fuel. He'd thrown everything from the van into the flames, including the fenceposts he ripped up driving into the field.

Tommy was about to drive the van itself into the fire to blow it up when the Cerro Gordo County Sheriff's Department stopped him. They dragged the singer kicking and screaming from behind the wheel, cuffed him and threw him in the back of a police car for a ride to the drunk tank.

It was the most exciting thing to happen around those parts since…well, Buddy Holly's plane crash. And as it turned out, Tommy hadn't even started his bonfire in the right field.

He was close, though.

CHAPTER TWENTY-FOUR

Getting Tommy out of this one took every last ounce of juice Gus had. Fortunately, Iowa was a state where the promoter did some business, so he had lots of employees and friends there, including a small army of law enforcement officers who moonlighted as concert security for Grandiose Productions. DeGrande paid all of them well enough that they were willing to look the other way when necessary. A special few, he paid well enough that they were willing to do more than that.

Two such plainclothes detectives showed up at the Cerro Gordo County Jail in Mason City an hour after Tommy was brought in, bearing warrants claiming jurisdiction over the entire case on behalf of the city of Des Moines. The legal justification was that the suspect began his rampage and did the most damage in Des Moines, so the charges he faced there would supersede anything in Cerro Gordo County.

Nevertheless, such a transfer in the middle of the night was highly irregular. It never would've worked, if not for the fact that a couple of deputies on-duty in Mason City that evening were also in DeGrande's pocket.

That got Tommy out of jail and into the custody of the two detectives, who pitched his inert body into the back of their cruiser. But instead of returning to Des Moines, they headed in the opposite direction – north, up Highway 65.

The officers' warrants were fake, as it turned out. So were the names they used, Friday and Krupke. They weren't really from Des Moines, either.

Across the state line, in the tiny hamlet of Gordonville, Minnesota, Tommy's bandmates cooled their heels in the deserted parking lot of a darkened gas station. They waited in a drab Ford Econoline van they'd just picked up from a used-car dealer in Mankato, an hour away. Gus wired the dealer the money, after chartering a helicopter to fly Ray and Michelle up from Des Moines.

Tommy was sprawled across the back seat, still unconscious and sleeping off his bourbon binge, when the police car pulled into the parking lot. He still wore the orange PRISONER jumpsuit from the county jail, and a bandage on his left middle finger. He didn't wake up when the two cops lifted him out of their cruiser, carried him across the pavement and slung him into the back of the van. Tommy never stirred and they never spoke, wordlessly vanishing back into the cold Midwestern darkness toward Iowa.

Ray drove in the opposite direction, north to Interstate Ninety and then east. When the sun came up several hours later, they were crossing the state line into Wisconsin and turning south, carefully giving Iowa a wide berth as per DeGrande's instructions. By the time anybody in Des Moines or Mason City figured out what had happened, TAB was long gone.

Several hours later, as TAB traversed rural Illinois, Ken Morrison sat at his desk, fighting off a garden-variety hangover with a cup of muddy coffee. The critic had just arrived at the office and was scanning the Associated Press newswire on his computer.

A brief item slugged ROCK-RIOT-TAB caught his eye:

DES MOINES, Iowa (AP)—A concert by the New York rock band Arrowhead was canceled after a riot broke out during the performance of the opening act, TAB.

Sixteen people were injured in the melee Wednesday night, most with cuts and bruises. Damage to the Des Moines Civic Center was estimated at $10,000.

The bizarre incident began when TAB guitarist Tommy Aguilar verbally abused the crowd with obscenities. It escalated when Aguilar played loud guitar feedback.

Civic Center general manager Howard Wilson claimed the volume exceeded the pain threshold of 140 decibels. The injuries and damage occurred when concertgoers stampeded up the aisles to escape the noise.

"I don't know what [Aguilar's] problem was, but he just snapped," said Wilson. "We were lucky nobody was hurt seriously. It could have been a lot worse."

Aguilar also damaged some of Arrowhead's on-stage equipment before fleeing the arena. Police were still seeking him late Wednesday night.

Management for both TAB and Arrowhead did not return phone calls seeking comment.

All hell broke loose in Iowa after the Des Moines debacle. There was talk of extraditing Tommy by force if necessary, bringing him back to face charges of everything from obscenity to attempted murder. From the hysterical tone of the editorials and letters in the Des Moines newspaper, the local populace seemed to find the former offense more alarming.

Gus told his Des Moines lawyer to stonewall for as long as possible. Then the promoter began making generous-to-the-point-of-illegal contributions to every politician, judge, district attorney, policeman's fund and political action committee that might have the slightest connection to the case of *Des Moines v. Tommy Aguilar*. If he dragged things out long enough and greased enough palms, Gus figured, he could get Tommy off with no jail time.

Besides, the bribes and legal bills were just another recoupable expense to write off against TAB's incoming record royalties. Those were going to be substantial because *Chorus Verses Chorus* was exploding literally overnight—in part because news of the "TAB Riot," as it came to be called, made such great copy. Coming the very same week that copies of TAB's album and video showed up in the mailboxes of every critic and media outlet in America, the riot provided an irresistible hook. The music video networks and syndicated daily entertainment shows endlessly replayed footage of the fictional riot from the video during their reports on the real fracas. Newspapers and magazines put together compare-and-contrast visual essays, juxtaposing news photos of the riot in Des Moines with stills from the video (eerily enough, they did seem to match up).

Critics were falling all over themselves, too, grinding out their reviews. All of them seemed to use the same handful of meaningless adjectives to describe TAB: "raw," "urgent," "searing" and, of course, "riotous." The nation's flagship alternative weekly paper, New York's *Vox Populi,* led its record review section with a long-winded and extremely pointy-headed essay by its self-appointed "Dean of Rock Critics." The headline: "There's A Riot Goin' On: TAB and Pointless (Un)Civil Disobedience as Self-Expression."

Whatever Tommy thought he was trying to accomplish in Des Moines, he had unintentionally created a masterpiece of marketing synergy.

TAB made good time on the trip home. Their stops were brief by necessity, since the bandleader's picture was everywhere and they didn't want to attract any attention. Keeping him out of sight was easy enough for the first part of the drive, since he was unconscious. Their longest detour was to a Goodwill store in a small Wisconsin town to get Tommy some new clothes after he woke up. Having burned everything in the Iowa cornfield fire, all he had to wear were the orange jail overalls.

Michelle refused to get out of the van or drive or eat, or even answer questions when asked if she was on a hunger strike. So Ray went into Goodwill and picked out the most garish pair of pants in the store— blinding bright yellow, the kind retirees wore on the golf course—and a tattered red T-shirt that read I'M WITH STUPID. For good measure, Ray completed the disguise with a greasy American flag baseball cap, even though a hat wasn't really necessary. The drummer had already cut off most of Tommy's hair while he slept, sawing off handfuls of it with a pocketknife. Between his hangover pallor and the missing hanks of hair, TAB's frontman looked like a cancer patient.

"Aw, gimmie a break," Tommy groaned when he saw the clothes. "I can't wear this shit! What'd all this cost, seventy-five cents?"

"Three dollars and twenty-seven cents," Ray said. "But don't worry about paying me back right away. I know you're good for it."

"Forget it. I'm not wearing this."

Ray grabbed his bandmate by the throat, pulling him close enough for Tommy to count the vessels in the drummer's bloodshot eyes.

"Oh yes you are," he hissed. "The clothes are supposed to be a disguise, which was Gus's idea. They're also punishment, which was my idea. So put the shit on and don't give me any more excuses to break your face. And keep down while you're changing, so nobody sees your hairy ass. That's all we need, for you to fucking get arrested again."

Tommy was no happier when he discovered the pants were two sizes too small. He suspected Ray did that on purpose.

He suspected right.

Five days later, Tommy walked into DeGrande's office and sat down. The promoter was expecting him, although he didn't expect his client's new look: bald. After getting back home, Tommy finished his band-mates' rough haircut with a straight razor. Not that he wanted to look like a cueball, but he figured his hair would grow back faster and more evenly if he cut it all off.

"Nice 'do," Gus said dryly.

"I call it my puppet zombie look," Tommy said, taking off his sun-glasses and eyeing his manager's pet piranha. "I got the idea from that video you made. You like it?"

"I'm sure the chicks'll dig it."

"Yeah, I'm sure they will, now that they'll be seeing more of me around here."

"Oh yeah?"

"Oh yeah," Tommy said. "I quit."

DeGrande didn't answer. He knew Tommy was going to come in and tender his resignation, then allow himself to be talked out of it. The only variable was how stubborn he'd be about it. So Gus simply sat with his arms crossed, looking impassively at his client. Thirty seconds went by.

"Well?" the bald bandleader finally said.

"Well what?" the bald promoter shrugged.

"Well, aren't you supposed to give me the speech about how I can't do that?"

DeGrande permitted himself a brief flicker of a smile. This would be even easier than he thought. "If you want to quit, Tommy, I can't stop you. Of course, you're walking away from a lot of money."

"I don't care about the money, Gus."

"You sure about that?"

"Fuck yes, I'm sure. However much it is, this ain't worth it. Shit, man, you *lied* to me. You said you could make things happen fast, but on my own terms. Well, now there's a cheesy pop record with my name on it that I don't even recognize, and a video that makes me cringe whenever I see it. I've been seeing the goddamn thing a lot, too."

"Good," Gus said. "That's my job."

"What, embarrassing me? Screwing me? Lying to me?"

"No, keeping you visible and exposed—and making you money. Remember, I didn't go looking for you. You came to me, and you sat in that same chair and said you loved Bob, but things just weren't happening and it was time for a change. So, I changed things."

"You didn't 'change' jackshit, you ruined it."

"C'mon, Tommy, get over yourself," DeGrande said, irritated in spite of himself. "You were just going to make the same fucking record all over again—the same record, you might recall, that you weren't even too crazy about yourself. It wasn't going to get you anywhere. So I just tweaked it enough to turn it into the record that *would* get you what you want."

"But it's not what I want!"

"Sure, it's not," Gus said, smirking. "Tommy, it's what every band wants whether they admit it or not. People always talk a good game about 'art' and 'integrity,' but sooner or later, everybody has to play the game. Even somebody as good as you, which is why people like you hire people like me. I know what you want better than anybody. Even you."

"Bullshit," Tommy interrupted.

Gus ignored him. "Do you have any idea how many people have tried to get me to manage them? Hundreds, maybe even thousands. I lose track. Every single one I turned down, except you, because you actually have talent. And even when you're trying to fuck up, it turns out okay. I could work for years and not come up with a marketing campaign as brilliant as that bonehead riot stunt you pulled out there. You can't *buy* the kind of publicity we're getting right now.

"Anyway," Gus concluded, "we still got work to do. I honestly don't understand why you're upset because things couldn't possibly be going better. The single's already in the top forty, the album is up to number fifty-seven. We need to get you back on the road to keep this going."

He paused to eye Tommy's hairless scalp, unconsciously patting his own head. "Interesting look, but I don't think it works. Maybe with the right wig—"

"Gus," his client finally interrupted, "what're you talking about? I'm done. I quit. I don't care. You want someone to tour for this record, get those mannequins from the video and send them out instead. That's what everybody wants to see."

DeGrande paused before continuing.

"All right, then. But you may want to reconsider. This album will only go so far on one single, and there's only so much Poly Brothers can do to promote it without your cooperation. Quit now and you'll be a one-hit wonder, never heard from again. Is that the career you had in mind? One and done?"

Tommy's only answer was to shrug. Gus decided it was finally time to raise the volume.

"For Christ's sake, will you just grow up?! Get back out there and do what you do, and let me handle the dirty work. I'm good at it and I've got no problem being the bad guy if you want to tell everybody I'm wrecking your life. Go write some more songs; convince everyone there's more to you than this horrible 'embarrassment' I've inflicted on you.

"Although," DeGrande continued after a brief pause, "the reviews are starting to come in, and I haven't seen a bad one yet. The critics are raving, all of them. They're calling you 'the new voice of a generation.'"

"Yeah, that's a laugh," Tommy spat. "So fucking what? Fuck the critics. Bunch of goddamned idiots, what do they know?"

"Tommy, sometimes you just have to accept that the entire world isn't wrong. You've got every musician's fucking *wet dream* right now. The public loves you and so do the critics, and that's not enough? Come on, you're getting away with it! If this album does well enough—and it will, if you cooperate—you'll be set. Then you can do whatever you want.

Producing the next record yourself might be the way to go on the follow-up. Then you'd really have complete control."

" 'Complete control,' " Tommy snorted derisively. "Sure I would, until I let the tapes out of my sight. Then you'd just hire another of your weasel remixers to ruin it."

"Like I said, every reviewer on earth seems to love this record. Anybody else would kill for these kind of reviews. Nothing wrong with good press, it don't hurt. But it don't pay the bills, either. There are only two kinds of records, hits and flops, and right now you've got the good kind."

Gus opened a desk drawer, pulled out an envelope and held it up. "This is your first royalty check, based on early sales reports—for eight thousand dollars. There are gonna be a lot more checks, for a lot more money. Do you really want to walk away?"

Tommy took the envelope, tore it in half and handed the pieces back to Gus. Then he said, "Fuck you"—very slowly, drawing both words out and almost crooning them—and laughed mirthlessly.

To Tommy's surprise, Gus laughed, too. It was not a pleasant sound; more like the cackle of a hyena settling in on its prey.

"Okay, then," the promoter said. "Fine."

He tossed the torn check into the trash, reached back into his drawer and extracted a thick sheaf of papers. Their management contract. Gus tossed it onto Tommy's lap and nodded.

"Go ahead," DeGrande said. "Burn it."

Tommy gave a start. "Just like that?"

"Just like that. I'll even throw in a light."

Gus produced a cigarette lighter and set it on the desk.

"Before you purge yourself of me, though, there's one more thing you should know. Keeping you out of jail over this business in Iowa is going to take lots of time and money. Between the criminal charges and whatever civil suits get filed, the whole thing will come to a couple hundred grand at least. Plus you could get a year or so in prison, to say nothing of all the time you'll have to spend hanging around courthouses or doing community service in Mason City, Iowa. Which might be worse than jail time, come to think of it.

"But I digress," Gus said. He leaned forward and flicked on the lighter, which flamed brightly. "Right now, I'm taking care of it. I look at Iowa as a promotional expense because it's helping sell the album while we figure out our next move.

"But if you quit," the promoter concluded, snapping off the lighter, "you're on your own."

Tommy was depressed after his talk with Gus. So he did exactly what his manager knew he'd do—put on a hat and took a long walk, at the end of which he just happened to find himself at the house of his drug connection. This, too, was well-timed.

As it turned out, his hometown connection was yet another Friend of Gus. After monitoring his client's heroin intake on the road, DeGrande decided that it was time to refine and cultivate Tommy's heroin habit to keep him under control. Tommy was simply too unpredictable a drunk.

But he'd be easier to handle as a junkie—especially with Gus controlling both the purse strings and the supply.

CHAPTER TWENTY-FIVE

Whatever its talent-scouting shortcomings, Poly Brothers Records could still be a formidable marketing juggernaut when given the right product in its pipeline. And now the label had not just one hot record to sell, but two: Arrowhead and TAB.

The hits hadn't arrived a moment too soon, either. Although Mo fended off his uncles' clandestine attempts to acquire Poly Brothers Publishing, Nehi and Adolph hadn't given up on re-acquiring their former empire's assets. They were still circling like vultures, trying to undermine the label through gossip and rumor. Mo spent a major chunk of each day putting out fires—reassuring nervous creditors or stockholders or band managers that, despite what they'd heard, everything really was just fine.

As soon as Poly Brothers had a few records on the charts again, he discovered that everyone found his claims a lot more convincing. And once it became obvious that TAB and Arrowhead were both going to stick and become enormous hits, he found he'd been magically transformed from village idiot to wise sage. Suddenly, people actually gave a shit what Mo Polydoroff thought.

The president sat in his office pondering this reversal of fortune while perusing a front-page story in the new issue of *Cashboard*. The headline read, "Turnaround at Poly Brothers: Hits by Old, New Acts Revive Label." As noted in the piece, Arrowhead had more than lived up to pre-release expectations, selling three million copies of *Rocks Off* in just over a month. Were Mo the sort of person who appreciated honorable gestures, he would have been thankful Arrowhead hadn't sandbagged him with an indifferent record, since this one was pure contractual obligation. Neither did he fully appreciate TAB, the gift hit Gus DeGrande coerced him into accepting. No, the only thing that really mattered to Mo was that *Cashboard* had to eat its own words:

> It wasn't that long ago that Poly Brothers Records' days as an industry pioneer seemed over (Cashboard, Nov. 19). But the breakthrough success of the North Carolina retro-rock trio TAB shows that the label may be regaining the touch that once made it among the most important nurturers of new talent among U.S. record companies.
>
> On the strength of the radio and video hit "Go As You Are," TAB's Grandiose/Poly Brothers debut album Chorus Verses Chorus has sold 378,000 units. This week, the album jumps seven spots on the Cashboard 200 to bullet at No. 14; 'Go As You Are' vaults six notches to No. 11 on the Hot 100 singles chart.
>
> Also enjoying a phenomenal chart run is veteran New York act Arrowhead, whose current Poly Brothers release Rocks Off is shaping up as the biggest album of its career. Rocks Off has logged five weeks at No. 1 and already passed the triple-platinum mark.
>
> Nevertheless, TAB is a more exciting story for the label. It marks a satisfying upswing for Poly Brothers president Mo Polydoroff, whose time running the label hasn't been entirely trouble-free.
>
> "The important thing about the success of this act is that it's all been completely organic and uncontrived," notes Polydoroff. "We haven't had to resort to any gimmicks or

arm-twisting. It was obvious from the start that TAB was a very special band, and they've made a very special record that people are really responding to. We're as surprised as anyone at how fast this happened. About all we're doing is shipping the records to stores."

All of which was organic, uncontrived, hundred-percent cornfed horseshit. Poly Brothers was pulling every string it had to make TAB a hit. A major reason their video was getting so much airtime was that the label piggybacked it onto Arrowhead's new video, promoting the two as a package deal. Poly Brothers let it be known that any channel wanting one had to play the other, which was enough to get the ball rolling. The Des Moines riot took care of the rest.

Of course, that was the off-the-record truth, and therefore nowhere in this story. That was the wonderful thing about *Cashboard.* The magazine's editorial policy was that the business of the music business was business, and it never met a hit record it didn't like. As long as business was good, whatever it took was fine by *Cashboard.* Had Mo credited TAB's breakthrough to the Easter Bunny, the magazine would've gladly taken him at his word.

Everyone in the industry understood that smoke-and-mirror fairy tales about "art," "special bands making special records" and "organic, uncontrived hits" were simply part of its protective coloration. No sense spoiling the illusion by letting the public in on too many of the gory details.

It was precisely this code of silence that kept Mo from telling *Cashboard* his next goal: to get the top two spots on the album chart simultaneously, a feat his label hadn't accomplished in fifteen years. He wanted TAB to knock Arrowhead down to number two, Poly Brothers' future overtaking its past—that would show everyone.

Mo wanted this all the more after the Des Moines riot, when Arrowhead tried to demand its pound of TAB's flesh from Poly Brothers.

The president had ample reason to despise Procter Silberman, Arrowhead's longtime manager, starting with his close friendship with Mo's uncles (who had signed his band twenty years earlier).

Moreover, Silberman was much smarter than Mo. That in itself wasn't unusual—most people were—but the manager pointedly made no effort to hide it from Polydoroff. The label chief was still smoldering from last year's company convention, at which Silberman regaled a table-full of executives with a story about some bad legal advice Mo once gave him regarding a foreign licensing deal.

"Good thing I'm a lawyer myself and know a little German copyright law, or it would've cost us a cool half-million," Silberman said, then delivered his punchline with a wink: "Especially since Mo here couldn't have made up the difference."

After Des Moines, however, the manager unwisely let his temper get the best of him. He was in no position to demand anything from DeGrande, who was booking Arrowhead's upcoming stadium tour; or even from TAB themselves, who Gus insisted on adding to the tour against Silberman's wishes. Instead of writing the whole thing off, he impulsively confronted Mo with an angry phone call in which he demanded Poly Brothers pay off his band's losses from the canceled Iowa concert—or else.

Mo laughed for a solid thirty seconds. The bluff was called. As long as Arrowhead's tour was a Grandiose Concerts production, Silberman wouldn't dare pull out and Polydoroff knew it. Nobody, but nobody, held a grudge like Gus DeGrande.

"That's a good one, Proc," the president said, purposely using a nickname he knew would irritate Silberman. "You think of any other dreams you want to come true, do let me know. Honestly, though, this sounds like a problem for your *next* record company."

Another missing detail from the *Cashboard* story was that TAB would be far less of a financial boon for Poly Brothers than anyone imagined. Gus had given the label a truly impressive hosing on their distribution deal. Just how impressive, Mo didn't realize until he saw the size of the first royalty check his accounting department was going to send to Grandiose—and thought it had to be a mistake. That's when Polydoroff finally went back and read their contract. What he found gave him a serious case of heartburn.

Poly Brothers' previous regime had done a careless, hasty job of negotiating with DeGrande, agreeing to outrageous terms on the assumption that the deal would never actually come to anything. Mo compounded the error by not paying attention when he still had the leverage to renegotiate (then again, he'd been a little busy fending off hostile takeover attempts). But Gus had paid very close attention to every last detail, carefully stacking the deck. While such distribution arrangements between large labels and small startup imprints usually favored the larger company, the Grandiose/Poly Brothers deal was the rare exception.

As stipulated in the contract, Grandiose made at least four dollars and twenty-five cents for every unit sold—even more than Poly Brothers typically earned in an ordinary pressing-and-distribution deal. The royalty rate escalated once TAB surpassed certain sales thresholds, topping out at five dollars per unit for everything beyond two million copies. With Poly Brothers' net profit coming to less than two dollars per unit, this was among the most one-sided such deals in industry history. Mo's label would do well on TAB, given the sales volume. DeGrande, though, would make a killing—with Poly Brothers doing all the manufacturing, distribution, marketing and promotional legwork.

Mo could have avoided this by paying Gus the hundred-thousand-dollar advance he'd asked for. That would've locked Grandiose Records' cut on every album sold to a flat two dollars and fifty cents, with no escalating clauses. It also would have given Poly Brothers an option on acquiring TAB's publishing rights (now worth millions) for the cut-rate price of another hundred-thousand dollars.

Eventually, not paying that initial hundred grand was going to cost the label about twenty-five million dollars in lost revenue—and there was nothing Mo could do about it, because DeGrande held all the cards now. If the president squawked and Gus made the spat public, it would involve a major loss of face, since TAB was being hailed as Poly Brothers' new franchise artist.

Mo's only option was to bite the bullet.

Had he ever been a recording artist, Mo would've realized that DeGrande was simply giving Poly Brothers a dose of its own medicine. The label routinely subjected its acts to unconscionable financial atrocities, just like every other record company. Polydoroff's predicament might have been amusing—except that Tommy, Ray and Michelle were the ones really paying the price.

The money coming in from TAB's record sales went first to Poly Brothers, which took its cut on the gross and earmarked four dollars and twenty-five cents per unit for Grandiose Productions. With Gus taking a cut as manager (twenty percent), another cut as record label (twenty percent), another as production company (ten percent) and still another as publishing company (fifteen percent), plus miscellaneous expenses (twenty percent), not much was left for the band. In fact, it came to just seventy-five cents per record sold.

Seventy-five cents, out of a wholesale price of ten dollars.

Tommy's share was higher than his bandmates, since he wrote the songs and therefore made additional income from publishing. He made thirty-five cents a record; Ray and Michelle each made twenty cents.

But the worst part was that, even after selling nearly four hundred thousand records, TAB's three members weren't even halfway to their first royalty check. In the music industry, virtually anything a record company spent on behalf of an artist was "recoupable"—meaning the artist had to pay for it out of his own royalties. Until those expenses were recouped, the artist got nothing.

Even netting such a tiny percentage of the gross, TAB would probably get out of debt—eventually. That was the only way anybody ever got paid, by selling so many millions of records that a label could no longer plausibly claim they were "still unrecouped." But even for acts doing substantial volume, creative accounting methods made getting paid about as simple as replacing a guitar string mid-song. If a deal was bad enough, in fact, a label could turn handsome profits while keeping the artist in hock forever.

In TAB's case, there were some extraordinary expenditures on top of the standard recording budget, video expenses and the cost of independent promoters to bribe radio stations and TV channels into playing the single and the video. TAB also had huge legal bills to keep its leader out of jail in Iowa, not to mention late-night van purchases, chartered helicopter flights and an open-ended line of credit with a heroin dealer, to say nothing of whatever else Gus tacked onto their account. The details were all spelled out in their contract. The one Tommy signed on behalf of his bandmates without even speaking to a lawyer. The one his manager offered to let him burn.

According to DeGrande's tally, TAB had run up over seven hundred thousand dollars in expenses before *Chorus Verses Chorus* even came out. At seventy-five cents a record, the band would have to sell almost a million albums before seeing its first penny of royalties.

Meanwhile, Gus was already in clover. While the band made just seventy-five cents per unit, he made three dollars and fifty cents—a rate that would soon go even higher thanks to the escalating clauses that increased his royalty rate (but not the band's). By the time *Chorus Verses Chorus* hit three hundred thousand units, TAB was still almost a half-million bucks in debt. But the manager had more than a million dollars coming from Poly Brothers, which would leave him three hundred fifty thousand dollars in the black.

Gus was actually sending checks to Tommy, Ray and Michelle. But that was just to keep the peace because he counted the money as salaries, and therefore as another recoupable expense. They were, in effect, paying to get money they had coming, which was being added to their debt.

What they didn't know, he figured, wouldn't hurt 'em.

CHAPTER TWENTY-SIX

The same *Cashboard* story about TAB, Arrowhead and Poly Brothers left Ken Morrison feeling vaguely queasy. He didn't know all the gory details, but was familiar with enough of the off-the-record manipulations to know that the band's success was anything but "organic and uncontrived." Hit records were a lot like pork sausage; the more you knew about the process, the less savory the end product tended to be.

The critic was reminded of this metaphor after tracking down Tommy for their first conversation since Des Moines. The bandleader wasn't answering his phone, so Ken gave up trying to call and started dropping by The Crypt several times a day, finally catching him there on the fifth try. Tommy was sitting on his porch eating a greasy sausage biscuit as Ken drove up. Breakfast. It was 3:45 in the afternoon.

Between his draftee-length crewcut and generally haggard appearance, Tommy was almost unrecognizable. He sat hunched over and sideways in a broken wooden chair, huddled against a nonexistent chill in the sunlight.

"Tommy, you're always eating some gourmet food item whenever I come around," Ken said, settling into a rocking chair beside him. "I didn't even expect you'd be awake yet."

Tommy didn't answer, just kept slowly chewing as he leveled a vacant gaze at his visitor. It was the sort of look one gave to acknowledge that one was no longer the only person standing in line at a men's room urinal.

"Want one?" he finally asked, holding out his half-eaten biscuit, which practically dripped congealed ninety-weight grease. Ken stifled a gag.

"Thanks, I already ate."

"What?"

"Huh?"

"What," Tommy asked, "did you eat?"

"Oh. Um…well, nothing too exciting. Sandwich, apple, candy bar, coffee chaser. The standard gulp-it-down-at-your-desk lunch."

"What kind?"

"What?"

"What kind," Tommy asked, "of sandwich?"

"Salami," Ken said. "Two slices, cheese and mustard on wheat—not white—bread. Followed by a Butterfinger and a Golden Delicious apple. I believe the coffee was Folger's, but couldn't swear to it."

"Is that all?"

"There might've been a Coke in there somewhere, too," Ken said. "Maybe some chips, maybe even a pretentious crouton or two. I forget. Why?"

"You should keep track of these things, Ken. Pay more attention to what you eat, control what you can. Very important."

"Mm-hmm," the critic said, still not quite believing that he was being lectured about nutrition by someone eating processed pork product. "Looks like you're in control of that biscuit, anyway."

"You know it," Tommy said, taking another bite.

While he ate, Ken studied the tree in the front yard and remembered the bandleader's mid-interview gunplay. Fortunately, today Tommy wore the ratty I'M WITH STUPID T-shirt Ray bought him on the road; nothing with pockets big enough to conceal weaponry.

"So, Tommy," Ken began, "now that we've covered the inadequacies of my eating habits, let's talk about you. How've you been? Why'd you shave your head? And what the hell happened with this record and this tour and this riot?"

"I...can't talk about it."

"You can't?"

"Nope. Lawyers, lawsuits, arrest warrants, restraining orders—it's all real fucked-up and complicated. Mostly, I have to stay away from Iowa."

"At least it's someplace easy to stay away from. Better Des Moines than, say, New York."

"Yeah, well, New York didn't do me much good, either. That's where that goddamned record got made."

"That's another thing. I was...surprised when I heard it. Sure didn't sound anything like I expected. What happened with that?"

"Can't talk about that, either."

"C'mon, Tommy, why not?"

"Because I can't tell you what the fuck happened, exactly—I'm still not sure myself. We're up there recording, then we're out on the road and next thing I know, there's this record and this video and all this crazy shit goin' on, and I'm supposed to go out and jerk off in front of Arrowhead's crowd. So I tried to...you know, change things. But all I did was make everything even more like it was than before, only more fucked up."

"What do you mean?"

"Figure it out."

"I'd rather not guess."

"Ken," Tommy sighed wearily, "For the last time—no fucking comment, okay?"

The critic whistled in mock-amazement. "Wow, *that's* a new one. Jesus, Tommy, I've never known you to be at a loss for words about anything. Especially yourself."

"Yeah...well..."

Tommy looked at Ken as he stuck a cigarette in his mouth and lit up. He had a way of sizing people up by staring from under cover of exhaled smoke. The gesture was supposed to look casual, but his eyes always narrowed when he did it.

"Everything's different now," he said, finally looking away. "Isn't it? I've got a manager and a video and a hit record and a subpoena, and I don't know what the fuck I should do about any of it. Probably just run away."

Tommy hauled himself to his feet, tossed the remains of his biscuit into Ken's lap and stepped off the porch.

"I've gotta go," he said. "Door's open and there's a whole bag of biscuits in the 'fridge, if you want any. Beer, too."

Then he turned and trudged off toward the woods. Halfway across the yard, in the shadow of his target tree, Tommy paused and turned around.

"Oh, and by the way—the answer to your next question is, 'No.'"

"How do you know the question?" Ken said.

"I don't, but that's still the answer. I can't tell you anything anymore, Ken. From here on out, you're just gonna have to pay attention."

Ken went back to the office and stared at his computer screen. It was still just as blank as when he left. He'd hoped this review would write itself, since Tommy hadn't been any help. No such luck.

The task at hand should have been simple enough—a review of TAB's album. The critic knew Tommy hated it, and wanted to hate it just as much himself. But he wasn't having much luck, even after three-dozen listens. There were times he had to admit it actually wasn't bad. Pretty good, in fact. Really good. Maybe even as great as every other critic in the country seemed to think.

It all came down to perspective. When he listened with his heart, Ken agreed that *Chorus Verses Chorus* sounded like a faint, distorted echo of Tommy's vision. Or rather, a cleaned-up echo. On-stage, the bandleader thrived on dissonance, unleashing chaotic energy by colliding together things that shouldn't fit. His genius was building a framework in which musical anomalies could co-exist—metallic jazz, classical rockabilly, sensual punk rock.

Chorus Verses Chorus blunted Tommy's wild unpredictability, scraping away the rough edges and leaving just the bubblegum at the center. At heart, the kid really was a popular artist whose biggest influences were hit records. Still, the obvious pop stuff was only one small piece of a very complicated puzzle.

The rub was that few people realized this. The people who knew TAB best didn't believe that *Chorus Verses Chorus* fit their idea of the band because it somehow seemed...wrong. Like a Picasso painting reduced to stick figures, with smiley faces pasted over the screaming, twisted mouths.

But the millions of people hearing TAB for the first time had only this record to go on. When Ken listened as one of them—with just his ears and not his heart, setting preconceptions aside as best he could—he had to admit that *Chorus Verses Chorus* sounded incredible. Sledgehammer hooks and angelic singing, big and shiny and obvious as a chartreuse Cadillac whizzing by. Its songs just leapt out of the radio, demanding to be heard. In this light, Tommy's tendency toward vague and evasive lyrics (which he claimed to dash off with a minimum of thought, almost as a point of pride) actually worked in the album's favor. When pressed about what specific songs meant, he was prone to make statements like, "That's a song where I was trying to say that I, um, didn't have anything to say."

Accordingly, *Chorus Verses Chorus* was full of snappy soundbites that didn't really add up to much of anything. One reviewer dubbed the lyrics "pun rock": "Don't get it let you down," "All I'll ever try is your patience," "If you read my mind, I'll write whatever you want," "Blow blow blow your mind, gently down the stream." At the same time, the intensity of the performances made all the songs *sound* as if they meant something terribly profound. The beauty was, they meant as much or as little as anybody wanted them to, every song a perfect blank slate. Or a mirror.

After comparing it with Clay Dickerson's rough mixes of the same tracks, Ken actually preferred the official album in some respects. The Dickerson version was truer to Tommy's conception of himself, and was so noisy and idiosyncratic it excluded the rest of the world. Gus, on the other hand, used Geoff Baker's studio wizardry to seize upon the sliver of Tommy's vision that was most accessible and blow it up to the size of a skyscraper. Where the Dickerson version was music for a few devoted fans, this was music for stadiums.

Chorus Verses Chorus was bold, Ken had to admit. Had Tommy been willing to try it himself—to see how much mainstreaming his music could endure, yet remain his—it might have even qualified as courageous. Instead, it was done for (or rather, *to*) him behind his back. Critics all over the country were hailing the bandleader as "a bold new voice" for evoking a sense of youthful alienation and angst that he never meant. To those aware of the compromises and betrayals involved, *Chorus Verses Chorus* sounded hollow to the core. But millions of other people found it resonant with their own lives and fears.

So: How on earth to review this record? Should Ken buck conventional wisdom, or not? Did it really even matter what wasn't there? And did the ends justify the means? Variations on these questions were being hotly debated around town. TAB's former peers in the local music community had their fangs out. Now that Tommy's band had left them behind, the consensus was that he sold out at the first opportunity.

Not that it was hurting business any. No matter what the hipsters thought, there weren't enough of them to matter. They were all downtown. Out at the suburban malls to the north, the kids in Tommy's hometown were snapping up *Chorus Verses Chorus* just like kids in every other town in America.

And Ken still hadn't reviewed TAB's album for the *Daily News*. He put off his editor for as long as he could—so long that she was threatening to run a syndicated wire piece from another newspaper. Now, the critic was trapped between the proverbial rock and a hard place.

Make that a *Rock Slide* and a hard place. With TAB on the way up and about to resume touring, the magazine wanted a longer feature on the latest sensation. By the time the story ran, the band would be at number one or close to it—and almost surely on the cover.

Ordinarily, one of the magazine's own staff writers would handle a cover story. But both *Rock Slide* and *Bounce* wanted an exclusive, which meant Gus DeGrande was in a position to set conditions. His primary demand was choice of writer. While *Bounce* refused to grant that privilege, *Rock Slide* said yes. Figuring that Ken would be easier to keep in line than a stranger without an emotional investment in the band, DeGrande told the magazine to direct the assignment to TAB's hometown critic.

The cover of *Rock Slide:* Bands dreamed about it, but writers did, too. Prestige, national attention and the best credit a critic could have—all worth far more than the actual seventy-five hundred dollar fee (plus expenses). It was something Ken would have killed for not too long ago. But now that the opportunity was at hand, he found himself tied in knots. He was torn between conflicting loyalties to Tommy, Bob and even (goddamn him for letting this happen) Gus, never mind the people who actually read him. Ken couldn't make up his mind. TAB's record was too good to dismiss out of hand. It was also, from his viewpoint, too flawed to endorse.

This was very bad, the cardinal sin of his profession: Thou shalt not get so personally invested that thy judgment becomes clouded. Ken had rationalized his earlier transgressions by brushing them off as minor sins. But this was different. Parroting DeGrande's TAB party line on the cover of the biggest rock magazine in the world when he knew better went beyond anything he could brush off. This was shilling, pure and simple.

If he went through with it, Ken knew, there would be no turning back.

Unsure what else to do, the critic called Bob Porter at Each. He wasn't looking for advice, exactly—this was one dilemma he didn't see how he could talk over with anybody, least of all Bob. He simply wanted to talk to someone whose opinions about TAB were as conflicted as his own.

"Each."

"Hey."

"Hey, yourself."

"What up?"

"Same ol' shit. Too many bills, not enough customers and everything sucks, as usual."

"Not if you're Gus DeGrande. You see that story in *Cashboard?*"

"Oh, yeah. Just what that bastard needed, a bunch more money."

"Should've been you."

"Yep," Bob sighed, then changed the subject. "So are you gonna do the *Rock Slide* story on TAB?"

"How'd you know about that?" Ken asked, surprised.

"Oh…I gots my sources."

"They must be better than mine, because they didn't even call until today."

"And?"

"And it's a tossup which is more embarrassing—how much they pay, or how little actual work is involved."

"This is something to complain about?" the clubowner asked.

"Well…no. But I still can't decide if I'm gonna do it."

"What are you, nuts?"

"Probably."

"You must be. What's to decide?"

"See, that's hard to explain," Ken said. "Everything I write on TAB seems to be just another cog in DeGrande's big master plan. I'm starting to feel like his goddamned publicist, especially since certain...you know, 'subjects' seem to be off-limits. There's this whole weird side to Tommy and Gus that nobody wants to talk about. It's like Tommy's been taken prisoner or something. Here he's got a huge hit record—which is supposedly what he wanted—and he seems just miserable. Their album will probably be number one in another few weeks."

"So I hear," Bob said. "You like it?"

"Well, that's a whole 'nother thing. I can't decide. I mean, it sounds great on the radio and all, but it's so...different. It doesn't sound like TAB, it sounds like a top-forty remix engineer's focus group version of TAB. Does that make any sense?"

"I guess."

"So what do *you* think of it?"

"Depends," the clubowner said. "Are we on or off the record?"

"Off, of course. Why?"

"Because," Bob said, "Gus DeGrande just hired me as TAB's new tour manager."

Chapter Twenty-Seven

For some time, it was obvious that somebody had it in for Each because strange things kept happening, too many to be coincidental. There were the DUI checkpoints the Raleigh police set up on the roads leading away from the club—not just once, but three straight weekends. Once word got out that Each was a target, the crowds dried up and the people who did come didn't drink.

Ugly rumors started going around, too: That Each had again become a front for a drug ring, that Bob Porter was ripping off bands, even that a woman was gang-raped in the bathroom. Although none of the gossip was true, it eroded the club's crowds even further.

Then the one night during the previous month when Bob wasn't there, Each got busted for serving beer to a minor. The liquor board spanked him hard for that one, a two-thousand-dollar fine and one year's probation. One more violation, and Each would lose its liquor license. But the final straw was a property tax bill delivering the news that the lot Each occupied had somehow just been reappraised for triple its previous value. The taxes went up accordingly: seven thousand dollars, due within thirty days.

Bob didn't have the money, or any realistic prospects for getting it anytime soon. He was already leveraged to the hilt, just barely hanging on. The fine from the liquor board was bad enough. But this was enough to bring on debtors' prison.

Sitting at his desk, the clubowner stared at the tax bill and sighed. The phone rang and he picked it up without taking his eyes off the piece of paper on his desk.

"Each."

"Bob?"

"Speaking."

"Gus DeGrande here."

Bob winced and rubbed his eyes as a lightbulb flickered on in the back of his mind. He figured the timing of this call was no coincidence.

"Gus," he answered flatly, without enthusiasm. "What an unexpected…well, *pleasure* it is to hear from you. How are you?"

"Couldn't be better. How's the bar business?"

"Swell, Gus, just swell."

"Had any good bands in there lately?"

"Nobody you'd be interested in, I don't think," Bob replied, failing to suppress the bitter edge from his voice. Since congratulating DeGrande on TAB's success was more than he could stomach, the clubowner decided to cut the obligatory chit-chat interlude short. "So Gus—what can I do for you?"

"Actually, I was wondering what I could do for you. I understand you have a little problem."

"And what 'little problem' would that be?"

"I know of several: Your liquor license is on probation; your crowds have sucked lately; and if the rumor I just heard is true, your property was recently reappraised and you owe the city a lot more taxes than you were counting on."

"None of which you had a thing to do with, eh?"

"I only know what I see and hear."

"Uh huh," Bob said skeptically. "Yeah. Right. Look, Gus, I'm not a bigshot like you. I just run a bar, and yes, I've got a few 'little problems,' as you put it. But what else is new? That's the bar biz, and have you ever met a happy bar owner?"

"Can't say I have."

"Me neither. You wanna know why?"

"Sure."

"'Cause it's bad for business. People drink more when they're unhappy and pissed-off, and the last thing they want to see pouring booze is a smiling face." The clubowner had no idea why he was telling Gus any of this. "So anyway," he continued, on a roll and not even trying to stifle his anger anymore, "I'm deeply touched that you care, Gus. Really. It's a gesture I'll treasure always. Okay? Now then, I assume you didn't really call to chat about the bar business…"

"No…"

"…Or to fill me in on your latest triumphs with a band you fucking stole right out from under me…"

"Now Bob, it wasn't like that—"

"Save it for the war crimes tribunal, Gus. You didn't call to apologize, either. So what the fuck do you want?"

"You."

"Come again?"

"Bob," the promoter said, "I want to hire you."

Bob cackled in disbelief. He stood up and stretched, standing on his toes while keeping the receiver to his ear. "You can't be serious," he said.

"Oh, but I am. TAB needs a tour manager, and you need a job."

"TAB may need a tour manager—fuck, Tommy must need a therapist after everything you've done to him—but I don't need a job. I've gotten through worse than this before."

"You can bluff all you want, Bob, but tax collectors tend to be pretty stubborn about getting their money. Soon as you miss the payment deadline, the city will foreclose on you."

"Then I'll appeal it, and if they close me down, I'll just do something else. I'd dig ditches—hell, I'd fucking *starve*—before I'd work for you."

"Before you say no, at least listen to what I'm offering: thirty thousand dollars up-front for three months, with an option for me to put you on retainer for the rest of the year if everybody's happy at the end of the tour. That should be enough to get you out of debt— although I'd ditch that place if I were you. But if you want to keep running Each, I'll take care of your liquor license problems and see to it that the cops lay off."

"Gosh, it sure is nice to know who's been leaning on me lately, Gus. How? Why? Do you own the fucking government and the police department, too?"

"Let's just say I've got plenty of friends in both places."

"You must," Bob said, "to have stayed out of prison for this long. Now I know why I gave up voting."

"The only thing voting gets you is jury duty," DeGrande said. "Politicians tend to be more responsive to your concerns if you buy 'em instead of just vote for 'em."

Bob couldn't help but laugh at the promoter's shamelessness. "You're amazing, Gus, truly one of a kind," he said. "I thought guys like you only existed in spy flicks. You really want me to work for you?"

"Yes."

"You could get anybody. Why me?"

"Because the band trusts you."

"And they don't trust you," Bob said.

"Of course not. Would you?"

"Fuck, no. Christ, I can't believe I haven't hung up on your sorry ass yet."

"But you haven't. And you still haven't given me an answer."

"You're right, Gus, I haven't. So let's see: First you screwed me and stole my band, then you screwed them. Then you screwed me again, tried to put me out of business. And now that the band has turned out to be more of a handful than you thought they'd be, you want me to come bail you out. Wow, that's a tough one. So listen closely, 'cause I'm only saying this once. The answer is…*fuck…you!*"

The clubowner slammed the phone down for emphasis, so hard his hand hurt, and started counting the seconds. The phone rang again just as he reached twelve, and Bob picked it up without saying anything.

"I don't think you understand me, Bob."

"Sure, I do. Everything's a big game, and we're all just pawns to you. You think you can buy anyone. Even me."

"Everybody's got their price," DeGrande said, "and so do you. Yours isn't even all that high."

"Oh, I'm cheap, am I?"

"Mm hmm. Thirty grand is what I already owe you. I tried to give it to you once, but you wouldn't take it. Will you now?"

"Not a chance."

"You're sure?"

"Positive."

"As I expected," the promoter said with a dramatic sigh, "you continue to have this martyr complex and won't accept anything to save yourself. But I think you will if it involves saving someone else, too."

"Who, Tommy? Nah, he's beyond saving."

"No," Gus said. "I'm talking about your cousin Mitch."

Bob gave a start, and sat back down. "What are you talking about? He's in the witness protection program. I haven't seen him in years. I don't know where he is. I don't even know what his name is anymore."

"I do," Gus said ominously. "And I know he's been violating the terms of his probation, which is enough to get him in some serious trouble with the feds. I also know some very nasty people who, thanks to your cousin, are doing hard time in prison and would love to find him when they get out."

Bob was stunned. "Are you telling me," he rasped incredulously, "that you're gonna have this cousin I haven't seen in years *killed* if I don't take this job?"

"No. I'm going to put out the word that you know his alias and his whereabouts. Soon after that, some very bad guys will show up on your doorstep with a few questions. If you try to run and hide, they'll find you. And if you want to make things difficult, they'll have no qualms about torturing it out of you. Either way, you'll be dead and so will he."

"But I don't know anything!" Bob protested.

"Brian Satterfield in Tuscon, Arizona. Now you do."

Bob tried to say something, but couldn't. He was almost gasping for breath. All he could finally stammer was, "How?..."

"All those friends of mine in law enforcement and government," Gus said. "It's not easy to find out things like this without tipping off the wrong people that you know."

"I'll bet," the clubowner said, trying to think of a way out. He couldn't.

"You want to do this," DeGrande pressed. "You must, or you would've hung up already. So...here we are. Have you reconsidered?"

"Yes." It was all Bob could think to say. Just uttering that one word felt as if he'd given a speech.

"Good," the promoter said, downshifting to a soothing tone. "This is the right thing to do, Bob. Trust me, there are a lot of vicious bastards out there who don't know when or where to stop."

"You're right, Gus. There are a lot of vicious bastards out there who don't know when or where to stop."

Only later did it occur to Bob that he should've demanded more money. But the entire exchange left him in too deep a fog to trifle with details as mundane as filthy lucre. Anyway, what was a few grand between mortal enemies? Mere pocket change in the psychic exchange rate.

DeGrande would have happily paid much, much more, because Bob solved all kinds of problems. His reentry made TAB more willing to get back on the road—which was to say, willing at all. Only Ray seemed to have any enthusiasm for carrying on. Years of struggling in terrible bands left the drummer hungry for a shot like this. But it took Bob to convince Tommy to do the Arrowhead tour. It was now a co-headlining bill, featuring the two hottest bands in the country. Naturally, there were some conditions.

"No more videos," Tommy said. "This is the only tour we'll do for this record, and I get complete control on the next one. I produce it, you keep all your little 'helpers' away and it gets put out exactly the way I give it to you."

"Done," Gus said. It's possible he even meant it.

With Bob and Tommy both in, Michelle also came around on touring, although she had some conditions of her own. The bassist wanted not just a separate room, nor just a separate hotel, but a separate *city* for each date—a private chartered flight immediately following each performance, to the next stop on the itinerary. She had a pretty good idea about the sort of post-show activities this tour would involve and didn't want to be anywhere in the vicinity. Michelle also wanted an option to walk from TAB at the end of the tour, no questions asked. In fact, she told Gus, she was pretty sure she'd quit no matter what happened.

"No problem," the manager said, and he definitely did mean this one. Not being a musician himself, Gus didn't understand the crucial role Michelle played in TAB and considered her expendable. She just played bass, after all. For now, DeGrande was more concerned with image control; the carefully maintained illusion might be damaged if somebody were to quit TAB so soon after the record came out.

Finally, Ken Morrison agreed to do the *Rock Slide* cover story on TAB. If Bob was working for DeGrande, he figured, all was forgiven—or the fix was in. Either way, the critic wanted a piece of it. Now that he had some company in the soul-selling department, no way was he bailing.

So by saying yes, Bob made up three other people's minds, too. All that, and he would even do live sound engineering for TAB on tour, as per Tommy's request.

Life was good.

Life was so good, in fact, that Gus impulsively decided to take a quick jaunt out to Las Vegas. He was on a roll with TAB and figured the time was ripe for reversing the one losing streak that remained on his books. His gambling trips hadn't been going so well lately, the last one having cost him almost eighty thousand dollars. Then again, they never went well. Gus was a rotten gambler, which was peculiar considering how he made his living. Every concert a promoter booked was a gamble, but not the way Gus did business. When it came to booking shows, DeGrande understood how to stack the deck in his own favor.

As shrewdly as he played people, however, the promoter simply could not play poker. His business skills at controlling situations and minimizing risks did not transpose well to literal wagering. Giving up control ran counter to every instinct Gus had, yet a certain amount of letting go was necessary to gamble successfully. He could never relax and let down his guard enough to pick up on a card game's rhythm— the ebb and flow that said when to press, and when to back off. All Gus knew how to do was press and press harder, an instinct that frequently took him over a cliff at the card table.

Successful gambling also required a belief in luck, and DeGrande's entire career had been a series of draconian measures intended to render luck irrelevant. Trusting to blind chance was something Gus never, ever did. Except on his trips to Las Vegas.

Gus went there often because he was a compulsive (as well as terrible) gambler. More than once, gaming losses put his company on shaky financial ground. The promoter had never gone completely broke. But thanks to his habit, Grandiose wasn't as flush as most outsiders thought. DeGrande always rebounded quickly from his mishaps, an advantage of running a vertically integrated, multi-tiered business. He could move money around and hide debts, staying a step ahead of bill collectors and taxmen whenever he gambled his way into cash-flow difficulties.

Because he kept getting off the hook, Gus eventually came to believe these losses were no big deal—even though they ran to six (and occasionally even seven) figures every year. Driven by ego, the promoter kept coming back for more, convinced he could master gambling the same way he mastered the music business.

Anyway, with so much cash about to pour in from TAB, Gus figured he could afford a pointless extravagance or two. Out in Las Vegas, they were expecting him.

There was no way he could lose this one. No way, no how.

The promoter was playing a private game of blackjack, straight-up and one on one. He'd had a tough night, followed by an even tougher morning. Gus was sweating heavily and had been for some time, ever since he ran through the one hundred thousand dollars in cash he brought in a briefcase.

Losing that first hundred grand hadn't taken very long, maybe an hour and a half. It was hard to tell because there were no clocks in here (and he'd left his watch up in his room). He actually won a few games early, then lost a few more and started doubling up on every bet to try and recoup. Then he got so mesmerized by the cards and the chips and the scotch passing in front of him that he hadn't even noticed his money disappearing until it was all gone.

He wired for another hundred thousand, lost that even faster and wired for more. After a while, Gus stopped wiring back for money or even keeping track and began signing IOU's. And he continued to press, praying for a sure thing he could bet the farm on.

A game just like this one.

The game began about as well as it could have. The dealer threw Gus two black aces, the club and the spade. Of the two cards the house took, the one showing was a six of diamonds. The dealer paused to see if DeGrande wanted to raise his bet by splitting his hand.

They were off the floor of the main casino and behind closed doors in a private room, where all the high rollers went. Just the two of them, Gus and the dealer, with a waiter ferrying in a steady stream of scotch and the casino manager checking in periodically. The room was dark and windowless and always felt like the middle of the night.

It was actually eleven forty-five in the morning, and Gus did indeed want to raise his bet. "Split 'em," he said. Now Gus had two hands going, each with an ace, and had doubled his bet from fifty to one hundred thousand dollars. The dealer still had six showing.

Next card, the dealer gave Gus…another ace, the diamond. Three aces. He gasped and felt his heartbeat quicken. "Split 'em again," he said.

Now Gus had three hands going—three aces, each representing either one or eleven points—and the bet was up to two hundred thousand dollars. He didn't see how he could lose. "Wait a minute," he said, stopping the dealer before he gave any more cards. The dealer paused, a quizzical look on his face as the promoter stared hard at the cards. He decided to put the hammer down.

"I'd like to raise my bet," Gus said. "Can I?"

The dealer pondered this, glancing in the direction of the manager. "It would be against house rules, Mr. DeGrande," he said. "But we've made exceptions before. I suppose it would depend on just how high you wanted to go."

Gus turned to rummage through his briefcase, and took out a pen and a piece of Grandiose Productions stationary. In bold strokes, he wrote out a promissory note beneath the gold "GP" logo and handed it over.

The man did a doubletake when he saw the amount: two million dollars.

"I'll, uh…have to get this approved," he murmured, signaling for the manager. The dealer was under standing instructions to let the promoter bet however much he wanted. His bosses knew Gus well, and always agreed to waive the house limit for him. Even if they took a hit now and then, they knew they'd come out ahead in the long run if they gave DeGrande all the rope he asked for and stayed out of his way.

Nevertheless, a seven-figure bet was different—especially one based on a handwritten note, in the middle of a game. The casino staffers moved away from the table and conferred in whispered tones as Gus looked on anxiously. He planned to wipe out his last three years of gambling debts with this one game and was worried they wouldn't take the bet.

The manager picked up a phone and had a brief conversation before conferring again with the dealer. Finally, he hung up, and the dealer came back to the table and nodded. Gus smiled broadly.

"You're sure you want to do this, Mr. DeGrande?" the casino manager asked, standing behind the dealer.

"Oh, yeah," Gus said, rubbing his palms together.

"Okay, then." The manager gave a slight bow and stepped back.

The dealer picked the cards back up and resumed dealing. First, he threw the nine of hearts at the ace of clubs. Twenty points.

"I like that," Gus murmured.

Next card, to go with the ace of spades—another nine, the diamond. DeGrande gasped. Now he had twenty points on two different hands.

"Yes!"

Finally, the ace of diamonds got another card. But this one wasn't so good, four of hearts. That left him at either five or fifteen points.

"Ouch," Gus winced, then pondered. It was an easy decision. "Hit me again."

Another card landed on the table, this one fortuitous: five of clubs. Gus didn't say anything, just smiled broadly. Now he was sitting on an almost-unbeatable twenty on three different hands—with two million bucks on the table.

"Anyway I could raise the bet again?" he asked, jokingly. The manager gave a small, strained smile. A few beads of sweat broke out on the dealer's forehead.

"Only if you want to split those nines," the dealer said.

"Thanks, no," Gus said, perfectly content to hold on to three twenties. "I'll stick."

His smile grew even broader when the dealer revealed his hole card: ten of hearts. Now the house had sixteen points, not a good number to be sitting on, and had to take another card. If it was anything other than a five—and Gus already had the five of clubs, so there was one less that could turn up—he was going to win two million dollars.

This had to be the one. *Maybe,* he daydreamed, *I'll get out of band management and go into gambling full-time.*

The dealer started to deal, then had a thought. What the hell, he was going to get fired over this anyway.

"Here," the man said to Gus, gesturing toward the deck, "you deal the card."

The promoter's smile somehow widened. "A noble gesture, sir," he said with mock solemnity as he picked up the deck. "You are a gentleman and a scholar and a fine sport."

I am going to enjoy this, he thought to himself.

Gus wanted to see the look on the dealer's face when he gave away two million bucks. So he peeled off the top card and threw it down without even looking to see what it was. He felt that sure it was a lock.

The promoter kept his eyes trained on the dealer's face to watch his reaction, expecting to see guarded dismay. Instead, he saw wide-eyed astonishment.

Puzzled, Gus's eyes moved to the manager, whose smile had shifted from strained to faintly predatory. The manager was walking toward the table, where he reached past the dealer to pick up DeGrande's promissory note, then moved briskly out the door.

Only then did Gus look down to see the card: five of spades. Without a single face card, the house had improbably turned up twenty-one—the only thing that beat his three twenties.

Gus was busted.

CHAPTER TWENTY-EIGHT

While Gus crashed, TAB practiced, convening for its first post-Des Moines rehearsal at Each. Bob Porter and Ken Morrison both dutifully attended—the clubowner to mix sound, the critic to take notes for his *Rock Slide* piece.

Ray arrived first, twenty minutes before the appointed hour. He busied himself setting up his drumkit, then noodled around playing rimshots, keeping his distance from Bob. Some ill will remained between them, because Bob knew the drummer had pushed hardest for TAB to go over to DeGrande.

Michelle showed up next, walking through the door at three o'clock on the dot. After setting up her bass and plunking for a few minutes, she retreated to the bar and perched on a stool drinking root beer through a straw. Even though it was dark inside, she kept her sunglasses on.

Just about the time Bob wondered if he should drive out to The Crypt, Tommy appeared in the room as if by transport. Not having seen him in a while, everyone was shocked at his wraith-like bearing. His eyes appeared to be receding into his head, which would've looked just like a skull if not for the dark hair slowly returning to his scalp. Ken figured the biscuit he watched Tommy eat on his porch the previous week was the last solid food he'd consumed.

Even weirder, Tommy wore a conservative double-breasted gray suit. His tie was a subdued shade of red, done up in a crisp Windsor knot; his shoes a battered pair of black wingtips. The jacket and pants were sharply pressed and creased, the ensemble hanging from Tommy's thin frame as if his bones were made of coathangers. Ken started to make a crack about the bandleader bucking to make partner, but the words died in his throat.

"Jesus, Tommy," Bob murmured.

Tommy didn't even look at any of them; just slowly carried an electric guitar to the club's small stage and hopped up. He plugged in and started deliberately strumming a vaguely familiar melody. Michelle shrugged and followed him onstage with her bass.

No one else recognized the song, but the bassist figured out the changes first and glided in with a rudimentary bassline. It took only a few beats for her to lock in; this was a slow song. Ray came in last, blowing right past the beat. He had to slow down to catch up, which took a bit of effort. The drummer's onstage fake-it skills were rusty.

Tommy kept right on strumming without acknowledging his bandmates, who figured this must be just a warm-up instrumental to riff on—right up to the point where he began to sing. This was a song TAB hadn't played in eons. It wasn't one of their regular covers, just a goofy old chestnut they sometimes dusted off and trashed for laughs. But there was nothing the least bit funny about this rendition. Tommy stepped to the microphone and began to croon in the lowest part of his still-intact choirboy tenor, more Frank Sinatra than Sid Vicious. It took a couple of lines before everyone else in the room recognized…"My Way," maybe the corniest statement of purpose ever.

As Tommy testified about facing the final curtain, traveling *each* and every *highway,* and doing it "myyYYYYYyy waaaaAAAAAAaaaay," Ray, Bob and Michelle all exchanged looks, as each had variations on the same thought simultaneously: *The boy has lost his fucking mind.*

Ken, on the other hand, thought it was brilliant. Cheesy, to be sure, but not without an edge of desperation; which made it…ironic. In years to come, the critic would actually remember this cover of "My Way" as one of his favorite TAB moments and wish he had it on tape.

He would also realize that, given what happened later, Tommy wasn't being ironic at all.

Gus put the phone down. The receiver felt as if it weighed several tons, the burden of news Mo Polydoroff had just dropped on him.

The good news was that TAB had, as expected, reached number one on the *Cashboard* chart, bumping Arrowhead down to number two. Sales were over a million and climbing, stoked by radio and video play of "Go As You Are." Even with TAB off the road, Poly Brothers' marketing machine had come through.

"Amazing, that we pulled this off without any touring," enthused Mo.

"Yes, amazing," Gus agreed. And he was just about to broach some logistical issues when Mo dropped the bad news on him: The Arrowhead-TAB tour was off.

The news would hit the next day's papers that Arrowhead singer Perry Rose had fallen off the wagon. After a decade of abstinence, he just went shopping, bought some heroin, took it home, shot it up and overdosed. No one knew why. Rose even made the classic backsliding "recovered" junkie's mistake of taking the same high dosage he'd been accustomed to when shooting up every day. Only this time, his resistance was lower and it nearly killed him.

"Guess he forgot that a little dab'll do ya," Polydoroff quipped.

Fortunately for Rose, his long-suffering wife discovered his comatose body before too much time elapsed and rushed him to the emergency room. She found the singer passed out on the marble floor of their upstairs bathroom, head on the floor by the toilet, a bandanna still clenched between his teeth, syringe still in his arm.

While it appeared Rose would recover, he was going to be out of commission for a few months. Mo actually viewed this as a positive development and (after the obligatory heartfelt expression of sincere concern) said as much.

"Now Arrowhead is completely out of our way," the president said. "We'll quit working their record and let it coast, and TAB will have everyone's full attention. So I think we should change gears—don't try stadiums yet. Pull back and set up a smaller TAB arena tour, maybe do another video."

"I'll have to get back to you, Mo," Gus said, hanging up.

For once, Mo was actually right. There was little crossover or empathy between TAB's self-conscious teenage following and Arrowhead's older blue-collar crowd. So packaging them together accomplished nothing beyond fattening the attendance. Video had gotten TAB this far, but it was time to back that up with some actual facetime. Doing it on their own, as sole headliner with no help from Arrowhead, made more sense even if it meant playing for smaller crowds.

But from the short-term perspective of paying off a gambling debt, this was a disastrous turn of events. DeGrande had run through about four hundred thousand dollars in Las Vegas, wiping out most of his on-hand liquid cash; plus he had an IOU for two million dollars sitting in the casino's fireproof safe, increasing by the minute at twenty-one percent interest.

Of course, Gus was worth far more than two million dollars. But most of his assets weren't liquid—buildings, houses, cars, publishing rights, contacts, reputation—things that were difficult to turn into cash right away, and that he couldn't afford to part with anyway. His problem was time, and cash flow. Huge sums of money were going to come his way on TAB record sales, but not immediately. Since royalties were paid quarterly, that would take a while. So the promoter had worked some complicated bookkeeping voodoo, cutting corners where he could and counting on the Arrowhead/TAB stadium tour. Two headliners meant high expenses. But with forty thousand people showing up at every date, the influx of cash would be massive enough for Gus to pay off his debt, balance his books and cover his tracks.

An arena tour would also bring in lots of cash, but not as much or as fast. For one thing, canceling all the scheduled stadium dates and starting over would take months, and he simply didn't have that long. For another, Tommy was adamant about not making any more videos. With a several-month gap of no touring or new videos, *Chorus Verses Chorus* would lose valuable momentum.

Blackjacked again, Gus had no choice. Against Mo's advice, he decided to continue the stadium tour with a sole headliner. It just might work. With Arrowhead off the bill, he'd have one less band to pay. And TAB was, after all, the most popular band in the country at the moment.

But the pressure was really on now.

The one advantage Gus thought he had was secrecy. He was wrong about that. Mo Polydoroff knew of his plight, thanks to an inadvertent tip from the promoter's secretary Natalie.

"You just missed him," she said the last time Mo called. "He's on his way to Las Vegas."

"Oh, really?" the president replied, perking up. "I didn't know Gus was a gambling man."

"Oh yeah. He goes out there at least once a month."

A little more chit-chat yielded the name of Gus's favorite casino hotel. It just happened to be an establishment where Mo had a friendly source—one of the few networking assets his uncles left behind.

Many years earlier, Adolph Polydoroff started giving bonuses to high-profile Poly Brothers acts in the form of all-expenses-paid trips to this particular gambling emporium. Casino management thought the presence of rock stars added glamour, which attracted suckers, and made sure the musicians always won a little money.

Mo continued the practice, and part of the quid pro quo was that it covered his own gambling indiscretions. Then again, he'd never lost nearly this much money. Discreet inquiries revealed the promoter's two-million-dollar meltdown, which Mo suspected was no casual loss given how much he'd spent to launch TAB. Gus's reaction to the Arrowhead cancellation confirmed his hunch.

DeGrande's problem, however, could be Mo's opportunity. The president wanted to quietly renegotiate Poly Brothers' deal with Grandiose Records to get a bigger cut of the money pouring in from TAB. This might be just the lever he needed.

Tommy's rehearsal declaration to the contrary, he seemed perfectly content with going along to get along. The bandleader came to rehearsals and played all the songs from *Chorus Verses Chorus* without complaint. He no longer introduced any radical new on-the-fly rearrangements, or obscure old covers, or any new songs at all. He and his bandmates just played the same eleven songs, over and over and over.

Rather than the nasty cutting contests of old, TAB's practices were no-nonsense and businesslike. Early into the second post-Des Moines rehearsal, Michelle wasn't paying attention and bricked a chord change so badly that she and Ray both winced. It was just the sort of glitch Tommy used to pounce on. This time, to her surprise, he gave a little shrug and actually slowed down to let her catch up. No muss, no fuss. Not even an obnoxious smirk.

Tommy seldom pushed himself or his bandmates anymore. Superficially, he still sang and played as beautifully as ever. But something intangible had been lost; not simply fire or spontaneity, but possibility. As she became certain of what was coming next on every song, Michelle found herself getting bored. That had never happened before.

It wasn't just Tommy's playing that seemed diminished, but also his stature. He looked somehow smaller and incomplete, almost translucent. It didn't seem obvious to anyone except her. There were times when Michelle seemed to lose sight of Tommy when he was standing only a few feet away, as if he blended in with the background scenery. He didn't occupy space so much as fade in and out of focus.

That, she figured, was the smack. While Tommy remained secretive as ever, there was little doubt. At a certain point, he'd been made to understand that his continued supply was contingent upon his cooperation. So he did what he had to do, all the way around, and looked frailer by the day. Ironically, the only person who could get any food down the guitarist was his drug dealer. At DeGrande's instructions, he'd make Tommy eat something before giving him a shot. If not for the forced feedings at the point of a needle, Tommy might well have starved himself to death.

The psychological toll weighed just as heavily as the physical wear and tear. Whether it was acquiescence or defiance, Tommy never did anything halfway. Lately, any request was good enough for him. Tell him to be somewhere and he'd probably be late, but he would be there.

Like the coffeeshop over by the university for his first official interview in months. With Ken's *Rock Slide* deadline fast approaching, he'd been pestering the bandleader for a sit-down chat. The critic had more than enough background color for the story, a few utterly useless quotes from Ray (who had become a grasping, crushing bore in the wake of TAB's success), and some weasely official statements from DeGrande. Michelle refused to talk, on or off the record.

So Ken needed some quotes from Tommy. He hoped to get more than the usual boilerplate soundbites about the onset of fame—how weird it was to see yourself at the top of the charts, how disorienting it felt to go from clubs to stadiums overnight—and maybe get into some of the bizarre intrigue surrounding *Chorus Verses Chorus*. Ever since he'd written the same glowing review as every other critic in America, Ken had felt uneasy.

They were seated in a booth by the coffeeshop's front window. The interviewer nursed a latte, the interviewee a steady stream of cigarettes. Neither ate, although Tommy did chew his fingernails. The bandleader's suit was long gone, never to be seen again, and he was back to tattered jeans and a dirty white T-shirt. He looked more cadaverous than ever, and didn't smell too appetizing, either.

As ghastly as he looked, Ken figured nobody would recognize TAB's leader. But about every fourth person who walked by on the sidewalk outside gave a start when they saw Tommy through the window. Raleigh wasn't a big city and had never before been home to an actual "rock star." Soon, people were coming in to ask for autographs, which Tommy was only too happy to sign. And shortly after that, two uninvited strangers were in the booth with them, asking questions.

Ken let them do it. This would be the easiest lead he'd ever write: The formerly obscure Tommy Aguilar, who was suddenly so famous he couldn't even get a cup of coffee without being accosted by strangers. Ten minutes of this, the critic figured, and Tommy would be trying to burn the place down to escape.

"Man," said one of the strangers, "I saw you guys in Richmond like a year ago. You remember that show?"

"Can't say I do."

"Yeah, you smashed the shit outta yer guitar. It was great. But then I saw you again a few months ago, and you didn't do that—how come? Seemed like you'd…I dunno, lost your edge."

Ken tensed, anticipating an explosion in response.

"Nope, still got the edge," Tommy said from behind a tight smile. "It's just…you know, pointing somewhere else right now."

The critic was dumbfounded.

"What's it like to be number one on the charts?"

"Weird."

"And now you're going out to play stadiums, huh, how 'bout that?"

"It's, um…disorienting."

"Hey," the second guy spoke up, "there's something I've always wanted to ask someone in a band: Which do you write first, the words or the music?"

Tommy glanced over at Ken, who smiled and almost answered the question for him. But the critic waited a nanosecond too long.

"The words," Tommy said, returning his gaze to the questioner. "What any song says, that's always the most important thing. Always."

The rock star did not look again at Ken, which was probably just as well. Ken wanted to ask Tommy if he'd brought along his gun.

Before long, the crowd at their booth grew into a mob. A score or so TAB fans crowded around, trapping them in the corner. They passed up napkins and menus for Tommy to sign (no breasts, alas), while more people stood outside gawking and pointing through the window.

Despite his concentration camp pallor, the bandleader worked the crowd like a pro. Ken watched him, realized he was actually enjoying this and felt physically ill. Tommy hadn't simply given up, he'd gone over to the dark side. He gave predictable rock star-type answers to every single question he was asked, often directly contradicting things he'd told Ken in the past. Tommy even claimed he was "proud" of *Chorus Verses Chorus.* The critic wanted to press him on that one, but not in front of an audience of newfound fans. So Ken forced his way through the crowd and left Tommy with his adoring public, saying he'd call later.

Ken decided he was going to let Tommy Aguilar have it, right there in *Rock Slide.* The critic was going to say all the things he should've said in his newspaper review of TAB's album—that *Chorus Verses Chorus* was an abomination and a betrayal, and that Tommy had apparently been bodysnatched and replaced with a zombie clone. That wasn't the story the magazine had in mind, Ken knew. But if the magazine decided to kill it, that was fine by him. Hey, Marty McPhail was always available.

But when Ken was sitting at his word processor trying to think of the perfect metaphor for selling one's soul to the devil, temptation intervened yet again in the form of a phone call. It was a New York publisher that put out a lot of quickie rock-star biographies, calling with an offer. The proposal was for Ken to travel with TAB on the first leg of their upcoming tour to get lots of juicy (but not *too* juicy) behind-the-scenes anecdotes, then crank out thirty thousand words to go with a lot of pictures. The book would be rush-released to cash in on publicity from the tour. It was another of DeGrande's ideas.

If the Rock Slide profile was easy money, this was highway robbery: a dollar a word, or thirty thousand bucks. More money than the critic made in a year, and it was there for the taking.

All he had to do was not blow it.

The story in *Rock Slide* was headlined, "No TABoo: The Next Big Thing Becomes Right Now's Big Thing." The three bandmembers were pictured on the cover, just below the magazine's scripted logo (which conveniently covered Tommy's upraised middle finger). Michelle hid behind a slump and a pair of shades, while Ray wore a deer-in-the-headlights expression familiar to anyone who has ever read a high school yearbook.

The look on Tommy's face was wide-eyed and perfectly blank. The bandleader posed for the photo in the same clothes he'd worn the day of the coffeeshop interview, with one added fashion statement. He took a green magic marker and scribbled on his T-shirt in big letters, "CORPORATE MAGAZINES (STILL) SUCK!" Since the picture just showed TAB's front side, none of *Rock Slide's* readers saw what Tommy had written on the back: "AND SO DO YOU."

Inside, Ken's story was as neutral as Tommy's thousand-yard stare. It led with the scene in the coffeeshop, then recounted TAB's quick rise. The only references to "selling out" involved tickets and records, and there was nothing at all about treachery, psychosis or drugs. Instead, the story quoted some randomly selected teenagers at the mall talking about how much Tommy Aguilar's songs meant to them—"He doesn't just speak *to* me, man, he speaks *for* me"—followed by the songwriter himself holding forth on the state of the world and his place in it:

> This is a scary time to be in your 20s. There's no youth culture left, no greatest rock'n' roll band in the world left. Could we be the new greatest rock 'n' roll band in the world? I dunno, maybe so. At first, you know, I was really upset that we went and made a "big" record. But then I got to thinking, what's the use of half-assing around? So we just decided to get the whole thing of becoming huge over with right away—just, you know, deliver the goods…

Altogether, it was a perfect package in which the dissonant elements canceled each other out. *Rock Slide* was happy to let TAB's leader give it a jab on the cover. The magazine looked hipper that way, Tommy could claim he was still fighting the power, and everybody got what they wanted. Everybody, including Ken. This was his first really big TAB-related score, and the book would be even bigger. Friends, relatives and colleagues the critic hadn't heard from in years were calling to glad-hand him—and angle for favors.

With the possible exception of the Charlie Holmes column, Ken had never felt worse about a story in his life.

CHAPTER TWENTY-NINE

Las Vegas was the opening date of TAB's "Come Go Away" tour, and the band went there a week early to log some rehearsal time at the concert site—Boyd Stadium, the University of Nevada at Las Vegas football field. It was hard enough to get any sort of musical point across in an arena, but this felt like setting up shop on the moon. The sheer size of the place, plus the hundred-foot video screens on either side of the stage, made for a weird combination of isolation and voyeuristic, one-way intimacy.

The first time Michelle saw herself enlarged on the screens, she was horrified—a huge stress zit on the left side of her nose was going to be visible from California. So she stood in profile with her right side facing the seats and instructed the video crew to keep their cameras on Tommy.

"He's the one everybody's coming for, anyway," she told them.

TAB practiced mornings, before the searing desert heat fully took hold. All things considered, the rehearsals went pretty well, even if the repetition of playing the same set over and over was numbingly dull. Due to the complications of sound and lighting cues in such a large and echo-plagued space, everything was scripted down to the last note.

There was, however, spontaneity aplenty in the surrounding parking lots, where thousands of kids congregated each morning to try and sneak into the stadium while the band played. One seventeen-year-old boy was nearly killed when he scaled halfway up a wall, lost his grip and fell fifty feet. An awning broke his fall, but he still suffered two broken legs and spinal injuries. After that, the police erected fences topped with razor wire to keep the crowds at a distance. Michelle felt like they were practicing in a holding pen.

TAB's hotel could've used some defensive fortification, too. Hordes of sullen kids lurked around the lobby, the stairwells and the street outside. Some wore T-shirts emblazoned with lyrics or song titles. A few took a cue from Tommy's current shorn look and sported shaved heads (girls as well as boys). And all of them were prepared to completely lose their shit at the mere sight of their idol.

The first time Tommy tried to get a drink in the hotel bar was also the last. Word spread, and close to a hundred young fanatics surged in with the force of a tidal wave, overturning tables and potted plants in their hysteria. When they spotted the bandleader, an animal roar went up. It scared Tommy to death. These kids weren't like the hometown fans, who just wanted autographs and maybe a little chit-chat. This crowd seemed to want a piece of him—literally. Within seconds, they tore his shirt off and were fighting over the shredded cloth. That gave him just enough time to flee through the fire escape, which triggered an alarm. It was just as well that the fire department showed up, because mace didn't even slow this crowd down. They had to be herded outside with firehoses.

After that, Tommy stayed in his room with the phone unplugged and the lights off, behind a deadbolted door he refused to answer. The only time he went out was for rehearsal, sneaking out with Ray to ride in separate limos over to the stadium. As per her arrangement with Gus DeGrande, Michelle stayed a half-hour away in Boulder City, eschewing limos to take a taxi to the stadium each morning.

Cooped up in hotel rooms for twenty-two hours a day was a miserable way to live, and all three band members quickly grew bored and irritable. Most of the babysitting burdens fell on Bob, who could've used some help keeping the band in line. He found DeGrande's refusal to come to Las Vegas irritating, and curious.

So far, this tour was shaping up as triumphant; Gus's gamble appeared to be paying off. Even as sole headliner with no opening-act support, TAB had sold out all forty thousand seats in less than a week. Ticket sales were brisk elsewhere, too. The promoter had no time to gloat, however. He was too busy putting in round-the-clock hours at the office to hold everything together long enough for this tour to start. Fraud, embezzlement and arm-twisting was not the sort of work he could delegate to others. More importantly, his casino creditors had a well-deserved reputation for unpleasantness when debtors were slow in payment. They expressed doubts about Gus's ability to pay in a timely manner, and even dropped some ominous hints about seizure and liquidation of assets. All the more reason to open TAB in Vegas, to reassure them.

But until his debt was paid off, Gus had no intention of going any-where near the city himself.

Ken Morrison, on the other hand, was already in town and making a nuisance of himself. He wanted to take a leave of absence from the paper to do the TAB book, but management refused to guarantee his job. The compromise was for him to file tour reports from the road for the *Daily News.*

Ken hadn't even checked into his room before he managed to get arrested in the hotel bar riot. Scribbling notes the whole way, he followed the crowd and arrived in the bar just in time to get caught up in a crush of riot police, who herded him into a police paddywagon at the point of a firehose. Unable to convince the cops that he was an observer and not a participant, the journalist wound up in a large holding cell with a few dozen soaking wet TAB fans. Bob had to bail him out.

"You, I didn't expect to have to do this for," the road manager said. "Doesn't your newspaper have lawyers to deal with shit like this?"

"They only handle libel suits. Besides, I'm technically here in the capacity of Official TAB Biographer, which makes you my problem."

"Just what I need—another fucking problem. So you're really doing a book?"

"Uh huh. The behind-the-scenes, no-holds-barred, whole-truth-and-nothing-but inside story of TAB's rocket ride to the toppermost of the poppermost."

Bob snickered mirthlessly. "Motherfucker, I wish you luck."

"What," Ken said, "getting the real truth?"

"No, getting anybody to believe it."

"They will if the book has the right title. I'm thinking of calling it *TAB: Behind Bars and On the Road With the Prisoners of Love.*"

As he spoke, the critic moved his hands as if posting the words on a billboard. "Whaddaya think?" he asked.

"That's the dumbest thing I ever heard."

"Of course it is. But you have to admit, getting arrested seems to be a quintessential part of the whole TAB paradigm."

"Yeah, and chanting, 'The whole world's watching' back in the poky there didn't exactly endear you to the cops. You're lucky they let you out without working you over. So let's not make this a habit, okay? You may be part of the organization, but that doesn't mean I've got time to babysit you, too."

"I'll do my best," Ken said. "So what does your ward think of Las Vegas?"

"You can ask him yourself. Near as I can tell, he seems to think it's cool because Elvis played here a lot."

"Dead Elvis, you mean. This is where he came to die."

"Yeah, well, I just work here."

"That you do," Ken said. "What's it like ladling shark chum for DeGrande, anyway?"

Bob sighed and shook his head.

"Ken," he said, "I should've just left you in jail."

Ken's first dispatch from the TAB tour was a first-person account of his arrest, liberally embellished to make him look like a First Amendment martyr. His editor loved it. Gus was less pleased, but let it slide. He had more pressing problems, like coming up with enough cash to pay deposits for the other two dozen shows he had pending with different bands at various venues all over the country. The promoter still had a business to run, even if TAB took up most of his time.

TAB took up most of Gus's money, too, because Las Vegas was costing him a fortune so far. The overhead—renting hotel rooms and a stadium for a week, paying production crews and security, covering miscellaneous expenses—was staggering. It came to fifty thousand dollars a day, a figure that would more than double once the tour actually started. The riot in the hotel bar took another ten grand to take care of, and the kid who fell off the wall was going to cost even more. Since his parents didn't have insurance, Gus covered the hospital bills, hoping to head off any litigation.

Des Moines was proving to be litigious enough, because that situation refused to go away. The judge had lost patience with DeGrande's delay tactics and refused any further continuances, while the district attorney spurned all talk of plea bargains. The local D.A. was even making noises about extraditing Tommy by force for the next hearing, scheduled in two weeks, which made Gus hesitant to send TAB to any states bordering Iowa. With Kansas City, Chicago and Minneapolis on the itinerary, this was a problem.

As if that wasn't enough, Gus was picking up disquieting vibes from Poly Brothers. A lawyer from the label's accounting department called one day out of the blue, asking strange questions about contractual details. Figuring that the man wouldn't be asking unless he was aiming to renegotiate, the promoter tried to brush him off. Still the lawyer persisted, expressing a peculiar level of concern about Grandiose's liquidity. DeGrande began to suspect his cash-flow difficulties were no longer a secret. No big surprise there; secrets were tough to keep in the music business, especially those revealing weakness.

The next question was whether or not Poly Brothers intended to pull a fast one on TAB's upcoming royalty payment. Under different circumstances, that would've been no problem at all. If Poly Brothers so much as twitched, DeGrande could consider it breach of contract and take his business elsewhere. But that scenario would take time the promoter didn't have.

Once he was off the hook, Gus had every intention of leaving Poly Brothers, maybe for the new label Adolph and Nehi Polydoroff were rumored to be starting. Short term, however, DeGrande needed Poly Brothers to pay up on schedule; for the first leg of TAB's tour to go off without any hitches, or empty seats; and for this ball-busting D.A. in Des Moines to back off.

His checking account was just about empty.

After Bob drove him back to the hotel, Ken finally checked in. He was assigned to the same floor as the TAB entourage. Room 1233, right next door to two guys from the lighting crew on one side and a couple of Poly Brothers flacks on the other—and directly across from Tommy in room 1232.

Ken rode the elevator up and started down the hall. Turning a corner, he saw a man leaving Tommy's room. It was someone the critic knew by sight from clubs back home, but had never actually met and didn't know by name—a tall, rangy, bald fellow. Ken figured the guy might be an instrument tech, although he was dressed a little too well for that.

"Hey ya," Ken said, about to add that he was glad to see TAB still hired locally while conquering globally. The man didn't answer, just gave a curt nod from behind his mirrored shades and hurried on by.

Ken shrugged, but thought it was a bit odd. He had pegged the man's role more or less correctly, however. Gus had indeed imported a local from back home to be Tommy's "personal assistant" on this tour. A personal assistant with some unique duties.

Ken didn't realize it, but he'd just met Tommy's drug supplier.

CHAPTER THIRTY

Leaning into the microphone, Tommy cranked away on a guitar riff and leveled his gaze at Michelle as he barked out the words to "Dumb and Number":

> Play dumb, baby,
> Not a stretch for yooooooooou!
> Or play numb, baby,
> Even better, that'll dooooooo!

Michelle pointedly avoided his eyes as she thumped away on the root. The bassist didn't like this song. She thought it was, well, dumb. She also hated Tommy's habit of staring at her while he sang it—an obnoxious bit of playacting that made anyone who saw it think the song might be about her. For all she knew, it was. He'd never actually told her otherwise, and she sure wasn't going to ask.

> Dumb dumber dumbest,
> 'Til you're numb number numbest.
> Then ya fall down
> And you're finally throoooooooooooooogh!!!

Jesus, what gibberish, Ken thought, watching from his perch at the mixing board on a platform tower forty yards from the stage. Behind him, Bob was in perpetual motion. He tried different mixes, tweaking this or that; listened through headphones at the board; then scurried around to different quadrants of the stadium to see what the crowd would hear, making notations on a clipboard tied to his belt. Bob had never mixed sound outdoors before, so these rehearsals were practice runs for him, too.

The critic hardly noticed Bob's comings and goings as he watched the band slog through still another version of the same exact set they'd drilled on for weeks. It was hard to believe this was the same group that, until a month earlier, he'd never seen play the same show twice. Subtly and gradually, TAB had turned into the band that was on *Chorus Verses Chorus.* The wild rough edges were gone, gone, gone—replaced by bloodless competence. If they never screwed up as badly as they used to, they never hit the same dizzying highs, either. All three of them looked as engaged and lifelike as the mannequins from their video.

Tommy was still human enough to break a string, however, which he did on the last verse of "Dumb and Number." Everyone took a breather while the guitar tech took the instrument away to replace the string and retune. Bob flopped down onto the floor of the mixing tower and took a long gulp of water from a canteen, thankful this was TAB's final practice. With the heat near ninety degrees, all his running made for a grueling workout. But even if the sound sucked at tomorrow's show, at least he would be standing still. The left leg shrapnel souvenir from Bob's long-ago military service ached and throbbed.

"So," Ken said, "whaddaya think?"

"I think," the road manager moaned, "that it's too fuckin' hot."

"Just think, if you were back home, you probably wouldn't even be awake yet."

Bob squinted up at the critic as he took another sip. "Like everybody back there says, you've gotta get up awfully early in the afternoon to beat Ken Morrison out of bed."

"Hey, why put up with all this shit if you still have to get up in the morning?"

"I get a mountain of shit every day before you get your first cup of coffee, pal," Bob murmured, watching the stage. The guitar tech was just about done. Tommy, however, had disappeared.

"Does this feel…you know…weird?"

The question slipped out. Apart from the occasional grim joke, Ken had carefully avoided the subject of the Bob-TAB-Gus triangle, until now.

The cuckolded manager merely shrugged. " 'Weird' is a relative term," he said. "I'm here, and…well, I'm here. That's probably all that needs to be said about it."

"But you're working for Gus, handholding a band he stole from you and turned into…I dunno, crash-test dummies. Hell, just look at 'em. We've been watching them play this same set every day for a week now, and the most interesting thing that's happened so far is Tommy breaking a string."

"And your point would be?…" Bob made no attempt to hide his impatience.

"My point would be yes, you're here—but I still don't understand why."

"It's not that hard to figure out. Same reason you're here: I've been bought."

That was true, but it still stung Ken to hear it said out loud. "Well, I hope you at least got a good price," he said.

"Good enough, I guess. I'll get control of my life back. Once this is over, I'll be out of debt and should be able to keep the club open for as long as I want."

"That's all?"

"That's enough."

"But I thought the whole reason you went into band management in the first place was that you wanted out of the bar business."

"Yeah, I did. Maybe I still do. But this"—Bob made a wave that took in the stage and the soon-to-be-filled bleachers—"is not it. Not anymore. Even if the bullshit with DeGrande had never happened, even if I'd kept Tommy and we'd gone slow and gotten to this point in five years like I planned…Well, hell, I don't even know if that's possible anymore. The record business is all or nothing, one or the other, right now. You have to be either a clueless screwball or a criminal to get anywhere. No thanks."

He paused. "So this is my farewell tour. I feel sort of obligated to be here, to finish the job. I'll see it through, get my fill of this shit once and for all—and have all the incentive I'll ever need to avoid getting mixed up with any more bands."

"So what you're really getting out of this," Ken asked in amazement, "is negative reinforcement?"

"Cheaper than therapy."

"Christ."

"But what about you, Mr. Celebrity Biographer? What do *you* get out of following this circus around? Money? The envy of all your geek critic pals? The chance to hit on Tommy's discards?"

Ken decided it was high time to change the subject. "Enough about us; what does Tommy get out of this?"

"You have to ask?" Bob said, laughing. "Hell, what doesn't he get? Fame, fortune, the adulation of millions, girls chasing him. And he don't have to mow lawns for a living anymore."

"But Tommy likes mowing lawns, Bob. You know that. The only thing I see him doing lately is hiding. Does he look like he's actually enjoying this?"

"Ask him if he is."

"I did, and he said he didn't understand the question. Used to be you couldn't get Tommy to shut up about anything. But every time a question like that comes up now, all you get is, 'I dunno.' What the fuck's going on with him? Is it the drugs or what?"

Bob didn't answer. The guitar tech had finally located Tommy, and it was time to resume rehearsal.

Ken knew he was asking for trouble. But the temptation was just too great. Tommy's room, the inner sanctum, beckoned. It was right across the hall, but might as well have been on another planet because he hadn't been allowed past the door. After practice, however, Ken was walking to his room when he turned the corner again, and literally ran right into the bandleader's "assistant."

"Sorry," the critic said. The man merely grunted and moved on down the hallway, not noticing that he'd dropped a key.

Ken picked it up, looked at the figure retreating down the hall, then at the key. Number 1232. Once Tommy's assistant was out of sight, Ken went and knocked on the door.

"Tommy? You in there?"

No answer.

Ken pondered his options. He could slide the key under the door. He could take it to Bob. Or he could go in.

Unlocking the door and stepping inside, he was surprised at the room's size. In contrast to his own modest digs across the hall, this was actually a large suite. Ken stood in the darkened entry, shivering in the air conditioning. All the curtains were drawn and the lights were out.

"Anybody here?" he called out.

There was an acrid smell in the air, sort of like burning vinegar. Ken followed the scent, toward a closed door. The crack underneath revealed a light on the other side.

"Tommy?" Ken rapped lightly. No answer. He wondered if Tommy had a girl in there.

Well, the critic thought, *here goes.*

It was somehow even more frigid inside; the air felt as cold as a meat locker. Despite the chill, Tommy sat nude on a king-size bed, his clothes piled on the floor and his back to the door. The only light in the room was a lamp, with a blue bandanna hung over the shade. The bandleader was so emaciated that Ken could count the ribs in his back, even in the dimness.

Except for the same necklace he always wore, all Tommy had on was a red bandanna tied around his right forearm. In his left hand—the one with TEMPT tattooed across the knuckles—he held a syringe. When he heard the door open, he looked over his shoulder and fixed Ken with a long stare. Then he slowly turned back to the business at hand. His right hand—the one with ME across the knuckles—rested on his knee in a tight fist. Tommy pulled the bandanna tighter with his teeth and tapped a vein in his forearm. Then he dug the needle in and pushed the plunger. Watching it, Ken winced.

Within seconds, Tommy went limp. His head rolled forward and his shoulders slumped. The critic watched the haggard muscles across Tommy's back twitch and relax, as if something was running out of them. He retained just enough consciousness to withdraw the needle and drop it on the floor before he laid down on the bed, curling into a fetal ball.

"This," said a voice behind Ken, startling him, "is off the fucking record."

He hadn't heard Bob follow him in.

Journalism textbooks didn't cover how to handle this—just what was the protocol for interrupting someone in the middle of shooting up?—and neither did Miss Manners. So Ken simply turned and walked past Bob out of the room, out of the hall, out of the lobby, out of the hotel and into the desert heat. He hoped a walk would clear his thoughts, but it only made his already-raging headache worse.

Tommy had turned into Charlie Holmes before his eyes. Seeing the bandleader physically in the act changed things, somehow. Ken had been hiding behind "on the record," but now he no longer had even that fig leaf of deniability. He felt dirtier, more tainted and angrier than ever before. He should do something, he thought. But what?

Ken went back into the hotel, rode the elevator upstairs and barged into Bob's room without knocking.

"Yes?" Bob said, not looking up from his laptop computer.

"We need to talk."

"About what?"

"About what?" Ken repeated. "Gee, Bob, I dunno. What would we have to talk about right now? The weather, maybe? It's raining needles and pins down the hall, I hear."

"Then my advice is to get an umbrella, and keep your head down so it don't get stuck."

"I'll keep that in mind."

"Good."

"Bob…How could you do this?"

"How I could I do what?" the road manager asked, wearily.

"You know, this deaf-dumb-and-blind routine of yours is wearing reeeeeeeal thin."

"Right back 'atcha, choirboy," Bob said, snapping the computer shut. "Yeah, let's talk about 'blind.' It's not like you didn't know about this. Fuck, I even told you he had a problem, remember? Is it all of a sudden a bigger deal just because you actually saw him do it?"

"Yes," Ken said. "Don't ask me to explain why because I can't. It just is. Before, I thought he just…you know, dabbled. But he shot that up like a real pro."

"Well, he's had a lot of practice," Bob said. "I tried to get him to quit before, and he wouldn't listen. He seems to think he can't write songs without smack, and if you take that away from him, what's he got left?"

"The rest of his life, maybe?"

"Ken, it's up to him. Whether you or I approve, he's an adult."

"If you can't stop him, how could you help him do it?"

"Hey, don't get self-righteous with *me*, asshole," Bob said heatedly. "Like I said, if it was up to me, he would've quit a long time ago. I wasn't in his room to help him shoot up, I was in there to make sure he was okay. Later, I'll go back and help him clean up. Try to get him to eat something, make sure he gets dressed, brushes his teeth."

"Brushes his *teeth?!*"

"Ask any junkie. The teeth are always the first thing to go."

" 'The teeth are always the first thing to go,' " Ken repeated numbly.

"It's true. And Tommy is proud of his teeth, paid good money to have them capped and everything. Be a shame to lose 'em."

"So let me see if I've got this right," Ken said. "Tommy has a heroin problem, and you're telling me with a straight face that you're worried about his teeth?"

"You should be, too. If he loses his teeth, he'll be too ugly for you to get on any more magazine covers or book jackets. Remember why you're out here in the first place."

"Right now, I'd just as soon not."

"Well, you'd better start, now that you've got what you came here for—that 'ugly, behind-the-scenes truth' you were talking about."

"What do you mean?"

"I mean, you need to ask yourself what you're going to do about this."

"You tell me."

"Nothing," Bob said.

"Nothing? What the fuck are you talking about? Why am I going to do nothing?"

"Because nobody wants to know. Everybody just wants to believe this horseshit fairy tale about Tommy being a poster child for 'generational disillusionment'—that's what all you rock critic jerkoffs have been saying, anyway. And that's what Gus and Poly Brothers and *Rock Slide* and your book publisher all want, so they can go right on selling the fantasy. Nobody wants to hear about the string-pulling or the drugs, because it destroys the illusion. This junkie shit is bad for business, all the way around."

"But I'm supposed to be a reporter," Ken protested, "not a flack."

"Not anymore."

CHAPTER THIRTY-ONE

The next day, Tommy Aguilar wandered onto the stadium stage at dusk as forty thousand voices screamed through the growing darkness. He strapped his guitar on over his black leather jacket and looked out. It was disorienting, seeing all these people where there'd been nothing for a week, especially with so many of them holding up those goddamn cigarette lighters. Tommy hated the whole lighter routine. It reminded him too much of cheesy rock bands.

He was about to look over at Michelle, when he froze. There in the front row was Susan—the first time he'd laid eyes on her since their game of sexual roulette a year earlier. Last time he'd seen her, she was holding a gun over him. Tommy wondered if she was armed, and wished he had one of his own guns. He almost ducked when he saw her throw something in his direction. A small felt ring box landed at his feet. He bent down, picked it up and opened it. The only thing inside was a folded-up scribbled note from Susan: "Play one of those songs about me."

Tommy stood up, drank in the evening air, pondered the forest of upraised cigarette lighters before him—and felt a long-dormant impulse go *click*. He flung the jewelry box as far and as high as he could, a morsel into the maw of the audience, then moved to the microphone.

"Hey," Tommy shouted, "cut the torches." He found he was shaking, and quietly strummed an unsteady C chord. Then he added, "Whodaya think we are, Arrowhead?"

The crowd laughed and cheered, thousand of lighters flicking off.

"Anyway," Tommy continued, "I've got a better idea. Everybody, come on down front!"

Back in the mixing tower, Bob Porter and Ken Morrison exchanged the same look that Ray and Michelle did onstage. This was…unexpected. Tommy had been so cooperative since Des Moines that he'd lulled the entire TAB entourage into an ill-advised complacency. It hadn't occurred to anyone that once he was in front of an audience again, the bandleader might revert to type.

For a long moment, nobody did anything. The crowd fell almost silent; cheers turned to murmurs of confusion as people tried to figure out how serious this invitation was.

"Everybody," Tommy finally hollered, "down front *right fuckin' now,* or we ain't playin'!"

Forty thousand people moved forward at once with a terrifying roar. Those already on the field surged toward the stage. The people in the stands followed right behind, hopping over the low walls onto the field. Security tried to hold back the tidal wave, but they were outnumbered a thousand to one.

In minutes, three-quarters of the crowd was on the field and stampeding forward, leaving behind piles of overturned folding chairs in its wake. Ken didn't see how somebody wasn't going to get trampled. The mob ebbed and flowed in front of the stage, the mixing tower swaying as people climbed up the sides to escape the crush of humanity below. Up front, bodies were wedged in so tightly that shorter people were lifted off the ground. The more claustrophobically inclined grew hysterical and began to flail, triggering skirmishes.

Susan was nowhere to be seen.

Everyone was so preoccupied with maintaining their own space, they almost forgot about the band onstage. Tommy reclaimed the focus of attention by winding up and hitting his guitar strings as hard as he could, at earsplitting volume. The chord of D rang out like a challenge, hanging in the air as the crowd cheered uncertainly.

KERAAAAAAAANG...

Bob took off his headphones and hurled them to the floor. This was not what the script called for. Tommy was to have greeted the crowd with minimal chit-chat, followed by the big hit single "Go As You Are." All the lighting, mix and video camera cues were set for that, timed to the nanosecond.

KERAAAAAAAANG...

But Tommy had other ideas, hitting the same riff again while bringing his right boot heel down hard. He began to march in place while looking back at Ray, who finally overcame his disbelief enough to figure out which song the guitarist was cueing.

KERAAAAAAAANG...

Not knowing what else to do, the drummer started pounding out a martial kickdrum beat in time with Tommy's marching. The crowd caught the rhythm and began clapping along, except for the people packed in too tightly to move their arms. Those who could jump did so, straight up and down in place. Those who couldn't were buoyed up, as if by ocean waves.

KERAAAAAAAANG...

Tommy nodded at Ray before turning to Michelle, who was busy watching the crowd batter the front of the barricades. People were passing out. Security worked frantically to haul the victims out, drag them away and deposit them behind the stage.

Got it? the guitarist mouthed silently at Michelle as he hit that deafening fuzztone riff again, harder than ever. It clanged like an alarm. Tommy's guitar-playing often assumed an almost physical presence. This time, it was a cloak of blackness descending over the stadium, which seemed to grow darker every time he windmilled his left arm down.

KERAAAAAAAANG...

The bassist nodded, numbly, still incredulous that Tommy wanted to do this—not in a bar in front of a hundred people they knew, but in front of a seething mob of forty thousand bloodlust-infected strangers. Ray's kickdrum continued, *boom-boom-boom-boom,* the rhythm of a column of jackbooted troops on the march.

"What the fuck is he doing?!" Ken asked.

"Wrecking my life," Bob shouted angrily, frantically trying to make on-the-fly soundboard adjustments for what was coming. His walkie-talkie crackled with bewildered questions from the lighting and camera crews. Bob turned it off so he could concentrate.

Onstage, all was ready.

Tommy took one last deep breath, reared back and let loose a sound that the word "shriek" doesn't even come close to describing. No one had ever heard anything quite like it before, nor would they again, which was just as well. Some noises stay with you well enough that you don't need to hear them more than once.

It was a bloodcurdling howl that didn't even sound animal, let alone human, from a time zone where flesh and blood barely registered; as if every piece of rock and stone and sand in the surrounding desert was somehow given a collective voice with which to reproduce all the sounds of a thousand years, boiled down to a single instant. People heard its echo from miles away and felt a vague, unsettling chill as they looked skyward, expecting to see an incoming meteor at the very least. People in the parking lots outside the stadium heard it and shuddered. Ken heard it from forty yards away and turned to stone. He wanted to cover his ears, but found he couldn't move his arms.

With the echo of his scream still stabbing everyone's ears, Tommy jumped three feet straight up, hit a split-leg pose at the apex of his leap and windmilled his guitar one last time.

KERAAAAAAAANG...

Ray followed the cue and hammered out a snare drum roll. As soon as Tommy came back to earth, he began pummeling his guitar at a fearsome pace, lurching across the stage. Even for old-school punk, this was ridiculously fast. Michelle had just about caught up by the time Tommy made it back to his microphone and started to caterwaul:

> I don't wanna holiday inna *SUN*,
> I wanna go to the new Bel-*SEN!*...*"

Ken gaped in astonishment, recognizing "Holidays in the Sun." Maybe a hundred people in the entire stadium knew the song at all, and even fewer still knew it had been the B-side of TAB's first single. It was an utterly bizarre way to open a supposedly triumphant breakthrough tour—the bleakest song from the bleakest band in rock history, a song about hurling oneself into a wall for no reason other than to tear down the false security it represented.

"The *Sex Pistols?!*" Ken yelled. "When did they practice this?!"

"They didn't," Bob shouted back, gamely trying to rein in the squalling guitar enough so that the vocals would be audible. If Tommy wanted to subject his audience to a vintage punk-rock lecture on fascism, Bob figured the least he could do was make the words intelligible.

Tommy radiated thermonuclear contempt, rolling his r's just like Johnny Rotten:

> I wanna see some his-to-*rrrreeeee,*
> 'Cause now I got a reason *FOR THE ECONOMEEEE!*

The rest of the verse imploded into incoherent, raving guttural noises. Tommy thrashed and wailed, stoking a guitar firestorm with no place to go but inside itself. Ray and Michelle could do little besides keep out of his way and stay within the eye of the storm. No sense them getting burned, too. From the stage, Tommy looked up toward the mixing tower, hidden in the harsh glare of the stage lights. He pointed his guitar neck straight at Bob and screamed, "I wanna go over the *waaaaaaaaalll!*"

Bob knew exactly what Tommy wanted him to do. He also knew what he should do, and wondered which would make Gus angrier— stop the show, or let it continue? He decided he didn't care just about the time his cellular phone began ringing.

That would be DeGrande, calling to listen in. The tour manager decided to let him do just that. He picked up the phone, turned it on and held it up for thirty seconds. Then he lobbed it as high and as far as he could toward the stage, and turned everything on the soundboard all the way up to maximum volume. For good measure, he turned all the house lights on, too.

Ken couldn't believe what he was seeing. "Aren't you gonna do anything about this?!" he screamed.

"Nope," Bob said, folding his arms. "He's doing just fine on his own."

"What are you talking about?! This is about to turn into a fucking riot!"

"You better take good notes, then."

"Holidays in the Sun" careened to a close, the ending an unrecognizable meltdown. Tommy screamed the last line over and over—"I wanna go over the wall, I don't understand this bit at all!"—each repetition less understandable than the one before; just twisted burned shards of words. Michelle gave up trying to keep pace and thumped steadily away, watching Tommy spin further and further out of control. Ray looked completely bewildered at what was taking place.

"Ah wanna go over thuh wallllll, Ah don unnerstan dis bit a'tallllll!!!…"

While hardly anyone in the audience knew the song, there was no mistaking the venom in Tommy's voice, and it spread through the crowd like tear gas. Some were completely mystified, some got off on the pure adrenaline rush and some thought this was supposed to be part of the show—a riot, just like the video.

The last group dutifully played its part, forming a huge moshpit in front of the stage. The pit quickly degenerated into a savage brawl between those who wanted to slamdance and those who didn't. Fists, elbows, knees, feet, blood, teeth and clothing flew, garishly lit by the fluorescent stadium lights.

"An wan gover thuh walllllllll, Ah don unnerstandis bit a'talllllllllll!!!..."

It didn't take long for word to go out that a riot was in progress. Within minutes after Tommy came onstage, every law enforcement patrol car in the region was screaming toward the stadium, lights blazing. So was a convoy of ambulances and firetrucks, plus a half-dozen police helicopters. Within a half-hour, the governor had called out the National Guard.

"Aaaaaaah w g vr dh wlllllll, A dn unr stn ds bt a ou lll!!!..."

People in the audience took the cue and started going over the wall onto the stage, then diving back into the crowd. Michelle shrank back, taking refuge behind Ray's drums—although her bassline never faltered.

"Aaaaaaaaaaaaaaaaaaaaaaaaaaaaaaaaaaaaaaaaaaaaaaaa!!!!..."

Even as the mob onstage grew and seethed around him, Tommy didn't budge from his microphone until one of the stagedivers stumbled and fell into him. He went down hard but kept right on playing as he rolled over and slowly climbed back to his feet. Blood from a gash on his forehead trickled down his face, but he kept playing, surrounded by flying bodies. He continued screaming, but nobody could hear because the microphone had disappeared. Finally, he stopped almost in mid-note, his bandmates lurching to a halt behind him. Ken looked at his watch as the echoes subsided. It seemed like the band had been onstage for hours, but it had only been ten minutes.

The crowd response was confused—scattered cheers, but a lot more pissed-off boos. About two dozen people from the audience were crowded onstage, uncertain what they should do next. Ken wondered how Tommy could possibly follow up an entrance like this one.

Without a word, Tommy took off his guitar, unplugged it and held the instrument over his head as if it were a trophy animal he'd just hunted down and killed. Then he gripped it by the neck with both hands and spun around three times, letting go to fling it as far as he could. The guitar landed in the front of the mixing tower, where it was instantly torn to pieces.

Tommy turned away as curses and angry boos rained down, the crowd onstage clawing at him as he tried to leave. Swinging his arms wildly, he cut a path like a cyclone through the mob, starting to run as he broke free.

As soon as the phone line went dead, Gus hit the redial button. All he got was a busy signal. That was…strange. Almost as strange as the brief maelstrom of noise he'd heard over the phone. What the hell was going on out there?

The promoter dialed another number and turned on the cable news channel. The second number was busy, too. But he soon learned everything he needed to know from his television set. The network had live footage from Boyd Stadium within minutes, via a Las Vegas TV station's news helicopter.

Something was terribly, grievously wrong. All the lights in the stadium were on, and the stands were almost empty. Virtually the entire crowd appeared to be on the field, except for the ones fleeing out the exits and into the streets. TAB didn't seem to be onstage, but several hundred other people were. The news anchor speculated that a terrorist act of some sort had taken place.

In fact, it was a full-on riot. Flames shot up at one end of the stadium where somebody set a T-shirt booth on fire. People ran all over, starting fights, tearing down fences, feeding the bonfire with whatever could be thrown in. Outside, lines of twinkling red and blue lights approached the stadium from every direction.

"Son…of…a…bitch," Gus stammered.

His phone began ringing, and he picked up the receiver without taking his eyes from the TV screen. Knowing it would be a certain casino representative, he didn't bother with a greeting.

"We have a problem," declared a voice on the other end of the line.

Gus would receive many such calls that night.

"If I were you," Bob told Ken, "I'd take that laminate off before trying to walk through this crowd. It'll be hard enough getting out of here, and if anybody thinks you're with the band, you're liable to get an ass-kickin'."

Bob took his own advice and pitched his tour pass from the tower. Now that the music had stopped, they could hear the approaching sirens. Ken looked down at his pass, which was the envy of all his critic friends because of the behind-the-scenes access it gave him. His colleagues covering the opening of the TAB tour had to make do with press conferences in which Ray was the only bandmember who showed up.

"Anyway," Bob continued, "it's just a useless piece of plastic now. This tour's over."

"It is?" Ken asked.

"Fuck, yes! You think there's a venue on earth that will touch this band now?" Bob said as he pulled a UNLV Runnin' Rebels baseball cap on, hoping he wouldn't be recognized as the guy at the mixing board. He started to climb down the side of the tower.

"Hey," Ken said, "where you going?"

"To find Tommy. Then I'm gettin' the fuck outta town. You should, too."

He was almost to the ground.

"Bob!" Ken hollered, and the tour manager looked up, bodies rushing by below him.

"What?!"

"Did you mean for this to happen?!"

Bob's answer was drowned out by a police helicopter that came in low over the stadium. Ken ducked instinctively and watched it scream by the mixing tower, then slow up and land behind the stage.

When he looked down again, Bob was gone.

One by one the faxes came in, all bearing bad news. Every venue on the tour was exercising its option to cancel. News traveled fast and nobody wanted any part of trouble like this. They weren't even waiting until the start of the next business day.

Long into the night, the machine hummed and the messages came. Drinking one tall glass of Scotch after another, DeGrande watched the sheets of paper pile up and overflow the in-basket. The machine finally ran out of paper, and he didn't bother putting any more in. The phone wasn't delivering any better news than the fax machine, so he quit answering that, too.

This wasn't just bad, it was catastrophic. No way around it, Gus was flat broke. He had cooked his books, spread himself paper-thin, robbed from one account to pay another—all on the assumption that millions of dollars were about to pour in. An assumption that his supposed cash cow Tommy Aguilar wiped out in ten minutes of work in Las Vegas.

Rock stars, Gus thought bitterly. *Fucking…prima donna…-artistic…ROCK…STAR…ASSHOLES!…*

By morning, every date on the tour would be off. And soon, very soon, people were going to demand their money back; money the promoter didn't have, unless he could unload some assets in a hurry. There was also a devastated stadium, an angry D.A. in Iowa, a twitchy record label and an impatient casino operator to deal with.

Gus was just about out of options.

Ken carefully made his way through the crowd and escaped the field just in time, just before the riot squad marched in under cover of teargas and opened up some heads. He climbed the concourse and headed for the stadium press box, where he had to hunt for a phone that wasn't in use. He finally found one, sat down, plugged in his laptop and began to type.

Just like every other reporter in the pressbox, Ken was filing a story about a concert that turned into a riot—but his had a little more background information than the rest.

This time, the critic finally told his readers everything he knew, off as well as on the record.

Everything.

Back at the *Daily News,* almost everyone working in the newsroom that Saturday night was focused on a spectacular apartment fire across town. Fourteen people died in the blaze, which started after a gas grill exploded. Arson was suspected; the police were searching for a disgruntled boyfriend who'd been heard making threats earlier in the evening.

As usual, a small skeleton weekend crew was putting out the paper. The night desk was holding space for Ken's review, anticipating no problems—the critic had been filing his dispatches from Las Vegas for a week, all without incident. Since most of the staff was busy dealing with the fire, it fell to a twenty-year-old copydesk intern with three weeks' experience to edit Ken's story. It sailed right onto the front page, virtually unchanged. About all the intern did was break up a couple of paragraphs. The kid's J-school professors had taught him that paragraphs shouldn't run longer than two sentences.

Had Ken's regular editor seen this, she would have immediately summoned the paper's libel lawyer for a ruling. The critic filed this story fully expecting it would not make it into print; he considered it his resignation speech, an appropriate finale to his tenure as TAB's unofficial propagandist.

Less a news story or review than an overwrought first-person confessional, the piece castigated everyone involved with TAB (including Ken himself) for ignoring Tommy's drug problem out of greed and cowardice. The word "heroin" appeared in the third sentence. Ken had been thoughtful enough to provide a headline— "Fear and Loathing in Las Vegas: Facing Up to the Ugly Truth About TAB"—which also went into the paper untouched. It ran at the bottom of page one, accompanied by a wire-service photo of Tommy looking wild-eyed, blood running down his cheek, his face contorted in a scream.

The fire stories ran at the top of page one in Sunday's paper, illustrated with equally spectacular photos. But the fire wasn't what everybody ended up talking about.

CHAPTER THIRTY-TWO

Ray and Michelle barely escaped the crowd's clutches, locking a backstage door behind them and scurrying out a gate. Once outside, they had to run several blocks before finding a taxi.

"Where are we going?" Ray asked. His voice was so flat and lifeless, it barely registered as a question. Michelle was practically leading him by the hand.

"The airport," she told the driver, pushing Ray into the backseat and climbing in after him.

"That's not very far, but it's gonna take a little longer and cost a little more than usual," the driver warned. "With all these crowds around, I'll have to take the long way."

"No problem. Just get us there."

The cabby scrutinized his passengers in the rearview mirror. "Hey, were you two just at the stadium?" He appeared to be about fifty, not the type who'd care anything about TAB. His radio was tuned to the local big band station, which just happened to be broadcasting Frank Sinatra crooning "My Way."

"Afraid we were," said Ray.

"I heard on the radio that that guy just flipped out. Tommy whatshisname, Aggravate? Agitate? Whoever he is, my kids are always talking about him. They were really upset they couldn't get tickets.

Anyway, the radio said he told everybody to rush the stage, played one song and split. That what happened?"

Ray was just about to answer, when Michelle squeezed his arm so hard he gasped. "We couldn't really tell what happened," she said curtly. "We were sitting too far away."

"Oh," the driver said, giving them another quizzical look in the mirror before turning his attention back toward the road. "Well," he added a bit later after a half-dozen police cars roared past with sirens blaring, "I hope they catch him."

Michelle and Ray glanced at each other, hoping he'd ask no further questions. He didn't, and was rewarded with a large tip at the airport.

"So," Ray said after the cab drove off, "I guess we're off to Denver." At the mention of TAB's next scheduled tour stop, Michelle looked at her bandmate with a mixture of wonder and contempt.

"Ray," she said with a weary sigh, "seeing as how it isn't ski season, what earthly reason could there be for us to go to Denver right now?"

"Isn't that where we're supposed to go next?" Ray asked.

Michelle dropped her backpack on the sidewalk and took his face in her hands, pulling it close enough to smell his breath. The drummer stank of craven desperation. "Listen closely, Ray, because I'm only saying this once: The tour is over. So is the band, and if you're not careful you will be, too. I don't know if there's such a thing as accessory to inciting a riot, but I'm pretty sure you and I just did it."

"But—"

"Ray," Michelle snapped, "the only thing you'll find in Denver is fifty thousand angry people who want their money back. That's somebody else's problem, so don't make it yours. Go somewhere far, far away, and try to forget the last two years ever happened."

"You mean this is it?" he asked, bewildered.

"Christ, just stop it," Michelle said, almost screaming. "Do I have to spell it out for you? Tommy's *crazy*, completely out of his mind. Somebody could've been killed tonight—for all we know, someone was.

Don't you get it? We're done, the band is over! And you're just too god-damned *stupid* to figure it out!"

"But—"

"Goodbye, Ray."

Before he could protest again, Michelle put her hand over his mouth. Then she picked up her backpack and walked away, leaving Ray sitting on the curb. Inside the terminal, she exchanged all her suddenly extraneous TAB tour plane tickets for a one-way ticket to Honolulu and as much cash as the airline would give her.

Somehow, leaving the continent seemed like a good idea.

By the time Bob waded through the mob and reached the backstage area, all three TAB members were long gone. The tour manager took a quick look around, wondering which path to follow. He figured Ray and Michelle could take care of themselves well enough. Tommy, however, would need looking after.

Bob guessed he would flee, which ruled out the hotel. He also hated flying and would never do it voluntarily, which ruled out the airport. But if Tommy held true to form, he would commandeer a car and head for the site of the nearest high-profile rock-star death. Bob went to his rented van and pulled out a U.S. road atlas, opening it on the front seat.

"Goddamn, Ken, where are you?" he muttered, studying the map. "Figures. The one time a rock critic might come in handy, you're nowhere to be found."

Los Angeles was one possibility, a four-hour straight shot down the interstate. No, too obvious, and too many options. Bakersfield, farther north? No, too far away. San Francisco was even farther. But what about?...

As soon as he saw it on the map, though, Bob knew where Tommy was headed. He tossed the atlas aside, started the van and slowly drove out from under the stadium. Once past the fences, he patiently steered through the crowds roaming the streets. A rock came flying out of the darkness and hit the back window with a thud, cracking it. Bob paid it no mind. The van was a rental, on Gus DeGrande's account. And tonight, a busted window was the least of the anyone's worries.

Bob finally broke clear and headed for Highway 95, turning south.

After Ken sent off his story, he unplugged his laptop and packed up to leave. There were about two dozen other journalists working away, covering the tour for magazines and wire services. One was his pal Marty McPhail, who waved Ken over from the other side of the press box.

"Jesus," McPhail said, typing away as Ken approached, "what a clusterfuck this little shindig turned out to be."

"I'll say," Ken sighed. He actually didn't know what *to* say. Having finally unburdened himself, he felt purged and also a little queasy. What he'd done was just starting to sink in.

"You already file?" Marty asked.

"Yep."

"What'd you say?"

"Oh, just that things here took an…unexpected turn."

" 'Unexpected,' " McPhail laughed with a snort. "God, Morrison, everyone else is writing that the sky fell down out there tonight, and you make it sound like a little rain."

"When in doubt, always understate."

"Uh huh. You get any quotes out of the road manager?"

"Only if 'HOLY SHIT' counts."

"So you've been out here all week. Did you have any idea this would happen?"

"Not a clue. Tommy's been nothing but well-behaved the whole time, until tonight."

"Until tonight, when he decided to start a riot. What'd he think he was doing?"

"Oh, hell, who knows?" Ken shrugged. "I don't think Tommy even does, really. It's just an instinct he has, and there never seems to be a reason. Back home, the cops call him a riot enabler."

"Riot enabler, that's good. Mind if I use it for a headline? 'The Riot Enabler Strikes Again?'"

"Be my guest," Ken said, watching the fire department struggle to bring the bonfire in the stadium under control. It was mostly fueled by trash, T-shirts and plastic beer cups. Clouds of acrid, probably toxic smoke billowed up into the night. "Anyway," he continued, "Tommy has cleared a lot of rooms in his day, but he's never blown a gig this big."

"Yeah, well, he fucked up, all right. He'll be lucky if he doesn't do time for this. I still don't get why he'd do it."

"Beats me," Ken said, keeping his thoughts to himself. "Listen, I should get going. I'm, um, sure they'll want me working on follow-ups bright and early tomorrow."

"Plus you've got a book to write."

"Plus I've got a book to write," Ken agreed, trying hard not to wince.

"So the question is, will this make it better or worse?" McPhail asked, looking out at the devastation on the field.

"We'll find out, won't we?"

As he slipped out of Vegas, Bob reviewed the possibilities and decided he'd picked the right destination. Joshua Tree, in the Mojave Desert east of L.A., was Tommy's kind of place—desolate, harsh, with a long tradition of catering to hermits with unsavory personal habits. It was also beautiful; lots of movies and album covers had been shot there.

In rock lore, it was best known as the site of country singer Gram Parsons' last stand. Back in 1973, Parsons set up shop in Room Eight of the Joshua Tree Inn and commenced to binge so hard on cocaine and Conmemorativo tequila that he killed himself. Two of Parsons' friends subsequently hijacked his coffin from the Los Angeles International Airport, drove his corpse back out to Joshua Tree and set fire to it at Cap Rock to fulfill a death pact. Parsons was twenty-six, the same age as Tommy. When he quit yowling and just sang in his naturally pretty voice, Tommy could sound quite a bit like Parsons' angelic tenor. Other than that, they had little in common beyond punky attitudes and self-conscious anguish. Tommy ran on rage, while Parsons exuded a near-Biblical sense of guilt.

Bob made the California state line in ninety minutes and continued south on the deserted highway. He forced himself to concentrate on driving because he didn't want to think too much about the task ahead. He was chasing after a crazy man with arrest warrants on his head, one who had betrayed him before and would not hesitate to do so again, on behalf of someone who had already no doubt fired him.

Well…no. This wasn't for Gus. Bob had already tendered his resignation by phone, so to speak, from the stadium. Which didn't make chasing after Tommy any more sensible. It was more a combination of loyalty, inertia and a need to see firsthand how this played out. He meant it when he told Ken he wanted out of the rock business. But part of his closing ritual involved finishing this job—whatever that entailed. So he planned to rescue Tommy one last time, out of pity if nothing else, after which he'd be DeGrande's problem.

Still, if he had any sense, Bob realized that he would abandon the chase and quietly leave the country. The border was tantalizingly close. He could be into Mexico by dawn. Instead, he was going on a fool's errand toward danger.

No percentages in this one, thought Bob. But neither had there been any percentages in turning the sound all the way up back at the stadium. Or letting DeGrande coerce him into this gig. Or even in becoming Tommy's manager in the first place.

Bob drove on.

After escaping the stadium, Ken went back to the hotel and hurriedly prepared to leave. He didn't expect to find anybody in the suite across the hall, but knocked on the door anyway—and was surprised to find himself face to face with the bald guy he'd seen earlier. Tommy's drug supplier, he'd finally figured out. They stood there glaring at each other, Ken keeping the door open with his foot. "Where's Tommy?" he asked.

"Not here."

"No shit. Where is he?"

"Not here. That's all I know."

"So since he's not around, what are you doing here? And just who the fuck are you, anyway?"

The dealer just shrugged.

"Here's another question," Ken said, "and I'd really like an answer to this one: Did tonight happen because of too strong a dose, or not strong enough?"

At that, the vibe between them escalated from passively unfriendly to actively hostile. "Wrong number," the bald guy said, firmly kicking Ken's foot out of the way and closing the door.

Yes, Tommy decided, the desert was a fine place to be at night. Empty enough that he could go virtually undetected, especially if he drove with the headlights off. The full moon made that possible. But it still wasn't a good idea, seeing as how he was driving a stretch limo, the only car he could find with the keys in it. Never having driven a land yacht like this before, Tommy was having trouble keeping it on the road.

He was having difficulty with a lot of things, in fact, like staying awake. He even tried pulling off the road to nap, but falling asleep proved even harder, though he'd never been so tired in all his life. This weariness would take more than sleep to cure.

Nothing to do, then, but press on. Stay in constant motion, like a shark. Go forward, never straight. Tommy remembered that one from drunk-driving joyrides in high school, a long time ago; skipping class to hot-wire a teacher's car and sneak off to the liquor store, the one on the other side of town where all the winos went. They never carded. Drinking was fun, although Tommy didn't do it so much anymore because other things had come to occupy his time. Well, one other thing, anyway.

Smack was…certainly not "fun" the way drinking was. It had its pleasures, sure, which was why he did it. Or rather, why he'd started doing it. But at a certain point, shooting up became less about pleasure and more about relief, avoiding the unpleasantness of not shooting up. It was a demanding drug, one that didn't leave room for much else.

Tommy could still find time for music, even if that had also become a dosage issue. If he kept playing, stuff kept arriving. Good stuff, too. Really, *really…good…shit…*

I wonder what happens after tonight? he thought. At the very least, a lot of things were going to change. Despite his exhaustion, Tommy felt truly awake for the first time since he'd been swept onto Gus DeGrande's merry-go-round. Tonight had been his attempt at jumping off. But had he jumped far enough?…

A jackrabbit darted across the highway, just ahead of the car. Tommy would have swerved, but his reflexes were running slow. Besides, any sudden movements in such a boat of a car would've been a very bad idea. So he closed his eyes and prayed. The rabbit escaped. Tommy opened his eyes just in time, as the car drifted onto the shoulder of the road and sent a shower of rocks and gravel shooting off to the side.

Steady, he thought, guiding the car back between the lines, holding the steering wheel so tightly that his knuckles were white. Tommy felt a chill and then a shudder, fighting down a yawning chasm of panic that would devour him whole if he even acknowledged it. He was going to have to cop, soon, and he knew it.

Tommy closed his eyes again and prayed about that, too, as he drove on southward. He opened them again when he felt something cold and metallic pressed against the back of his neck. It felt like…the barrel of a gun. After a few seconds, Tommy heard Susan's voice from the backseat.

"You didn't play my song."

Ken didn't realize it, but he followed after Bob and Tommy, although only far enough to get out of Las Vegas. The critic wanted a quiet place for a day or so before heading home to face the music. He'd never actually been fired before, and wondered what that would be like. *Guess I'll finally have to get a real job,* he thought, steering his rented car out of the hotel parking lot.

Twenty minutes down the road, he stopped in Boulder City, checked into the first cheap motel he came to and went directly to his room. He'd picked up a bottle of bourbon on the way, and slammed down three tall glasses. Ken didn't just want to sleep, he wanted to pass out.

He did.

Early the next morning, a ringing phone jangled him awake. He reached for it through his hangover.

"You," said a voice Ken thought he recognized, "have *really* fucked up this time."

Click.

Music industry convention was to treat substance abuse with a nod and a wink, paying lip service to the evils of drug use while stridently denying all allegations of same (often up to the moment of death by overdose). But Ken's story about Tommy was too specific, too high-profile and too catastrophic for anyone to brush off. By noon Sunday, the word was out that everyone involved with TAB had been ignoring a volatile powderkeg, which blew up onstage in Las Vegas. Reporters from all over the country bombarded the offices of Grandiose Concerts and Poly Brothers Records with phone calls and faxes.

Mo released a statement that his label was "deeply troubled by the events in Las Vegas, and the allegations surrounding them," and would have no further comment. Gus had his secretary take messages he didn't return. But he finally took Mo's call late Sunday afternoon.

"What the hell is going on?!" Mo screamed. "I can't believe you're not out there! And what's this business about Aguilar having a heroin problem? Is it really on the front page of the goddamned newspaper down there?!"

"Yes," the promoter said, holding the receiver away from his ear. Mo sounded like a yapping Chihuahua when he was angry. Gus had been through so many bottles of scotch that he was beyond drunk. Cocaine was the only thing still keeping him awake.

"Jesus! I've been getting calls about this all day, even from the networks! Was it that same writer from down there? Ken Morrison?"

"Yes."

"I thought you said he was discreet, and could be trusted."

"I thought he was."

"You thought he was. Well, fuck, that's just great."

Gus moved to cut off the lecture before it got started. "Mo," he said, rubbing his eyes behind his dark shades, "I'm kind of in the middle of a lot of shit with this. So unless you have something specific that we need to—"

"Is it true?" Mo interrupted.

Gus was taken aback. He looked down at his tape machine, recording their conversation, and wondered if Mo had his end of the phone wired, too (he did). This could be a dangerous exchange to have on tape. "I don't think you have any business asking that question," the promoter said evenly.

"But that's where you're wrong," Mo said. "According to last year's collective record label agreement, all participating companies have morals clauses in their contracts now. That means we have an obligation to make inquiries into the personal habits of our artists, if we suspect them of drug use. And if there's evidence of a problem, our policy is to suspend royalty payments. Which I'm doing with TAB, effective immediately."

"What?!" Gus sat up, yanked off his sunglasses and winced. The light was blinding.

"All part of the industry's anti-drug efforts," Mo said breezily. "Haven't you heard? There's a war on drugs, and I'm on the committee. So it wouldn't look good if Poly Brothers was perceived to be bankrolling your client's addiction. You want to do it yourself and can keep his nose clean, fine. But you can't control him. This riot shit has got to stop, Gus. It's bad for business."

" 'Bad for business?' What the fuck are you talking about? The album's been number one for two months!"

"Yeah, no thanks to you," Mo retorted. "Where've they been since the record came out? Not on the road, because you couldn't keep that little fuck out of trouble. As I see it, TAB has not lived up to its promotional obligations. We'll get a nice short-term bounce out of this riot, but not as much as from a full-scale tour—and that obviously can't happen now."

DeGrande's head spun into overdrive. Desperate, he started reaching for straws that weren't even there. "But what about Ray and Michelle? They're not gonna get paid because of something Tommy did?"

"What, you're actually *paying* those two?" Mo laughed harshly. "That's not like you, Gus, you grow a conscience all of a sudden? You want to pay 'em, you go right ahead. But until further notice, it's on your nickel, not mine."

The promoter didn't have a nickel, and Polydoroff knew it.

"Now, then," Mo continued, lining up his final jab. "There may be one other option: Perhaps you'd care to renegotiate our contract?"

"Mo, you cannot do this!" Gus sputtered. "I don't care what your 'collective agreement' says, the contract I signed doesn't say anything about any of this shit. And no way are we renegotiating *anything*."

"Fine," Mo said. "Sue us. Goodbye, Gus."

Click.

CHAPTER THIRTY-THREE

Bob Porter hit Joshua Tree just before 3 a.m. and took a quick look around. It didn't take long because there wasn't much to it, a hamlet of two thousand people. While there was no visible sign of Tommy, Bob felt certain he was in the vicinity—probably somewhere inside the vast Joshua Tree National Park. But continuing the search in the dark was going to require more energy than he could summon up after the long drive from Las Vegas. He considered sleeping in the van, but decided to get a room so he could begin the next day better-rested. With nothing in Joshua Tree open at that hour, Bob back-tracked fifteen miles to the larger town of Twentynine Palms and checked into the first motel he found.

He signed in using his real name, a mistake he would've avoided had he been listening to the radio. The airwaves were full of reports on the events in Las Vegas. Tommy was classified as "At Large," wanted on charges including assault and inciting a crowd to riot, while Bob was identified as a possible accomplice. Television reports even carried a picture of Bob, the photo from the laminated tour badge he discarded at the stadium.

Viewers and listeners alike were advised that both Bob Porter and Tommy Aguilar might be armed and dangerous and should only be approached with extreme caution.

"Hey, Norm, this is Evelyn over at the Sands."

"Hey, Evelyn, how you?"

"Oh, fine."

"How's your mom 'n' them?"

"Good."

"Everything okay?"

"Well...Are you watching the news?"

"Yeah."

"You see the thing about that riot in Las Vegas last night?"

"Yeah."

"Well, I thought you'd want to know that one of those fellows they say caused it is in room fourteen-A over here."

"Oh, yeah?"

"Yeah. I thought I recognized the picture on TV, and the name matches. Bob Porter. He checked in a few hours ago, and asked for a wakeup call."

"Well, we'll be right over to give him one."

Bob awoke from a deep slumber to one of his least-favorite sounds—someone pounding on a door. He had not quite roused himself enough to remember where he was when the door splintered and a mob of cops stormed in.

"LET ME SEE YOUR HANDS!!!" was the last thing Bob heard before a billyclub crashed into the side of his head.

He tumbled off the bed in a heap, landing on the floor with a sheriff's deputy grinding his face into the carpet. By the time his ears stopped ringing, Bob was handcuffed and sitting in the back of a squad car.

After his own rude awakening, Ken Morrison unplugged the phone and tried to go back to sleep. He couldn't, his drunken stupor having congealed into a vicious hangover. Obviously, then, the only solution was to resume drinking. So he gulped down another glass of bourbon—and swooned, barely making it to the bathroom before he threw up. After his purge, he rinsed his mouth out with water, forced down some more bourbon and passed out all over again.

By the time the critic came to several hours later, it was early afternoon and he was almost too weak to stand up. But that was okay; he wasn't going anywhere. Maybe fasting was the answer, or a hunger strike. His growling stomach gave Ken something to think about besides the reasons why he was holed up in a cheap motel room in Boulder City, Nevada. Every time his mind wandered anywhere near TAB, Ken was overcome with an urge to find the nearèst cliff and hurl himself over it.

So he sat and he stared and he brooded, and most of all he drank. He did not turn on the television or the radio, or plug the phone back in, or look out the window, or even open the curtains. When he finally got so hungry he couldn't bear it any longer, he ordered takeout food. When it arrived, he slipped money under the door and told the delivery person to leave it in the hallway.

He lost track of time, spending what seemed like a week in Boulder City. It was actually just two days. Even so, the maids were starting to wonder why the guy in 212 wouldn't let them in to change the sheets.

By then, he was beginning to stink. So on the morning of day three, Ken shaved and took a long hot shower. Then he removed the battery from the room's smoke detector, lit a small fire in the trashcan and burned his TAB file, one piece of paper at a time. Interview transcripts, performance notes, random observations, magazine clips, photographs, even a cocktail napkin he'd once gotten Tommy to sign ("Ken—Fuck you for everything. Love, TA"). It took a while, but he burned every last scrap, flushing the still-smoldering ashes down the toilet for good measure. Then he checked out of the motel, drove to the Las Vegas airport, turned in his rental car and bought a ticket for the next flight home.

Thinking about what awaited him in Raleigh made Ken's stomach knot up, which was how he knew the booze was wearing off. He didn't want to be sober just yet. So he headed for the airport bar and ordered up a whiskey sour, even though it was only ten thirty in the morning. He was just about to take a sip when the television set behind the counter caught his eye. The top left corner of the screen displayed a particularly sullen-looking photo of Tommy, superimposed over a helicopter-borne camera shot of the desert. The critic vaulted over the bar to turn on the TV's sound.

"Hey," the barkeep said, but Ken silenced him with a look and turned his attention to the screen:

"...Repeating our top story: Tommy Aguilar of the top-selling rock band TAB was found dead early this morning in the desert east of Los Angeles, an apparent drug overdose the cause. Also found at the site was the body of a woman identified as Susan Barwick, from Aguilar's hometown of Raleigh, North Carolina.

"Aguilar was last seen Saturday night fleeing Boyd Stadium in Las Vegas following an abbreviated performance that culminated in a riot, injuring fifty-seven people and causing over a half-million dollars in damage. A hiker in the Joshua Tree National Park discovered the bodies, as well as drug paraphernalia nearby.

"Aguilar's manager and record label had no comment..."

The authorities in Twentynine Palms never could figure out what to do with Bob. After the bodies were found, there was some talk of charging him with accessory to murder. But that was a stretch. Both deaths appeared to be drug overdoses, although of a particularly sordid nature—Tommy and Susan were nude, and appeared to have been engaged in some manner of rough sexplay at the time of death—and Bob was locked up when it happened.

Reluctantly, the police let him go without filing any charges. He bailed out the van (he'd been charged twenty-five dollars a day in "storage" during his jail stay) and put Twentynine Palms in his rearview mirror as fast as legally possible.

It was time to head home. Mexico was still tempting. But one way or another, Gus DeGrande was going to find Bob if he wanted to, regardless of where he ran. Might as well make it on his own turf.

Bob did, however, feel compelled to warn his cousin Mitch that the heat was on. After he was down the road a bit, he found a truckstop payphone and dialed directory assistance.

"What city?"

"Tucson."

"What listing?"

"Brian Satterfield."

"One moment."

After a wait much longer than a moment, the operator returned to the line.

"I'm sorry, sir," she said, "but that number has been disconnected."

Ken drained his whiskey sour in a gulp and ordered another. After slamming that one down even faster, he turned and walked out of the terminal. The late-morning desert heat hit him like a slap in the face but did nothing to snap him out of his daze.

He walked faster, passing the airport's taxi stand and moving purposefully in the direction of I-15. Once there, he went to the southbound lane and put his thumb out.

The critic had no idea where he was going, other than away.

Michelle had just settled in for an afternoon of reading on the beach in front of her hotel in Honolulu. She turned on her radio headphones, just in time to hear the chorus of TAB's "Go As You Are." Wincing, she spun the dial, only to discover that the next station over was also playing her old band.

"What is this?" she wondered, and kept spinning the dial until she finally found a deejay talking.

"...do have to wonder why this keeps happening to so many bands. I guess some people just can't handle success, and it's too bad and all, but...hey, at least the guy went out with a smile on his face, heh heh heh. And he left behind one really kiiiiiiller album, too. Anyway, weather today: mostly sunny, high in the mid-eighties, small chance of evening showers. Tomorrow, more of the same. On the way, more music and remembrances of TAB and Tommy Aguilar—who, if you haven't heard, died this morning of a drug overdose..."

Michelle turned off the radio, looked out over the ocean and felt...absolutely nothing. Not even surprise. She'd been expecting this for so long, it didn't even register as anticlimactic. The details, like whatever the deejay meant by that asinine "smile on his face" crack, mattered even less.

Well, she thought, closing her eyes, *I guess you finally joined the club, you stupid asshole. Is this why we spent so much time looking for places where people died?*

Ray was back home in Raleigh, hanging around the instrument store, when he heard the news about Tommy. Like Michelle, he was not the least bit surprised.

He was, however, much angrier about it.

As soon as reports of Tommy's death came in, Mo Polydoroff got to work. Step one was to call his product manager to make sure the label had enough TAB records in stock, and to crank up the pressing plants. Sick but true: In the record industry, death was great for business. Mo figured this would get *Chorus Verses Chorus* at least another month at number one.

Step two was to buy a full-page "In Memory Of" advertisement in next week's issue of *Cashboard*. It was crass and exploitative, since

Mo had just been putting the squeeze on Gus. But it created the appearance that Poly Brothers cared about something other than the massive sales they'd get from Tommy's very timely demise. Mo billed the ad's fifteen-thousand-dollar cost to the TAB royalty account—the same one he put in escrow. He dictated the ad over the phone, a dozen words of text in white letters on a black background with the Poly Brothers logo:

"Only the good die young. Goodbye, Tommy. Your music will live forever."

Tommy didn't have any family that anybody could find except for his institutionalized mother, who was far too unwell to leave her room. So he never had a formal memorial service. But it hardly seemed necessary, given TAB's omnipresence on the airwaves in the weeks following the bandleader's death. All anyone had to do was turn on a radio to hear Tommy's ongoing benediction for himself.

Fans listened raptly, dissecting every word of every song for clues that would reveal why he flamed out so spectacularly. But aside from some cryptic references to guns and needles, his lyrics were too inscrutable to yield much insight.

Media pundits got plenty of mileage out of Ken's first big TAB profile, in which Tommy talked about fishing for songs and shot the tree in his front yard. Ken's paper sent it out over the wire again, along with the critic's piece outing Tommy as a heroin addict. Although the paper's management was initially furious at Ken's post-riot confessional, they were only too happy to claim credit for breaking the story once Tommy was dead—and the story therefore rendered safely libel-proof.

It was, but not for the reasons they thought. Where Tommy's drug use was concerned, Gus had done much more than simply look the other way, which was why he didn't dare sue. The last thing he wanted was any further scrutiny of Tommy or Susan's death. DeGrande made some public blustering about Ken and "sensationalism," mostly because it would've looked suspicious for him not to complain. But the story actually gave him the perfect cover.

So Ken's account of the Las Vegas riot stood unchallenged as the on-the-record version of events. The *Daily News* even entered the piece in the annual state press association awards, in the "commentary" category. It won second place, after which management reprinted it in an advertisement boasting that the paper was "Telling The Stories That Count." No one seemed terribly concerned that, by then, Ken himself hadn't been heard from in months.

Other publications sank to even lower depths. A supermarket tabloid printed what it claimed was Tommy's suicide note, even though he didn't leave one behind. And one of the big national newsweeklies ran the infamous photo of the bandleader with a pistol in his mouth on its cover. The headline: "Death Wish? What's Wrong With Kids (And Their Music) Today."

That same gun-in-the-mouth picture soon appeared on bootleg TAB T-shirts all over the world—except they weren't bootlegs, exactly. True, they did use a copyrighted photo without permission. The shirts were, however, authorized by the estate of Tommy Aguilar, though no one knew it. Gus secretly had them made, then arranged to sell them through black market channels. It was the perfect scam. Since the shirts were supposedly bootlegs, people expected shoddy quality (which they got) and exorbitant prices (which they paid). The manager cleared a hundred fifty thousand dollars within a month. He did even better with a similarly bogus "bootleg" recording of TAB's truncated final show, *Leaving Las Vegas*.

Those were just two of the many deals Gus cut, practically before his client's remains were cold—he'd died in the desert, after all. Susan Barwick's family had disowned her years earlier, so DeGrande took care of her as well. He had both bodies cremated in California and the ashes scattered at Cap Rock, the site of Gram Parsons' funeral pyre, in deference to Tommy's fascination with death sites.

"Since he became an important rock-star death himself, it just seemed like the right thing to do," Gus told a *Cashboard* reporter, as he broke down in tears.

"He was like a son to me, you know," he added, weeping.

In public, Gus did a great deal of crying over Tommy. Behind the scenes, though, he was all business because there was so much of it to take care of. Just as Colonel Tom Parker had insisted that Elvis Presley being dead was no different from when he'd been in the Army, DeGrande wasn't about to let a little technicality like death get in the way of Tommy's career. Dead or alive, he would have a career, by God. And as Tommy's sole heir (another provision of their management contract), Gus controlled the rights to every aspect of his late client's music and image. Generating revenue from Tommy would actually be easier now that he was no longer around to cause trouble.

Tommy had, once again, played right into Gus's hand—and bailed him out.

Within a week of Tommy's death, DeGrande severed all ties with Poly Brothers. "Better to just start all over," he told the press by way of explanation.

What Gus didn't say was that he planned to make Mo Polydoroff's existence a living hell, starting with where he took TAB and the Grandiose Records imprint: Fold-Hi Records, the new start-up label run by Mo's uncles Adolph and Nehi. It was hardly surprising that Fold-Hi's first artist acquisition was a Poly Brothers act. The elder Polydoroffs had already hired away their former label's best staffers and were angling to make new free agents Arrowhead their second signing.

Even though TAB no longer existed, the band would still have plenty of posthumous releases. Tommy left behind hours of work tapes, to go with twenty-nine songs in various stages of completion from the New York sessions. Grandiose/Fold-Hi's first release was *Second Verse: Unfinished Business, Volume One.* Eight of the album's twelve songs were

Chorus Verses Chorus outtakes, padded with four tracks assembled from the bandleader's stash of homemade tapes.

As on the first TAB album, Gus brought in Geoff Baker to handle the mixing and tweaking. Not that it was necessary, except to give the pretense that this was something besides exploitative profit-taking. Coming barely a month after Tommy's death, the album was going to sell millions no matter what was on it.

In fact, *Second Verse* displaced TAB's first album from the top of the charts, despite Poly Brothers' best efforts to keep *Chorus Verses Chorus* there. That galled Mo, who was legally powerless to stop either TAB or Grandiose Records from leaving. Once again, Mo was on the short end of a contract his uncles stuck him with.

Adding potentially grievous injury to insult, DeGrande took Mo's parting advice and sued Poly Brothers for a hundred million dollars. Immediately after Tommy's death, Mo unfroze Grandiose's royalty account and sent Gus a two-million-dollar advance. But Gus was unmoved. His suit asked for all profits from *Chorus Verses Chorus* plus hefty punitive damages. It alleged fraud, bad faith, restraint of trade and reckless malfeasance, especially in the timing of Mo's suspension of TAB's royalty payments—"an obvious attempt to drive apart plaintiff and client that may have contributed to client's subsequent and untimely death," the suit claimed.

Mo countersued, mostly because there was nothing else he could do. He also asked for an injunction to halt the release of *Second Verse,* but the judge turned him down. So the album rolled into stores, and Gus and Mo entered into what promised to be a protracted legal struggle. DeGrande didn't really expect to win, but figured he could take Poly Brothers, or at least Mo, down if he made the label look bad enough.

It was payback time.

CHAPTER THIRTY-FOUR

Ken Morrison had seemingly vanished off the face of the earth. The trail went cold with the plane ticket from Las Vegas to Raleigh, purchased but never used. After that, nothing. Friends, relatives and co-workers' attempts at finding him came to dead-ends. The critic's landlord waited a month and then rented his apartment to someone else, putting Ken's things into storage. A month after that, his paper hired another rock writer. The replacement's work was solid, though he lacked his predecessor's flair for self-promotion. Since the new guy was fresh out of college, he was cheap.

Bob Porter made it a point not to read the new guy's column, even when it concerned his club. Not that he felt any lingering loyalty to Ken; the clubowner simply no longer cared. For reasons no one could fathom, Bob came back to Raleigh after his TAB misadventures and resumed his place behind the bar at Each. Bands still came and went, but he stopped hearing them despite being in the same room night after night. They were all just so much noise. If he could've gotten away with it, Bob would've worn construction earmuffs.

In spite of his obvious apathy, several times a year bands approached Bob to ask if he'd manage them. As disastrously as his tenure with TAB ended, he still had an unwanted reputation as a guy who could get you somewhere. That TAB's fate was something bands actually thought they wanted was far too disturbing to dwell on.

Bob gave the same answer every time. "Nope," he'd say, "I don't do that anymore. So if you want to keep playing here, don't ask again." Only one band had been stupid enough to ask more than once, and he made good on his threat to ban them.

Always a bit of a mystery to Each's clientele, Bob faded into the background as he withdrew inside himself. He no longer engaged the regulars in small talk, just silently poured drinks and kept to himself. The common assumption was that he felt a sense of guilt or responsibility for what happened. But it wasn't anything so simple. He felt…cheated. Denied, somehow.

Rather than a father figure, Bob fancied himself Tommy's last, best conscience. That was why he'd done nothing to stop what happened in Las Vegas. To Bob's way of thinking, inciting a stadium-full of ill-gotten new fans to riot was the truest TAB's leader had been to himself or his music since going over to Gus DeGrande. That was a sign of life—a signal flare that made Bob think he had one last shot at rescuing Tommy from his heart of darkness.

Not that Bob even knew what he would've said or done had he found his former client in the desert. Would he have lectured Tommy? Yes, at the very least. Beaten the shit out of him? Most likely. Kidnapped him, taken him hostage?

Hmm. Maybe…

Or would he have killed Tommy himself?

The first time this occurred to Bob, he was humming an old Dylan lyric—the one about God telling Abraham, "Kill me a son," and Abraham replying that God must be puttin' him on—and the thought stopped him cold. The clubowner had to admit he might've done it. And the more he thought about it, the more he believed he *should* have been the one to do it. Tommy so loathed what he'd become that he could see no other way out. Which was, Bob thought, the message he was sending out by screaming, "I wanna go over the waaaaaaaall," again and again in front of forty thousand oblivious onlookers.

Through dumb luck, Bob had been spared the burden of deciding Tommy's fate. But this knowledge gave him no relief, or peace. Rather than undoing anything, the bandleader's sudden demise froze him in amber—and gave DeGrande a posthumous icon he could mass-produce and peddle like goddamned popsicles. It made Bob ill to think about.

Late at night, when he was trying to sleep, the clubowner usually found himself wondering about details. Pointless details of what was happening out in the desert while he'd been locked up in jail: What Tommy did during his last hours. And this Susan Barwick woman, who Bob vaguely remembered seeing at Each once or twice—who was she and what was she doing with Tommy that night? Where, when and from whom did they get that final dose? How did they decide where to shoot up? Which one of them went first? And most of all, why? Had they been careless? Reckless? Stupid? All three?

Bob was never going to get any answers out of Tommy. His only hope of a final reckoning was from Gus DeGrande, which was why he came back to Each, and waited.

That was going to take a while, because Gus had much more impor-tant fish to fry. Specifically, a double-crossing little eel by the name of Mo Polydoroff.

DeGrande's lawsuit against Poly Brothers was merely the opening salvo of a jihad, which continued with the promoter exacting retribu-tion on every one of the label's acts that came his way. Lawsuit or no, bands couldn't avoid working with Gus unless they wanted to forgo touring the eastern half of the United States.

So Gus played hardball. He put Poly Brothers bands in the wrong venues, on the wrong nights, up against the wrong competition. He put tickets on sale the wrong days, at the wrong outlets, for too much or too little money. Computers crashed, money vanished, contracted advertising and promised radio airplay mysteriously failed to materialize. All the dirty tricks the promoter used to steal TAB away from Bob Porter, he applied on a grand scale.

It didn't take much to cripple a tour, and Gus was a master at conjuring up disasters while covering his tracks. Now that he finally had a positive cashflow coming in from TAB, he could afford some day-to-day operating losses in the name of a larger purpose. As long as the hits hurt Poly Brothers, too, the promoter was more than willing to take them—especially when he had such a ready scapegoat when anyone complained.

"Your problems," he told one disgruntled band manager, "start with your record label. Poly Brothers, let me tell ya, I've been there and it's just not a good situation. That company is a shadow of what it used to be, and you're the one suffering. You're out here busting ass, but they're not getting you the record sales or the airplay you need to mount a profitable tour. Tell me, for an act of your stature, is Poly Brothers giving you the attention you deserve?"

"Well…no."

"And is your record selling like it should?"

"No."

These were classic leading questions, as Gus knew from years of listening to bands and managers bitch. "Well, there ya go. You need to get out of there and hook up with a real label. Hell, I get more out of Fold-Hi now for a band that doesn't even exist anymore than I got out of Poly Brothers for the same act when it was still around!"

He paused to let that one sink in before asking, "How many more records you owe Poly Brothers?"

"Two."

"Ouch," Gus said sympathetically. "Well, at least it ain't four or five. Ask if they'll let you finish out the contract with a two-disc best-of, then go elsewhere."

"Good idea."

"Son of a *bitch!!!*"

Mo flung the magazine wildly across his office. It tumbled onto a coffeetable and knocked over a potted plant, the vase shattering as it hit the floor.

Rubbing his eyes, the president didn't notice. The offending publication was the new issue of *Rock Slide,* which Mo had hoped would bring good news in its record review section for two Poly Brothers acts.

One was the Nematodes, a band from Florida. Three years earlier, the Nematodes' first album picked up a lot of airplay and sold pretty well—seventy-five thousand copies, solid numbers for a debut and good enough for the label to pin some hopes on the follow-up. The other act was Tailgate Jerk, a new all-female band from Los Angeles that was longer on looks than musical ability. Mo had signed Tailgate Jerk himself, against the advice of his own A&R department.

Between recording costs and marketing setup, Poly Brothers was in for a cool million bucks on the two bands' new albums, which came out on the same day. That was Mo's idea, for the label to flex its muscles by showing off two promising new artists. Unfortunately, early returns were not encouraging. Radio stations simply weren't adding either record to their playlists, despite massive cajoling from Polydoroff's promotional minions. For the first time Mo could remember, stations actually turned down payola.

"I'm sorry, Mo," one program director told him, "but I can't help you this time. It would just be too obvious why this one got on the air."

Both bands had also made very expensive videos—which were going nowhere just as fast as their singles. And no radio or video exposure meant no sales. Mo figured his last shot at saving either project was building buzz through the press. On their own, favorable reviews didn't usually sell records. But good reviews sometimes led to airplay, and it never hurt one's standing within the industry to put out critically respected work.

Mo had already primed the pump at *Rock Slide,* personally taking pre-release copies of both albums down to the magazine's offices. This sent the message that these acts were a priority, since the president of the company was personally involved. The record review editor agreed to review both albums, so Mo bought two half-page advertisements to run in the same issue. If the reviews were positive enough, the plan was to buy ad space elsewhere and reprint them.

Polydoroff made one significant miscalculation, however. In spite of all the time and money Poly Brothers sank into the Nematodes and Tailgate Jerk, neither band's record was very good. The reviews in *Rock Slide* weren't simply bad, they were more like what you'd do to a housefly. The Nematodes review began:

> Paying homage to one's influences is fine, but there's still a difference between homage and regurgitation—or outright thievery. There's not a single song, riff or note on this boneheaded Florida outfit's thoroughly tedious second album that you haven't heard before, done better elsewhere.

At least the Nematodes received a two-star rating out of five, which translated as "fair." But Tailgate Jerk earned an almost-unprecedented half-star rating—half of what the magazine deemed to be "poor." Mo had become enamored of Tailgate Jerk after seeing the group's live show, which involved soft-core porn, more than a little nudity and, for the encore, tattooed six-foot-three guitarist Julie Serrano stripping down to a G-string and literally breathing fire. But none of that had anything to do with making a record, and *Rock Slide's* review was unusually harsh:

> Times must be dire indeed, if this much-hyped all-femme band is anybody's idea of the future of rock 'n' roll. As it is, Tailgate Jerk's big-league debut is one for the ages—

the dark ages, that is. Possibly the worst-conceived record of
the year, *Tailgate Jerk* is laughably inept, proving only that
all the smoke, mirrors, kerosene, cleavage, hairspray and
tattoos in the world can't compensate for a lack of actual
ideas or talent.

Mo stopped reading after the next paragraph, which speculated that
the only reason Tailgate Jerk got a record deal at all was the group members' rumored prowess at blowjobs (which made him wonder if his
office was bugged). So he threw the magazine at the potted plant, and
wondered: Could he build an advertising campaign around how much
critics hated these bands?

Labels had done creative things with embarrassing situations before.
A few years back, after one of its British bands was denied performance
visas to do a U.S. tour because the INS ruled the group had "No Artistic
Merit," another record company actually used that phrase as an advertising tagline.

But these reviews were so awful that anything Mo did now would
only make things worse. *Rock Slide* hadn't simply defied Mo but
mocked him, in a way the magazine would never have dared when
the elder Polydoroffs were running Poly Brothers. A further helping
of salt in the wounds lay in the placement of the ads for the
Nematodes and Tailgate Jerk—which, at the president's instructions,
referred to both albums as "critically acclaimed"—on the same pages
as each slam-dunk review.

From New York to L.A., everybody in the industry was opening up the
new issue of *Rock Slide,* turning to the record review section and having a
good laugh at Mo Polydoroff's expense. They'd all passed on signing
Tailgate Jerk themselves.

This represented a serious loss of face. It also left Mo with few options,
or hopes that either band could turn things around for Poly Brothers. The
label's last successful release was TAB, which continued to sell. He wanted

to pull the plug on *Chorus Verses Chorus,* but didn't dare because it was the only hit he had. Even after Grandiose/Fold-Hi's posthumous followup knocked TAB's debut out of number one, it lingered in the top-ten. Sales were at six million and counting, with no signs of slowing down.

And if DeGrande's lawsuit went badly for Poly Brothers, the label would have to hand over every dime it made on TAB—and than some.

It was a strange Christmas that year. Mercifully, the Nematodes and Tailgate Jerk were both long-forgotten. But TAB wasn't. *Second Verse* sold more than respectably, passing the three million mark before the end of the year. By then, Fold-Hi had another posthumous volume of TAB tracks ready to release.

As the year came to a close, holiday shoppers could also snap up another TAB product—*Go As You Are: The Official History of TAB*—the book Ken was to have written. In his absence, the ever-opportunistic Marty McPhail inherited the book deal and proved to be the perfect stand-in. Gus made the agenda perfectly clear, and McPhail delivered with a tome that was long on rhapsodic bullshit about What It All Meant, but short on ugly details. It glossed over Tommy's drug problem as a regrettable frailty that had been "blown out of proportion," painting his death as a fluky exclamation point that only made TAB's music that much more poignant.

Chorus Verses Chorus and *Second Verse* both showed up in most critics' top ten lists, with the debut topping all the big year-end polls. That gave the music glossies yet another excuse to put Tommy on their covers again. Gus and Mo weren't the only ones to realize that dying was the most profitable thing Tommy ever did.

In its yearly recap, *Rock Slide's* competitor *Bounce* included an interesting little story on Tommy's partner in death, Susan Barwick. Prior to her death, she'd been working in Los Angeles making pornographic movies. One of them, in fact, starred Peg Camper—the porn actress working name of Tailgate Jerk guitarist Julie Serrano—with a bizarre plotline involving rape and Russian Roulette.

Susan had a major supporting role.

Ken was deliberately unaware of most of this. By the fall, he'd settled in Seattle, which was as far as he could get from Raleigh without actually leaving the country. He lived under the radar, alone in a cheap efficiency on the rundown side of town. His landlord didn't require paperwork, references or deposits, just that the rent show up on time. Ken scrupulously paid on the first of each month, in cash. He made his rent money working for a shady temp agency, which also paid in cash and didn't report its workers' income to the IRS.

Ken was one of the agency's few employees who wasn't an illegal alien, and therefore one of its only workers fluent in English. That made him useful—he could do clerical work, which he didn't mind a bit. He saw no reason for his penance to include physical labor on top of psychological anguish.

Life in exile was hardly glamorous. Every day began at precisely six fifty-seven a.m., when Ken snapped awake. It was one of the odder side effects of the jolt he got in Las Vegas. After years of late nights and leisurely late-morning rising, he found he could barely sleep past dawn anymore, even if he drank himself into a stupor the night before. That had its upside, of course. He no longer needed an alarm clock.

After starting his morning with a cursory scan of the morning paper over an equally cursory breakfast, Ken showered, dressed and walked to work. Driving wasn't an option, even when the weather was bad—he no longer owned a car. By the end of his first year in Seattle, in fact, Ken no longer had a driver's license. He never bothered applying after his old North Carolina one expired. No need. He no longer drove, didn't have a checking account and never got carded at the liquor store anymore. He didn't have a phone, either, as there was no one he wanted to talk to.

Ken's daily destination was a small unmarked storefront that housed the temp agency, fourteen blocks from his apartment. He arrived by eight-fifteen most mornings, staking out the chair farthest from the door to await the day's instructions. Usually, he passed the time with a paperback; he found he could better deflect his fellow day laborers' inquisitive stares from behind a book.

By eight-thirty, the waiting room was crowded with up to two dozen people. They were a sad lot, mostly run-down men who weren't nearly as old as they looked. The majority of the firm's employees were in the U.S. illegally, either from Central America or Asia. For whatever reason—not enough nerve or too many prior convictions, usually—none of them could risk either legitimate employment or outright criminality. So they came here in search of honest labor in the gray zone of the local underground economy.

They seldom had to wait long for work. There were ditches to be dug, loads to be hauled, trees to be cut, dishes to be washed, toilets to be scrubbed, nails to be hammered, vegetables to be picked. The agency was popular with independent contractors, especially small-time mavericks who didn't bother with details like inspections or permits or taxes.

A steady stream of employers came in each morning, walking through the waiting room to knock on a door to the inner office. They disappeared into the office and reappeared a few minutes later, silently pointed out the workers they wanted and left with the day's laborers following behind them. The room was usually empty by nine. Except for the sound of shoes shuffling across scuffed and dirty floor tiles, the process was deathly quiet. Entire mornings went by without a single word being spoken in the waiting room.

Ken was, as far as he knew, the only employee ever permitted past the door to the office in back, where he occasionally did typing, file-sorting or simple bookkeeping. He carried out these assignments with an unthinking competence, asking few questions. His employers appreciated his lack of inquisitiveness.

Most days, Ken was sent elsewhere, riding the bus if it was too far to walk. Most of the work was pretty cut-and-dried—word-processing, answering phones, sorting mail, running errands. The closest he got to his former profession was a weeklong stint compiling calendar listings at a weekly paper. Being around a newsroom again threw him into a hideous depression that lingered for weeks. He was relieved when the paper folded.

He was paid by the hour, and paid every day. If he put in a full day, he usually took home fifty dollars, which he stashed under his mattress. He made more than enough to cover his minimal rent and living expenses. Very occasionally, he ate out at a restaurant or went to a movie—alone, always. But he didn't get out much at night, preferring to go to sleep when the sun went down and rising when it came up. Sleeping twelve hours meant he didn't have to be awake thinking about anything half the day.

Of course, in his sleep, there was still no escaping his own relentless nightmares. Every night, in Ken's dreams, Tommy Aguilar and Charlie Holmes remained very much alive.

CHAPTER THIRTY-FIVE

With TAB's posthumous career going so well and Poly Brothers Records falling apart right on schedule, Gus DeGrande turned his attention to finding his next managerial client. He needed a band that actually still existed, preferably one that was already established. With another proven hitmaker in hand, Gus would then be well-positioned to take on a brand-new act—one that would be more cooperative than Tommy.

The promoter didn't have to look hard, finding his mark in another ex-Poly Brothers group: Arrowhead, gearing back up after frontman Perry Rose's near-fatal overdose. Once Rose recovered enough for the band to map out future plans, they collectively decided a change was needed. The band's first step was to fire longtime manager Procter Silberman.

The second was to sign on with Gus. For a band with a problematic drug situation, hiring someone whose only previous client died of a heroin overdose made little outward sense. Moreover, Silberman was one of the most respected managers in the industry. His integrity and loyalty were both beyond question—Arrowhead was the only group he'd ever worked with.

But one thing outweighed loyalty or logic, and that was simple greed. Gus was the man with the keys to the vault at Fold-Hi Records. Never mind Silberman's friendship with label heads Adolph and Nehi

Polydoroff, which went back decades. Thanks to TAB, DeGrande had more leverage there.

So Silberman was odd man out, his twenty-five-year association with Arrowhead dissolved by a single curt phone call. The band didn't even have the decency to fire him in person, figuring a seven-figure contract buyout was decency enough.

To get Arrowhead, Gus promised the moon. He delivered, and then some: a five-album deal paying an unheard-of advance of twenty million dollars per album. A hundred million bucks, guaranteed. It was an insane amount of money to give anyone, let alone a band in which all five principles were pushing fifty. Each Arrowhead album would have to sell at least four million copies for Fold-Hi to break even.

But there was a message in the money. Fold-Hi had lots of it to spend, thanks to the deep pockets of its overseas investors. Adolph and Nehi wanted to make a statement. They intended their new label to be the biggest dog on the block—much bigger and more important than their old one.

Thanks to Silberman's tutelage, Arrowhead was more savvy about business matters than Tommy. They at least knew enough to hire their own lawyer, ensuring that the conditions of DeGrande's management weren't as onerous as the terms he gave TAB. But the sheer volume of up-front dollars more than compensated.

"Management is a horrible way to make a living," he mockingly cackled to a *Cashboard* reporter when the deal was announced. "Who wants to do all this work, then give eighty-five percent of your money to the artist?"

Gus could afford to be glib. His cut as manager meant he stood to make fifteen million dollars from the Arrowhead deal, plus millions more by having the Grandiose Records imprint on their releases. A few more scores like this, and the promoter would no longer need Fold-Hi. He could upgrade Grandiose from an imprint to a freestanding label; push the buttons himself instead of leaning on other people to do it. Maybe even go multimedia, take the jump to movies.

But that was still down the road. In the meantime, Gus had a few loose ends to tie up.

Given the peculiar circumstances of his employment, Ken Morrison was accustomed to unusual assignments. Nevertheless, the work he did was seldom as brazenly, transparently fraudulent as this particular job.

It involved processing files for a Las Vegas-based insurance company in the midst of declaring bankruptcy. Criminality aside, the work was stupefyingly dull: Open a manila folder, punch up the corresponding computer file and see if the figures matched. A lot didn't, with some of the differences running to tens of thousands of dollars. Apparently, this particular firm was involved in some highly questionable ventures, cooking the books to hide money-laundering, land flips and god knew what else.

Ken's' task was to make the numbers in the paper files match up with the numbers in the computer files. On any that didn't match, he was to shred the paper file and replace it with a printed copy of the computer record. Soon into the process, he realized what he was doing: reconciling discrepancies between the company's real books and its fake ones before any creditors, prosecutors or judges saw them. Just to be on the safe side, Ken started wearing gloves so he wouldn't leave fingerprints on anything.

It was slow work because the files were a mess, randomly stuffed into boxes as if they'd been moved in a hurry. They had. One reason they were in Seattle at all was to keep them out of Las Vegas while the insurance company's lawyers stonewalled on a number of subpoenas. Once Ken finished cleaning everything up, the records were scheduled to reappear in a bonded warehouse in Las Vegas—where they would be "discovered" soon after several key statutes of limitations ran out.

There were fifty-seven boxes to get through, piled haphazardly into a small dank storage warehouse in an office park. The room was equipped with a desk, lamp, portable computer, printer and paper shredder. Ken had already spent three weeks on the project, with at least that much still to go.

One rainy Tuesday afternoon, Ken settled in after lunch and started to shift his mind over to autopilot. He opened a new box, reached in and pulled out a file folder from the middle of the stack. Out of habit, he looked at the name on the folder strip. He didn't know why he kept doing it, as he had yet to recognize a single one. In fact, he was just about ready to conclude that the names were as bogus as this company's bookkeeping, until he saw:

"AGUILAR, THOMAS W."

It was neatly typed. Just below the name, the label was a little sloppier. Someone had hurriedly scrawled in red ink, "(deceased)." There were a lot of other cryptic scribblings on the two-dozen sheets of paper inside the folder, including the name of a casino and some staggeringly large numbers.

Ken didn't get much work done the rest of that afternoon.

Four days after Ken stumbled across Tommy's insurance file, the phone call Bob Porter had been waiting on finally came—one year, eight months and twenty-two days after Tommy's death.

"Each."

"Please hold for Gus DeGrande," said an inhumanly businesslike female voice on the other end. That gave Bob a few unexpected moments to prepare; it wasn't like Gus to give up the element of surprise.

He must be pretty confident, the clubowner thought. *Or else he just doesn't give a shit.*

"Bob," the promoter said when he finally came on the line, "Gus DeGrande here."

"Gus. What a delightful surprise, after all this time."

"Oh, the pleasure's mine," Gus said. "All mine. How's business?"

"Can't complain. You?"

"No complaints, other than my biggest act no longer being around."

"Well, that doesn't seem to be holding you back much."

"One does what one can," Gus replied, deflecting Bob's sarcasm. "What was it you said about Tommy, that he was 'beyond saving'? Guess you turned out to be right after all."

"Guess so."

"Not that you knocked yourself out trying to save him," DeGrande jabbed.

Oh, if you only knew, Bob thought, but said nothing.

"You know," DeGrande continued once it became clear the clubowner wouldn't take the bait, "you and I never did settle up over TAB."

"Well, Gus, somehow I figured you wouldn't be picking up my option, seeing as how that tour ended before it even got started."

"Yes, exactly. There was no tour, and I wound up paying you a lot of money for services that weren't rendered—in part because you stood by and did nothing in Las Vegas."

Bob laughed harshly. "Since when did you ever think thirty grand was 'a lot of money,' Gus? Jesus, you must make more than that off TAB in an average day now. Anyway, you hired me to manage a tour and run sound, not put down a riot. Besides which, what you paid me wasn't a salary, it was a finder's fee—a 'cheap one,' remember? So you and I are even."

"Not exactly," DeGrande said. "You have something I want. Or, more precisely, something I own."

"And that would be?…"

"The mastertape to TAB's first single."

Bob laughed again, this time incredulously. "You mean the single I recorded? 'Rock Hit Back to Black'?"

"Yes. That one."

"Wow. Suddenly, it all makes sense. I just heard from my pal Gerald, who owns the studio where we did that record. Seems they had a break-in the other night, and the only thing the burglars took were some mastertapes from the library. No instruments, no equipment, just worthless old tapes. Strange, huh?"

"I'm sure," Gus said, "that I have no idea what you're talking about."

"Just like I'm sure the timing of this call is a complete coincidence. Right? So anyway, I guess you discovered that 'Rock Hit Back' is not on any of those tapes from the studio."

"Do you have it?"

"Let's just say it's stashed someplace where you'll never find it," Bob said.

"I wouldn't be so sure of that. You really want me to come looking for it?"

"Be my guest. Just don't waste your time breaking into my club, because it's not here. But tell me something: We did that single before you even knew who TAB was. So where do you get off claiming you 'own' it?"

"Because," Gus said, "as the sole heir to Tommy's estate, I own the rights to everything—his property, his image and, yes, his music."

"Not this tape, you don't."

"I'm pretty sure a judge would disagree."

"Especially if it just happened to be *your* judge."

"They're all my judges, Bob."

"Right. Thanks for the reminder. Anyway, just for the sake of argument, let's say you do own this tape. Why do you even want it?"

"For the next TAB compilation. We tried taping it off a copy of the single, but you had that thing so cheaply pressed it sounded like shit—too much hiss for CD. So we'll take the tape and tweak it."

"Just like you tweaked that album, eh?" Bob jabbed.

"Just like we tweaked that album," Gus agreed. "It worked—ten million sold worldwide. Whether you like it or not, *Chorus Verses Chorus* made Tommy a legend."

"Yeah, and it's a real shame he's not around to enjoy this hall of fame you've built for him. But you know, Tommy didn't much like that album. And to tell you the truth, he didn't even like this single too much, either. So if you want to put out a bunch more records of Tommy making fart noises, Gus, knock yourself out. But you ain't putting my single on any of 'em."

"Did I mention that, as producer, you'll get a cut of the royalties? Our last TAB compilation did three million units, so this is serious money. Maybe even six figures."

"The answer," Bob said, "is still an emphatic, six-figure no."

Gus paused to ratchet the pressure up a notch. "Bob, I respect the fact that you're driving a hard bargain. Given our past history, I'd expect nothing less. But one way or another, you are going to let me have this. We can do it easy, or we can do it hard. So let's try easy for a change: How much you want for it?"

"I already told you, it's not for sale."

"Oh, yes it is," Gus said darkly. "It better be, or we're going to court and you can take your chances there."

"If I lost, I'd just erase it."

"Do that," the promoter warned, "and you're a dead man."

"Was that a threat?"

"You heard me."

"Good," Bob deadpanned. "Just checking. You seem to be losing your touch, Gus, because this time I'm sticking with my first answer: No."

"You *will* regret this. Count on it."

"I'd be disappointed if I didn't."

It was a photo finish who hung up first.

Ken took his time getting home. He didn't want to fly and make the trip too fast, or hitchhike and get too distracted. For once, he didn't want to escape any of his memories. He wanted to just sit in a captive transportation situation, and think.

So he packed up the few belongings he wanted to keep, abandoned his apartment and got on a train. The trip to Raleigh took five days, which he spent staring out the window at the scenery rolling past the rails.

Re-reading the insurance file, Ken thought about Tommy and Bob and Gus, and himself. And money, lots more than he'd ever imagined. Three million dollars, which a now-bankrupt insurance company from Las Vegas paid DeGrande after Tommy's death. The timing of that was certainly convenient. Funny how, no matter what happened, Gus always seemed to get paid. The world could end, and that fucker would somehow still get his fifteen percent

By the time Ken stepped off the train back home, he thought he had a rough picture sketched out. All that was left to do was detail work.

CHAPTER THIRTY-SIX

Immediately after arriving at the downtown Raleigh Amtrak station, Ken headed straight for Each. He did it without giving himself time to reconsider, because this was one conversation he truly dreaded. The nightclub looked as though he'd never left—same sign with the burned-out 'B' on the roof, same weed-filled potholes in the parking lot, same stale smoky air inside. He walked in and wasted a few minutes watching the band. It was comforting, in a small way, to discover that the old rule of thumb still applied: Bands always sounded better from outside.

This one seemed typical enough, four scruffy kids making a godawful racket, most likely playing their first-ever show outside of somebody's basement. They'd at least learned the valuable lesson that volume concealed a multitude of sins. They had plenty of sins to cover up, too, especially the drummer's wavery rhythms and the frontman's off-key vocals. But the chunky kid on the right, the lead guitarist, seemed to know what he was doing. In fact, he was all that stood between the rest of the band and total chaos. He fought a brave, doomed battle.

Bad as this band was, seeing them up there hacking still lifted the critic's spirits a bit. There is a certain poetry to awful bands, thanks to the courageous, foolhardy leap of faith it takes to get up on a stage and pretend to know what you're doing. Ken had a leap to take himself. At least it would involve a drink.

Trying his best to look casual, Ken finally turned and ambled over toward Each's bar—where Bob Porter had been staring at him from the moment he walked in. As he approached, Ken aimed a look he hoped would be interpreted as friendly at the clubowner, who made no such effort in return.

Ken reached the bar, levered himself onto a stool and planted his elbows on the stained and pitted counter, hands folded under his chin. His left elbow fit perfectly into the crucible of a heart someone had carved into the wood years before. He started to order, then stopped because his request would've been inaudible over the noise of the band. Bob let his gaze drop long enough to turn around, open the cooler and extract a green twelve-ounce bottle of Rolling Rock.

Bob pried the cap off with his teeth (one of his better party tricks) and slid the bottle down the bar. It bounced through some rough spots and almost toppled over before Ken caught it and took a nervous sip. As if on cue, the band on-stage crashed to a halt, leaving a silence as thick as their music.

There was very little applause.

"Kenneth," Bob said quietly.

"Robert," Ken answered with a nod, wondering why they both felt compelled to use such formality. All he could read in the clubowner's tone was irritated bemusement. There followed an uncomfortably long pause, while the chunky lead guitarist changed a string on his Gibson and tried to retune. He'd been beating the hell out of it, overplaying in a vain attempt to keep the rest of the band in line, and broke the E-string. He picked and tuned, over and over: A-D-G-B-E, A-D-G-B-E...

Bob didn't move or take his eyes off Ken, just stood there behind folded arms. The critic fought an urge to jump up and run from the room.

"Ken," Bob finally said.

"Bob," Ken replied.

They seemed to have reached an impasse, although Ken was encouraged they had progressed to informal names. The pause was shorter this time.

"Been a long time," Bob said.

"Going on two years," Ken agreed, nodding. Bob dropped his gaze to study his nails a moment. Then he looked up with a glare so intense that Ken nearly winced.

"So Ken...Just what the *fuck* are you doing here?"

Onstage, the chunky guitarist was finally ready.

"We need to talk," Ken said.

A spasm of anger flickered across Bob's face. "I got nothin' to say to you," he said. "And that'll be a buck-seventy-five for the beer."

Ken laid two one-dollar bills on the bar.

"You never did tip worth a shit," Bob muttered, ringing up the sale and pocketing the quarter. Ken finally felt brave enough to risk a quip.

"Who said anything about a tip?"

Bob's reply was lost as the band started into another song. The chunky guitarist resumed hammering away, again locked in mortal combat with the rhythm section, while the singer screamed to be heard. Halfway through the first verse, the guitarist realized his instrument wasn't as in tune as he thought. It sounded like the four of them were playing four different, totally unrelated pieces of music.

Bob watched Ken watch the band and shook his head. Finally, he walked down to the end of the bar closest to the stage, reached into a breaker box out of sight near the floor, and threw a switch. Instantly, the band's amplifiers and microphones went dead. Ken smiled in spite of himself, remembering the clubowner's secret gong system.

"We're closed," Bob announced to the room after the echoes died away. No one argued.

After clearing the room and locking up, Bob turned and walked into his office. Ken trailed him in.

"So…how's the club biz?" Ken asked.

"Just swell," Bob answered, shutting the door behind them. "Fabulous, wonderful, terrific, turn-away crowds every night—all those other phrases that get used whenever it's on the record."

"Like you used to say, 'The truth is always off the record.'"

"So's this conversation, Mr. Reporter," Bob said, settling into a chair behind his desk and folding his arms. "You do remember off-the-record, don't you? It's a concept I remember you having some trouble with."

"Only when it turns out to be the truth."

The clubowner laughed harshly. "Fuck, don't even get me started."

This wasn't going to be easy. Ken decided to try waiting him out, so he said nothing for a while. But the silence grew more awkward and Bob didn't budge. He seemed perfectly content to just sit there silently glaring all night. The critic cleared his throat and tried to laugh.

"Glad to see you're still your same ol' talkative self, Bob."

"You're the one who said we needed to talk. So talk, already."

"Ever hear of foreplay, Bob?"

"Fuck you."

"See, that's just what I—"

"Ken," Bob interrupted, "cut the shit. Get to the fucking point. What do you want?"

"All right, all right," he sighed. "I'm here about Tommy."

"So I figured. Well, Morrison, you can rest easy—he's still dead, and Gus DeGrande is still making a mint off of him."

"Too bad."

"Yeah, well…" Bob snorted. "I guess you and I both blew whatever shot we had at that. Where the fuck you been all this time, anyway?"

"Seattle."

"What'd you do, throw a dart at a map and miss wide left?"

"Sort of. It was a long way from here and nobody asked any questions. That seemed good enough at the time."

"And all of a sudden, you're back. Why?"

"To try and figure out what happened in Las Vegas."

"What's to know?" Bob asked. "He fucked up, he died. End of story."

"But why?"

"Why? Why do you even think there's a 'why' involved? Hey, wait a minute—are you trying to weasel another book out of this?"

"Nope," Ken said. "No books, newspapers, magazines, tabloids. This is personal, confidential and off the record."

"It fucking well better be," Bob warned. "Anyway, I was in jail when he died. So why do you think I'd know anything?"

"You might know something about this woman Tommy was with when he died, Susan Barwick."

"Nothing beyond what I saw in the papers. I might have seen her at a TAB show or two, and Tommy went off with her at the end of the night. But that's it."

"Did Tommy ever tell you anything about her?"

"Nope. I didn't even know her name until after Las Vegas, when I saw her picture. She was never a regular. I don't think I ever saw her at a show here other than Tommy's."

"Doesn't it seem weird that, of all the people Tommy could have been with that night, it was an old girlfriend from back here?"

"I guess. It's either a really weird coincidence, or she was one devoted fan. So what?"

"So I don't think Tommy's death was an accident."

Ken expected Bob to be surprised. Instead, the clubowner shook his head with a smirk.

"And here I used to think you were an idiot when I had to read your column every week. But that's giving you too much credit—you're not just an idiot, you're a moron."

"For thinking Tommy was murdered?"

"No, dipshit, for taking so long to figure that out. Now get outta here."

"So you already knew?"

"Out," Bob said. "Now."

"I'll be in touch," Ken said, moving toward the door.

"Not if you know what's good for you."

On his way out of the club, Ken made a stop in the men's room. And there it still was, on the wall above the urinal near the ceiling, a piece of vintage graffiti that had somehow survived. He recognized his own handwriting: "TOMMY AGUILAR RULES THIS TOWN WITH AN IRON, ALBEIT SHAKY, HAND."

After looking up Bob, Ken knew conclusively that no one in Raleigh was going to be happy to see him again. He thought he'd try Ray next, since he'd be easy to find—still giving lessons over at Dick's Drum Head, one of the big local instrument dealers.

His second day back in town, Ken showed up at the store just before noon and asked for Ray. "He's in back giving a lesson," the clerk said, nodding toward the practice rooms behind the main showroom. "Can you come back in an hour?"

"Sure."

"You want to leave a message?"

Ken thought for a moment, wondering if that was a good idea. "Yeah, tell him Ken Morrison was here and I'll be back later."

"Will do."

Relieved that the clerk didn't recognize him, the critic turned to leave. Dick's used to be enemy territory. When he'd been the *Daily News* critic, the technique fetishists who made up the store's employees and clientele universally loathed Ken Morrison. Strike one was that he was a critic at all, strike two that he didn't play an instrument himself. And strike three was that he tended to like bands they all regarded as incompetent frauds who couldn't play for shit. Things got particularly hostile after a column in which Ken claimed the worthiness of a band could be predicted by their dayjobs. "Members of good bands work in record stores, while members of great ones work in restaurants," he wrote. "But members of bad bands invariably work in instrument stores."

That was worth a few lines of choice graffiti on the bathroom walls at Each, plus a broken window. Someone duct-taped a broken guitar tuner to a brick and heaved it into Ken's car outside the club one night. Taped to the brick was a message—"Tell those shitty bands you DO like that they need to learn to TUNE their FUCKING INSTRUMENTS"— scrawled on the back of a Dick's Drum Head brochure.

Oy, Ken thought, looking around Dick's showroom. *How soon they forget.*

On his way out, he paused by the drumkit display in the front window. Covering one wall was a blown-up black-and-white photo of TAB with Ray flailing away at his drums, a smirk on his face as he and Tommy looked at each other. The guitarist was charging forward and appeared to be on the verge of pitching face-first into the drumkit—which was exactly what subsequently happened. The collision cracked a cymbal, bloodied Tommy's nose and left Ray with a black eye.

Great picture, though. *Rock Slide* used it to illustrate Ken's TAB cover story, an enlarged copy of which was framed next to the picture. Ken looked closer and noticed that his byline had been whited out.

Figures, he thought, then looked at the picture again and noticed Tommy's necklace. Ken was just about to take out his notebook to write something down when he heard a crash from the back of the store. A door flew open and Ray came storming into the showroom, the thoroughly alarmed clerk and one very perplexed drum student trailing behind.

Ken tried not to gawk, but couldn't help himself. Ray had always been an avid body Nazi, working out religiously so he'd look good playing shirtless. But his body had seemingly lost the will to stay in shape. Less than two years since the last time Ken saw him, the drummer looked like he was carrying an extra ten years and fifty pounds—plus a lot less hair and almost no pride. He looked pudgy, yet somehow shrunken.

The shocked look on Ken's face only made Ray angrier. He turned and addressed the clerk in a loud voice. "Tell Ken Morrison," he said, "that I have nothing to say to him. And tell him that if I catch him anywhere near here, I'll make him sorry he was ever born."

"Ray—"

Ray wheeled on Ken in a fury, stalking forward with his fists balled. Even having gone to seed, he still looked capable of snapping the critic in half.

"There aren't many people I'd risk ruining my hands over, Morrison, but you top the list. So get outta here before I decide to go ahead and do just that."

"All right, I'm going," Ken said, holding his hands up. "But if you change your mind—"

"Go fuck yourself," Ray spat contemptuously. "I won't. Now get lost."

Ken nodded, turned and walked outside. Instead of immediately leaving the premises, he ambled around to the back of the store, where the employees parked. He was looking for Ray's car, which was easy to spot—the oldest but best-kept one in the lot. The drummer may have let himself go, but he still took care of his cars.

As Ken scribbled the plate number in his notebook for future reference, he heard someone start to play in one of the store's practice rooms. It was so loud that the metal back door was vibrating. Whoever was back there, they were really beating the hell out of a drumkit.

It didn't sound like much of a lesson.

Chapter Thirty-Seven

Stop number three was Michelle's old place of employment, the bookstore over by campus. Ken didn't expect to find here still working there, and he didn't. But the owner gave him directions to her new job at a greenhouse just west of town.

Michelle tended plants for a living now. They were less trouble than people, especially the ones she'd been hanging around. She hadn't touched a bass since fleeing the stage in Las Vegas, and found she didn't miss it. She was alone in the greenhouse repotting a small shrub when Ken arrived. He walked in and stood in the doorway, waiting for her to notice. When she finally looked up, she gave a start.

"Hello, Michelle," Ken said, feeling awkward.

She said nothing and simply stared, still gripping a small spade, her knuckles turning white inside their work gloves.

"Michelle?…" he said after ten seconds went by, wondering if she'd heard him.

Finally, she answered. "Give me one good reason why I shouldn't plant this in your throat," she said, holding up the uncomfortably sharp-looking spade.

"That it would be silly and pointless to get yourself fired over the likes of me?"

"Never happen," she said.

"No? Does the boss know you threaten the customers?"

"She knows, but doesn't care."

"Sounds like my kinda job," Ken said. "Where do I apply?"

"Nah, you'd never do," Michelle said. "Even though you'd be useful for fertilizer. But I've already got all the help and all the fertilizer I need right now."

"All the help you need? Wait a minute, you're the boss?"

"Uh huh," Michelle said. "I own this place."

"No way," Ken said, giving the small but well-kept greenhouse a closer look. "How'd you manage that on a bass player's salary?"

"Oh, the salary wasn't too bad. Plus I made Gus DeGrande pay me in advance before that last tour—the one that never happened."

"And I guess you've made a pretty penny on record sales, too."

"Nope," Michelle said, shaking her head. "Not a penny, let alone a pretty one."

"How is that possible?"

"Last time I bothered to check, I was told we were 'still unrecouped,' though I can't imagine Gus spent *that* much. But I didn't push it. He never asked for the tour money back and he's left me alone, so we'll call it even. I came out okay."

"He probably figured you earned it," Ken said. "Battle pay for putting up with Tommy and Ray for as long as you did."

"You don't even know the half of it," Michelle sighed, her frown finally softening a bit.

"I might, actually. But tell me anyway."

"Tell you what?"

"Anything you can remember," Ken said. "You know, gory details about TAB and Tommy and Las Vegas. War stories, stupid things Tommy said or did, any girls he talked about."

" 'War stories'?" Michelle repeated, her eyes narrowing. " 'Stupid things Tommy did?' How about *dying,* was that 'stupid' enough? Jesus, Ken, what planet have you been on? Isn't it a little late to still be trying to do 'The TAB Story'?"

"Probably. But I'm never gonna get caught up if I don't start sometime."

Michelle's angry scowl was firmly back in place. "I really can't fathom why you're here, Ken, and you know what? I don't even want to know. I don't spend much time nowadays thinking about Tommy or TAB, or Ray or Bob or Gus—or you. That's all in the past, and I'd like to keep it there. So, ah, thanks for the opportunity to reminisce and all. But I'd really like it if you went away and didn't come back."

"Everybody keeps saying that," Ken sighed.

Michelle laughed derisively. "What'd you expect, just showing up out of the blue like this? Why should anybody trust you? The only thing you gave a fuck about was what you could scam out of hanging around us. So you sucked up to Tommy, then you sucked up to Gus. You'd have sucked up to me and Ray, too, if you thought it would do you any good. But no, we were just the hired help—just like you."

Ken tried to protest, but Michelle cut him off. "Oh, don't even try it. We all knew exactly what you were doing. Ray and I used to joke about the screenplay you were writing, 'I Made Him What He Is Today: The Tommy Aguilar Story.' But then the whole thing finally got so obvious that even *you* were embarrassed by it, so you pulled this bullshit self-righteous trip of being shocked—*shocked!*—to discover Tommy had a drug problem. Yeah, right!"

Stunned by Michelle's vehemence, Ken tried to rally. "That's all…um, pretty hard to dispute," he sputtered. "But I…I was…trying to tell the truth. And that last story, the one about Las Vegas, it *was* the truth—he had a problem we all ignored. You, me, everybody."

"Yes, it was true," Michelle said quietly. "But it was also nobody else's goddamned business, just like with Charlie Holmes. He was a friend of mine, too. And with Tommy, by the time you finally decided to start telling the truth, you didn't have the right anymore. Truth is not something you use as a last resort, Mr. Journalist. What the hell did you think you were doing? If Tommy hadn't died, did you really think spilling your guts in the newspaper was going to help?"

Ken didn't answer.

"Well?!" Michelle prodded, pointing her spade at him.

"I...don't know," Ken finally said. "You're right, it was something I should've done earlier or not at all. Finally, I got tired of going along with DeGrande's master plan, and I was looking for a way out. Just like Tommy, I guess."

Michelle exhaled and shook her head. "Where'd you go after that, anyway?"

"Seattle," Ken said.

"Seattle?" she snickered. "Yeah, that's a great place to get away from drug problems. And now you're back. Why? Therapy? Or is this your idea of a vacation?"

"Nothing like that. I'm trying to...well, I can't say I'm trying to put things right because that's beyond doing."

"Duh."

"So let's say I'll settle for finding out what really happened out there," Ken said.

Michelle put down her spade and applauded sarcastically. "Well, we'll all sleep better knowing you're on the case, Sherlock," she said. "How come you're looking here and not in California, or Las Vegas?"

"Because I think the answer is here, not there, and I need your help."

"Why should I help you?"

"Well, I'm hoping you'll want to know the truth about Tommy, too."

" 'The truth about Tommy?' What does that mean?"

"I don't think him dying out there was an accident."

Michelle gave no visible reaction beyond a brief fluttering of the eyelids. She looked away, shucked her gloves and pulled a pack of cigarettes from a shirt pocket. She lit one and inhaled deeply, finally letting her eyes again come to rest on Ken. She was tempted to pick her spade back up and chase him off. But curiosity got the better of her.

"How do you figure?" she finally asked.

"I didn't know you smoked," Ken said.

"I needed another bad habit after I gave up hanging around musicians. Don't change the subject."

Ken shook his head. "I can't—shouldn't—really say just yet. Right now, it's mostly a hunch based on some papers I've seen and a few other things I found out. The next thing I need to do is find Tommy's drug dealer. The bald guy from here who was out in Las Vegas, you remember him?"

"Who, Skull?"

"Skull is the guy's name?"

"I don't know his real name," Michelle said. "No one does, I don't think. Everybody calls him Skull because he's bald, and he's always wearing these butt-ugly skull rings."

"Hmm. Skull rings, eh?"

"Yeah."

"So do you know him?"

"Not really. First time I noticed him was when we were touring with Arrowhead. He was around quite a bit after that, but Tommy was the only one he ever dealt with. He and I never really talked, which was fine by me. Mostly, he did a lot of leering. Creepy guy."

"Is he still around?"

"Can't say I've kept up with him, but as far as I know, Skull is still smack dealer to the stars. DeGrande must keep that guy on retainer. You want to find him, best place would be the next big arena show through here."

"That's where I need your help."

"Why?" Michelle asked. "I just told you where to find him."

"Because," Ken said, "you can pass for a groupie easier than I can."

Afterward, Ken borrowed Michelle's car and took a drive out to The Crypt. He was not surprised to find Tommy's shack gone, apparently burned to the ground. Nothing was left, not even the foundation, and the dirt was still gray and barren.

But the elm tree still stood in the front yard, bullet holes and all.

Two days later, Michelle found herself standing before a full-length mirror at an intimate apparel store, gawking at her own reflection. She wore spiked heels, fishnet hose, a low-cut red top and a high-cut black miniskirt. The outfit was painfully tight, especially the shoes.

"Wow," Ken whistled from behind her, "you look just like a stripper."

Michelle shot him a dark look in the mirror. "Was that supposed to make me think you're *less* of a weasel?"

"Don't get all touchy. I only meant I've never seen you like this. You should fit right in."

"Swell," she said, fidgeting uncomfortably. "I always wanted to be just another slut in the crowd. So tell me again, why am I going out in public dressed like this?"

"To find out where Skull lives and, if you can, how hard it'll be to break into his house."

"Oh, great. Breaking and entering always was one of my favorite hobbies. Especially drug dealers' houses—they tend to really like visitors. Why can't you just go find some junkies and ask them?"

"Asking around might tip him off."

"As opposed to me dressing up like a tart and hanging around the sperm dock of the Enormodome. Yeah, *that's* inconspicuous. What am I supposed to do, give Skull a blowjob and then ask if he's got a business card?"

"Only if you really want to," Ken said. "But this should be pretty simple. If I remember correctly, the VIP parking places there are inside the arena, right by the backstage area. All you have to do is hang around long enough to figure out which car is Skull's. You get the license plate number, and I'll do the rest. Anything else you find out is gravy."

"You know, I have played the Enormodome before, with TAB. It's possible somebody there will recognize me."

"Doubtful. That was years ago, and given the turnover they must have, there's probably no one from back then who still works there. Besides which"—Ken indicated her groupie outfit—"nobody's ever seen you dressed like this before."

"Good thing."

Ken paid cash for the clothes.

The next day, Michelle borrowed a large quantity of garish makeup and mousse from a friend who worked as a hairdresser, claiming she needed it for a costume party. Getting ready took most of the afternoon.

By dinnertime, she had transformed herself—sort of. As long as she sat or stood still, she was pretty convincing. But she couldn't get comfortable enough to walk in the stiletto heels without a pronounced wobble. Her hands were a problem, too. Even with bright red nailpolish, they were just too rough and gave her away as someone who worked with her hands, rather than other bodily regions.

"Try to keep the hands out of sight," Ken told her.

"Right."

That night's pre-concert traffic was as bad as for any show Ken could remember. The mere sight of the Enormodome looming in the distance made him and Michelle anxious. This was like sneaking in to visit a former job, one they'd both quit without giving notice. Showtime wasn't for another two hours, but all the roads leading to the arena were gridlocked. The concert was almost sold out.

"God," Michelle said, nodding at the car stereo. "What is this you're playing?"

"Tonight's band," Ken said. "The Blasting Concept. They're from Toronto. I went out and bought their record to see what we'd be getting into."

Michelle tried to listen more attentively, but could only put up with one more verse before reaching over and turning it off. They sounded like an inept TAB tribute band.

"Just think," Ken said. "If TAB was still around, you'd have bands like that opening for you every night."

"I suppose I should feel flattered, but somehow I don't."

"Hey, it's The New Sound of Young America."

"Young America can have 'em, then," Michelle said. "That record's actually selling?"

"Number six on the *Cashboard* chart, with the proverbial bullet."

"And I presume Gus has something to do with them?"

"Correct," Ken said. "First thing he did after Tommy died was to sign Arrowhead—"

"Arrowhead? Really?"

"Uh huh."

"I had no idea. Wonder how he managed that?"

"Same way he 'acquired' you guys," Ken said, "by muscling somebody else out of the way. Anyway, Blasting Concept was the next band he signed after Arrowhead. They were already pretty far along by the time he got ahold of them. He put them in the studio with Geoff Baker, made a real slick video, greased a bunch of radio programmers' palms and then stuck them out on the road with Arrowhead. Sound familiar?"

"First us, and now this Blasting Concept," Michelle sighed. "Arrowhead must have saddle sores by now, the way Gus keeps riding them."

"Maybe so, but it's been worth their while. He got them a hundred-million-dollar record deal."

Michelle gave a low whistle. "A hundred million bucks, are you serious? Nobody's worth that. I can't believe Poly Brothers has that kind of money to throw around."

"They don't," Ken said. "Gus had the good fortune to acquire Arrowhead right after their contract with Poly Brothers was up, so they were free agents. He got them the deal with Fold-Hi, Adolph and Nehi

Polydoroff's new label—two scary bastards who are even more 'old school' than DeGrande, if you can believe that. After losing TAB and Arrowhead, Poly Brothers collapsed. Their Japanese owners fired the president—Adolph and Nehi's nephew, and a real bozo by all accounts—laid off a bunch of people and dropped most of their bands. They also settled a very large lawsuit Gus had pending against them."

"How do you know all this?" Michelle asked.

"You obviously don't read the papers."

"Nope," Michelle said, then watched in silence for a while as they drew closer to the Enormodome. The prospect of attending her first rock concert in nearly two years filled her with dread.

They were almost to the parking lot, close enough to smell the tailgate cookout parties. Scalpers lurked by the side of the road, holding up tickets while dodging any police who might be out. One came over to Michelle's window and tapped on it.

"Hey, baby," he shouted through the closed window. "Need any tickets?"

She shook her head no.

"Well, then, you need somethin' else?" the man hollered, waggling his tongue with a suggestive thrust. Michelle flipped him the bird, locked her door and turned away.

"I can't tell you," she said to Ken, "how much I don't miss the music business."

CHAPTER THIRTY-EIGHT

After parking the car, they split up. Ken went to the ticket window, bought a seat in the nosebleed section (which was all they had left) and went on inside. Michelle headed to the backstage entrance to see how far a short skirt would get her. Fortuitously, she arrived just as a stretch limo from one of the local strip joints, GAZONGA'S, was discharging a half-dozen women who looked as if they'd all bought their wardrobes at the same store as Michelle. She loitered behind the car, then fell in behind them as they marched into the arena.

A roadie with a walkie-talkie held a door open for them, leering admiringly at each passing chest. "Evenin', ladies," he said. "Right this way. The hospitality suite is just down the hall to the left. If you'll—"

"Shut up. We know where it is."

The Enormodome's hospitality room was already crowded with similarly clad women, chatting and sipping drinks while waiting for the musicians to arrive. The room was a forest of spandex, tights and short skirts. Michelle felt like she was corralled in a holding pen.

Doing her best to blend in, she edged toward the bar. She shakily lit a cigarette and gulped a beer, then remembered her hands. So she went to the nearest wall and leaned against it, setting her beer can on a table and keeping her hands behind her back. She tried to eavesdrop without being too obvious, hoping to overhear some mention of Skull. Instead, she just heard snatches of conversation about clothes, makeup, jobs, boyfriends, boob jobs, other bands, other parties.

"The party for Arrowhead last month was better," said the same woman who'd dressed down the roadie on her way in. She sipped a fluorescent daiquiri.

"Maybe so," said another, "but at least this one has booze."

Michelle found groupies horrifying. Mostly, that was because she was constantly mistaken for one when she played in TAB, despite never dressing the part. Her worst-ever humiliation came in St. Louis, when the head of security refused to believe she was in the band and demanded sexual favors before letting her backstage. She wanted to have the bastard charged with solicitation, but Ray talked her out of it. "C'mon, Michelle, he just didn't know better."

The hell of it was, he probably didn't. Big arena shows drew a different class of groupie than club shows. When TAB played small dives, the girls who came around for Tommy were mostly college co-eds who fell for his vulnerability schtick—naive, sweet young things. But there was nothing in the least bit naive, sweet or vulnerable about the crowd of women assembled for The Blasting Concept's pre-show festivities.

"Bathroom?" Michelle asked the bartender. The fewer words she spoke, she figured, the smaller her chance of being found out.

"That way," he said, pointing down the hall.

She nodded thanks and left the room as casually as possible.

Folding her hands beneath her arms, Michelle toddled unsteadily down the hall. It was almost impossible to walk in a straight line in her heels, but she finally made it to the women's room without running into anything. Once inside, she decided not to try peeing because shedding her skirt and hose would've been too much trouble. She locked herself into a stall and smoked another cigarette instead, trying to work up enough nerve for her next move.

Michelle took a deep breath and one last look in the mirror, then went back outside to stroll the maze of corridors backstage. Roadies, go-fers and instrument techs bustled back and forth, ferrying instruments and gear. Despite having no credentials, Michelle walked unchallenged past three different uniformed security guards. A tight skirt was better than any backstage pass.

Rounding a corner, Michelle entered the sidestage area. A few steps up a ramp was the stage, and the crowd; nineteen thousand people waiting for something to happen that would be worth their thirty-five bucks, murmuring in anticipation. She was surprised to discover the sound still gave her an adrenaline-fueled stomach ache.

She turned around to begin retracing her steps—and almost fell down at the sight of two familiar bald heads. Skull and Gus DeGrande were standing down a hallway not thirty feet away, huddled with a third man who Michelle guessed was a tour manager. The dealer and the promoter both held cellular phones, while the tour manager wore a headset. From the body language, the conversation appeared to be tense.

Tracking to her right to give them a wide berth, Michelle walked slowly in their direction. Gus and Skull both had their backs to her, murmuring separately into their cell phones. She paused by a wooden door with a window, pretending to fix her hair in its reflection. After she couldn't tease it anymore, she pulled out some lipstick and applied a second layer; then a third. She was spared a fourth layer when the conversation finally broke up. Gus and the tour manager walked one way and Skull the other. Michelle followed at a discreet distance, hoping he was headed for the backstage VIP lot. He was.

The dealer walked briskly to a nondescript blue Ford and opened the trunk. Michelle couldn't see what he was doing, but that wasn't important. She ducked back into the bathroom and returned to her toilet stall, sat down, lit another cigarette and counted to one-hundred, trying to steady herself. She hadn't planned on ever seeing Gus DeGrande again.

After finishing her cigarette, Michelle walked back out and went to Skull's car to get the plate number—only to realize she didn't have a pen, or paper. Improvising, she wrote the number on her wrist in bright red lipstick: PFZ 115. Mission accomplished. She dropped the lipstick into her purse and was about to turn around when she felt a hand on her shoulder.

"Excuse me, miss?"

Michelle flinched. She turned around and found herself face to face with the tour manager she'd seen talking to Skull and Gus. "Y-yes?"

"Would you come with me, please?"

Her stomach tumbled to the floor. "Is there…something wrong?"

The man was a blank, impossible to read. He didn't answer, just took Michelle by the elbow and guided her away with just enough firmness to prevent her from escaping. Michelle walked in a daze, trying to keep her lipstick-marked wrist out of sight without smearing it. She hoped she was simply being thrown out of the arena.

Instead, after a painfully long walk, they arrived at a remote suite of rooms on the far side of the backstage area. The man used a key to open a door, wordlessly ushered Michelle inside the candlelit room and closed the door behind her. From the plush furniture and well-stocked table of food and drink, Michelle guessed this was The Blasting Concept's dressing room.

A moment later, it dawned on her why groupies were summoned to such places. She hastily turned to leave.

"Wait," said a voice, and she stopped with a wince. "Turn back around."

Groaning inwardly, Michelle complied. Once she got a good look at the speaker, sitting on a couch across the room, it was all she could do not to laugh. The guy was probably in his early twenties, but barely looked old enough to drive. His leather pants, white ruffled shirt and fringed vest made him look like a childish rock-star parody—a little boy dressing the part for a Halloween party.

"I thought it was you!" he said excitedly. Michelle looked closer, trying to figure out if this kid was someone she was supposed to know. He acted like he was. Somebody's younger brother, maybe?

"Do I know you?" she finally asked.

"You really don't know who I am?" he asked in a hurt-sounding voice.

"Well…No."

"Then why are you here?"

"Because," Michelle said, "your tour manager dragged me in here."

"No—I mean, why are you here at all? In this arena, tonight, at this show? Dressed like…uh…like that?"

"Oh. Right," Michelle stammered. He had a point. "Well…um…"

Stumped, she finally just shrugged and smiled—and instantly regretted it. Encouraged, he smiled right back, stood up and walked across the room. Michelle towered over him, only partly because of the spiked heels.

"My name's Peter," he said, and they shook hands. "Peter Ringwald. The Blasting Concept is my band. I sing, and I play bass. Just like you."

"Excuse me?"

Peter misinterpreted Michelle's confusion. "Well, not *just* like you," he said hastily. "But I do the best I can. I can't tell you how much of an honor it is to meet you, Michelle. I was out by the stage a little while ago and saw you—even though you're pretty hard to recognize right now. Is that a wig?"

He reached up to touch her hair. Michelle shook her head no and knocked his hand away, trying not to let the alarms going off in her head register on her face.

"Oh," he said. "Sorry. Anyway, the rest of the guys are down at the hospitality room now. But I wanted to meet you in private, so I had Rusty bring you here. TAB was my all-time favorite band. I once drove all night from Toronto to St. Louis to see you play, and it was incredible. Best show I ever saw, especially you. All my friends were talking about Tommy afterward, but I just thought you were the shit. In fact—" Peter laughed a bit sheepishly, then nodded to a corner of the room where a Fender

Precision bass sat. It looked virtually identical to the one Michelle played in TAB. "—In fact, I considered myself a guitarist before that show. But after seeing TAB, I switched to bass. Because of you."

Michelle didn't know whether to burst out laughing or recoil in horror.

"I'll admit I'm nowhere near the player you are," Peter said. "But...say, do you think you could show me a few things? I've memorized most of the records, but there are a few lines I've never quite been able to figure out."

Michelle would've sooner had her arms ripped off than to touch a bass in Peter Ringwald's presence.

"Hey, I've got an even better idea," he exclaimed. "You want to sit in with us tonight? Having you onstage would be a dream come true. Why don't you come out for a song during the encore? We can at least fake our way through everything on *Chorus Verses Chorus*. How about we do...Oh, I know! That Sex Pistols song! The one that started the riot in Las Vegas! Yeah, that'd be great!"

Michelle would have given anything to be sucked into the depths of hell at that moment. An eternity spent burning in the hereafter couldn't possibly be any worse than this kid, the clueless spawn of her former band. Oblivious to her rising panic, Peter babbled on. "...And, um, later...Afterward, I mean...If you wanted to...you know...we could..."

He really was just a little boy, Michelle decided. Very sweet and not without a certain amount of charm. Cute, even. But also very accustomed to getting his way—especially now that he was Number Six With A Bullet—and he was coming toward her with that look in his eye. Michelle put a hand up.

"Peter," she finally gasped, and he stopped. She took a deep breath and continued, managing a schoolteacher's firmness. "Listen...thank you for...well, for your very kind offer. I'm speechless. It's, ah, good to know we had fans as dedicated as you out there. But I really don't play anymore; haven't even touched a bass in years, in fact. I'd only embarrass myself. So I do appreciate you asking, but I have to go now."

"You do?" he asked, looking puzzled. "But why? You just got here and we won't play for another hour and a half. The opening act hasn't even gone on yet."

"I've, um, got to get back and meet my friends," Michelle improvised.

"Oh? Where are your seats?"

"Somewhere," she said with a vague wave.

"Well, at least let me get you onto the front row," Peter said. "I'll call Gus, our manager, and have him take you there personally. Then we can have a drink while we wait."

He walked across the room and picked up a phone. "Hey," he said, "didn't Gus used to…"

When Peter turned back around, Michelle was gone.

"…manage you guys, too?"

Out in the hall, Michelle took off her heels and pitched them into a trashcan as she strode briskly in the direction of the stage. She passed by the starboard side and walked onto the floor of the arena, heading for the mixing board at the back of the floor. Just like old times, Ken was seated in the back row of the mezzanine level. Through binoculars, he watched Michelle pause by the board, look straight up and wave. That was the signal. He hoofed down to meet her on the concourse level.

"You don't look so good," Ken said, noting Michelle's rattled demeanor.

"Yeah, no shit."

"So what happened?"

"Well, I at least got Skull's number," she said, displaying her wrist.

"Good work," Ken said, laughing at the lipstick.

"But then one of the Blasting Concept's flunkies dragged me back to their dressing room."

"You're kidding," Ken said. "Did they want to, um, you know, squish?"

"Worse! This one wanted me to *play* with them!"

"What?! He knew who you were?"

Michelle closed her eyes and nodded, shuddering. "God, it was fucking horrible," she moaned. "The bass player in this band, I'm apparently his idol. He wanted me to come out during the encore and do a song with them—'That Sex Pistols song, the one that started the riot, that'd be great!'—and then go back to his dressing room and let him ravage me afterward."

Ken was turning crimson from trying to contain his laughter, much to Michelle's anger. She glared daggers.

"Oh, come on!" he protested. "You have to admit, that's at least a little funny."

"It's *not* funny, it's creepy and oedipal. He looked like he was twelve years old, and I could tell he had this sick 'older woman' fantasy of consummating my musical influence on him by fucking me. It felt like meeting a stalker I never knew I had. He said he'd memorized all of TAB's songs, and he even had a bass that looked just like mine."

At that, Ken could contain himself no longer. He finally burst out laughing.

"What," Michelle fumed, "is so goddamned funny?"

"I'm, uh, not sure how to tell you this, Michelle, but…Well, that *was* your bass."

"What?!"

"*Rock Slide* had an item last month about that guy 'inheriting' your bass. Peter somebody, right?"

"Right. Peter Ringwald."

"That's him. Hey, it makes sense. You left it onstage in Las Vegas, so Gus obviously wound up with it and bequeathed it to his latest hitmakers."

"Yeah, like it was his to give," Michelle fumed.

"Maybe that's why Gus never asked for his money back."

"That fucker! And *you!* How come you didn't tell me?"

"Because," Ken said, "I didn't want you to do anything stupid, like try to get it back. How'd you get out of there, anyway?"

"Peter started to call DeGrande to have him move me up to the front row. I figured I should leave before Gus showed up wanting an autograph, too."

"Wait a minute," Ken said. "That means Gus must know you're here."

"Yeah, probably."

"Come on, we'd better get out of here."

CHAPTER THIRTY-NINE

As the Enormodome's houselights went down for the opening act, Ken and Michelle fled into the night, hotfooting it downtown to the *Daily News*. It was a drive the critic remembered making many times after shows, trying to beat deadline to file concert reviews for the next day's edition. Tonight's deadline was even tighter.

They arrived at the paper's office fifteen minutes later, parking in an alley around back. It was a poorly kept secret that the back door by the printing presses was left unlocked for slack employees who lost or forgot their magnetic ID badges. Ken had chucked his into Puget Sound a year earlier.

Inside, Ken and Michelle hurried past the whirling presses printing up the early edition, trying to look nonchalant for the security cameras. They made it to the freight elevator and rode up to the news research department on the third floor. Research stayed open at all hours in case of a news-related emergency—you never knew when you'd have to look up the governor's middle name, or which time zone Italy was in—but it was usually deserted at night. No one was around. Ken went to a computer terminal and started typing.

"What happens if we get caught in here?" Michelle whispered.

"You offer to give whoever it is a blowjob, maybe?" Ken murmured, and she smacked his arm. "Ow! Okay, okay. I'll point out that since they didn't give me a pension, the least they can do is let me borrow their computer just this once for old times sake. Now let's hope they haven't changed the password."

Michelle watched him type: S-H-I-T-4-B-R-A-I-N-S. Ken sighed with relief as the screen flashed, "LOGON SUCCESSFUL."

"Well, with a password that clever, I can see why they wanted to keep it," she said. "What are you doing?"

"Logging into the state DMV database to do a cross-reference search," Ken said. "You can enter a license plate number and get somebody's name, address, social security number, driving record—all kinds of juicy stuff. Tonight, though, we'll settle for finding out where our pal Skull lives. What's he drive, anyway?"

"A really boring blue Ford," Michelle said. "You'd never notice it."

"Which is why he drives it, I'm sure…Okay, here we go. Let's have that plate number." Michelle held up her wrist, and Ken typed in the number: PFZ 115.

The search took an agonizing two minutes, which Ken spent watching the door, hoping no one would show up. Finally, the computer concluded its search with a beep.

"Yee-ha," Ken said, opening the file on the screen. "Cecil Wallsby— yikes, no wonder he doesn't go by his real name—at 427 East Shaw. If we had the time, I'd do some more snooping on Mr. Wallsby. But that'll have to wait. Come on, let's go."

"Right now?"

"Yep," Ken said. "After Gus hears about your Blasting Concept encounter, he'll be onto us. Tonight might be our only chance."

Skull's house was as nondescript as his car, a small two-story affair in a neighborhood a realtor would euphemistically call "transitional." Several large trees blocked the view from the street, but the driveway was clearly empty. Ken and Michelle parked one street over and slipped around to the back of the dealer's house. A quick survey revealed a kitchen window as the easiest break-in point. Ken opened a duffle bag and extracted a pair of gloves, pulling them on. Then he removed the window screen, took a roll of electric tape and began peeling off long strips.

"How do you know there isn't an alarm?" Michelle whispered, watching him apply the tape to the windowpane.

"I don't. But if there is, it won't be one that calls the police department. Drug dealers generally don't want the cops making house calls."

"Oh," Michelle said. "Right."

Ken finished taping the window and pulled a hammer from his bag. Then he handed a plastic Tupperware container to Michelle. Inside were two baseball-sized chunks of hamburger.

"When I break the window," Ken said, "throw those in."

"Both of them?"

"Both of them. And if you don't want to lose any fingers, don't touch anything—and especially *do not* let your hand get inside the window. Ready?"

Michelle nodded.

A commotion broke out inside as soon as Ken broke the glass. Something very large (though curiously silent) was scrambling around in there. Michelle carefully lobbed the meat in, and they both ducked and waited. Nearly a minute went by before they heard a thud.

By the time Ken counted to fifty, all was quiet again. He took a deep breath and climbed through the window, landing lightly on the floor. After a quick scan of the kitchen, he pulled Michelle in after him. She flinched when she got a look at the very large Doberman lying on the floor—the biggest, meanest-looking hellhound she'd ever seen. Even unconscious, the dog radiated viciousness. A puddle of drool gleamed in the moonlight, dripping from teeth the size of stalactites.

"Man," Ken said, "I can see why he's only got one dog. That thing's the size of a cow! Good thing I brought along enough to finish him off."

"Please tell me that wasn't poison I just threw in here."

"Nope, doggie tranquilizers. Looks like he ate both pieces before they got to him, so he should be out for a while. Probably won't feel so great after he wakes up, but he'll be fine."

"Why wasn't he barking?" Michelle asked.

Ken reached under the dog's neck. "Feels like his vocal cords have been severed. Useful, if you don't want the neighbors to know you keep a dinosaur-sized attack dog inside your house."

"Or if you want the dog to eat prowlers instead of just scare 'em off."

"Looks like he's eaten a few in his day."

"Great," Michelle said. "Okay, here we are—now what?"

"We look."

"For what?"

"For where Skull keeps his jewelry."

"Why?"

"Just start looking," Ken said. "Trust me, you'll know why when we find it."

After closing all the curtains and turning on as many lights as they dared, Ken and Michelle began searching. Despite his seemingly lucrative profession, Skull appeared to live like any other single male. Dirty dishes filled every square inch of kitchen sink and counter space. Piles of trash and papers and magazines were scattered across the worn and mismatched furniture throughout the house. And everywhere, doggie landmines gave pungent evidence of the dealer's pet attack beast.

"What a dump," Ken said, holding his nose. "This place sure could use a woman's touch."

"There are a few backstage at the Enormodome who probably wouldn't mind auditioning for the job," Michelle said with a grimace.

The kitchen yielded no clues, nor did the living room or downstairs bathroom. A quick search of the closets and dresser drawers in the two upstairs bedrooms also turned up nothing. They finally found it in the upstairs bathroom, in the cabinet under the sink—an old wooden jewelry box. Ken opened the latch and almost recoiled at the sight of row upon row of rings decorated with skulls. The dealer had them in every conceivable shape, color and design. There were creepy ones, goofy cartoonish ones, scary ones; mostly human skulls, but also a few animal. They were made of gold, silver, platinum, turquoise, tin.

Ken lifted the felt ringholder out of the box, scattering rings across the floor and revealing another ring-studded piece of felt underneath. The second layer held just as many rings as the first, all of them equally repulsive.

"Jesus," Ken whistled. "How many ugly rings can one guy wear? He must have a couple hundred in here."

"Ugh," Michelle said, wrinkling her nose. "Is this what we came here for?"

Ken didn't answer as he removed the second ringholder. There were more rings and a few coins and random gewgaws beneath it, as well as a small flat box. Inside the box was a silver necklace with an oval crucifix-and-skull medallion, slightly larger than a silver dollar.

"No, this is," Ken said, holding the necklace up. "Look familiar?"

"That looks just like the necklace Tommy used to wear," she said.

Ken turned the medallion over and showed Michelle the inscription: "TWA."

"It *is* Tommy's necklace!" she said, reaching for it.

"Was he wearing it the last time you saw him in Las Vegas?" Ken asked, dropping the necklace into her palm.

"Sure was," Michelle said, turning it over. "I can't remember ever seeing him without this on. How'd you know it would be here?"

"A hunch. I'd actually forgotten about Tommy's necklace until I went to Each the other night, and saw it in some TAB photos Bob has in his office. Then when I went looking for Ray the next day, I noticed the same necklace in the picture on the wall at Dick's. Then when I looked you up, you alluded to Mr. Wallsby's skull-jewelry fetish, so there you go."

"So why would Skull, of all people, have Tommy's necklace?"

"The short answer is that he's a man who appreciates fine jewelry," Ken said, starting to gather up the rings that had fallen on the floor. It took some time because they were scattered all over the bathroom floor.

"Is there a long answer?"

"Well, since DeGrande inherited everything of Tommy's, it's possible he gave it to Skull—but not very likely. Since when does Gus ever give anything away?"

"Other than my bass, never," Michelle said.

"Right. So it's more likely that Skull got this directly from Tommy, out there in the desert. Maybe he found the body before the cops did. Or maybe he was actually there when Tommy died."

"Which proves…what?"

"On its own, nothing," Ken said. "But put it together with a few other things, and it suggests DeGrande was probably doing more than just looking the other way where Tommy's smack habit was concerned. You said Gus must keep Skull on retainer, right?"

"Yeah. I even saw them talking at the arena tonight."

"Okay. So after Gus signs TAB, his underling Skull starts following you around, and Tommy's habit starts to get worse. It peaks in Las Vegas, where Tommy freaks out, starts a riot and flees. Then he turns up dead—and this necklace proves Skull was most likely there when he died. How could Gus *not* be pulling the strings?"

"I'm confused," Michelle said. "You're saying Gus supplied Tommy through Skull, right? I don't understand why he'd do that."

"Neither do I," Ken said. "Tommy's heroin habit did, however, wind up killing him—which put three million dollars in Gus's pocket. Did you know he had a life insurance policy on Tommy?"

That startled Michelle. "I had no idea," she said.

"Yep," Ken said. "Three million bucks, bought through an agency in Las Vegas that was deep into more bad shit than you can imagine. Numbers rackets, prostitution, drugs, money-laundering, crooked land deals. A casino out there seemed to be involved, too. If you ever get a chance, you should read the bankruptcy court file sometime. It's pretty amazing."

Ken finished replacing the rings in the jewelry box. But he had a hard time getting the box closed again. "Here's how crooked this company was," he continued. "On a life insurance policy that big, the insurer almost always tries to get out of paying if there's the slightest hint the death was drug-related. Tommy was found dead with a needle in his hand, but these cowboys didn't even flinch. They paid up within two weeks after Tommy died. Given everything else going on with this company, my guess is the insurance payoff to Gus was a way to launder some money and solve a few problems for a third party. Maybe it involved a drug deal—in which case I wouldn't be surprised if our man Mr. Wallsby was in on that end of it, too."

Michelle had gone stark white. "Wait a minute," she said. "Are you telling me that Gus actually had Tommy killed?"

"Think about it," Ken said. "Who's the one person in the universe with the most to gain from Tommy being dead?"

"DeGrande?"

"Bingo. He gets a gigantic insurance payoff, and he can go right on making tons more money putting out shitty posthumous records. Tommy isn't around to complain, or run up his legal bills by getting into any more trouble. And having this dead rock icon gives DeGrande the perfect leverage to escape one slimy record company and go to another for a whole bunch more money."

Ken finally got the lid closed and latched again. He carefully replaced the box under the sink and closed the cabinet door. "All that," he concluded, "plus Gus comes out of this a made man. Before, he was just a crotchety old troll everybody hated. But now, he's got the Midas touch. He uses his kingmaker reputation to sign up the old TAB, Arrowhead, and to launch the new one, Blasting Concept. You've got to hand it to him, the whole thing is brilliant. Evil and twisted, but brilliant."

Michelle's head was spinning. "Can you actually prove any of this?"

"Nope," Ken admitted. "It's all conjecture and circumstance, not to mention off the record. I can't figure out where this Susan Barwick woman fits in, unless she was just unlucky enough to get caught with Tommy at the wrong time. And I still don't have a motive beyond greed—which, in Gus's case, might be enough. But you'd like to think—"

Few sounds are as distinctive and alarming as the cold metallic *thwack* of a pistol's bolt action being cocked. It was precisely such a noise that interrupted Ken mid-sentence. He and Michelle were sitting on the bathroom's filthy tile floor. They turned around to find themselves staring at the business end of a drawn gun.

Ken tried to speak, and found he could not. Skull spoke instead.

"I should've killed you in Las Vegas."

CHAPTER FORTY

Skull had a car waiting in the driveway, a stretch limo. He handcuffed Ken and Michelle behind their backs, then tied them together at the elbow and shoved them into the backseat.

"Gee, Cecil, I didn't know you were a limousine hack on the side," Michelle said. "Nice wheels. I guess whoever you drove to the show tonight will have to take a cab home?"

The dealer didn't answer, merely stared at them in the rear-view mirror, poker-faced. His gun sat on the seat beside him, still cocked and loaded. Ken found the lack of a chauffeur or blindfolds ominous.

No other words were spoken in the twelve minutes it took to drive to the offices of Grandiose Concerts, where Skull pulled into the underground parking garage. They rode the elevator up to the third floor, encountering no one in the halls. Everyone on the night security detail had been sent home.

Gus awaited them in his office, which was almost as dimly lit as The Blasting Concept's dressing room. He sat behind his massive desk, the blinds drawn. When the prisoners entered the room, he nodded toward two chairs. They sat down—Ken in the same chair from which he'd once interviewed DeGrande.

Skull followed, untying the rope and unlocking the handcuffs. Then he dropped Tommy's necklace on Gus's desk. DeGrande looked at it uncomprehendingly, until he turned it over and saw the inscription. Then he glared up at the dealer, who shrugged and retreated to stand by the door.

"That was indiscreet," Gus snapped.

"Sorry. Won't happen again."

"It better not," DeGrande said, then turned his attention to his two captives. "And speaking of indiscreet, here we have our intrepid rock critic and bass player. Ken and Michelle. I'll be honest: I had hoped never to lay eyes on either of you again."

"Likewise," Michelle said, rubbing her sore wrists. Skull had not been gentle with the handcuffs.

"Yes, well, whose fault is that?" Gus asked, eyeing her miniskirt with bemusement and a trace of arousal. "I was perfectly willing to live and let live, so long as everybody minded their own business. But now—" He paused to take a cigar from a box on his desk and light up, leaning back with a pensive look on his face as he expelled a noxious cloud. "— I'm afraid that's no longer possible. Cigar?"

"No thank you," said Ken.

"You never did have any style," Gus sighed, almost sadly.

"All right, then," he continued as he smoked. "Would either of you"—puff—"care to explain"—puff—"why"—puff—"you broke into this gentleman's house?"

He then stared at Michelle and, using his cigar as a pointer, said, "While you're at it, you can explain what you were doing backstage at the Enormodome tonight dressed like a hooker."

Another puff, and then he turned to Ken. "And you—where've you been the last two years? Never mind that, how come you didn't stay gone? Why'd you go to Each the other night? And what were you doing at Dick's Drum Head, asking for Ray?"

Neither said anything.

"Don't everybody talk at once," Gus said.

"Maybe I wanted a drum lesson," Ken said. "Been thinking about starting a band. You think you'd want to manage me?"

DeGrande took a few more puffs from his cigar, then tossed it into a trashcan by his desk, where it began to smolder. He didn't appear to notice the gathering smoke as he leaned forward, tensing like a cobra about to strike.

"Morrison," Gus said through clenched teeth, "you have no idea how deep the shit is that you're in right now. You've already got me *annoyed,* but I am about to get *angry*—and believe me, you don't want that to happen. So why don't you just start explaining what you're doing back here, before this gets any worse?"

"Tell me how it could possibly get any worse," Ken said, trying to sound brave but unable to suppress the quaver from his voice.

"I could feed you to the fish over there."

"Sort of like what you did to Tommy, eh?"

"Oh, is that so?" Gus asked, drumming his fingers. "Please, do tell me more."

His supply of snappy retorts exhausted, Ken just looked away. The promoter turned to Michelle, who was able to match his gaze but didn't say anything, either. Finally, Gus summoned Skull back, asking, "Why don't we, as the sportscasters say, go to the videotape?"

Skull set a tape player on the desk and turned it on. Ken felt his stomach plummet as he heard his own voice explain about Tommy's necklace, insurance policy and probable murder. He loathed the sound of his voice on tape, but never more so than at that moment.

DeGrande betrayed no reaction as he listened. He simply sat with his chin resting on his clasped hands. The tape ended with the sound of Skull interrupting the conversation. Gus reached down and clicked the tapeplayer off.

"In case you were wondering," he said, "Skull's house has a very sophisticated security system. It doesn't call police when there's a break-in, but it does page him, and activates a system that records every room in the house. Videotape, too. Can't be too careful nowadays."

"I guess not," Ken said.

"Anything you'd care to add to your spiel there?"

"No, I think that about covers it."

"How'd you find out about the insurance policy?" Gus asked.

"Lucky break."

"You might not think so for too much longer."

Ken didn't have a clever comeback for that one, either. But Michelle interrupted.

"Listen," she said as she stood up, "this, um, really seems to be between the two of you, and I don't have anything to add. So if it's all the same, I think I'll just be going, and you two can—"

From behind, Skull came up and put his hands on Michelle's shoulders, roughly forcing her back into the chair.

Gus cackled wildly. "Oh, that's beautiful! Well done, Michelle! You always did have an underrated sense of humor. But no, I'm afraid I can't trust you any more than I can trust detective boy here. So you just stay right there."

Whatever slim hope either had of escaping the situation unharmed was well and truly gone. Michelle closed her eyes and took a deep breath. Ken was shaking so hard that he had to grip the edge of his chair to steady himself.

"Now, then," Gus continued. "I don't know what the hell you two thought you were doing. But you've become rather pesky, breaking into houses, prying into matters that are of no concern to—"

"So it's true, then?" Michelle interrupted.

"What?"

"That you killed Tommy."

Before answering, Gus gave Michelle's eyes a good long look to see if she really wanted to know the answer—and understood that she'd never live to repeat it. He saw that she did.

"Actually," he said, "I prefer to think of it as saving him from further embarrassment."

"Jesus," Michelle said in exasperation. "Like destroying a village to save it?"

"C'mon, Michelle." The promoter's tone was almost chummy. "You were there. You know as well as anybody how miserable he was by the end. His drug habit was getting worse, he felt isolated, trapped—"

"But *you're* the one who trapped him," Michelle pressed. "Who made the record he hated? The image he hated? And who gave him the smack? You did all of that!"

"It was what he wanted," Gus said, waving dismissively. "I knew him better than you did—better than he did himself, even. The kid wanted to be a star, but didn't want to blamed for 'selling out.' He just wanted somebody else to make the whole thing happen. So I did. And when it did happen, he couldn't handle it. So I took care of that, too. Trust me, it was better that it ended when it did. Tommy would've been a one-hit wonder because he was such a fuck-up. This way, he wound up a legend."

"Bullshit," Michelle said. "He wound up dead, and you wound up rich. You used him up, then you killed him."

DeGrande finally erupted, able to contain himself no longer. "I did him a *favor*, don't you understand?!" he boomed. "He was turning into a fucking vegetable! Three more months and he would've been in diapers. You think he'd have wanted that? Fuck no. Killing Tommy was the best thing I ever did for him."

That last line hung in the air, settling over the room like fallout. Even Skull seemed a little stunned by DeGrande's declaration.

"Gus," Ken finally broke the silence, "you may be even crazier than Tommy was."

"Ken," Gus said patiently, as if lecturing a child, "nobody cares what you think. Nobody. That was always your problem, thinking anybody else gave a flying fuck about you. As long as you were just fingerpainting by the numbers, you were harmless and occasionally even useful. But then you deluded yourself into believing you had to tell 'The Truth,' only it was something you didn't understand. So all you did was tell even bigger lies. How do you think I got away with this? I couldn't have asked for better cover than what you gave me in the newspaper.

"And you," Gus continued, turning to Michelle. "You always thought you were so much better than everyone else, but you're *nothing*. You were just scenery. I could've put anybody up there in your place and it would not have changed a thing. You didn't make Tommy. *I* did."

Gus paused again to let them squirm before continuing. "Well," he said, beckoning Skull back over, "tonight you're both gonna discover how truly insignificant you are, because you'll be disappearing. Skull here will take you to a meatpacking plant over in Wilson. It'll be messy and painful for you, I'm afraid, but it leaves no traces and that's what's important. If you try to escape, he'll just shoot you both before processing. But you can take comfort in the knowledge that you won't have died in vain. You'll be feeding others—literally."

He chuckled. Then regaining his formal composure, Gus said, "Any questions? Well, then, good evening to you both."

Skull grinned, nodded and opened the door. He turned around and took the handcuffs from his pocket, when a blast from the hallway knocked the dealer forward. He screamed as he went down, his gun clattering across the room, a twelve-gauge hole in his back. The shotgun roared again, buckshot tearing into Skull's skull and finishing him off. His body lay twitching in the doorway, thick pools of blood spreading rapidly across the carpet.

Everything happened so fast that Ken, Michelle and Gus just sat and stared, frozen. A moment later, Bob Porter walked in carrying a shotgun, stepping carefully over Skull's body.

"Hidy, Ken," Bob said. "Hey, Michelle, long time no see." He walked up to DeGrande's desk with the shotgun. Michelle thought he was going to shoot again, and braced herself. Instead, he stuck the still-smoking barrel into Gus's open mouth.

"Um, Bob?" Ken said unsteadily. "As glad as I am to see you right now—"

"Shut up, Ken," Bob commanded, keeping his gaze steady on his target. "Okay, Gus. Now that I've got your attention, we're gonna have us a little talk."

The heat of the barrel was scalding his tongue, but Gus didn't dare flinch.

"Here's how this'll work," Bob continued. "After I pull this here gun out of your mouth, I'm gonna ask a few questions. Answer them honestly and you'll be fine. But as soon as I think you're bullshitting me, I'll splatter your head all over the blinds. Capece?"

DeGrande looked into his captor's eyes and was certain he meant it. The promoter nodded, then gagged when Bob pulled the gun out, leaning over to vomit in a trashcan.

"While you're collecting yourself, Gus, let's have us a little preamble," Bob said, setting a tape player on the desk and pressing "play." DeGrande gave a start when he heard the conversation immediately before Bob's entrance. The fidelity was remarkable, even the recording of the recording of Ken.

"Nice speech, Gus," Bob said, turning the deck off. "Very impressive. Maybe not quite as good as some of the lectures you've given me over the years, but solid. I'm sure all your industry pals will love it."

"How?..." Gus started to ask.

"You're not the only one who can play cute games with tape decks, Gus," Bob said. "Yeah, you've gotta love these newfangled supersensitive microphones. This one can even record through a keyhole. Sounds pretty good, too, don't you think? But let's see how it does at gunpoint."

Bob turned the deck back on and hit the "record" button, then turned on the deck Skull left behind. "Shall we begin?" he asked

DeGrande looked wildly around the room, his gaze coming to rest on Michelle and Ken—as if he somehow expected them to help him. Bob turned the decks off and raised the shotgun again as he nodded toward Skull's corpse behind him. "Gus, whether it's the cops or your mob pals after me, or a single- or double-homicide rap, it makes no never-mind to me. Last chance: You want your brains inside your head or out?"

The promoter sighed and reluctantly nodded. The decks came back on.

"Alright, Gus, we've already established that you had Tommy killed—yes?"

"Yes."

"Very good, Gus. See, that wasn't so hard. Next question: Did Skull do it?"

"Yes."

"How?"

"Gave him a hot shot."

"A hot shot?" Michelle asked.

"A too-strong dose of smack, laced with a few other things to cause a heart attack," said Bob. "What else was in it, Gus?"

"I don't know. I left that part to Skull."

"Yeah, well, he would be the expert. What about the girl?"

"Skull gave her one, too."

"Why?"

"Because she was about to shoot Tommy."

For the first time that night, Bob was shocked. "Come again?"

"Skull told me that when he found the two of them, she was holding him hostage with a gun," Gus said. The other three people in the room exchanged a look.

"Why?" Bob asked.

"She claimed Tommy wrote a bunch of songs about her."

"What'd she want?"

"She was so strung out, it was hard to tell," Gus said. "Near as Skull could figure out, it had something to do with wanting co-writing credit."

"Wow," Ken piped up, "now *that* would be one strange publishing deal."

"Shut up, Ken," Bob said. "Well, Gus, that's so fucking weird I almost believe it. But riddle me this: If you were gonna kill Tommy anyway, why not just let the girl do it for you?"

"The cops would've asked too many questions."

"Easier just to kill her, too, eh?" Bob said. "That, I'm not so sure I believe, which means we've come to the tricky part. We've all heard your for-the-cameras rationale about doing Tommy a favor by killing him. I'll be honest, there was a time when I thought I should've done something like that myself. But somehow, I have a hard time buying that you were concerned about his place in history. So—" He put the shotgun barrel right up against DeGrande's forehead. "—This better be good, meaning you better convince me. The off-the-record, no-bullshit truth: Why'd you do it?"

"Money," Gus said weakly.

"Hallelujah, we have a winner!" Bob said. "But there's gotta be more. Go on."

"I owed some people a lot of money."

"Who?"

"Some people in Las Vegas."

"How much?"

"More than I had."

"How much?" Bob pressed harder with the gunbarrel.

"Two million."

"That's all? You've got to have more money than that!"

"Not then, I didn't. Tommy cost me a lot of money before I made anything off him."

"Wait a minute," Ken chimed in again. "These people you owed in Las Vegas—did they run a casino?"

"Yes."

"That's it!" Ken exclaimed. "It was a gambling debt…Wait a minute, you mean you killed Tommy to pay off a fucking gambling debt?!"

"Fuck you," DeGrande said wearily.

"Well, Gus, that's where you're wrong," Bob said. "Because you, my friend, are the one who's about to find himself fucked."

Bob turned off both tapedecks and passed them over to Ken, who noticed for the first time that the clubowner was wearing gloves. "Stand up, Gus," he said. "Now put your hands out, palms up."

DeGrande did as he was told and, to the surprise of everyone else in the room, Bob placed the shotgun in his hands. The promoter looked down at it, bemused, then looked up. He raised the gun, pointed it at Bob and pulled the trigger. It gave a hollow click.

"Sorry, Gus, I burned all the shells on Skull here."

The look on DeGrande's face changed from confusion to anger—he'd been held hostage with an unloaded gun.

"That gun belonged to Skull, by the way," Bob continued. "He was a little careless all the way around tonight. He was in such a hurry to get over here that he left without doing anything about the hole in his kitchen window. So after he split, I went in, took a look around and found that gun. Then I set his house on fire."

"You *what?!*" Michelle said.

"Not to worry, I moved the dog outside first."

"Oh," she said, relieved. "Good."

"He was a heavy fucker, too. Anyway, Gus, Skull's house should be just about gone by now. And since I wiped down that gun pretty good before coming over here, the only fingerprints on it are yours."

Bob retrieved the late drug dealer's pistol from across the room and leveled it at Gus.

"By the way, you can sit back down now."

Numbly, DeGrande complied, still clutching the useless shotgun.

"Is this room wired?" Bob asked, and Gus nodded. "I figured. That leaves you with one hell of a predicament."

"What do you mean?" the promoter asked. "Isn't that more of a problem for you?"

"Well, sure, the tape could prove you weren't the one who shot Skull," Bob said. "But it also has you confessing to two murders, and plotting two more. With Skull, you can maybe claim self-defense—although that probably won't wash, seeing as how he was shot in the back—or temporary insanity. Tommy, though, that's premeditated and for profit. That one could get you the chair.

"Guess you'll just have to pick your poison," Bob concluded. "If I were you, I'd forget about the tape and take my chances on Skull here. He's just a drug dealer anyway, so who'll miss him? And if you get one of those judges you own, maybe they'll just give you twenty years instead of life."

Bob picked up the phone on DeGrande's desk, unscrewed the receiver, put a vocal-scrambling chip into the mouthpiece to alter his voice and dialed 911. Michelle felt as if she were watching James Bond at work.

"Oh, you're probably thinking the building's security cameras might bail you out," Bob said as the phone rang. "Maybe they would have, if I hadn't turned them off. I expected it to be harder. Getting in here was a lot easier than it should've been. For such a high-powered operation, your security really sucks, Gus."

The operator finally answered.

"There's been a shooting at 1600 Industrial Drive," Bob said into the phone, then hung it up and removed the scramble chip.

"Gotta go, Gus," he said, screwing the receiver back together. "You've probably got just enough time before the cops get here to erase your tape."

DeGrande gave him a withering glare. "You have not heard the last of this. You're dead. All three of you. You can count on it."

"Nah, I don't think so," Bob said. "If you get any ideas about sending your thug pals after us, just remember: We've got a taped confession that can bury you. And if anything happens to any of us, it will do just that. *You* can count on *that*."

Bob turned to leave, Ken and Michelle standing up to follow.

"Oh, I almost forgot," Bob said. He tossed a metal tape reel onto DeGrande's desk, where it landed with a clatter. "You said you wanted that."

It was the master tape of TAB's first single.

CHAPTER FORTY-ONE

Michelle climbed out of Bob Porter's car and stood on the curb outside her apartment.

"You got a friend you can stay with for a couple of nights?" Bob asked.

"Yeah, I guess."

"Do it, then. It's probably not necessary, but better safe than sorry. You should also think of an alibi for why your car was parked in Skull's neighborhood tonight. Just in case they trace the license plate, and an arson investigator knocks on your door."

"Okay."

"You all right?"

"Oh, sure," Michelle said. "It's just a little…overwhelming, that's all. I mean, I always knew TAB was a weird situation. But I didn't realize just how much intrigue was going on until tonight. Anyway, I'm glad it's all over. Finally. Thank you, I think."

"Anytime," Bob said, with a bow and a wave.

"No," Michelle said, "let's hope not."

She turned to Ken.

"And I guess I should thank you, too."

"What for?" Ken asked. "For getting you into this when you didn't want to, and then almost getting us both killed?"

"Well, yeah. But none of this would've happened without you, and Gus DeGrande is gonna spend tonight in jail. Not for the right murder, and he won't get put away for as long as he deserves. But you take revenge where you can get it."

Before either man could say anything else, Michelle gave a final wave, turned and left. They watched her go, looking bedraggled in her miniskirt.

"Damn," Bob said, "how come she never dressed like that when I was around?"

"Here, you left this at Skull's house," Bob said after they got back to Each, handing Ken his duffel bag. "If I were you, I'd get rid of that."

"Will do," Ken answered. It was past closing time, Each was deserted and they were sitting alone at the bar. "So what are you going to do?" he continued.

"Leave the country. First thing tomorrow, I'm gone."

"Where will you go?"

"Not telling."

"How come?"

"Trust me, it's better for you not to know. Deniability. I'm going into a sort of private witness protection program."

"Oh," Ken said. "Do we really need to be worried?"

"Probably not, but you can't be too careful. DeGrande won't forget who did this to him, but he'll have enough problems without worrying too much about us."

"You really think so?"

"Oh, yeah. It's not like everybody in the business didn't already know about his thuggier tendencies. A few might even suspect he iced Tommy. But as long as he had plausible deniability, he was untouchable. Knowing Gus, he probably won't even get that much jail time. But he's still finished. For a heroin dealer to turn up murdered in your office, that's just a little too dirty. He's damaged goods, and these big corporations that are taking over everything don't like that. After this, he'll have a hard time finding anybody who wants anything to do with him."

"A music business without Gus DeGrande," Ken said. "That almost makes me want to be back in it again. But I can't help thinking someone even worse will take over."

"Maybe so, but that's not our problem," Bob said. After a pause, he continued, "So I've been thinking—what are *you* gonna do now?"

"I don't know."

"I do."

"You do?" Ken asked. "What?"

"You're gonna stay here and run Each after I'm gone."

"Are you serious?!" When Bob nodded, he sputtered, "But that's crazy! What do I know about running a bar?"

"No less than I did when I took this place over. But I'm leaving some money behind to help you out. Besides, as you were always saying in print, running a nightclub ain't rocket science."

"When did I ever say that?"

Bob stood up and walked over to a bulletin board where a yellowed newspaper clipping was tacked up—one of Ken's old columns. Bob read aloud:

> The way clubowners in this town talk, you'd think that booking a nightclub was impossible. But all it takes is a little more imagination than anybody around here seems to have. Because no matter what they say, it ain't rocket science.

Bob walked back to his seat, giving Ken a light elbow in the ribs. The critic swatted it away. He hated it when his own words were turned back on him.

"All you ever did was complain about how inept and evil everyone else was," Bob said. "Or how stupid people were for not liking the same stuff you did. Okay, here's your chance to make a difference—to do something besides bitch. Hell, what are you worried about? You were right, it really isn't *that* hard, as long as you don't drink too much of your stock. And if you go out of business, you just start over."

Bob paused to take a sip from his bottle. "Besides, you may think running off to hide in Seattle was penance. But that was just avoidance behavior, because you were too chickenshit to clean up a mess you made. Tonight was a good start, but only a start. It's time you paid up for real."

Ken sighed. "Okay, you win. Why not? It's not like I've got anything better to do right now anyway."

"Good. I've got all the paperwork in the office. We'll take care of it before I leave."

"Hey," Ken said, "you still haven't explained how you just happened to materialize in time to save us tonight."

"I've been trailing you ever since you came back to town."

"Aw, c'mon—really?"

"Military surveillance training can come in handy, sometimes," Bob said. "I also made a few discreet inquiries of my own—I've always had my suspicions about Gus—so I sort of figured out which direction you might be heading. I was at the Enormodome tonight, watching you and Michelle from a distance. I followed you to Skull's house. Then when he showed up, I figured he'd take you to DeGrande. The rest, I more or less made up as I went along. My goal was to get Gus on tape. He's impressed enough with his own cleverness that I figured he'd get around to bragging about it, even though he had no reason to other than sadism. As for the chance to kill Skull and pin it on Gus, that was a bonus."

"Yeech," Ken said. "I couldn't have done it."

"Surveillance wasn't all they taught us in the military."

They both paused to drink.

"Did you really mean what you said to Gus, about thinking you should've killed Tommy yourself?"

"Aw, hell, I don't know," Bob said, shrugging. "I used to think that, usually late at night. But I never realized just how crazy it sounded until I heard Gus say he'd done Tommy a favor by killing him. All I've ever done with Tommy is pick up the pieces afterward, it seems like."

They paused to drink some more.

"So Tommy Aguilar is avenged, finally," Ken finally said.

"If not Susan Barwick. That was the one unexpected curveball of this whole thing. Just think—if Skull had let her shoot Tommy, Gus probably would've gotten away with it. But that's Gus for ya, he just has to be in charge of everything."

"We should drink a toast," Ken said. "To Tommy and Susan."

"We should," Bob agreed, and they silently clinked bottles.

"Bob…What about the tapes?"

"What about 'em?"

"What do we do with them?"

"Nothing," Bob said. "I'll keep one copy, and so will you. But you can't let *anyone* else hear it, except in extreme circumstances—like death. Keep one copy in the safe here and another in a safety deposit box, and file instructions with a lawyer you trust that the tape be played for the district attorney if either you or Michelle ever turn up missing or dead."

"It's mighty tempting to use it on Gus right now."

"Nope," Bob said. "The tapes are like nuclear missiles, insurance that we hope we'll never need—mutually assured destruction and all that. Remember, they implicate me in a murder, too. But as long as Gus knows they're out there, he should leave us alone. And as long as he does that, this will stay our little secret."

"But why?" Ken asked. "As much as you must hate Gus—why?"

"Because like I always used to say," Bob said, "the real truth is always off the record."

ABOUT THE AUTHOR

David Menconi is the music critic at the *News & Observer* in Raleigh, North Carolina, where he lives with his wife Leigh and three children Aaron, Edward and Claudia. His byline has also appeared in *Spin, Billboard, Request, No Depression, Oxford American, Mother Jones,* the "MusicHound Album Guide" series and a host of other publications that no longer exist. For the record, Mr. Menconi would like it known that he is not the Ken Morrison character depicted herein—but he will acknowledge that they've met a time or two. "Off The Record" is his first novel.

APPENDIX

Song credits

Sex Pistols Residuals (ASCAP) & Glitterbest Ltd. for "Holidays in the Sun." Words and music by Paul Cook, Steve Jones, John Lydon, Sid Vicious. Copyright © 1977, administered by Warner Bros. Music Corp. All rights reserved, used by permission.